CONTENTS

ILLUSTRATIONS

(between pages 232 and 233)

KEY TO ACKNOWLEDGMENTS

1 R. J. Stopford, Esq.
2 The National Library of Ireland
3 The Mansell Collection
4 Richard Collier, Esq.
5 The *Daily Mirror* Picture Library

MAPS

Where there are variations of spelling in the names either of
people or places, I have ordinarily followed Casement's: e.g.
'Kinchasa' rather than 'Kinchassa' or the modern 'Kinshasa'.

To my mother, who loved Ireland, and had many close friends in Ulster. Her hope was that this book would help people to understand the problem, and that nothing in it would create, or revive, bitterness. So is mine.

Preface to the Paperback Edition

When I was writing Roger Casement's biography I was under the impression that the issue whether or not his 'black' diaries were forged had been settled: that apart from a few die-hards, impervious to argument, nobody now still believed in the forgery theory.

A visit to Dublin shortly after the book had been published removed this misconception. The influence of the late Herbert Mackey, who actually saw the diaries in the Public Record Office, but returned to Ireland to re-assert his belief they were forged, remains quite pervasive—not, admittedly, in academic circles, where only a handful of the faithful, like Professor McHugh, remain; but among readers of, and writers to, the newspapers, notably the *Irish Times*, in which a correspondence on the subject continued for several weeks.

I was consequently tempted to revise and strengthen the final chapter, 'The Ghost of Roger Casement', by including additional information to support the case that the diaries are genuine. On reflection, however, I decided that it would be more sensible to leave the biography as originally written, and to provide the additional information in an appendix. For this purpose I have used a letter which I wrote to the *Cork Examiner*, in reply to points raised by their reviewer—who happened to be the only critic who attempted seriously to argue the forgery case, as distinct from simply reiterating the conviction that the diaries were forged. So, the text of the biography itself remains unchanged, except for an emendation for which I am indebted to Mrs. Geraldine Plunkett Dillon: that it was her father, Count Plunkett, who was the 'friend of James Malcolm' and who got the letter from 'James Malcolm'—Joseph Plunkett—to Casement in Germany in 1916.

Brian Inglis

This book was originally published in hardcover form by Hodder and Stoughton Ltd. in 1973, and it is in that edition that students of the subject will find a detailed Bibliography, of both original and secondary sources consulted.

INTRODUCTION

In the summer of 1956 Peter Singleton-Gates, a London journalist, came to the *Spectator* office to show us the typewritten transcripts of Roger Casement's 'black' diaries — wrapped up, as I recall, in a paper parcel; we watched him untie it with some trepidation, as if it might contain an explosive device. And, in a sense, it did.

I knew little at the time about Casement's career; no more than the average Irishman knows about his country's patriot heroes (though this, as Bernard Shaw must surely somewhere have observed, is more than the average Englishman, or for that matter the average American, knows about his). I knew that as a member of the British Consular Service, early in the century, Casement had investigated conditions in the Congo Free State, and produced a report so damning it was generally credited with destroying Leopold's empire there; that a similar investigation which he conducted a few years later into the rubber industry in the Putumayo region of the Amazon had had similar consequences; that he received a knighthood for his services; that when war broke out, he went to Berlin to try to secure armed assistance for the Irish independence movement; and that when he returned to Ireland, just before the Easter Rising in 1916, he was captured, tried for treason and found guilty. I knew, too, that diaries alleged to be his had been used to blacken his reputation, to prevent him from obtaining a reprieve; and that he had been hanged.

Scanty though this information was, I felt more of a sense of identity with Casement than with the other men of 1916. Like him, I had been brought up as a Protestant, a Unionist, loyal to the British Crown. I could appreciate why Casement's family, who had been friends of my own, should prefer to forget that he had ever existed. Looked at from their viewpoint, his record was uniquely disgraceful. Here was a man who had once believed that Ireland was an integral part of the United Kingdom, yet had become a militant separatist; who had served his King and country, and accepted their honours, yet in their hour of need had deserted to the enemy; who had been brought up a

Protestant, yet had turned Catholic just before he was executed. And, if the rumours about his diaries were correct, he was a man who had appeared to be strictly honourable in his private life, yet had in fact been a practising homosexual.

I could also understand, though, how Casement had come to turn against England. By the time the Second World War broke out, although like most of my Irish friends I joined the British forces as a matter of course, I remained sufficiently Irish to realise that if a conflict of loyalties arose — as one nearly did, over rumoured plans for British invasion of Ireland in 1940, to secure the use of her ports — I would take the Irish side. As no such decision had to be made, the conflict in my case was painlessly resolved; but it gave me some insight into how Casement, having taken the same road as Swift, Tone, Emmet, Mitchel and Parnell, had felt compelled to follow it to the end — though in his case, as he knew, the end was likely to be the gallows.

For the British to have executed him for being a traitor to the Crown did no harm to his reputation among his fellow-countrymen. It was the noblest of deaths he could have died. What enraged the Irish was the method the British Government had used to silence the campaign for a reprieve. A great many people in public life — politicians, churchmen, journalists — saw copies of what were claimed to be his diaries, at the time; but after they had fulfilled their purpose, they were withdrawn and subsequent attempts to secure an examination of them were fruitless. Inevitably, the suspicion arose that they had been forged.

For years, controversy about Casement tended to be less on his career than on whether the diaries were, or were not, forgeries. But actual evidence of what they had contained was lacking, until Singleton-Gates produced this typed version of two of them, for 1903 and 1910. They had come into his possession, he explained, in the early 1920s. He had intended using them in a book on Casement, but he had been told by the then Home Secretary that if he did so, he would expose himself to prosecution under the Official Secrets Act. The simple act of showing them to us, in the 1950s left him (and us) technically liable to prosecution; but after consideration, it was deemed safe for him to write an article on the subject, which appeared in the company of a denunciation by Robert Blake of the uses to which the Act had been put, in the past. There was no official reaction; Singleton-Gates was emboldened to accept an offer from Maurice Girodias to have the transcripts published in a book, in Paris and New York. The Home Office at last gave way. In 1959, the Home Secretary, R. A. Butler, gave instructions that the originals should be made available for inspection in the Public Record Office.

I go into the history of the forgery controversy later;* suffice to say that inspection convinced me that they were genuine. And at the time that seemed to be that. But with the forgery issue out of the way, the fact that Casement had been a practising homosexual, however disgraceful it had seemed in 1916, ceased to be important. Why, after all, should it be any more destructive of his reputation, from the standpoint of half a century later, than it was of the reputation of his contemporaries — Wilde, or Gide, or Proust? At most, it could only help to explain some puzzling features of his career. And on that career, a mass of fresh material was soon to become available, following the termination of the 'fifty year rule', and the opening of the Foreign Office files up to and beyond 1916. From this source, and from the growing Casement collection in the National Library of Ireland, it is now possible to try to answer the questions which for so long were rarely asked, owing to the forgeries controversy. Did Casement really elicit the truth about King Leopold's Congo — or was his report as biased as his critics, then and since, have alleged? Did his work there, and in the Putumayo, have any lasting effect? What was the extent of his influence on the course of events which led up to the Easter Rising; and on later Irish history? And what drove him to break with his past in 1914, when he went to Germany, though he realised it would be the loss of his reputation, and probably of his life?

* See Part Seven. (I should add that my request to be allowed to reproduce a page from the diaries, which would have made it easier to illustrate my objections to the forgery theory, was refused by the Home Office.)

AUTHOR'S NOTE

Writing the amount he did, in longhand, Casement was occasionally careless in his syntax, spelling and punctuation. To avoid interrupting quotations from him with corrections or 'sics', I have silently altered, where necessary. I have also filled out some abbreviations, rather than explain them.

Casement often made and kept a draft of letters he was intending to post. It is not always possible to tell if he despatched them, but I have used the drafts as evidence of what was in his mind at the time — even if they were not actually sent.

In dealing with finance — trade figures and so on — I have levelled up or down to the nearest round number. Where the figures are given in the original currencies, they are easy to translate into each other: 25 Belgian francs = 5 U.S. dollars = one pound sterling. The worth of those francs, dollars and pounds in present-day terms is much less easy to gauge: somewhere between a fifth and a tenth of what they could purchase then.

PART ONE

KING LEOPOLD'S CONGO
1884–1905

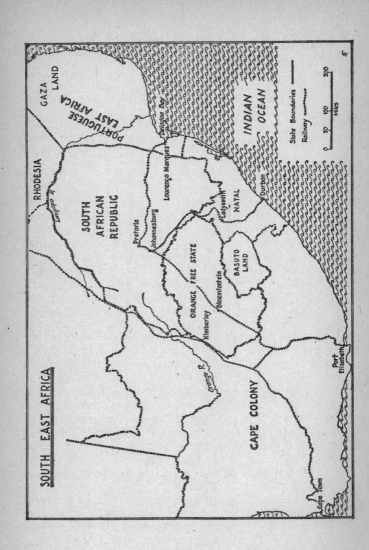

SOUTH EAST AFRICA

GAZA LAND

PORTUGUESE EAST AFRICA

RHODESIA

Limpopo R.

SOUTH AFRICAN REPUBLIC

Pretoria
Johannesburg

Delagoa Bay
Lourenço Marques

ORANGE FREE STATE

Kimberley
Bloemfontein

BASUTO LAND

Ladysmith

NATAL

Durban

INDIAN OCEAN

State Boundaries _____
Railway ....

0   50   100   200
        Miles

Orange R.

CAPE COLONY

Port Elizabeth

Cape Town

CHAPTER ONE

THE DARK CONTINENT

Stanley's Men

'A great map of the Dark Continent hung on the walls of my classroom,' Casement's close friend and colleague-to-be Edward Glave recalled in his *Six Years of Adventure in Congoland*. 'The tentative way in which the geographers of that day had marked down localities in almost unknown equatorial regions seemed to me delightful and mysterious.' Why the Congo basin should have remained almost unknown for so long is still something of a mystery, as the mouth of the river had been discovered by Portuguese explorers four centuries earlier. But cataracts a hundred miles up stream made it unnavigable; and the precipitous cliffs on both sides had discouraged portaging. Slaves (who could be compelled to march across country) and ivory (which the slaves could be compelled to carry) were brought down through forest tracks to the Atlantic; but no trade route had been opened up into the interior, and although the Arab slavers had long used the alternative route to the Congo basin, from the Indian Ocean, it was not explored by a westerner until Lovett Cameron started across the continent from east to west in 1873.

In 1874 Henry Stanley set out from Zanzibar with an expedition to follow the river from its source down to the Atlantic. If he succeeded, the last of the remaining unmapped regions of Central Africa could be opened up. But for whom? The project attracted Leopold II, King of the Belgians. As Crown Prince, he had tried without success to interest his countrymen in colonial ventures, and he had been unable to rouse them when they became his subjects. The Congo, he realised, represented his last chance; but he would have to look for financial support outside Belgium. In 1876 he called a conference in Brussels of explorers, geographers and scientists, and put to them the idea that the Congo offered humanity its last chance to set up a colony whose aim would be, from the start, to benefit the indigenous population. In case the delegates to the conference should be sceptical—protestations of disinterestedness had been heard commonly enough before from ruthless colonial exploiters—Leopold pointed out that nobody could accuse the Belgian people of imperialist aspirations; he had failed utterly to interest them in his ideas. His own sole ambition was 'to open up to civilisation the only area of our globe which it has not yet penetrated'. For this purpose, he proposed, they should form themselves into an international trust, to take over responsibility for the Congo. It was an unprecedented offer; and the explorers, geographers and scientists were deeply impressed. An International African Association was set up for the purpose, with Leopold as its first chairman.

A few months later, Stanley reached the mouth of the Congo; and his despatches describing his journey down the river created a sensation greater, if possible, than that which had greeted the news of his discovery of Livingstone. It had taken him 999 days to cross the continent; and he had been in constant peril from rapids, from storms, from cannibals, from crocodiles, and from fever. None of the white companions with whom he had begun the journey had survived; he himself had almost perished from hunger when within only a few miles of his destination. There had never been an adventure story to compare with it. But it was not calculated to raise hopes of easy pickings; when Stanley unfolded his plans to develop the region, he could find no British backers. Reluctantly, he decided to listen to Leopold's proposals.

Leopold had been having a struggle to hold his enterprise together. The national committees which had been set up to help run the International African Association had taken their own divergent courses, leaving him to rescue it out of his own pocket. Now, reconstituted as the Congo International Association, he offered it to Stanley, with a free hand to recruit men to survey, and then to administer, such territories as the Association would acquire. And among those who came out to join Stanley's men on the Upper Congo was Roger Casement.

The Congo Free State

Casement had been born on September 1st, 1864, at Sandycove (where James Joyce was to set the first scene of *Ulysses*) near Dublin; and christened Roger David. He had two elder brothers, Charlie (who later emigrated to Australia), and Tom; and a sister, Agnes—'Nina'—eight years his senior. As adults, Charlie and Tom were continually in financial difficulties, and Nina was a possessive and quarrelsome woman; but Roger loved them.

Both parents died before Roger was ten years old; he and his sister and brothers, wards in Chancery, were taken to live with their guardian, a member of his father's family, in Ulster. He went to school there, and was always to think of himself as an Ulsterman. His closest family tie, though, was with his mother's sister, who had married Edward Bannister, an agent in West Africa for one of the great Liverpool trading companies. His aunt looked on Roger as if he were her own son; and he often stayed with her family in their Liverpool home. To his cousin Elizabeth, four years his junior, he had 'the dignity and graciousness of some fairy prince'.

He spent many of his holidays with us, and we came to look on him more as an elder brother than a cousin. He was devoted to my mother, who, unlike his own mother, was very small. He always spoke and wrote of her as 'Dear Wee Auntie'. During his holidays he would play games with us and entertain us for hours. I never remember him to lose his temper, nor to become rough in his play, as occasionally the two older boys would do in their exuberant high spirits. He was always fond of painting and of inventing stories and I believe if he had seriously cultivated these gifts he would have made a name for himself.

Roger's favourite cousin, though, was Gertrude—'Gee'—nine years his junior. They became, and remained, devoted to each other. Gertrude remembered him spinning her long fairy tales, and dressing up in weird improvised African costumes. 'Roddie'—as the family called him—was musical, with 'a beautiful baritone voice, and an absolutely true ear'; he liked to sing Irish airs, to his sister's accompaniment. He read voraciously, chiefly history and poetry—the story of Greece, and of Rome, and any work on Ireland he could lay his hands on. He was also athletic, though not in the conventional sense of being good at games. And he was passionately fond of animals. Gertrude was to recall him.

In appearance Roddie was strikingly handsome. He was over six feet when he was seventeen; his eyes were grey and deep-set, his face rather thin; and his hair nearly black and curly. He had good teeth, and a very clear skin. When he was in Africa he grew a beard, and this was his habit ever since. The beard was a shade lighter than his hair, and he kept it short. His speaking voice was beautiful—he never lost a very slight Irish accent, but his English was that of a cultured gentle-man. His demeanour in society, or in public, was always quiet and unobtrusive—he hated publicity and loathed being 'shown off'. When he entered a room, he seemed to make the other people in it seem commonplace . . .

There had been some plan that Roger should enter the Civil Service; but his uncle got him a job in Liverpool in the Elder Dempster shipping line. He soon felt, as he must have looked, out of place as a desk-bound clerk. 'I must have an open air life,' he had told his sister Nina, 'or I shall die.' As a boy he had delighted to paint imaginative scenes of wild beasts roaming through exotic tropical forests; and the fact that Elder Dempster ships did the West African run now gave him his opportunity to visit them. He persuaded the company to let him go out as a purser on one of their ships to Boma, where his uncle was stationed. What he saw while he was there determined him to return; and when he was just twenty, he joined the volunteers—they were unpaid—who were working for Stanley.

It was not a promising moment to arrive. The Congo Inter-national Association appeared to be under sentence of death. In an unguarded moment, Stanley had claimed that whichever European power controlled the mouth of the river could control the trade of the whole Congo basin, and the Portuguese had decided that, by right of their four-hundred-year-old occupation of the territory, the control should be theirs. Just before Case-ment arrived to join the Association, a treaty was announced between Portugal and Britain, conceding Portugal's territorial claims and, in so doing, delivering what appeared to be a fatal blow to the Association's prospects.

Up to this point, nobody had taken Leopold seriously. Striking though he was in appearance, with his great height and his formidable-looking spade beard, he had inspired neither the respect of his own people nor the friendship of his royal contemporaries (the Prince of Wales, the future Edward VII, detested him). But now, he showed the qualities which Casement was to come to know so well: foresight, determination, and pre-ternatural guile. For a start, he commissioned an article reveal-ing just how slippery the Portuguese had been over such treaties in the past, had it translated, and circulated it to influential people in Britain. Then, he let it be known that the Portuguese had actually offered the same deal, but with better terms, to the French. Such was the indignation at this disclosure that the Liberal Government had to back down; the treaty with Portugal was not ratified. He was also courting sympathy in the United States, with the help of the former U.S. minister in Brussels, Henry Sanford. President Arthur praised the Association's aims, and the Senate foreign affairs committee recognised the Asso-ciation's flag. But the decisive intervention came from Bis-marck. Little though he liked or trusted Leopold, he was de-lighted to be able to humiliate Britain, which had so frequently blocked Germany's African ventures. The future of the Congo, he insisted, must be determined by an international conference, to which he would play host in Berlin. The Gladstone Govern-ment—distracted by the fears for General Gordon, beleaguered in Khartoum—did not feel in any position to refuse; and Leo-pold judiciously bought off the French with a promise that they should have the reversion of the Association's territories, should it be unable to survive. When the delegates to the Berlin Con-ference assembled in November, they found they needed to do no more than ratify the sanctions already given by the individ-ual powers to the Association; and in February 1885 the Congo Free State—as it was now to be called—came into being.

For Stanley's men, who had had good reason to fear their work would be overturned, it was wonderful news. The Berlin signatories pledged themselves to ensure that the Association's aims—to work for the improvement of the Congo natives' moral and material conditions, and to suppress slavery—re-mained unchanged. 'The most rigid injunctions enforcing free trade, absolute religious liberty and freedom of worship are guaranteed,' the Congo missionary, W. Holman Bentley, exulted. 'We cannot fail to see the hand of God in this result.' That Leopold had been prevailed upon to become the sovereign of the new state, Bentley felt, was itself a guarantee that the Berlin terms would be kept. And this would give Stanley's men an opportunity, never offered to any such group before, to mould the destinies of a new nation, unhampered by the usual pressures of imperial pride or commercial greed.

It would be a formidable undertaking. Casement and his colleagues would have to develop and administer an area the size of western Europe. Much of the territory was still unexplored; much of it still under the dominance of the Arab slave-traders. It was an opportunity, and a challenge, without parallel in history.

Casement himself left no account of his experiences working for the Free State; but Edward Glave, Fred Puleston, and Herbert Ward were to describe the work of Stanley's men. Even allowing for explorers' licence, the wonder is that they survived. They had to face the same hazards that had confronted Stanley on his first voyage down the Congo: savage cannibal tribes; unpredictable weather—frequent storms; stifling hot days followed by chilly nights—and menacing wild beasts: buffaloes, leopards, crocodiles. Pervading everything was the swarming insect life, ants, tsetse flies, gnats, mosquitoes, and countless others 'there to torment you to death', Puleston recalled, 'and drive you almost insane'. Always, too, there was the threat of fever, ranging from mild attacks of malaria to the often fatal 'blackwater'. Of three men who came out with Glave, a few months before Casement, one died on the journey up to Stanley Pool, and the other two had to be left behind before they reached their assigned posts—one also soon to die, the other to return, broken in health, to England.

In one respect, it was even harder for the agents of the new State than it had been for Stanley. As an explorer, he had won a reputation for ruthlessness; he liked to have a substantial well-armed force of Zanzibaris with him, and to use them, if necessary, to fight his way through opposition—as he often had to do, on that first voyage down the Congo. But for the purpose of developing territory, after it had been opened up, he believed in following the principles laid down by Livingstone, whose memory he venerated. When the objective was to ameliorate the condition of the natives, Livingstone had insisted, only peaceful persuasion could work; then, 'any act becomes ennobled. Whether exchanging the customary civilities at a village, accepting a night's lodging, purchasing food for the party, asking for information, or answering polite African inquiries as to our objects in travelling, we begin to spread a knowledge of that people by whose agency their land will yet become enlightened and freed from the slave trade.' Stanley imbued his followers with the same spirit. 'We travelled through the Congo,' he could claim,

> making roads and stations, negotiating for privileges, surveying the vast area, teaching and preparing the natives for the near advent of a bright and happy future for them, winning them by gentleness, appeasing their passions, inculcating commercial principles, showing them the nature of the produce that would be marketable when the white man should come; and everywhere, we were accepted as their friends and benefactors.

Stanley went back to Europe for the Berlin negotiations; but he was allowed to nominate his successor, the respected Sir Francis de Winton, and it is clear from the memoirs of the men he had recruited that they remained loyal to his principles. Even Fred Puleston (who had come out to Africa simply as an adventurer) regarded Stanley as a 'demigod'. In his *African Drums*, Puleston was to couple Casement's name in the dedication with Stanley's—'my dearest friend', Puleston described him, recalling that he had been given two nicknames by the Congo natives: 'Swami' (Woman's God) and 'Monafuma' (Son of a King); 'he deserved both, for a more charming, lovable man never lived.' And in the chapter of the book in which he described some of the characters he had known in the Congo in those years, Puleston made an attempt to do justice to his friend's memory.

> Casement's disposition and make-up was the gentlest imaginable; he was always sweet-tempered, ready to help, condemning cruelty and injustice in any form. Indeed he was so emotional, tender and sympathetic that, when his fox terrier (Spindle, I think he named it) got at cross-purposes with a wild hog and had his stomach ripped open, Casement was unable to control his feeling and wept like a girl.

His whole nature, Puleston insisted, was strongly opposed 'to anything in the nature of double dealing'.

Puleston wrote his memoirs nearly half a century later, when time might have glossed over some of Casement's deficiencies. But in *A Voice from the Congo*, published in 1895, Herbert Ward—soon to win an international reputation as a sculptor—had shown he shared Puleston's estimation of their colleague. There could be no better opportunity to test a man's true worth, Ward pointed out, than working with him in so barbarous an environment. 'Under such circumstances the true disposition of a comrade soon becomes apparent. A man's courage or tendency to faintheartedness are soon betrayed; all men must perforce reveal their latent qualities, good and bad.' And of his Congo comrades, Ward singled out Casement for praise. 'A tall, handsome man of fine bearing; thin, mere muscle and bone, a sun-tanned face, blue eyes and black curly hair. A pure Irishman he is, with a captivating voice and a singular charm of manner. A man of distinction and great refinement, high-minded and courteous, impulsive and poetical.' It was to be the beginning, for the two men, of a close friendship.

The Sanford Expedition   *1886–1887*

With only a handful of men available to develop and administer so huge an area, the immediate problem was communications; and, from the start, Casement was involved in building up the new State's transport system. But it was soon clear that the State's resources—still, in the main, Leopold's private resources—were inadequate, and in 1886 Henry Sanford was called upon to obtain financial backing in America for a survey of still unexplored areas. Casement was invited to join, along with Edward Glave. For this work, he was to have a salary—£150 a year to look after the expedition's supply problems at its base in Matadi. It was a dull job; but Casement was described by one of his colleagues as 'a good, hard-working man; a gentleman, with some principle about him'. Emory Taunt, the officer in charge, felt that he had found the right man for the job; if the expedition were successful, Casement would be given a more responsible post, up country.

He duly got the job, succeeding Glave in charge of the trading station which the expedition established at Equator, on the Upper Congo. But it did not give him more responsibility. There was little to do, because trade had not developed; and such development as there was disconcerted him, revealing that the

Sanford expedition had been designed as a commercial enterprise, rather than directly for the Free State. There were dissensions; Casement came in for criticism; and although Glave loyally reported that he must have been made the scapegoat for the faults of others, he decided to resign, in order to take charge of another survey, for the proposed railway between Matadi and Stanley Pool.

He was under no illusions about that project, either, as a letter he wrote to Sanford, explaining his resignation, reveals. 'The difficulty here,' he explained, 'is not that the country is not fertile, but that the people do not work.' The Association was finding, as colonial developers everywhere in Africa tended to find, that the low wages offered meant little to natives, set off against the need to work for them. In the circumstances, he felt it was wasteful to build a railway; the money spent would be better employed in organising a more efficient administration and seeking to educate the natives, 'quickening their good instincts (and they have many) and repressing their bad'.

At the Mission Station   1887–1888

It was a perceptive letter, save in one respect: Casement had not grasped that whereas funds might be made available for any project which could ultimately bring profit to those who put up the capital, the State had no source of income through which its administration, or the education of the natives, could be improved. Looking for ways in which the State might cease to be maintained out of his own pocket, Leopold was beginning to find the idealism of Stanley's men a nuisance; and he was embarking on what even his admirer Bentley, the British missionary, felt was a deliberate policy of getting rid of the non-Belgian element in the Congo administration. In his letter to Sanford Casement had claimed with some pride that his survey for the railway was going so well that he hoped to finish it before the rainy season began in November. He did—only to find himself out of work, and with no prospect of re-employment by the State. It happened that owing to the high wastage rate from disease and death, Bentley's mission had been in difficulties, and he had sounded out his head office in London about the possibility of using lay helpers. The trouble, he admitted, was that the level of salary he could afford was likely to attract only men who could find no other work; and the reasons why Europeans could find no other work in the Congo had not usually been of a nature that would commend them for employment on a mission station. If any candidate should appear, Bentley promised, he would be very carefully vetted. Head office had given its sanction; and in November 1887, Bentley reported that a fellow missionary had mentioned that Casement was looking for a job. Bentley had accordingly made discreet inquiries why, and found that it was because of the State's policy of employing only Belgians, and not from any fault of his own. 'I was especially glad to hear it,' he commented, 'for Casement is very highly esteemed by everyone out here, a perfect gentleman, and very good and patient with the natives.' He had also, Bentley had heard, been 'recently led to Christ', and he appeared to be 'the fittest man we could find anywhere to help us'. Nevertheless Bentley had taken the precaution of inviting him to stay at the station for a day or two, before actually offering him the job—managing the transport, building, planting, accounts and correspondence, and the general work of the station, for a salary of £10 a month, exclusive of board, until the end of the rainy season.

Soon, Bentley was able to report that the lay helper was giving satisfaction:

> So far I am sure that we could not have done better either in terms or type of man . . . His general bearing and all that I have learned mark him as a gentleman. His treatment of the natives is all that can be desired so far as I can learn; I managed also very delicately to get an assurance that there had been nothing in his manner of life out here which would cast reflection on us did he become identified with us. I do not think we have any grounds of apprehension on those lines. Then as to his religious convictions and experience. He speaks very definitely of his conversion and faith in Christ, which he dates from the early part of this year.

The only fault Bentley had to find was that his lay helper lacked ruthlessness when buying food from the natives in the local currency, brass rods:

> He kept up our prices of barter stock; but, left entirely to himself, would have lowered them, and would rather give 20 rods, for one thing, than bargain and beat down to 12 rods,

the proper price. Of course such haggling is a great nuisance, but unless we keep firm to prices they would run up no one knows where to. If he sold a fathom of cloth he would wish to give six inches more than a fathom, and so on. There is far too much of this throwing away money out here, on the part of State men, and we in the missions have great difficulty in keeping prices down. A man travelling who has no meat for dinner will give a very long price for a fowl. I only mention this to show how fair, generous and good-hearted he is. His work was well done and the books well kept.

And when he departed, at the end of the rainy season, Casement donated £3 10s. of his earnings to the mission.

The searcher after a faith; the perfect gentleman; the friend of the natives—all these came to be accepted as characteristic of Casement by those with whom he worked. Even the belief that his private life was beyond reproach lasted to almost the end of his life. And always, there was to be the desire to be doing something useful, something which stretched him, even if there was little money in it. He had worked for no more than his keep before, in the service of the Free State, and doubtless he would have stayed in it, if there had been anything for him to do. But, as he was to explain a few years later, although he still had all the love of Africa in him, he had no wish to continue in what was clearly becoming a Belgian enterprise. Still, he had managed to do a great deal of exploring 'and making friends with the natives; I liked them, poor souls—and they me'. And young though he had been, he had left the Congo with no discredit, and 'no enemies, only friendships'.

Heart of Darkness   1890–1891

Casement was in fact to return, a few months later; but as his job did not take him to the Upper Congo, he did not think of it as a continuation of his earlier work. Following his survey, a company had been formed to construct the railway from Matadi to Stanley Pool, and his experience and reputation made him an obvious choice as manager. One of Stanley's men, Major Parminter, who was one of the directors of the company, was deputed to persuade him to come back. This time, he could afford to make his own terms. Past experience had made him cautious—it had taken him months to extract his salary from the syndicate backing the Sanford expedition. He went to Brussels to ensure a satisfactory contract, before leaving for Matadi.

There, he met the young Captain Korzeniowski, soon to be better known as Joseph Conrad. Conrad, too, had been attracted by the romance of the Congo. When he acquired his master's ticket, he had come out there in the expectation of being given the command of one of the fast-growing fleet of river steamboats which were being brought up in sections along Stanley's road, and reassembled on Stanley Pool. His stay turned out to be a disturbing experience, forming the basis of his *Heart of Darkness*. The climate began to undermine his health; the Congo depressed him; and the Belgian authorities, jealous of a foreigner, would not give him his promised command. But—as he recorded in his diary—making Casement's acquaintance at Matadi, in the summer of 1890, was 'a great pleasure under any circumstances, and now it becomes a positive piece of luck. Thinks, speaks well, most intelligent and sympathetic.' When Conrad had to return to Britain, their parting was 'most friendly'. As he was to recall, in a letter to R. B. Cunninghame Graham:

> I can assure you that he is a limpid personality. There is a touch of the conquistador in him too; for I've seen him start off into an unspeakable wilderness swinging a crook-handled stick for all weapons, with two bulldogs, Paddy (white) and Biddy, (brindle) at his heels, and a Loanda boy carrying a bundle for all company. A few months afterwards it so happened that I saw him come out again, a little leaner, a little browner, with his stick, dogs and Loanda boy, and quietly serene as though he had been for a stroll in a park.

Time had embroidered Conrad's recollection. Casement himself described what the construction work entailed, in a letter to his young cousin Gertrude Bannister—the first of many; playful, as she was nine years younger; always to be suffused with deep affection. The countryside through which the railway was being constructed, he told her, consisted of grassy plains covered with scrub—inhospitable, but hardly unspeakable. The work was not exacting enough to satisfy him for long. When his year's contract expired, he decided not to renew it, and returned home. His employers expressed their opinion of him by describing him, in their testimonial, as an *agent exceptionnel*.

CHAPTER TWO

ON HER MAJESTY'S SERVICE

Old Calabar   *1892–1895*

At some point in the next few months, Casement went to the United States—perhaps on a lecture tour, in connection with Sanford's project. But in 1892 he was back in West Africa, in a job more to his liking than any he had undertaken since the break-up of Stanley's team. A few years earlier, a British company which had obtained a trade concession on the Niger had been detected abusing the powers granted in its charter; it had been superseded by the Niger Coast Protectorate; and he was appointed to the Protectorate's Survey Department. This presented him with a variety of tasks—including, if he was not being flippant, the Acting Director-Generalship of Customs. But his main work was to survey those regions of the Protectorate which had not previously been visited by white men, except the occasional trader.

What such surveys entailed was described in his reports to the Protectorate's Administrator, Sir Claude MacDonald, in the spring of 1894. Sometimes the natives were courteous, sometimes surly, sometimes menacing; once, he was forced to return after an incident when his party had been surrounded by warriors—dancing, shouting, 'clashing swords and machetes in our faces'—who seized some of the porters, and the loads they were carrying. In the confusion, however, a woman appeared who led him by the hand to the local chief, on whose orders the porters and their loads were released. But if the chief had not been friendly he could have done nothing; for his party were unarmed. He could have made his way through the hostile territory by force, he explained to MacDonald; but not without loss of life on both sides, which 'would certainly result in a widespread feeling of hostility and resentment'. It was best, he felt, to accept the necessity of opening up the country gradually and peacefully. Only then would the natives become friendly, and co-operate.

Evidently he had not forgotten Stanley's admonition that real, heart-felt sympathy with the natives was the prerequisite; and how heart-felt it had become can be sensed from some verses he wrote while he was in the Protectorate, in 1893, on hearing the fate of Lobengula's army in Matabeleland. When Herbert Ward described his friend as 'poetical', it was not just a matter of temperament: Casement aspired to be a writer. In 1893 he had actually had a story published—though as the conclusion was accidentally left out, it can hardly have helped to make his reputation. And he continually wrote, and rewrote, poetry. It could be painfully derivative; odes after the manner of Keats, ballads in the style of Thomas Davis. But feeling seeped through the stilted construction and vocabulary, as in his lament for Lobengula's warriors, mowed down by the Maxim guns of Cecil Rhodes's mercenaries, under Dr. Jameson's command.

To Stanley's men, what was happening in Matabeleland was what they had tried in the Congo to prevent. For British consumption, Rhodes had promoted it as a beneficent colonial development for the protection of the natives. In reality, it was a commercial venture relying for its profits on the ruthless exploitation of native labour; a threat to the whole idea of bringing civilisation to the natives by inducing them to work for themselves, rather than by forcing them to work for their white conquerors. Rhodes, as Sir William Harcourt assured the Commons, was a very reasonable man. 'He only wanted two things. Give him Protection and give him Slavery and he will be perfectly satisfied.' Now, having got rid of Lobengula, he could have them both:

> Old King of Zulu sires, had you but known
> The word the white man spake
> Stood only till his cannon fires, your fallen throne
> Had not today been hid in far Zambesi's brake

—Casement's lament began, and it ended:

> Prate not of England's valour in the field
> Her heart is sick with lust.
> The gold she wins is red with blood, nor can it shield
> Her name from tainted league with men of broken trust.

This did not mean that he felt, as yet, any serious conflict of loyalties. Many Englishmen were repelled by what Rhodes and his like were doing. And in the Niger Coast Protectorate, at least, Casement was able to do something to show that the natives could be won for civilisation by precept, and by sympathy. Unorthodox though his methods might be, they won the admiring approbation of the Protectorate's administrator. Transmitting the reports of his surveys to Whitehall, MacDonald echoed Casement's arguments in his covering letter. A passage could have been forced through those regions of the Protectorate which still remained to be surveyed, he wrote, with the help of the Maxim gun. But it was desirable to try the conciliatory approach; and that was why Casement had declined armed protection. 'It would have been difficult,' MacDonald added, 'to find anyone in every way more suited to the work.'

Lourenço Marques   1895–1898

When Casement came back on leave from the Niger Protectorate in the summer of 1895, it was to find that his reports, and MacDonald's comments, had been published as a White Paper, and that the British Association wanted an account of his Niger experiences. It was his first taste of public recognition. Evidently his worth was also recognised in Whitehall; he was told there that his services would now be required on a mission to Uganda, where Rhodes's British South Africa Company had run into difficulties. The region was still so ill-defined that its boundaries tended to be left undrawn on contemporary maps of central Africa, and it was coveted by the French, the Germans, the Italians, and Leopold; it would need colonial administrators of courage and quality to secure it for the Crown. Casement could consider himself flattered to be one of them.

In June, however, when the Conservatives returned to power under Lord Salisbury, he was informed that his services were required in a post which the new Government thought was even more important; he was asked to cut short his home leave so that he could proceed at once to Lourenço Marques, in Portuguese East Africa, to be Her Majesty's Consul. 'I have only to say, my Lord,' he wrote to Salisbury (who had decided to be his own Foreign Secretary), 'that I am deeply sensible of the honour the Queen has done me in entrusting the duties of that post to my care; and I can only express the hope that I may prove myself not unworthy of this gracious expression of Her Majesty's pleasure.' The wording of the reply might sound as if it owed something to a Foreign Office manual of etiquette; perhaps it did, as similar cadences were common in the consular correspondence of the time. But he had good reason to be pleased—especially as the Foreign Office was so anxious to have him that they were prepared to spare him the usual qualifying entry examination. The Foreign Secretary retained the right to appoint consuls. Ordinarily, he used it to dispense patronage; in this case, to avoid delay.

Casement was not entirely new to the work. As Nigeria was in theory an independent native state, with Britain merely the protecting power, there had been consular functions to perform until (as, nearly twenty years later, he was to describe the process to a Royal Commission investigating the Civil Service) 'the protecting Power became the annexing Power', rendering Consuls unnecessary. But in Nigeria, he had not been established. Now, he was an accredited member of the Foreign Service.

From the moment he arrived in Lourenço Marques, Casement began to send a stream of letters and memoranda to the Foreign Office; and they reveal that even at this early stage of his career, he was remarkably self-assured. He was determined to be his own master. 'It is glorious to be independent,' he had told his cousin, Gertrude, to encourage her to work harder at school (years later, she found an old exercise book in which she had written 'WORK, for R's sake'); and he behaved less as a humble consul than as a proconsul, vested with authority to take such courses of action on Her Majesty's behalf as he thought fit. He was also determined to live in the style becoming Her Majesty's representative. It happened that an inquiry from the Foreign Office greeted him on arrival, whether the local contractors had put in a damp course, as they had undertaken to do, in the walls of the consulate. It was hardly worth tearing down the walls, he replied testily, to find out; what was more to the point were the building's numerous other deficiencies, which he listed, and continued to remind the Foreign Office about. He demanded more land to make the consulate worthier of the name, and new flags, to communicate with British ships in Delagoa Bay—and to celebrate the Queen's birthday; an occasion on which, he suggested, it would not be fitting that Her Majesty's consulate 'should be lacking in, and forced to borrow, the means of dressing the flagstaff'. He did not plead, or cajole. From the start, in his despatches to the Foreign Office, he showed that he regarded himself, and expected to be regarded, as master in his own house.

The British Consul's main function in Lourenço Marques had been to try to give some protection to British subjects from arbitrary exactions, and sometimes arbitrary arrests, by the Portuguese authorities. His predecessor had been pestering the Foreign Office to make formal protests, in such cases, to Lisbon. It did not take Casement long to realise that it was easier to obtain redress through informal approaches to the appropriate authority locally. As in the Niger Protectorate, the method might be unorthodox, but it worked. 'I am to inform you'—he was told by the Foreign Office, after he had secured the release of a British trader who had been held for some time without trial, in spite of the efforts of his predecessor—'that your conduct in the case meets with His Lordship's entire approval.'

There were some cases of injustice, though, where he found himself unable to intervene effectively; and they aroused his compassion. In particular, he was outraged by the treatment meted out to the native king who ruled in Gazaland: Gungunhana.

The territory of Gazaland had been disputed between the British and the Portuguese; and Gungunhana had decided to place his people under the protection of the British Government, as the less untrustworthy of the two. But the British Government, from diplomatic considerations, decided to relinquish its claims; Gungunhana was told he must make his peace with the Portuguese authorities. Reluctantly, he presented himself to them, accompanied by his wives and children. The Portuguese arrested them, and lodged them in Lourenço Marques gaol, periodically taking them out to exhibit them on a stand to passers-by, as a testimony to Portuguese military might. 'I understand from those who were present at the public exhibition that the Chief and his son Godede appeared to be overcome with shame and resentment at their exposure,' Casement reported; 'I cannot but feel that the ready surrender of Gungunhana was due as much to the representations of Her Majesty's Government, conveyed to him on more than one occasion since the recent troubles began, as to any achievements of the Portuguese troops.' *

* Gungunhana was later exiled to the Azores, where he died.

But deeply though he felt about such cases, he came to realise that the Portuguese officials could not be held responsible. It was the system of administration which was at fault; a system by which the Portuguese trader was also often the local magistrate, which enabled him to exploit the natives and harass British rivals with impunity. To secure the removal of men who were found guilty of perpetrating injustices, after inquiry, would make no appreciable difference; they would merely be replaced by others who would behave in the same way. The real fault, Casement observed, lay in the attitude of mind which allowed such a system to exist. 'The wide divergence of views upon the question of personal liberty entertained by Englishmen and Portuguese,' he thought, accounted for 'much in the public conduct of officials of the latter nation that to any ordinary Englishman's sense of justice seems unfair.' The Foreign Office agreed with the diagnosis, at least to the extent of realising the futility of expecting reforms in East Africa at the Lisbon Government's behest. A minute attached to one of his despatches admitted that representations in Lisbon about 'the rather Haitian administration of justice' in Portuguese East Africa had indeed proved a waste of time.

But Casement had not been despatched to Lourenço Marques simply to look after British subjects there. The real reason for sending him became apparent a few weeks after he arrived. From Cape Town, Cecil Rhodes had watched with apprehension what was happening in the Transvaal, where the Boers had been consolidating their independence. The British Government was not yet ready to go to war on behalf of the non-Boer element, the *Uitlanderss*; but if they rebelled, Rhodes was privately told (or claimed he had been), they would be supported, provided that the rising could be represented as having been forced on them by intolerable tyranny. That was enough for Rhodes. Again, Dr. Jameson was to be the instrument. But the 'rising', in December 1895, ignominiously sputtered out, and Jameson's raiders had to surrender. The only beneficiary was President Kruger. The Boers, he could now justifiably claim, must have arms, to protect themselves from further incursions. Instead of executing the ringleaders, which might have brought British intervention, Kruger commuted the death sentences to heavy fines —ransoms, in effect, out of which the money would be found to pay for the arms. And the obvious route through which to import them was through Delagoa Bay, by the new railway from Lourenço Marques to the Transvaal, thereby avoiding British territory.

Even before the Jameson raid, Casement had confirmed the Foreign Office's fears that the Boers were planning to exploit the railway. In November W. J. Leyds, employed by Kruger as a roving emissary, arrived for a short stay in Lourenço Marques, ostensibly for his health — though 'if undertaken for such an object,' Casement commented, 'the visit would be without parallel in the annals of the admittedly unhealthiest port in South East Africa.' Leyds's real object, he suggested, was to investigate the strategic possibilities of the new railway and to confer with the German Consul, Count Pfeil, and with the head of the German shipping line which was 'the only serious competitor to the English carrying trade in this port'. But to the Foreign Office's anxious inquiries whether German soldiers and arms were being landed at Lourenço Marques, and brought to the Transvaal, Casement off-handedly replied that he could obtain no reliable evidence. Some Germans had arrived, but he did not feel they were likely to play a military role: as for the arms, all consignments for the Transvaal were labelled 'Government Goods', so he could not say what was being transmitted. That summer, however, he managed to find a way to examine the despatch manifests for the freight which had been carried on the railway — presumably, by bribing some official. In the previous three months, he reported on June 16th, sixty-five cases of rifles, a hundred cases of Maxim guns, and cases containing four million cartridges, had been taken to the Boers; and another four million cartridges were awaiting despatch. If the British Government had been able to make use of the information, Casement's stock would have risen even higher; but they were helpless — as Arthur Balfour was to admit, after the Boer War had begun: 'our hands were tied,' he explained, 'and our mouths closed, by the Raid'.

There was another possible threat to British peace of mind in Africa, which aroused Casement's concern: the possibility that the Germans might come to terms with the Boers, and appropriate Portuguese West Africa. Early in 1896, he transmitted to the Foreign Office the gist of a long conversation he had had with Señor Lança, the Acting Governor-General of Mozambique.

Portugal and Britain, Lança had suggested, should get together, to foil German plans. This would suit the interests of both countries, 'England's being to ensure the maintenance of British supremacy in the Transvaal—that of Portugal, to retain the sovereignty of her territories'. As Casement had no inhibitions about pointing out the flaws in arguments of this kind, he was presumably impressed by Lança's thesis; and it was understandable that he should sympathise with the Portuguese, menaced as they rightly felt themselves to be, by the other colonial powers. Nevertheless, on their own record, the Portuguese had a poor case for continuing as the protecting power in the region; nobody knew better than he did just how incompetent, corrupt, and cruel their rule had been. He was, in fact, to document the case against them only a month after his conversation with Lança, in a report he had prepared for the Foreign Office on the condition of the harbour at Lourenço Marques, backed by an impressive array of statistics and press cuttings. In spite of the obvious advantages to be gained from encouraging trade, he showed, the port had been allowed to rot. The harbours, piers and warehouses were inadequate, and sometimes unsafe; the native labour, demoralised, was idle and incompetent; and he warned of 'the nemesis of neglect that one day may seriously imperil the welfare of the white race generally in these regions, hopelessly out-numbered as it is by a native population, this being steadily and wilfully brutalised by drink'. If this was what their rule had done for the natives, Casement's sympathy for the Portuguese was by his own standards misplaced—even if they were likely to be the victims of the colonial ambitions of Britain and Germany. It was an example of the flaw that was later to mar some of his judgments; the inability to work out the full implications of projects to which his ready sympathy attracted him.

Casement's investigation appears to have made him realise just how much he was coming to loathe Lourenço Marques, and its climate; and three weeks' holiday which he took in Cape Town after he had sent off the report, did nothing to restore his equanimity. When he returned, he found that the growing fear of being taken over by one or other of the colonial powers was provoking a growing resentment among the populace against white foreigners. Stones were thrown at the British consulate, and natives working there subjected to persecution. But he still rejected the idea of a formal protest to Lisbon: 'so long as Portuguese methods prevail at Lourenço Marques, there will be, I feel sure, constant strain, and constant kicking against these methods, first by foreigners and then by their consuls; and the successful man will be he who gives the highest kicks and keeps the best temper'. Such a man, Casement thought, would make an ideal Governor; 'and, I may add, an ideal consul'.

He obviously thought of himself as conforming to the ideal. Perhaps he even envisaged the possibility that he might become a proconsul. If so, Lourenço Marques offered no more scope for his talents; and the strain to which he referred was having its effect. It was not the hard work, though he had certainly been a tireless worker, listening, inquiring, and reporting. Nor was his interest confined to the port; his knowledge of the interior impressed a visitor, Poultney Bigelow, one of the best-known American foreign correspondents of the time. At first, Casement's ready flow of information excited Bigelow's suspicions: but going behind his back to make inquiries, Bigelow realised that his suspicions had been unjust. He was the sort of man, Bigelow thought, depicted in Jules Verne's novels, 'the man who is everlastingly exploring and extricating himself from every imaginable difficulty by superhuman tact, wit and strength. . . . It is not saying more than the truth when I testify that Mr. Casement knew more of the natives between Basutoland and the shores of Mozambique than any other white man.'

It was not the everlasting exploration or the difficulties that wearied Casement; it was consular routine. 'I find it a severe strain upon my time and temper,' he complained to the Foreign Office, 'as well as being incompatible with the best discharge of my duties, to be forced as I now am to interview anyone, whether black, white or Indian, who calls throughout the long day at this consulate, often upon trifling business or in quest of unimportant details, sometimes being even compelled to rise from bed when ill, to listen to a drunken sailor's complaint, or the appeal to my charity of a distressed British subject.' He had used the excuse of the need to recuperate after an illness to go to Cape Town; and in March 1897 he again used the state of his health to ask for some home leave, explaining that he had found a suitable substitute—Alfred Parminter, the nephew of his former employer, and himself one of Stanley's men. Casement was taking no risk of refusal. When he had gone to Cape Town, his choice of a substitute—the local Anglican clergyman—had alarmed the Foreign Office; and although the Rev. J. H. Bovill had performed his functions satisfactorily, Casement had been left in no doubt that he had exceeded his powers. Suspecting that the Foreign Office might again be concerned about an unknown substitute, he cabled to say that it was necessary for him to return at once on 'urgent private affairs'; and the Foreign Office, who had planned to send a qualified replacement, found themselves landed with young Parminter.

When his home leave was over, Casement found that the Foreign Office expected him to return to Lourenço Marques. Although he could hardly refuse, he lingered as long as he could over the journey, breaking it at Cape Town to go to Pretoria— excusing himself by reminding the Foreign Office that they had asked him to remain in close contact with their agent there, and getting the agent to write to them how useful their consultation had been. As a result, he did not report back at the Lourenço Marques consulate until November 2nd. The next day he announced—his formal expressions of regret inadequately concealing a note of triumph—that the doctor there had told him he must go back home at once for an operation. If he had merely pleaded illness, the Foreign Office might have insisted that he should stay. With surgery involved, they would not dare to.

It is hard to believe that Casement had not planned this move; but his mind may have been made up by the condition in which he found the consulate. It had become little short of a scandal, he told the Foreign Office in his last despatch; and, in mute evidence, he referred to a discoloured patch on his letter:

The blot of rust mould upon this piece of paper—one picked at random from my desk—is a specimen of the continual dropping that takes place from the iron ceilings of every room of the upper storey, and which has already spoiled books, pictures, photographs, table cloths, hangings and bed-covers in most rooms; to say nothing of the inlaid wood flooring, the pine blocks of which now, after three years exposure to this metallic rain, seem in parts rather to be samples of some unclassified product of the iron age.

There was no point in trying to repair the building, he

asserted; it would have to be sold, and a new one built, on a better site.

In this final despatch, he also snatched a minor but still satisfying victory. Few of the applications which he had made for improvements to the consulate had produced any results; and the first he had made—the request for flags—had been made in vain. Now, he enclosed a bill for 5s. 11d. from the captain of H.M.S. *Philomel* (the fact that he had an Irish name suggests the possibility of collusion) with a covering letter explaining that in view of the deplorably dilapidated nature of the flags at the consulate, orders had been given for their replacement from his ship's stores. And back went Casement—via Zanzibar. It would make a change, he felt.

His time in Lourenço Marques had been important for him, not merely in establishing him in the British Consular Service, but in giving him experience of the ways of the Foreign Office. For their part, irritated though they must have been with him for exploiting a disorder which, even if real, was palpably also diplomatic, they could not dispute that he had been hard-working, shrewd, and efficient. Self-assured from the start, Casement could now feel confident that his services had become too valuable to be let go.

As in the Congo, too, he had made close and lasting friendships: with two adventurous young Irish peers, Lord ffrench and Lord Ennismore; and with Count Blücher, a direct descendant of the German commander at Waterloo, and heir to the princedom. In his memoirs, written after Casement's execution, Blücher did not give a personal opinion (or, if he did, it was cut by his English wife, who was anxious to play down the connection). But he did quote the view of Count Richard Coudenhove-Kalergi, as if to justify his long friendship.

Coudenhove-Kalergi wrote:

All I can say from personal experience, and long friendship, is that I always found him sympathetic, clever, and fascinating, and that I have met very few men during my whole life who had such an exceptional personality. He possessed an absolutely genuine though somewhat exaggerated idealism; nothing whatever would stop him assisting the weaker against the stronger, because he simply could not help it.

Casement arrived back in England early in the new year of 1898, and asked for four months' leave. Awarded only two, he nevertheless managed to spin them out to four with the help of a mixture of ingenious flattery – praise for the Foreign Office's decision to up-grade the status of the Consul at Lourenço Marques (which he still was, in theory)—and sombre bulletins on the state of his health, including a medical certificate from an Irish doctor pronouncing that he was suffering from the effects of malaria, neurasthenia, haemorrhage, and weak circulation. In May, when he was finally due to return, he asked to be allowed to remain on unpaid leave—again, to deal with urgent personal affairs (probably connected with his family: Nina was headstrong, and possessive; Tom continually required rescuing from scrapes, marital and financial). He still assumed he would eventually be sent back to Lourenço Marques, and continued to send comments and advice to the Foreign Office on the state of affairs there; but perhaps he hoped that if he delayed his departure long enough, some other post might be found for him. If so, he was right. At the end of July, it was announced that he had been appointed Her Majesty's Consul at St. Paul de Loanda, in Portuguese West Africa.

The Loanda post might ordinarily have been considered a come-down, after Lourenço Marques. But the Foreign Office were concerned about something that was happening within its consular territory; Casement was being sent there for much the same reason he had been sent to Portuguese West Africa, three years before. In 1898, a French force occupied Fashoda, a trading post to the south of Khartoum; and the Foreign Office learned that it was being supplied, and would be reinforced, through the Congo. Casement's experience in Lourenço Marques—and, earlier, in the Congo itself—made him an obvious choice to find out what the French were doing. On the way to take up his Loanda post, therefore, he stopped off to visit Matadi, the railhead to the Upper Congo; and he reported on December 18th, that 'considerable numbers of French officers and men, and large quantities of ammunition, said to be destined for the Bahr El Ghazal, have been recently despatched'. Once again, though, by the time his information reached the Foreign Office it was of little more than academic

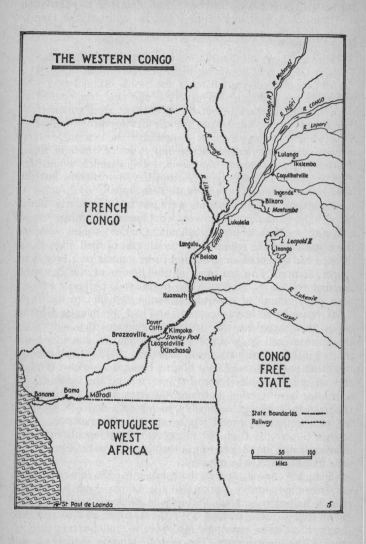

THE WESTERN CONGO

FRENCH CONGO

R. Sanga

R. Likwala

R. Oubangi (R.)

R. Ngiri

R. CONGO

R. Lopori

Lulanga

Ikelemba

Coquilhatville

Ingende

Bikoro

L. Mantumba

Lukolela

Lungulu

Boloba

R. CONGO

L. Leopold II

Inongo

Chumbiri

Kuamouth

R. Lukenie

R. Kasai

Dover Cliffs

Kimpoko

Brazzaville

Stanley Pool

Leopoldville

(Kinchasa)

CONGO FREE STATE

Banana

Boma

Matadi

PORTUGUESE WEST AFRICA

State Boundaries ------

Railway +++++++

0   50   100

Miles

St Paul de Loanda

5

interest. In September, Kitchener had defeated the Dervishes at Omdurman, and moved on south to confront the French. While Casement was on his way out to West Africa, they had withdrawn.

There had been another reason, however, for sending him: the Foreign Office was becoming disturbed about the Congo Free State. Leopold had carried out some of his original promises; the slave traders had been expelled, and the river opened up with trading stations linked by an efficient river steamer and telegraph system. But to pay for the development, he had requested permission to grant Concessions in certain areas to private companies, and to impose import duties—both in breach of the Berlin agreement. And soon, foreign traders found that they were not merely excluded from the Concessions, but discriminated against in the rest of the Free State.

For a time, their complaints were not taken seriously. But in 1895—the year Casement went to Lourenço Marques—news came of the fate of an Englishman, Charles Stokes, who had been trading in the region to the south-east of the Congo basin. Stokes had accepted an invitation to be a guest of a Free State agent, Captain Lothaire, one of the heroes of the campaign against the slave traders; when he arrived, Lothaire arrested him on a charge of gun-running, subjected him to an illegal trial, refused him leave to appeal, and had him hanged. Hearing what had happened, the British Government demanded that Lothaire should be brought to justice; and so convinced was Lord Salisbury that justice would be done that his main concern was that Lothaire should not himself be hanged, in case it might set up 'a sort of blood feud between us and the Belgians'. He need not have worried. Lothaire was arrested and brought over for trial in Belgium—ostensibly, as his guilt was not disputed, to ensure that he would not escape the consequences of his crime. But at the trial, the prosecutor threw up his brief, declaring it was impossible to impeach 'this brave Belgian officer'; and Lothaire had to be released.

Soon afterwards, Reuters had transmitted a report from an American missionary working in the Congo, John B. Murphy, which helped to explain the episode. Stokes's real crime had been that he was trading with the natives; and in the Free State, the natives were now forbidden to trade, except through the State's own agents. The reason, Murphy explained, was the growing profitability of rubber, of which the Congo provided an important source of supply—and of profit to the State. The State's agents therefore had been instructed to see that rubber was collected:

Each town and district is forced to bring in a certain quantity to the headquarters of the *Commissaire* every Sunday. It is collected by force; the soldiers drive the people into the bush. If they will not go, they are shot down, and their left hands cut off and taken as trophies to the *Commissaire* . . . these hands, the hands of men, women and children are placed in rows before the *Commissaire* who counts them to see that the soldiers have not wasted cartridges. The *Commissaire* is paid a commission of about 1d. a lb. on all the rubber he gets. It is therefore in his interest to get all the rubber he can.

In 1897 a Swedish missionary working in the Congo, the Reverend E. Sjöblom, corroborated Murphy's account, adding that after the hands were cut off they were smoked, in small kilns, to preserve them until they could be shown to the *Commissaire*; 'I have many times seen this done.' And if death resulted from such maltreatment, the corpse provided a welcome addition to the native soldiers' rations.

It might have been difficult for Casement, when he went to the Foreign Office for his briefing before setting out for West Africa, to credit these and similar allegations which were in their files. But it happened that three of the reports were from men whom he knew, and could trust. One was his uncle, Edward Bannister, who in 1892 had been appointed a British Vice-Consul in Loanda, with the Congo as his special responsibility. British subjects from West African colonies, he found, who had been recruited to work in the Free State, were being illegally employed as soldiers—'sentries', as they were described, nominally to protect the rubber gatherers, but really to ensure that the prescribed quantity was collected. If the sentries failed, the punishment—also illegal—was a flogging. He had protested to the Free State authorities, only to be told that as a Consul, he should confine himself to commercial questions. Realising, though, that he would relate what he had found to the Foreign Office, the Free State Government decided to anticipate him.

Investigating a report that a ship was bringing British West Africans illegally to the Congo, he had boarded it, brushing aside a State official who tried to stop him, in order to examine the men's papers. For this, he was charged, convicted of assault, and fined. Complaining to the Foreign Office about Bannister's behaviour, the Free State authorities had to admit they had been detected in an illegality; they promised to stop using British West Africans as sentries, and waived the fine. But the Foreign Office allowed themselves to be persuaded that Bannister had acted in a manner unbecoming to his station, and he was asked to resign.

The second of the reports from the Congo Casement must already have heard at first hand, as it had come from Alfred Parminter, his successor as Consul at Lourenço Marques. In the autumn of 1896 Parminter had given Reuters an interview in which he described how, working on the Upper Congo—one of the very few non-Belgians, other than missionaries, who were still employed there—he had watched the condition of the natives deteriorating. The Free State had not liberated the slaves. It had merely offered them what, in effect, was another form of slavery—seven years' service as 'sentries'. Sitting smoking after dinner one evening, Parminter had seen a group of them returning from the pursuit of some natives who had tried to escape into the jungle. When the sergeant triumphantly held up a collection of human ears, strung together, the *Commissaire* had congratulated him on his achievement.

But the report which was most likely to impress Casement had come from his old Congo companion, Edward Glave. After leaving the Congo, Glave had won an international reputation as an explorer; and in 1893, he decided to try to repeat Stanley's voyage down the Congo. But at Matadi, he died. On his way down the river, Glave had met the American missionary, Murphy, and told him he had written an account of what he had seen. 'Unfortunately,' Murphy reported, 'his effects fell into the hands of the State, and I am told by the missionary in charge of the station where Mr. Glave is buried that the majority of his papers shared the same fate.' Confident that the papers had been safely disposed of, the Free State's headquarters in Brussels felt they could dismiss Murphy's allegations as 'pure calumnies'. But some of Glave's papers survived; and when they were published in 1897, in the *Century Magazine*, they showed how his initial pleasure in returning to the Congo had changed to revulsion, when he saw that the Free State had not suppressed slavery, but had merely re-established it in a new form, designed for the purpose of 'wringing rubber from these people without paying for it'. A quota, Glave had found, was demanded for each district. Natives who failed to collect enough were flogged with a *chicotte*, a whip of raw hippopotamus hide, 'trimmed like a corkscrew, with edges like knife blades, and as hard as wood'. Resistance, or an attempt to escape, meant mutilation or death. Everywhere in the State, he had heard the same story: 'rubber and murder, slavery in its worst form'.

On hearing of Glave's death, Casement had composed an 'In Memoriam', beginning

> He sleeps himself, whose hand has often made
> The simple grave wherein lost comrades lie
> His last long tranquil slumber, duty-crowned ...

Along with Herbert Ward, Glave was the colleague he remembered with the greatest affection. The fact that all three men, Bannister, Parminter and Glave, had been in agreement would have been enough to convince him that the condition of the natives in the Congo must be as bad as the missionaries, Murphy and Sjöblom, had described. But their reports had only covered the period between Casement's departure from the Congo and 1896; and in that year King Leopold, on being confronted with some of the ugly evidence, had personally intervened to set up the Commission for the Protection of the Natives, consisting of Catholic and Protestant missionaries — among them Casement's former employer on the mission station, Bentley, and the respected George Grenfell. Leopold, too, did not lack supporters to point out that in a region the size of the Congo, so recently the scene of the war against the slavers, some latitude must be allowed. 'The officials are but men,' Stanley claimed in a letter to *The Times*; 'and missionaries must not forget that they themselves are not free from human weaknesses.' Stanley also wrote an introduction to a book on the Congo, published in 1898, written by one of his protégés, Guy Burrows, and dedicated to Leopold. It would set the mind of journalists at rest about conditions there, Stanley hoped; reading it had reminded him 'what great gratitude the civilised world owes to King Leopold—for his matchless sacrifices on behalf of the inhabitants of the region . . . who can doubt that God chose the King for his instrument to redeem this vast slave park?'

Privately, Stanley was expressing a very different view. When extracts from his notebooks 'were published, many years later, they showed that as early as 1896, disillusionment had set in. Leopold had often invited him to return to the Congo; but he had refused, 'because to go back would be to see mistakes consummated, and to be tortured daily by seeing the effects of an erring and ignorant policy'. Stanley, however, kept these opinions to himself; and the Commons were left under the impression, when Charles Dilke brought up the subject in 1897 on behalf of the Aborigines Protection Society, that Leopold's active intervention would soon set matters to rights.

Reports from Casement's predecessor as Consul at Loanda, however, suggested that Leopold's intervention was not proving effective: so ugly were his stories that Salisbury ordered the opening of a Congo Atrocities file. Naturally, Casement's first thought when he arrived was to investigate for himself. But in the meantime, the Foreign Office had given consular accreditation to a British officer, Major Pulteney, who had told them he was going to travel in the Congo, to help him with his inquiries; and when Casement requested permission to go to the Upper Congo, it was thought best to refuse—so that (as a minute to his request commented) 'they should not be roaming up and down the river at once'.

Still, as virtually all the Congo's trade was channelled through Matadi and Boma, he was able to do some investigating there, of much the same kind as he had undertaken in Lourenço Marques, by studying the trade returns. From the Upper Congo, he found, load upon load of rubber arrived, destined for Antwerp. In return came virtually nothing, except guns and ammunition. So, far from the Upper Congo being opened up to receive the benefits of civilisation, it had actually been closed to them.

From this, Casement was able to deduce what the Free State authorities had done. They had abolished slavery—only to replace it with forced labour. The guns and ammunition were required to arm the 'sentries' needed to compel the natives to collect rubber without payment (if they had been paid, they would have been able to buy goods with their money, and this would have been reflected in the trade returns). And the system applied, Casement reported, in the Concessions and the Free State alike. In 1897 Stokes's murderer, Lothaire, had returned to the Congo to run a hitherto undeveloped Concession, a region many times the size of Belgium. By 1899, its profits, which had been negligible, had risen to over 4,000,000 francs a year; and this had been achieved—according to reports reaching Casement from missionaries—by methods so cruel that they had provoked a rebellion, in which several agents of the company had been killed. But Lothaire, he emphasised, had not been simply acting on his own, or his company's account, without the sanction of the Free State. Investigating the company's financial structure, he found that it did not even have a separate existence, except in name. It conducted its business not through a bank, but through the Finance Department of the Congo Free State in Boma; 'Major Lothaire is nothing less than a State Official, of special and undefined powers.'

As the Foreign Office was unlikely to be interested in the fate of the natives for their own sake, Casement was careful to stress the illegal use that was still being made, in spite of the Free State's promises after the Bannister affair, of British West African subjects. The statistical evidence had a sinister ring. In 1896 the number of deaths reported among British subjects in the Congo had been 5; in 1897, 54; in the first seven months of 1898, 88. Why? It was another good reason, Casement felt, why he should personally investigate conditions on the Upper Congo. The Free State authorities would have taken good care, he feared, to ensure that Major Pulteney saw only what they wanted him to see; 'the Lothaires of varying notoriety will have been given the word to assume an air of almost missionary forbearance, tempered by military fortitude'. But so long as Pulteney was there, the Foreign Office insisted, Casement must keep away. His information about the continuing illegal use of British subjects was passed to the Governor of the Gold Coast, where they had been recruited; and the Governor asked that his thanks be conveyed to the Consul at Loanda. But the issue was not taken up with the Free State Government. There was nothing more to be done, Casement realised, until Pulteney returned; and on March 17th he left Boma for Loanda, there to resume the old consular routine.

There was little to do in Portuguese West Africa, he found; and he whiled away the time writing poetry. His notebooks reveal the processes of composition. He began one poem:

> Were it not that the lowliest act can be
> Stripped of unworthiness by love, and made,
> One thing were a heaven-reflecting sea
> Let fall on shores where Christ might walk afraid!

Then, experimenting:

> Sends to a shore where dawn is mist-delayed.

Or, as an alternative,

> Sends to a shore in deepest dark embayed.

And, then, a fresh start:

> Were it not that the lowliest act can be
> Stripped of unworthiness by love, and made
> One tiny wave a moon-reflecting sea
> Sends to a shore where dawn is long delayed . . .

The verses did not lack humour. He parodied, as well as imitated, Tennyson—as in 'Lockjaw Hall', about a newly-married couple suffering from London's early morning din:

> O my darling, when the milkman comes upon the morning
>   round
> More in sorrow than in anger are thy little molars ground.

That autumn, he actually had one of his poems, 'The Sphinx'—

> What secret keep'st thou on the desert's rim?

—published in *The Outlook*. He even had visions of persuading somebody to publish his poems as a book:

> To one I love,
> I dedicate this song
> That she may know how strong
> The bond that binds me is
> Where'er I rove.

But at this point, he was called upon to resume his roving. When the Boer War broke out in October 1899, he was told his services were more urgently needed in South Africa.

Cape Town   1899–1900

In view of Casement's ultimate Congo destiny, the events of the next few months can only be regarded as an interruption. For anybody else, the experiences which he was to have in South Africa could have been the most absorbing of a lifetime; a fascinating story to tell to the grandchildren. His first assignment was to go back to Lourenço Marques, to find out what war materials the Boers were receiving through Delagoa Bay, and in what quantity. To allay suspicion he went there 'on holiday'. He called on the head of the Customs, with a bribe of £500 — almost as much as his salary when he was Consul there. In return, he was allowed to examine import manifests. The result was negative; the amount of help the Boers had received through Delagoa Bay was insufficient for 'even a minor engagement, let alone a campaign'. Presumably the Boers no longer had the means to purchase Germans arms.

If, though, the Government was worried that German munitions might begin again to flow through to the Transvaal, Casement had a plan, which he had worked out when he was in Lourenço Marques before. As there seemed no point in staying there (and he could hardly have remained 'on holiday' for long without exciting the derisive comments he had made on Leyds's visit), he asked for permission to go to Cape Town; and from there, he cabled his plan's outline to London. A military expedition, he suggested, should be despatched from Natal to cut the railway line from the Transvaal to Delagoa Bay; he would be prepared 'to give personal assistance, and to bring several useful helpers from Lourenço Marques.' The attraction the scheme had for him was obvious. It had a Wild West aura — the hold-up of the train; the destruction of the track; then, the escape, along with the expeditionary force, to Natal. For the military, too, it had its appeal; if successful, it would do something to offset the humiliating reverses suffered in the early stages of the war. Sir Alfred Milner, the High Commissioner, asked him to stay on in Cape Town until a decision on the scheme was reached. If it came off, Casement wrote to explain to the Foreign Office: \

> it is possible I may take a more active part than by merely assisting in discussions. I hope so, and I conclude there would be no objection on the part of the Foreign Office to my giving the matter any personal help I could—even if by doing so I must remain still longer absent from Loanda and the Congo. I feel it somewhat on my conscience being so long away from my post; but then the question to be settled here is so urgent and of such transcendent importance that any help that can be given here is of greater moment than anything I could do to help British coloured people on the Congo.

At the end of March Lord Roberts, the Commander-in-Chief, sanctioned the project—'practically as I proposed it', Casement boasted. But the details were not finally completed until May; and although he set out with part of the expeditionary force, too much time had been wasted. There were other areas, Roberts decided, where the force might be used to better effect, and it was recalled.

Casement may have been justified in telling the Foreign Office the expedition was urgent, in the sense that if it was to succeed it must be done quickly. But it was hardly of 'transcendent importance'. 'If the bridge had been blown up,'—a Foreign Office minute noted—'it would have been repaired in a fortnight'; in any case, goods could have been moved by road. The affair, in fact, was another example of how hard he found it to preserve detachment about ventures in which he was involved. Nevertheless his absorption was understandable. He, a civilian, had put forward plans which had been accepted by the highest military authority; and they would have been carried out, but for the army's procrastination and inefficiency.

They would also have meant he was doing something which could help to defeat the Boers, whom he now loathed, because of their treatment of the natives; and for his country—the United Kingdom of Great Britain and Ireland. He was still as loyal as Ulstermen of his upbringing ordinarily were. The fact that the Boers enlisted a 'Brigade' from among Irishmen they had taken prisoner of war, to fight against the British, seemed to him 'only another proof of the methods of those in power in

Pretoria, to leave no weapon untried to induce men loyal to their Queen to be false to their own allegiance, and to be false to themselves'.

Once his expedition had been called off, there was no reason for him to remain in South Africa. He had continued to regard himself as only seconded from his West African post; and when he returned to England Sir Martin Gosselin, who had become head of the Foreign Office's African Department, confirmed that he was to return there. But he was to set up a new consulate, in the Upper Congo: at Kinchasa—the former Leopoldville—on Stanley Pool.

CHAPTER THREE

INTO THE INTERIOR

Edmund Morel

Among the reasons—Casement found when he saw Gosselin—for siting the consulate at Kinchasa was that it was close to Brazzaville, the capital of the French Congo, which would also be a part of his territory. British firms were complaining they were being discriminated against there, too. As it happened, Casement was to have relatively little to do with the French Congo; but in the files relating to it, before he left London, he read for the first time the work of a man with whom he was soon to be associated: the journalist E. D. Morel.

French business men with interests in the French Congo had watched with growing envy the growth of the Concession companies in the Free State. Inevitably, they had begun to ask themselves why their region of the Congo, which was potentially as profitable as that of the Free State, was not equally lucrative. In 1899 the French Government had been induced to authorise Concessions on the Free State model; and the Concessionaires promptly began to squeeze out foreign rivals. In the Free State, when this had happened, the foreign firms had been too scattered and insignificant for their protests to carry weight. But one of the businesses affected in the French Congo was John Holt and Co., of Liverpool; and Holt, unable to obtain satisfaction in the French courts, was influential enough to make his protests heard.

Among those who heard them was Edmund Morel. Like Casement, though ten years later, he had begun his career in the Elder Dempster line, where his knowledge of the French language—he was French by birth—had led the company to use him in its transactions with the Belgians, and with the Free State authorities in Brussels. In the course of his work, Morel became curious about the Free State's trade figures. The object of setting up the State, he knew, had been to benefit the natives, rather than the colonial powers. Yet the trade returns revealed to him what Casement had reported from Boma: the flow of rubber out of the Congo into Belgium was rapidly increasing, but there was no increase in the trickle of imports into the Congo. And the explanation struck Morel when he found that almost the entire value of the rubber, apart from transport costs, was represented as a credit. Labour costs were negligible; there were few imports because the labour force was not being paid.

The Congo, evidently, was being systematically milked for the benefit of . . . whom? Pursuing the answer, Morel found another clue. In the last financial year for which full figures were available, the value of exports—mainly rubber—from the Free State carried by Elder Dempster (which had a virtual monopoly in the trade) was given as £820,000. The same figure appeared in the Antwerp brokers' lists. But when the goods were actually sold, they fetched £1,350,000. While the Free State was systematically milking the Congo, somebody was systematically cheating the Free State of two-fifths of its income. Again, Morel asked himself, who? There was only one man in a position to embezzle the State's funds: Leopold. His authority was absolute: all the Free State's functionaries, in the judiciary as well as the administration, were his nominees, their appointments terminable at whim. And he (or companies in which he held the majority of shares) controlled the Concessions. The culprit, Morel was forced to realise, could only be Leopold himself.

Morel had been eking out his clerk's income with freelance journalism; now, he won Holt's confidence by articles in which he exposed the facts about the Concessions. Up to this time, only the Aborigines Protection Society had taken up the cause of the Congo natives, and the Foreign Office had paid little attention to it. But Holt, Morel found, was a close personal friend of Gosselin; and with Gosselin as an ally, the Foreign Office might be persuaded to act.

Luncheon with Leopold 1900

When he returned from South Africa, Casement did not actually meet Morel; but he read what Morel had been writing on West Africa, and presumably he also heard from Gosselin of the developments. Before he returned to the Congo, it was decided, he would pay a visit to Brussels, to find out as much as he could about the Free State Government, which had its headquarters there. And on his arrival Constantine Phipps, the British Minister, informed him that King Leopold had expressed a desire to make his acquaintance, and would be pleased to entertain him to luncheon.

The two men met on October 18th, 1900; and Casement was invited to come again, the following day, for further discussion — the gist of which he set down in a memorandum for Lord Lansdowne (who had just succeeded Salisbury as Foreign Secretary, Salisbury retaining the Premiership). Leopold, Casement wrote, had insisted that his chief desire, now as always, was 'the well-being and good government of the natives'—a fact which, he claimed, was 'continually being impressed upon his officers'. But it had also to be impressed on the natives that if they were to earn civilisation's benefits, they must work. Why not simply make them pay a just tax, Casement had suggested, rather than employ forced labour? It was not forced labour, Leopold replied, it was labour in lieu of tax. But why, then— Casement asked—the cutting off of hands, and other atrocities? Leopold admitted there had been some cases of misconduct. It was impossible to be sure of selecting the right men as the State's officials; and the climate, he feared, had had a deleterious effect on some of them; but the atrocity reports had been maliciously exaggerated. And the allegations that freedom of trade did not exist in the Congo were incorrect, Leopold insisted, except in the small region which he had preserved as his private domain. Even there, the revenue collected was used for the public good and not, 'as was sometimes untruthfully asserted, for His Majesty's pocket'.

Leopold's main concern, though—Casement realised—was less with the Congo than with Anglo-Belgian relations. And as he felt certain that Leopold expected his views to be passed on, in the hope that they would secure more considerate treatment from the Foreign Office, there would be, he hoped, 'no violation of a confidence in repeating them'. Germany, Leopold had assured him, was the danger. Yet instead of worrying about Germany, the Foreign Office were concerning themselves with the Congo Free State! Belgium was a tiny country; all that he wanted for her was 'a few—only a few—of the crumbs that fall from your well-stocked British table. And yet in England you are suspicious of us!'

Phipps believed Casement had been impressed by Leopold. If
so, there is no indication of it in his memorandum; but neither
is there any hint that he felt Leopold was not to be trusted.
There was a simple way to settle the issue. Leopold had had
ample time to institute reforms; if investigation showed that
they had not been introduced, then it could be assumed there
had been no real intention of making them. Casement determined to see for himself. It had been decided not to open a
consulate at Kinchasa, after all—Boma, as the seat of the Free
State administration, was more suitable; but as soon as he got
back to the Congo in the new year of 1901 he visited Kinchasa,
and went on to tour some of the villages around Stanley Pool.

What he saw and heard convinced him that Leopold had been
lying. Leopold, for example, had claimed that there was free
trade except in his private domain. Apart from a few isolated
and relatively unprofitable areas of the Congo, Casement found,
free trade nowhere existed. The entire State, he reported to
Lansdowne in May, 'has become by a stroke of the pen the sole
property of the governing body of that State; or, it should be
said, in truth, the private property of one individual, the King
of the Belgians'.

Leopold must have planned it, years before. An edict of 1885,
for example, making all vacant lands the property of the Free
State, had been represented as a means to prevent unscrupulous
traders from exploiting the natives; but it had really been
designed, and was being used, to enable the State itself to
exploit the natives. They could not escape, except deeper into
the jungle, or over the border into the French Congo, or into
Portuguese West Africa—where, according to the missionaries,
many tribes had gone. The boom in the rubber trade, admittedly,
Leopold could hardly have foreseen. But what he had done
earlier enabled him to make the maximum profit from it. The
administration of the State cost very little, because the State's
agents, the *Commissaires*, relied for the greater part of their
earnings on the commission they obtained on the rubber they
collected. This was illegal, under the Berlin agreement; but as
the *Commissaires* were also the police officers, and the magistrates, the risk that they would suffer if they broke the 'law'
was small. If a sentry cut off the hands of some natives, for

refusing to work, he need only fear trial by the officer who had ordered him to get the work done, and whose pay was determined by the amount of rubber which the sentry compelled the natives to gather. If a sentry jibbed at carrying out his orders, he would be charged and tried for insubordination by the officer who had given them.

This, then, was the 'system', as Casement began to call it. And although it might not have been planned in advance in all its aspects, the way in which it had developed made it clear that Leopold had worn the philanthropist's cloak only because he could see no other way to secure the Congo. And so long as the system continued, Casement argued, with Leopold in control, there was no point in agitating for reforms. New regulations might be introduced; they would never be implemented. The Commission for the Protection of the Natives was powerless— as Leopold had always intended it should be: it rarely even met, and still more rarely investigated complaints. No wonder Leopold had just given it a fresh mandate! The only solution was for the Berlin powers to intervene. The Free State—he urged in a memorandum to Lansdowne at the end of June—'should it continue to be governed by the Belgians, should be subject to a European authority responsible to public opinion, and not to the unquestioned rule of an autocrat, whose chief preoccupation is that his autocracy should be profitable'.

Lansdowne did not care for the idea. His tutor at Eton had described him, perceptively, as 'talented without imagination'. The talent, lent buoyancy by rank, had brought him high office first under Gladstone, who had made him Governor-General of Canada, and then under Salisbury, who had appointed him Viceroy of India. He tended to think in imperial terms. It was going to be hard enough to restrain the colonial ambitions of Germany and France, he realised, without giving them the additional opportunity, which they would greatly relish, of being asked to decide the future of the Congo. Each would demand her share—as would Portugal. Britain alone would have nothing to gain.

Casement's despatches from the Congo, too, made less impression on Lansdowne than his account of his conversations with Leopold in Brussels. Preparing the way for what became the Entente with France, Lansdowne was concerned in case

Leopold should be pushed into allying himself with the Germans. He judged Casement's memorandum on the Congo to be of sufficient importance to be shown to the Prime Minister; but Salisbury, although he recommended that the Congo Atrocities file should be kept up to date with any additional material which was collected, agreed that no action need be taken.

The Rabinek affair   1902

The succeeding few months were a difficult time for Casement —not least in that T. Fisher Unwin, the publisher to whom he had sent his poems, was unenthusiastic about them. In November, Unwin offered to publish them at the author's expense, but added a crushing 'I do not look forward to a remunerative sale'. That winter, too, Casement had a recurrence of his old malarial fever. In the spring of 1902 he requested, and was granted, permission to go to the Canary Islands to convalesce; and on April 28th, while on board the ship taking him back to the Congo, he wrote what was clearly intended to be a valedictory survey of the Congo situation, in case his ill-health might lead to his being transferred to another post.

It was improbable, he feared, that he would be able to stand the Congo's unhealthy climate and depressing conditions for more than another year. But he still hoped that, before he left, he could see 'its rotten system of administration either mended, or ended'; and he suggested that when he recovered his health he should go back to Boma and proceed at once to the Upper Congo, to conduct a more extensive inquiry. It would, he was sure, confirm his verdict, that 'there is no free trade in the Congo today; there is, it might be said, no trade, as such, at all in the Congo. There is ruthless exploitation at the hands of a savage and barbarous soldiery of one of the most prolific regions of Africa, in the interest of and for the profit of the Sovereign of that country and his favoured Concessionaires.' And in the meantime, he proposed, the British Government should assert free trade rights in the Congo, confident that the commercial self-interest of all of the Berlin signatories would attract their support.

But would it? The shrewd Harry Farnall, of the Foreign Office's African Department, had already commented that the public in Britain and in Europe were not yet ready for decisive action on the Congo. 'During recent years various letters have been published in the press, but they have not made any mark. Neither this country nor any other is likely to take active steps in the matter unless more or less forced to by public opinion.' This view was shared by Morel, who had realised that public opinion in Britain would have to be roused, and who persuaded Holt to help finance a campaign against the Concession system. With Holt's backing, and with H. R. Fox Bourne providing the organisation through the Aborigines Protection Society, a public meeting was held at the Mansion House on May 15th, 1902, with Dilke, Holt and Morel among the speakers; and a resolution was passed *nem. con.* calling on the signatories to the Berlin agreement to redeem the pledges which they had made seventeen years before.

The Foreign Office remained cool. Acknowledging a copy of the resolution, Lansdowne replied in the stock formula that the matter was one which was 'engaging his careful attention'. The meeting, however, served to awaken the British press, which had earlier displayed little interest; and a story which otherwise might have got no further than the Congo Atrocities file received some publicity.

Early in 1901 Gustave-Marie Rabinek, an Austrian who had been operating for some time in the Southern Congo, was arrested for trading in rubber (in spite of the fact that it was officially a free trade area, in which he was licensed to operate) and sentenced to a year's imprisonment, with confiscation of all his property. Unlike Stokes, Rabinek was given leave to appeal; but this, he found, would entail his being taken in custody some 2,000 miles down the river to Boma. Before he left, he smuggled out a letter saying that if precedent was anything to go by he would be unlikely to reach Boma alive. His forecast proved correct. The news of his death, and his letter predicting it, understandably aroused more indignation in Austria and Germany than it did in Britain; but Morel seized on a point which made it a British concern, too—Rabinek had claimed he had been arrested on a British ship, in British territorial waters. If this proved correct, it would be useful ammunition in the campaign.

Civis Romanus Sum 1902

Knowing nothing of the course events were taking in England, Casement returned to Boma from the Canaries in a depressed state. 'I hope that I may last out to the end of the year,' he wrote to Gosselin on May 16th, 'but I must say when I saw the Congo again—when its vast and gaunt waters broke on my view, and the blaze of its intemperate sun made me close my eyes in sheer physical pain, I felt like turning tail at the mouth of the river, and not drawing breath till I saw the peak of Teneriffe.' He would have been more depressed had he known that the minute attached to his letter, expressing concern that he might not stand the climate much longer, was the last that Gosselin was to write in his old capacity: he had just been appointed to be British Minister in Lisbon. But the moment he received a batch of press cuttings about the Mansion House meeting, his gloom lifted. At last, the British public had been told about the Congo.

In a despatch written on August 10th, he reiterated his view that all the Government needed to do to break the system, and end the atrocities, was to insist that the Free State should obey the terms of the Berlin agreement, and restore free trade. Tellingly, he recalled some of Stanley's pledges; one, in a speech in 1884, insisting that not only would there be free trade, but also 'paternal care of each of its subjects' rights, whether black or white'; and another, the following year, when Stanley had pointed out that only one British firm was exporting cotton goods to the Congo, their value being a derisory £138,000 a year—whereas when the Congo was opened up, he estimated, it would be worth over £25 million a year to Britain. Well, the Congo had been 'opened up'; and what was the result? The value of British cotton goods exported to the Congo in 1901 was less than half of what it had been sixteen years before, when there was no road, and no railway, to the interior.

Casement also now decided that it was time for him to do what he had earlier deliberately refrained from doing; he began to invoke the Palmerstonian principle of *Civis Romanus Sum* on behalf of British subjects in the Congo who had grievances. In July, he heard that some Sierra Leone men were detained in Matadi gaol. Of the twelve originally arrested, he found seven had died, and one had escaped; the remaining four were lodged in a mud-walled, cement-floored hut, with no bedding, and only the clothes they had been wearing when arrested, in which they had to go out to work as part of a chain gang. He managed to secure their release and repatriation; and in his report, he made the most of the fact that seven British subjects had died as a result of this illegal and cruel treatment. 'A very terrible state of things' a minute from the West African Department of the Foreign Office admitted, suggesting that the Colonial Office should warn men from the West African colonies not to go to the Congo, and that a strongly-worded representation should be made to the Free State Government. Lansdowne agreed; it was, he thought, 'a terrible story'.

To Lansdowne, it was terrible in the same sense as an earthquake involving a few fatalities. He did not regard it as in any way attributable to his own or his Government's negligence. Still, his reaction was the first sign that the Foreign Office might eventually be goaded into making a move. Heartened, Casement revived his project of a visit to the Upper Congo; and at the end of August, he cabled to say that if he were given the necessary authorisation, he would set out in October.

Before the Foreign Office had time to reply, he abandoned the idea, cabling instead for permission to return to England—a change of mind made no easier to understand by the explanation he gave for it: 'existing consular accommodation Boma most uncomfortable, rendering difficult work there. I think it better to hasten plan for house than go journey interior.' Edward Clarke of the West African Department was baffled. 'I really think the poor man must have gone off his head,' he minuted. 'There is nothing, I presume, to do but sanction his return.' One of the under-secretaries of state, Ronald Campbell, was more charitable: 'he is a good man, has had fever, and he would not telegraph like this unless it was really necessary.' But Casement demonstrated it could not have been really necessary, by staying on not for five days, as he had proposed, but for nearly five weeks, continuing his work and writing reports as if nothing had happened.

In all probability, nothing *had* happened. Casement was indeed concerned about the Boma consulate. He had had to live in a two-roomed hut; and the local authorities had been frustrating his efforts to secure a site. But if exasperation over the consulate was his reason for not going to the interior, it would equally have been a reason for not returning to England. The most likely explanation is that he acted, as he often did, on impulse. For some reason—his state of health, perhaps—the prospect of a visit to the Upper Congo had suddenly ceased to attract him. As it had been his own idea, and as the Foreign Office had shown so little interest, he could well have assumed they would not object if he changed his mind. And, after all, why put himself out, when they already had ample information on their files about the Upper Congo, if they wanted to act on it?

The likelihood is, too, that it would have been a waste of time for him to undertake the tour that autumn. Believing that he had been impressed by Leopold, Phipps had orginally welcomed the idea of a tour, assuming that Casement would be able to exonerate Leopold from the charges levelled against him. But when Phipps saw the report on the Sierra Leone men, and heard the Foreign Office's reaction, he became convinced that Casement must have picked up some unworthy grudge against the Free State. He set to work to convince the Foreign Office that Leopold and his ministers could be trusted to take the appropriate action, whenever such cases of injustice were brought to their attention. The Free State, he was sure, was being unfairly pilloried; 'I should be sorry,' he wrote privately to Campbell, 'to become the apologist of King Leopold or his regime, but surely there must in that country be some progress!' Still anxious not to alienate Leopold, Lansdowne allowed himself to be convinced. Nothing that Casement could have reported from the interior would have been likely, that winter, to move him.

Man about Town   1903

In the meantime, however, Morel was continuing his efforts to arouse public opinion. His book, *Affairs of West Africa*, which included a savage indictment of the Congo Free State, appeared in December. Fox Bourne, too, mustered the evidence collected by the Aborigines Protection Society for his *Civilisation in Congoland*, sub-titled 'A history of international wrong-doing', with a preface by Dilke denouncing the Free State as 'the home of appalling misgovernment and oppression'.

The campaigners were also joined by a recent convert to the cause. Guy Burrows had written another book describing his later experiences in the Congo, entitled *The Curse of Central Africa*—the 'curse' being the administration of the Free State. When Casement got back to England, he found that there was some ground for optimism—though he still felt that his official position precluded him from linking up with the Congo reformers.

The last few days of his leave, he spent in London; and he described his daily round there in a diary for 1903. The first few pages, containing the entries up to February 13th, are missing; they were torn out in 1916, so that they could be shown to journalists as proof of his homosexual activities. Most of the entries are such as anybody might have written.

> February 18. Beautiful frosty morning. Busy writing all day. Intended leaving 'Bonny' today, too late for her. Nina went Kings. Drew £50 and cheque book for 50. Sent clothes (two packages, hat box and trunk) to 55 Ebury Street, E. Peacock. Went to Aladdin with Nina. Awfully stupid piece. Wrote G.B. to New York . . .

But the meaning of a mysterious entry, 'saw enormous—youthful', during the stay in London only becomes clear when, after a week on the *Jebba*—'a tub, and rolling fearfully'—he reached Madeira, where he was to stay for a few days; and a new Casement emerges; the young man about town, lunching and dining in fashionable restaurants, and going to dances. He was not extravagant. Although he often stayed at good hotels, wherever he found himself, this to some extent was dictated by what was expected of him, in his position; and hotels at that time were cheap (in 'The Adventure of the Noble Bachelor', Sherlock Holmes tracked a man down by realising that he must be staying at one of the most expensive hotels in London because a fragment from his bill showed that his room had cost him eight shillings). Although he gambled at the casino, it was for modest amounts, his exact winnings and losses always meticulously recorded; he drank only in moderation, though he smoked, on one occasion, 'too much'. He was introduced to Lady Edgecumbe, to the Duke of Montrose, and to Mrs. Raglan Somerset (who shortly before he left, after nearly three weeks on the island, gave him a hymn book). But when he slipped away from time to time to private assignations, he recorded them; and they were with youths. Sometimes they were named— Agostinho, 'kissed many times'. Sometimes they, or their physical attributes, were simply noted in passing: 'saw very beautiful near Casino'; 'enormous at 10 o'clock in Square'. To express satisfaction he broke into a kind of crooning chant

> In street and to Avenida. Juan mua mu ami diaka N sono 18 p. 20 years. Back to Olsens. Pepe, 17 brought cigarettes much bueno, diati diaka moko mavebela mu mami mucho bueno fiba, Fiba X . . . p. 16.

'Very beautiful', referred to youths who caught his eye; 'enormous' to his estimate of the size of their penes. The 'p' was for pesetas; but the fact that he recorded the financial side of the transaction makes the entries appear more commercial than they were—he happened to have a compulsion to record everything he spent, down to a penny for a newspaper, a halfpenny thrown to a beggar. The tone of the diary, too, suggests that— unlike so many of his contemporaries, who felt guilty about their sexual appetites—he thoroughly enjoyed his relationships with young men. Sexual encounters were not for him a form of release, to be indulged in furtively, and recollected in shame. They were a delightful pastime, which it was only fair to pay for, as he would pay for a game of billiards. And he used the diary to record his experiences, so that he could again savour the pleasure when re-reading them (he would sometimes add an exclamation of delight in the margin, later).

Yet he did not attempt to justify what he was doing, even to himself. He gave a clue to his attitude in the 1903 diary, in the entry on the day he heard of the death of Sir Hector MacDonald. MacDonald had risen from being a private in the Gordon Highlanders to be the commander of the Highland Brigade in the Boer War; but early in 1903 he had been charged with homosexual practices, and he had shot himself, before the case came to court. 'Pitiably sad,' Casement commented. 'The most distressing case this, surely, of its kind, and one that may awake the national mind to saner methods of curing a terrible disease than by criminal legislation.' To Casement, a man was a homosexual in the same way as he might be a diabetic. It was his misfortune, not his fault.

He accepted that it was a disorder of which a man ought to be cured, if a cure were known. And this helps to explain him. He was a split personality; not in the sense the term was generally then used, a Jekyll and Hyde; nor in the sense it was coming to be used—a schizophrenic; but in the sense that his personality was compartmentalised. Sections of it were cut off from each other. There was the Casement whose friends so admired him—the Arthurian knight. There was the Casement revealed in his correspondence with the Foreign Office; calculating, as well as honourable. There was the poet: only his closest friends, apparently, were aware of the highly charged emotional force that found its way, with such difficulty, into his verses. And there was also, as the diary daily and incongruously reveals, the Edwardian masher—except that it was youths, rather than girls, who caught his eye.

Other aspects of his personality emerge from the diary. He was still an avid reader. To some extent his choice of books was imposed on him—by, for example, the exigencies of ships' libraries, and friends' bookshelves. On the last stage of his journey back to the Congo, on the *Anversville*, he read a great deal, including a number of books in French—presumably because the library stocked them, though he may have felt it would be useful, as French was the official language of the Free State; Loti's *Mon Frère Yves; Les Carnets du Roi* ('stupid exposition of a beast king'); *La Double Maîtresse*. In English, there was *Smart Set* ('very hot indeed'), Marie Corelli's *The Soul of Lilith*, on which he made no comment; and Conan Doyle's *Mystery of Cloomber* ('rather good'). Burrow's book on the Congo, which he had asked the Foreign Office to forward to him, reached him while he was on Grand Canary; and soon after his young cousin Gertrude sent him Somerville and Ross's *The Experiences of an Irish RM*, which he found 'delicious'. But a better idea of his literary tastes can be gleaned from the frequent references to books and writers made in his correspondence, often casual and oblique enough to suggest easy familiarity rather than a desire to show off. He was widely, if not deeply, read.

When he arrived in Boma, however, he tended to slip into what he obviously felt was a congenial social round—at least when there was no work to absorb his attention.

May 9th. Very cold morning. Wrote of Whittindale before breakfast. 'John' * better, poor old soul. A lot of men came with complaints, but I sent them all away refusing to give ear to their grievances, only pointing out the notices in their own colonies warning them against seeking work here upon local contracts. Swerts to tennis. Also Van Damme. I played —first time since August last year—played very badly. In evening at billiards with Trust and McKay. They beat us by 20 out of 126. But we should have won! I played U. after for 20 for who should pay the losses and beat him easy. A lovely night. John ever so much better. 'Craw Graw' troubling me dreadfully.

'Craw Craw' was not the only disorder that troubled Casement; his diary reveals him as rarely without some symptom of illness. In Madeira he had to stay in all one day—'not feeling well. Lay down in afternoon with three overcoats on'. In Las Palmas, a week later, 'To bed. To w.c. 11 times, awfully bad attack, half dysentry ... feeling very ill, lots of blood passing'— symptoms which recurred on the *Anversville*; 'feeling very seedy indeed'. He also continued to suffer attacks of malaria. The entry in his diary for April 29th, after he had arrived in West Africa, described how he had had fever all night; and his comment, 'first attack since I came out', indicated how much a part of his life it had become.

After a visit to Loanda—where he caught up with his consular work, was maddened by sandflies, and suffered from insomnia after he found a centipede in his bed—Casement returned at the beginning of May to Boma, paid his formal call on the Vice-Governor-General, Fuchs ('very amiable—too much so'), and inspected the proposed site for the new consulate. But this time, he was determined not to allow his interest in it to interrupt his plans to visit the Upper Congo. On May 6th, he cabled the Foreign Office to say that he proposed to start at the end of the month.

The Foreign Office had not shown much interest in his project, before he left. Their chief concern was still with British subjects in the Congo, who might be better served if he stayed at Boma. But hardly had he returned there, when they were forced to realise that the Congo reform campaign was beginning to attract

* His dog.

public support. In March the respected *Fortnightly Review* had an article by the Irish writer Stephen Gwynn on a theme so similar to Casement's that it seems likely that they had met — certainly they came to know each other about this time. More important — from the point of view of impressing the Foreign Office — John Holt persuaded a joint meeting of British Chambers of Commerce to pass a resolution calling upon the Government to consider, in conjunction with the other Berlin powers, what reforms were necessary in the Congo Free State. And following some parliamentary question, Herbert Samuel successfully moved that there should be a debate on the subject.

Up to this point, few Liberal M.P.s had shown an interest; but the results of two by-elections in March — Casement noted them in his diary: 'Rye has followed Woolwich, giving Liberal huge majority' — had put fresh heart into the party. In his barnstorming election tours, Gladstone had shown that the electors could be moved by stories of atrocities in remote places they had rarely, if ever, heard of; the Congo might offer even greater scope because British subjects were involved. Even *Punch* — no longer the crusading journal it had once been — took up the cause early in May with some barbed verses on 'The Congo "Free" State':

> The Congo State
> Is a thriving speculation
> For the happy Belgian nation
> The receipts are great
> And are getting yearly bigger
> — But I'm glad I'm not a nigger
> In the Congo State

Lansdowne now realised in what a vulnerable position his readiness to appease Leopold had left him. The Congo Atrocity files had been continually replenished; he could not plead ignorance of what had been happening. The only way out, he decided, would be to persuade Leopold to agree to the appointment of a commission of inquiry into the allegations; this decision would be announced in the debate, and the Government could say that until the Commission reported, it would be only fair to refrain from further comment. Still believing that an inquiry would exonerate Leopold, Phipps was not averse to the idea; he had suggested something of the kind himself. But to his, and to Lansdowne's, chagrin, Leopold staged a diplomatic disappearance. He could not be found, to give his consent. And by coincidence, or oversight, on the day of the debate, May 20th, 1903, the report of the British High Commissioner for Central Africa on the Rabinek affair confirmed Morel's allegation, which Free State spokesmen had denied, that Rabinek had been arrested on a British ship, in British territorial waters.

Opening the debate, Herbert Samuel had no difficulty in showing that the terms of the Berlin agreement had been flouted. Throughout almost the whole of the Free State, free trade had disappeared. The Concessions, utilising their monopolies, were able to make enormous annual profits—in one case, almost 500 per cent on its capital. To obtain these profits, the natives had been slave-driven; and in case anybody should think that the atrocity stories were a thing of the past, Samuel was able to cite the evidence of an American missionary who had just arrived in England after seven years in the Congo, and had given a talk about his experiences to the Aborigines Protection Society. So conclusive was the evidence, in fact, that not a single Conservative M.P. could be found to come to his Government's rescue. For the Government, Lord Cranborne fell back on such excuses as that the Congo was not the only part of the world where atrocities had been committed; and that the existence of restrictions on free trade had not been fully substantiated. But it was obvious that the House, even with its still substantial Conservative majority, was unimpressed. And Balfour, who had succeeded Salisbury as Prime Minister, though he warned that it would be unwise for the Commons to condemn another country's government without a preliminary inquiry, was unable to get the motion withdrawn. Any attempt to do so, Lansdowne explained to Phipps, would have met with ignominious defeat. It read:

That the Government of the Congo Free State having at its inception guaranteed to the Powers that its native subjects should be governed with humanity, and that no trading monopolies should be permitted within its dominions, this House requests His Majesty's Government to confer with other Powers, signatories of the Berlin General Act by virtue of which the Congo Free State exists, in order that measures may be adopted to abate the evils prevalent in that State.

Casement had been referred to in the debate, though not by name; Dilke had asked why the British Consul's reports had not been communicated to the Commons. Travel difficulties, Cranborne explained, and the need to look after the interests of British subjects, had meant that they had not been considered sufficiently comprehensive. As he had got out of going on the tour the previous autumn, he would not be in a position to take offence at the explanation. But the reference to him, apparently, gave Lansdowne an idea. He was still anxious to avoid another conference with the Berlin powers. With the Commons in so hostile a mood, though, he would have to find some way to convince them that the Government really was determined to act. Two days after the debate, he cabled to Casement sanctioning his projected tour of the Upper Congo.

On the Upper Congo   1903

Casement had already started on the first stage of his journey, to the railhead at Matadi, the day before these instructions were sent. 'Old Queen's birthday', he noted in his diary for May 24th, while he was there; and two days later her South African Medal, which he had been awarded for his services in the Boer War, reached him. While at Matadi, he also dreamed the plot of a novel: 'got up at 3 a.m. and sketched it out, would make a splendid story'. He was not going to have the chance to write it; that morning—June 2nd—he was told that three Foreign Office cables had arrived for him in Boma. He had planned to go on into the interior on the morning of June 5th; so he packed, and generally made ready, while waiting for them. Two proved to be undecipherable, but the third contained Lansdowne's instructions to proceed on his projected journey. He was on his way the following morning.

'Send reports soon' the cable requested, and he did so—though not the reports which they were wanting. Having arrived at Stanley Pool, he settled down there for a while to discuss the Congo situation with people he knew who were living in Kinchasa, and to revise his memoranda on various matters which had come up since his return to the Congo ('they'll curse me at the F.O.' he noted with some satisfaction. 'I have really got through a lot of writing for F.O. of late. It would make a big book if published'). Then, he set about making the arrangements for the journey. It would be risky, he felt, to allow himself to be beholden to the authorities; the sensible course would be to charter a steamboat privately, and he was fortunate enough to be offered the *Henry Reed*, which belonged to the American Baptist Mission. While it was being got ready for him, in early July, he went for a tour around Stanley Pool: 'beautiful Dover cliffs, lovely view ... hippo downstream. Saw three pelicans feeding, close to us. Also saw a beautiful Egyptian ibis, black body, white wings, a lovely fellow in full flight over us for his home in the woods.' Observations of that kind had not been common in his diary; they were soon to cease altogether. He was due to leave on the morning of July 9th. At the last moment there was some hitch ('delayed in starting by the infallible cause of all delay and every miscarriage since Eve first upset Adam's apple—curst woman'). But eventually they got away, making for the Bolobo Mission Station, where he could hear what the mission workers felt about the Free State.

Their opinion was not flattering; and Casement understood why, from the contrast between what he now saw with what he had seen when he was there in 1887. Many of the settlements he had known were deserted, the forest covering their abandoned sites. Bolobo had been one of the largest native settlements in the region, a centre for an industrious tribe trading with Stanley Pool and numbering, he had estimated, 40,000 people. Now, he found, they had been reduced to fewer than 8,000. Their trading canoes had disappeared, and their trade. They had nothing to do except perform whatever services the State required, like cutting wood for fuel, or clearing the undergrowth around the telephone lines.

The complaints he heard, though, were of the arbitrary ways in which services were exacted ('if the local official has to go on a sudden journey, men are summoned on the instant to paddle his canoe, and a refusal entails imprisonment or a beating') rather than about the compulsion to render them. At least at Bolobo, as at all the main river trading stations, they were paid for; and those who provided them could expect to be fed. But while he was there he heard that a large influx of refugees from the Basilingi tribe, which had formerly lived in one of the Concessions, had settled not far away. He decided to visit them, as soon as the *Henry Reed*, which had been taken up the slipway for an overhaul, was ready. He had not told the Foreign Office he was intending to charter a steamboat, presumably because he feared they might object (they would certainly have done if they had known that under the contract, he was responsible for paying compensation if she was wrecked, 'how much I don't know'). But now, when it was too late for them to stop him, he explained his decision; it was necessary to preserve his independence, and to enable him 'to provide an accurate and faithful representation of the state of affairs prevailing'. And on July 20th, after paying his debts, sending his Bannister aunt £5 (July 14th, he had remembered was her birthday; 'poor wee soul. I will send her a present'), and writing to his sister, he set off to find and question the refugees.

Four times a month, they told him, each of their villages had been required to bring in twenty basketfuls of rubber, for which the chief (who was responsible for ensuring that the right amount was collected) was given only a fathom of cloth and some salt. The men who actually gathered the rubber received nothing. When the rubber supply locally had been exhausted, they had to begin to go deeper into the forest to look for rubber vines; some had died from exposure, or starvation; some had been killed by wild beasts. 'We tried always going further into the forest,' he was told, 'and when we failed and our rubber was short, the soldiers came into our towns and killed us. Many were shot, some had their ears cut off ... the white men sometimes at the post did not know the bad things the soldiers did to us, but it was the white men who sent the soldiers to punish us for not bringing in enough rubber.' And eventually, realising that nothing remained for them at home but to be killed for their failure to bring in enough rubber, or to die looking for it, they had decided to abandon their homes, and to seek the hospitality of a friendly tribe a week's march away.

Although the natives gave their evidence with conviction and sincerity, Casement for a while felt that the stories, if not false, must be greatly exaggerated. But soon he was being plied with corroborative evidence. One of the excuses given by the Free State authorities for the falling population was the incidence of sleeping sickness, and a questionnaire had been sent out by the Governor-General on the subject to, among others, the Congo missionaries—among them the Rev. J. Whitehead, at Lukolela. With Whitehead and his wife, he went to inspect native villages, finding the population dreadfully decreased.

The population at Lukolela had been around 5,000 in 1887; it had since fallen—according to an exact count which Whitehead had made, to answer the questionnaire—to 352. Sleeping sickness, Whitehead was certain, was not responsible. In a letter he wrote to the Governor-General, inspired by Casement's visit, he blamed the pressure under which the people lived. They were being fatally weakened by the labour they were forced to undertake to bring in rubber, by the cruel punishments they recieved, by lack of adequate nourishment, and, Whitehead emphasised by fear, which left them an easy prey to disease. There were only eighty-two men of working age in Lukolela, Whitehead told him; adding, 'I can see the shadow of death over nearly twenty of them.' And by the time he returned that way, six weeks later, nine of the twenty were already dead.

After Lukolela, Casement visited Lake Mantumba, in the heart of Leopold's private domain, and there he remained for seventeen days. The lakeside population, he found, had been heavily reduced; some of the tribes had fled across to French territory, but most of the losses were for the reasons that Whitehead had given. On August 13th, a message arrived to say that five natives from Bikoro who had had their hands chopped off wanted to meet him; as he was ill, he sent for them to come across the lake, but hearing that he had gone, they had left. Very soon, though, there was no shortage of evidence. One youth who had no hands described how they had been beaten off against a tree with rifle butts; and a boy of eleven, whose hand had been chopped off, explained that he had remained still because he knew that, if the soldiers had realised he was alive, they would have killed him.

As he continued his journey, memories of his earlier Congo days were continually revived by what he saw. On August 15th he was at Ikenge; 'State post now, a few huts showing. In 1887 when I passed up a fine big town. Everywhere the same tale.' At Bolingi, he sent a man for wood from a nearby island; 'Poor old Ted Glave. His land.' And 'old Ted's beach, ah! in September 1887, what a change.' In one settlement, the sentry whose duty it was to ensure a steady supply of food for the nearby trading station at Coquilhatville freely admitted that he had volunteered for the job because: 'his own village and country were subjected to much trouble in connection with the rubber tax, he could not live in his own home; and he preferred, he said, laughing, "to be with the hunters rather than with the hunted".'

By the end of the month, Casement had reached Bongandanga, in one of the Concessions. Here, he had an opportunity to
see how the system worked through the eyes of the *Commissaire*, Lejesme, on whom he called. As he wrote in his diary:

> August 29 ... saw rubber 'market', nothing but guns—about
> 20 armed men. ... The population 242 men with rubber, all
> guarded like convicts. To call this 'trade' is the height of
> lying. Lejesme a gentlemanly man.
>
> August 30 ... Spent quiet day. In afternoon, saw M. Lejesme
> at ABIR. Sixteen men and women tied up from a village,
> Mboye, close to the town. Infamous. The men were put in the
> prison, the children let go at my intervention. Infamous!
> Infamous, shameful system.
>
> August 31 ... Went with Lejesme to the Landolphia Planta-
> tion, something like a million plants there. In evening a
> dance organised in my honour; all the local chiefs and their
> wives, etc. came (at Lejesme's orders) to it. Poor souls. I was
> sorry for it, of all the forced enjoyment I ever saw, this took
> the cake.
>
> September 1st ... My 39th birthday here up the Lopori, in
> the heart of Africa indeed ... terrible oppression of these
> poor people.

At Lake Mantumba Casement had heard about the system
used to compel the natives to collect rubber; at Bongandanga, he
actually saw it in operation. It reinforced the point he had first
made in Lourenço Marques; that injustice and atrocities were
not, or not necessarily, the work of criminals, or of men who
had become unbalanced (the excuse which Leopold and his
spokesman made, when atrocities could no longer be concealed).
It was the system which imposed injustice and cruelty on all
who served it.

As word got around that Casement was not just another State
official, but was collecting information which might lead to an
improvement in conditions, more and more natives came in to
display evidence of mutilation, including a boy of about fifteen
years old, Epondo, whose left arm, wrapped in dirty rags, had
recently been hacked off by the wrist. Epondo claimed that the

sentry responsible, Kalengo, was still in the village; and when
he had been found, the boy accused him to his face. Kalengo
blamed another sentry; but witness after witness stepped forward to identify him as responsible, and to charge him with
other crimes. Epondo, Casement decided, was just what he
needed as proof. He took the boy with him to Coquilhatville,
where he related the whole story to the Commandant. The
episode, he explained, was significant not only for itself, but
for the fact that although the mutilation had been carried out
within a few miles of the ABIR headquarters, and the guilty man
was known, the crime had not been reported.

'There is some act, design', he had quoted, at the beginning
of his 1903 diary,

> —some holy strife
> That leads us soon to a larger life.

He had known what was happening in the Congo before, and
he had known why; but it had been an intellectual, rather than
a felt knowledge. Now, he was filled with rage, and compassion.
He had seen enough; and he decided to return direct from Coquilhatville to Stanley Pool. Although he had not been able to
visit all the places from which there had been atrocity reports,
everything that he had already seen and heard suggested that
he would have found nothing substantially different in other
areas; only fresh examples of oppression and cruelty. He reached
Kinchasa on September 15th, sitting up all night working on his
report; the next few days were spent on it, and on letters to the
Free State authorities concerning cases of injustice which he
felt ought to be investigated. He was 'very tired and used up
over the excitement of the last few days'; he suffered from
toothache, and deafness; his eyes were troubling him, and he
was paying the penalty for what he described as 'Les Cloches de
Corned Beef, Opera en 365 Actes'. So irritable was he that he
broke his stick, thrashing his dog (thrashing dogs—or children
—was not then considered cruel—even the gentle Major Yeates,
the 'Irish R.M.', did it—but to break a stick on a dog suggests
he was in an uncontrollable temper). By the 24th, he felt worn
out. Taking the train for Matadi, he went on to Boma, to hand in
a letter to the Governor-General.

It was dated September 4th—because it was based on a speci-

fic complaint he had received that day from missionaries, whose
food supplies were being curtailed by restrictions on trading
with the natives. But he took the opportunity to say that the
complaint was against the system, 'which is in my opinion, in
conflict with the principles of an international obligation it is
one of my duties as Consul to seek to see maintained in its integrity'. Although he expressed his conviction that the Governor-
General would feel as indignant as he had, he did not fancy
having to discuss the contents of the letter. He spent only a
night at Boma—which enabled him to excuse himself for not
calling in person—before continuing by ship to Portuguese
West Africa, where he could stay at the consulate until the
Foreign Office issued its instructions.

The British Note   1903

In ordinary circumstances the Government would have used the
fact that Casement was making his investigation to postpone
further action until he had reported. But the Commons resolution had been too widely supported, to permit such tactics. A
note was drafted in the Foreign Office, to explain to the Berlin
powers why the Commons were uneasy about the Congo Free
State; and before it was sent, it was transmitted to Casement
for his comments. It had reached him while he was still in
Kinchasa, before proceeding into the interior. 'At last they are
moving,' he noted in his diary, 'my despatches have sown the
good seed.'

The move, however, was tentative. The original idea had
been to reinforce the note with some of the evidence already
available in the Congo Atrocity files. But Farnall, who had a
weather eye for political repercussions, pointed out that this
might get the Foreign Office into trouble; 'we must not make the
circular too strong, or we shall be blamed by the House of
Commons, to whom the circular is in one sense as much
addressed as it is to the powers, for not having made a representation long ago'. Lansdowne took the point; the final version,
sent out on August 8th, made no reference to the evidence in
the files. The attention of His Majesty's Government, it said,
had been drawn in recent years to reports of the existence of
forced labour in the Free State; of ill-treatment of the natives
there; and of the existence of trade monopolies. These allega-

tions, coming in memorials from philanthropic societies and from commercial bodies, in newspaper articles and in consular despatches, could no longer be ignored by the signatories to the Berlin agreement. Their views would be welcome on what should be done.

So general were the note's terms, so mild its tone, that none of the Berlin powers felt called upon to do more than acknowledge it. The only European capital where it provoked any reaction was Brussels; and there, its moderation had an unexpected consequence. On September 17th, a spirited reply —which, according to Phipps, had virtually been written by Leopold himself, and which he obviously had thoroughly enjoyed composing—derided the British note as no more than a string of hypotheses—'it was alleged', 'it is reported', 'it is also reported'. In effect, Leopold suggested, this constituted an admission that the British Government did not know whether the allegations were true. And how could they be true? How could there be cruelty and oppression, when the Free State was dedicated to the principles of 'that International Act which binds all signatory and adhering Powers'? It was true that the Congo natives paid their taxes to the State in labour, rather than in currency. But had not Joseph Chamberlain, when he was Colonial Secretary himself, justified such a form of taxation, to induce the natives to work? It was also true that there had been isolated criminal acts; but they had been punished. And such acts were not exclusive to the Congo. Had there not just been over sixty convictions in eighteen months in a British West African colony, Sierra Leone, for 'flogging, plundering, and generally maltreating the natives'?

To divert attention from the impending revelations, it was useful for Leopold to be able to accuse the British of hypocrisy; and to do this more effectively, he realised, he must seek to discredit Casement in advance of his report. Was he not— Leopold asked—the same British Consul who had written to the Governor-General of the Free State, in July 1901: 'Pray believe me, when I express now, not only for myself, but for my fellow-countrymen, in this part of Africa, our very sincere appreciation of your efforts on behalf of the general community—efforts to promote goodwill among all and to bring together the various elements in our local life?' And he had not just arrived when he wrote those words; he had come to West Africa as Consul as far back as 1898. . . .

Outside the Free State, few people would know that Casement was referring in the letter only to the Boma community, for which he felt genuine goodwill. Nevertheless Leopold's dig was unwise, because the letter suggested that Casement had arrived with no prejudice against the Free State, which might make his later hostile evidence all the more convincing. This, however, was a trivial tactical error compared to the one Leopold made by holding up the Foreign Office to public ridicule. The feeling of corporate loyalty was strong there, particularly when the Foreign Secretary and his officials were in general agreement, as they were about Leopold. Casement's investigation, which up to then had been little more than a device to allay suspicion in the Commons, now became a weapon they could employ in self-defence. He had cabled them at the end of his tour that he had 'convincing evidence of shocking misgovernment and wholesale repression'. A few days before, the information might have caused misgivings, as likely to stir up trouble with Leopold, which they had not wanted. Indeed, they had gone out of their way to avoid it—only to be humiliated for their pains. With the help of Casement's report, they should be able to pay him back.

CHAPTER FOUR

THE CONGO REPORT

'A man indeed' 1903–1904

For a while Casement was left to stay on at Loanda, feeling 'hopelessly lazy' after his exertions, and unable to write; playing tennis, dining out. There was little work for him to do except answer occasional Foreign Office queries. He had informed them of Grenfell's decision, at his prompting, to resign from the Commission for the Protection of the Natives; would Grenfell allow this information to be published? Casement replied that he would have to ask Grenfell; and then retired to bed, seedy. Three days later, on October 20th, he received his orders: he was to prepare his report in London. Anxious though he now was to get back, he had to hang around for two weeks until a cable reached him telling him that his substitute, Arthur Nightingale, was on his way out to take over the consulate. The *Zaire* was sailing for Lisbon, two days later, he decided to sail with her.

The voyage was uneventful. Apart from noting that *The Woman in White* kept him sitting up until four in the morning, his diary contained little more than the methodical record of the day's run, until they reached Lisbon. There, he had lunch at the legation with the Gosselins, before catching the *Ambrose*; enduring again the unpleasant Biscay gales, reaching Liverpool on November 30th, continuing to London by the night train, and going round to the Foreign Office in the morning. It was a depressing experience. 'Saw many men, including Villiers [the head of the West African Department]. They are a gang of stupidities in many ways.' He could not know why they were unsympathetic; Ronald Campbell had recommended that he should be brought back to London because 'he has the system on the brain', and it would be necessary to watch what he wrote. Depressed, he retired early to bed, feeling a cold was coming on. The next morning, it was worse: 'shall be seedy, I fear'.

But then, a note came from Farnall to say that Lord Percy, who had succeeded Cranborne as Parliamentary Under-Secretary to the Foreign Office, wanted to see him. They had a long talk, which Casement felt gave Percy 'some eye-openers'. Evidently it did; he was told that Lord Lansdowne would see him, the following day. After hearing him out Lansdowne commented, 'proof of the most painfully convincing kind, Mr. Casement'. It was arranged that he should have the use of a typist, for his report; and after an evening at *Richard II* ('not good') he got down to work on it.

There were interruptions; a man came to see him from Reuters, who had been given a tip-off that he had a sensational story, and on December 7th a number of papers, ranging from the staid *Morning Post* to the lightweight *Daily Mirror*, named him as having investigated what the *Mirror* described as the 'Horrors of the Congo'. There were also distractions. On December 6th, Casement dined alone at the Comedy Restaurant, 'First time there in life. ... Then walked. Dusky depredator huge, saw 7″ in all. Two beauties.' Still, that day he had written 6,000 words, and done some revision. By the 12th, he had a draft of the report ready, to show Farnall.

Again, the immediate reaction was disappointing. Even Farnall, he noticed, seemed despondent; and Francis Villiers was indecisive, one day saying the final version of the report would be needed before the end of the year—the next, that it was unlikely the report would be called for until February, when Parliament met. 'An abject piffler', Casement noted. This was unjust to Villiers; it was his political masters who were responsible for the indecision. Leopold, Percy had suggested, should be told that publication of the report would be withheld, if the Free State agreed to accept an International Commission of Inquiry into the allegations that had been made. Farnall disagreed. If he was despondent, it was not on account of the report, which he described as 'terse, full of matter, and written in a quite dispassionate style'. Even Villiers conceded the report seemed 'very well prepared, and free from all traces of exaggeration'. But what Casement did not know was that the request for delay in publication had come from his former employer, Sir Alfred Jones, who ran the Elder Dempster line. Its Congo monopoly depended upon Leopold's favour; and its contract was due to expire in 1904.

Jones's intervention came too late. The newspapers had got hold of the story, and so had Morel. What Casement had seen on his tour had decided him to write to Morel from Loanda, urging him to make contact with Poultney Bigelow, who was in London, and with Joseph Conrad, to enlist them as allies in his campaign; and when he arrived back in London he requested, with his usual punctiliousness, official permission to consult Morel. As the feeling in the Foreign Office was that Leopold must be taught a lesson—a project in which Morel would be a useful ally —permission had been granted; and the two men had met for the first time. 'No man walks the earth at this moment who is more absolutely good and honest,' Ward had earlier told Morel, enclosing a letter from Casement; and in his autobiography, Morel was to recall the effect the letter had made on him: 'I feel no shame in confessing that the perusal of the enclosure unmanned me—those burning words penned from the midst of the Leopoldian hell would have melted a stone image.' On December 10th they met, had dinner together, and stayed up so late in Casement's rooms, talking, that Morel had to spend the rest of the night on a couch in the study.

'The man is as honest as the day.' Casement's diary recorded of Morel; and Morel was similarly impressed by Casement:

> It was one of those rare incidents in life which leave behind them an imperishable impression. I saw before me a man, my own height, very lithe and sinewy, chest thrown out, head held high—suggestive of one who had lived in the vast open spaces. Black hair and beard covering cheeks hollowed by the tropical sun. Strongly marked features. A dark-blue penetrating eye sunken in the socket. A long, lean swarthy Van Dyke type of face, graven with power and withal of great gentleness. An extraordinarily handsome and arresting face. From the moment our hands gripped and our eyes met, mutual trust and confidence were bred and the feeling of isolation slipped from me like a mantle. Here was a man indeed.

Casement told him what he had found on his tour, occasionally breaking off his narrative to mutter 'poor people, poor people!'

> the scenes so vividly described seemed to fashion themselves out of the shadows before my eyes. The daily agony of an entire people unrolled itself in all the repulsive terrifying de-

tails. I verily believe I *saw* those hunted women clutching their children and flying panic-stricken to the bush; the blood flowing from those quivering black bodies as the hippopotamus hide whip struck and struck again; the savage soldiery rushing hither and thither among burning villages; the ghastly tally of severed hands.

Casement had arranged to spend Christmas in Ulster with his aunt at his old Ulster home in Ballycastle. It was not a success; nobody was at the train to meet him: 'cold and black, I will not go up there again'. Most of Christmas Day was taken up in making further revisions to the report; and he was cheered to have Farnall's praise of it, 'could not be better, both in style and substance'. When he returned to London on New Year's Day, it was to find himself eulogised by Poultney Bigelow in the *Morning Post* as 'the sort of man depicted in Jules Verne's novels, the man who is everlasting exploring and extricating himself from every imaginable difficulty by superhuman tact, wit and strength' (his diary comment on the article was 'a rummy one') and to be complimented again by Farnall, and by Villiers. He was even, he was told, to have a say in how the report would be used—'I am to decide its fate, practically.' He handed it in on January 8th; and with that day's entry, the diary ended.

Command Paper   1904

Casement had been told he must undergo another operation—for what, his letters did not disclose. As soon as the final version of the report was with Farnall, he went back to Ulster, and entered a Belfast nursing home. During his stay there, and while he was recuperating afterwards, he kept in close touch with the Foreign Office; and for a few weeks he had no reason to worry about the fate of his report.

The Foreign Office, however, were in occasional need of reassurance—on two issues in particular. One concerned the Congo missionaries. Why had they not been more vocal earlier? George Grenfell was to provide the explanation. When the missionaries had first begun to hear stories of atrocities, their initial reaction had been incredulity; and when they had eventually made protests, they had been reassured by the setting up of the Commission for the Protection of the Natives. When they could

deceive themselves no longer, they reported to their societies in
London; but these, in their turn, had been deterred from re-
leasing evidence of the atrocities by the fear that, if they did,
Leopold would withdraw his favour. But they could only continue to disguise what was being reported from their Congo
missions so long as it was not passed on to other quarters; and
it was here that Casement's tour had had an important consequence. If their criticisms were being suppressed, he had suggested, they should pass them to Morel, who could use them in
his magazine. John Weeks did so—the first British missionary
publicly to denounce the Free State. Soon, Grenfell and others
were co-operating with Morel; and Casement was able to reply
to the Foreign Office by quoting their admission that they had
been misled.

The other issue about which the Foreign Office was nervous
was mutilation. By confronting the Free State authorities with
the boy Epondo, and by denouncing the practice of mutilation
in his letter to the Governor-General, Casement had given advance notice that this was going to be one of his lines of attack;
and the Free State authorities had gratefully seized the opportunity to anticipate it. *La Dépêche Coloniale*, their organ in
Brussels, told its readers all about the existence of mutilations
in the Congo—but explained that they were a long-standing
feature of tribal warfare there, which the Free State was doing
its best to eliminate. Phipps, who assiduously forwarded anything which reflected favourably on the Free State to the
Foreign Office, argued that if it were not an old tribal custom, it
must surely have been introduced by the slavers. To the Foreign
Office, this looked reasonable. But Casement was able to secure
confirmation of his own recollection—that neither the tribes nor
the slavers had used mutilation as a punishment—from Ward,
from Conrad, and from missionaries who had been out in the
Congo at the same time as Stanley's men.

Reassured, the Foreign Office began to prepare the report for
the printers. But there remained the question how best to exploit it. Should it be shown to Leopold, first, in the hope of
frightening him into offering genuine reforms? It would be wise,
Lansdowne decided, to ask Lord Salisbury, who in his retirement was still consulted on important issues. The report, his
advice was, should be published as planned, in time to present
to Parliament. It was useless trying to do a deal with Leopold.

He might make a bargain, in exchange for agreement not to publish; but he could not be trusted to keep it, and to withhold publication would make a bad impression. Besides, it was important that the report should be seen: 'the picture is appalling. The publication will make a great noise.'

Leopold made one last attempt to shake the Foreign Office's confidence. Casement's tour—a letter from his Secretary of State claimed on February 5th—had been undertaken in order to make trouble among the natives, by inflaming them against the State. He had deliberately avoided meeting the Free State authorities. The districts he had visited were in a state of ferment; and the evidence he had accepted was of an *ex parte* character. In short, Casement had chosen to be the spokesman of the anti-Free-State campaign fomented on the one hand by the Liverpool merchants, 'who had found their pecuniary interests injured by the comprehensive scheme of exploitation organised in the interest of civilisation by the Sovereign', and on the other, by the Protestant missionaries who 'sought to combine self-interest with religion'.

Lansdowne was unimpressed. Even a visit which Leopold chose to pay to the German Emperor, at the end of January, did not worry him. The Belgian press might boast of the happy accord he had established there, but the visit failed in its real purpose; nowhere, other than in Belgium, did it receive much attention—certainly not in Germany. The decision was therefore taken to go ahead with publication. Phipps, informed, sent a panicky cable begging for a postponement because, on February 10th, he 'must unavoidably meet the King of the Belgians'. Lansdowne charitably agreed to delay publication until the 11th; and the Report eventually appeared on the 15th.

For a preface, the Foreign Office had decided to use some comments it had received from Lord Cromer, the British Government's agent in Egypt, one of the last of the great imperial proconsuls, who had just paid a visit to the Upper Nile. The contrast between British and Belgian territory, Cromer had found, was remarkable. There was hardly a sign of a village on the Belgian side of the river. The reason for this was obvious: 'the Belgians are disliked. The people fly from them, and it is no wonder they should do so, for I am informed that the soldiers are allowed full liberty to plunder, and that payments are rarely made for supplies.' These observations, he felt, afforded sufficient evidence of the spirit which animated the Belgian Administration, 'if indeed Administration it can be called. The Government, so far as I can judge, is conducted almost exclusively on commercial principles, and even judged by that standard, it would appear that those principles are somewhat shortsighted.' The denunciation was less impressive than it looked, for Cromer could hardly have been described as a disinterested observer. Early in the new year, a Belgian force had moved into the Southern Sudan on a 'scientific reconnaissance', and he was irritated, as he realised it was only a ruse to secure a base there. But the British public would not know this. They would be impressed by the fact that the famous Cromer had observed the same evils in his visit that Casement was describing from other areas of the Congo.

Casement's Report followed, beginning with a brief summary of his itinerary, and a mention of the fact that he was able to contrast the condition of the natives with what he had found fifteen years before. In one respect, there had been marked improvement—communications. Admirably built and maintained river stations greeted the traveller, the steamboats offering regular access to some of the most remote regions of Central Africa; and the railway between Matadi and Stanley Pool saved the traveller days of bodily fatigue. But the contrast, he had found, was otherwise a sad one; 'perhaps the most striking change observed during my journey into the interior was the great reduction observable everywhere in native life. Communities I had formerly known as large and flourishing centres of population are today entirely gone, or now exist in such diminished numbers as to be no longer recognisable.'

Why? The sleeping sickness, an incurable disease of which the cause was unknown, was certainly partly responsible, as the natives agreed. But 'they attribute, and I think principally, their rapid decrease in numbers to other causes as well'; and it was these Casement had felt it his duty to investigate.

A description of his tour followed, interspersed with his comments. Almost the only praise he felt able to bestow on the Free State for its achievements was that it had got rid of the slave trade. No action it had taken, had produced more laudable results. But, 'while the suppression of an open form of slave dealing has been an undoubted gain, much that was not reprehensible in native life has disappeared along with it'. The ivory

trade had passed from native hands; and at formerly prosperous
trading centres like the Bolobo region none of the products of
native industry, not even fish, was now used in trade. The natives
of that region, though, were relatively well off compared with
those in the rubber producing areas, further into the interior.
Careful investigation of the conditions of native life in those
areas had confirmed, for Casement, the truth of the allegation
that the great decrease in the Congo population, the wretched-
ness of the towns, and the shortage of food, were to be 'attributed above all else to the continued effort made during many
years to compel the natives to work india-rubber'. The compulsion had been applied by native troops: with the chiotte, to
punish those who did not bring in their quota of rubber; and
death for those who tried to escape—along with mutilation of
the dead (and sometimes of the living) to provide evidence that
duty had been done. The cutting off of hands was the deliberate
act of the soldiers of the administration, 'who never made any
concealment that in committing these acts they were but obeying the positive orders of their superiors'. The Free State, Casement concluded, was no more than a gigantic and ruthless
commercial enterprise.

Leopold's Reply   1904

The Report, in its published form, ought to have given Casement
lively satisfaction. It did not. Although he had been assured
that he was going to be allowed to decide how it was to be
handled, in the event he had not been in London in the critical
few days before publication. He had been in Ireland, and on
the move. Recovery after his operation had been slow, and he
had decided to go to the south of Ireland in the hope of finding
a little sun. The Foreign Office had tried to keep him informed
about what was happening, but communications in that region
proved to be as erratic as Somerville and Ross had described
them in *The Irish R.M.* Two telegrams sent to him in Ballyhooly, County Cork, had only reached him (he explained to
Villiers) after twice being redirected from the other end of the
country. And, as a result, he was unable to get his view across
on a point which had come up just before publication.

At the time he was writing the first draft, in December, he had
included the names of places and of people—agents, mission-

aries, natives—referred to. But in the published Report, he had
told Farnall that the names of the Free State agents should be
omitted. This was not simply because some of them were
charged by the natives with the responsibility for mutilations,
castrations, and murders—crimes for which, if their names appeared, they would in effect be condemned unheard. It was also
because these men were themselves victims of the system. Some
of them he liked—even Lejesme; and he had received hospitality
from them which it would be ungentlemanly to repay by pillory-
ing them. In the final revision of his Report, therefore, the names
of Lejesme and the others were left out; and before returning
to Ulster he had written to remind Farnall to keep them out—
'it has been a pain to me all the way through to have to refer to
these poor men by name'.

As he shared Casement's view that the system was more
blameworthy than the individuals, Farnall had raised no objection. Neither had Percy, though he felt it would look a little odd
if the accused men remained anonymous, while their accusers
were named. But Salisbury had intervened. The only thing which
made him uncomfortable about publishing the Report, he wrote,
was 'the possibility that those wretched blacks will be still
worse used in consequence'; it would be better if the names of
the victims, as well as of the tyrants, were omitted. To be on
the safe side, Lansdowne suggested that the names of tribes
and of the villages where Casement had heard their evidence
should also be left out, in case it might make it easier for the
Free State authorities to identify them. And finally, just before
the Report was due to go to the printers, it was decided that as
the names of agents, native witnesses, their tribes and their
villages had all been removed, the names of missionaries ought
to go, too—except where, as in the case of Whitehead, there
was specific authorisation.

When the news reached him in Ballyhooly, Casement wrote
setting out in detail his reasons why all names, except those of
the agents, should be put back. What was the use of omitting
them, when the Free State authorities knew where he had been,
and whom he had seen? All that leaving them out would do
would be to leave him open to the charge that he was unable to
stand over his evidence. Or, worse, it might seem as if the
Foreign Office had left them out because it doubted the authenticity of the information which he had provided. 'The onlooker

will say', he complained to Farnall, 'that the better role and the braver role is with the accused, not with their accusers.'

This letter, Casement feared, might arrive too late. It did; he only posted it on the day of publication. He must have realised, therefore, that the Report would be a disappointment. It turned out to be worse even than he had feared. The method adopted by the editor to disguise the actual names of towns and tribes was to substitute a single capital letter: 'At F., I spent four days'; and for witnesses, two letters — presumably representing Christian and surname. The idea might have sounded reasonable enough when it was put forward; in practice it led to absurdities like 'I am N.N. These two beside me are O.O. and P.P., all of us Y.' And whoever had edited the report had eventually run out of letters:

R.R.'s statement:
I, R.R., came from N.N. . . . N.N. and R. fought, and they killed several R. people and one R. man. O.O.O. took a man and sent him to L.L.L. to go and tell the white man to come and fight with Nkoko. The white man who fought with N.N. first was named Q.R.

'Ringing changes on the alphabet,' Casement protested to Farnall, 'cannot produce the same effect as putting the alphabet to its right use.' Other changes too, had been made in his Report without his being told. Statements had been attributed to him, for example, which had been made to him in the 1890s; 'put into my mouth they lose all value — as well as being, frankly, quite dishonest when offered thus'. If the Free State Government discovered them the consequences would be embarrassing. The Foreign Office would find it hard to explain, without admitting that they had issued a 'cooked and garbled report'. In the circumstances, the Report should not have been attributed to him, as he was 'clearly not responsible'. Much of his work, he felt, had been wasted, and his aims compromised:

It is disheartening, in more senses than one — and it renders my position in regard to the Foreign Office a somewhat difficult one. I am not clear what my course should be, but it would seem that my resignation is called for. I cannot well continue to serve a Department which has so little confidence

in me, and so little regard for my opinion, as to give to the
world as mine statements made by another, and to make such
vital changes in face of my strong protest.

Farnall was not to consider that he himself was referred to by
these remarks, Casement insisted — or indeed any other individual; but 'indecisions and vacillation of this kind will give the
whole case to the Congo authorities, who at least are able to
know their minds'. And for a while, he preserved an aggrieved
silence.

His irritation was justified; the Report caused less of a sensation than the findings deserved. Of the influential newspapers,
the *Morning Post* grasped its significance, devoting almost four
columns to a summary, and commenting in an editorial that
the secret of the Free State was that it was 'not a State at all,
but a gigantic trading concern, a monopoly run for the benefit
of its share holders'. But of the column and a quarter that *The
Times* gave to the Report, most was devoted to Cromer; and it
expressed no editorial opinion. The way the Report had been
edited, too, precluded its achieving any popular appeal, and
made it difficult for those who bought a copy to wade through it.

In Belgium, Phipps claimed, the effect of the Report was to
promote a lively reaction in Leopold's favour. As Casement knew
too much, Poultney Bigelow had forecast in his *Morning Post*
article, 'we must prepare ourselves soon to hear that this same
Mr. Casement is capable of every crime in the calendar'; if he
told what he knew, 'he will surely become the target for all the
abuse of the Belgian and affiliated press'. He did. And Phipps, so
far from objecting, actually put it about in diplomatic circles in
Brussels that the report was designed merely as a sop to the
Commons, and need not be taken seriously. Although this was
not known till later, his despatches left little doubt where his
sympathies lay. They were sent to Casement at the end of
February, for his comments; and they were just what was
needed to rouse him from his sulks — 'How Phipps can believe
all these people tell him puzzles me,' he replied; 'or rather, it
doesn't.'

After the success of his reply to the Foreign Office, Leopold
could not resist trying to repeat the performance; and in his
'Notes on Mr. Casement's Report' he too set about discrediting
it by casting doubt on the trustworthiness of its author. So

rapid and hasty had his visits to the Upper Congo been, Leopold argued, that his observations could only be superficial; and as he had represented himself to the natives as a redresser of wrongs, they had naturally been encouraged to air all the grievances, real or imaginary, they could think of. And what did his charges amount to? They could be reduced to two: depopulation, and mutilation. But the depopulation had demonstrably been caused by sleeping sickness; and the mutilations were the product of tribal feuds. Significantly the only actual case of mutilation which Casement had brought to the attention of the Free State authorities, the boy Epondo (his name had been omitted from the Report, but the case had been easily identifiable), was actually a good example of how Casement had allowed himself to be misled by prejudiced missionaries and lying natives. Epondo had since confessed that his hand had not been cut off; it had been bitten off by a wild boar — as an American missionary, the Rev. E. E. Faris, who had heard the confession, would testify. Doubtless the rest of the Consul's report was on the same level of veracity. . . .

The wild boar story had in face been passed on to Casement earlier in January, but he had laughed it off: 'the only question I should suggest to the boar,' he had commented to Farnall, 'is where he got his gun from' — Epondo had shown him the wound from a bullet in his arm. It was also inherently improbable that the sentry would have made the excuse that it had been chopped off by another sentry, if it had really been bitten off by a boar. In any case, the circumstances in which Epondo had made his 'confession' were suspicious. Only when he had been taken away to a distant Free State post, and kept there alone, had he retracted his accusation against the sentry. Faris, too, had subsequently denied that he had testified to the truth of the wild boar story. He had not believed a word of it. All that he had been asked to do, he claimed, was testify that this was the version Epondo gave in his presence, which it was. Suspecting that it was a forced confession, he had tried to find out what had really happened, but he found the boy drowsy, disinclined to talk — as if he had been threatened. If he had, Faris thought, the threats had certainly been effective.

As the story was presented in Leopold's 'Notes', though, it looked circumstantial — and damaging; and in the memorandum which Casement sent to Lansdowne on March 30th, replying to them, he concentrated on rebutting their version of the Epondo affair. The fact that they had made so much of it, he suggested, was itself significant. They had even pretended that of all the events on his journey, it had been the one which engaged his main attention. This was manifestly untrue, it was only one of many such examples he had given of mutilations in the Report, and he had disposed of it in a single paragraph—whereas the Free State's reply accounted for more than half of the 'Notes'. Obviously the Free State Government was less inclined to deal with the evidence presented than 'to discredit, if possible, at the outset, the capacity and good faith of the writer'.

The Free State Government was not Casement's only target, here. He still felt strongly that the Foreign Office had made it easier, by the way it had presented the Report, for its critics to cast doubt on his capacity and good faith. It must be clear to the Foreign Office that the 'Notes' were a striking vindication of his work, because if they were the best the Free State could do by way of reply, his Report could not have contained any serious errors. But was it clear to the general public? The 'Notes' had described his visit as 'hasty and rapid', and although he had managed to cover a lot of ground in the two months, while he was on the Upper Congo, it was true that he could not have hoped to present a comprehensive picture. But he had assumed he would not need to, because the Foreign Office already had such a mass of evidence, from years back, in the Congo Atrocity files. To convince the public, therefore, that his Report was not superficial, he suggested that a selection of stories from the files should be brought out as a Government White Paper.

Paradoxically, this was a view which Phipps, in Brussels, was also urging on Lansdowne; not in Casement's interest, but in his own. The reaction to the Report in Belgium—as *Indépendance Belge* expressed it, on February 20th—was that Casement had been a pliant tool on a commercial mission; 'we know in what spirit the London Government has ordained this inquest; we know how the London Government has looked for justification for the benefit of the Liverpool merchants who have organised the campaign against the Free State!' The British Government, Phipps felt, must prove that they were not relying on Casement's evidence alone. But Lansdowne refused to allow the reports in the files to be used. They were hearsay, he told Phipps, and 'lacked the authority of personal observation, without which H.M. Government were unwilling to come to any definite conclusion unfavourable to the administration of the Congo State'. In the margin of the copy of Lansdowne's letter, when it reached him, Casement commented, 'a deliberate lie!' He must also have been outraged at another of Lansdowne's excuses—that some of the material in the Congo Atrocity files was of very old date, and that as the State had recently been active 'in pushing forward occupation of the country, it would be unjust to bring forward statements regarding a condition of affairs which may have entirely passed away'.

There was a domestic reason for these excuses; the political situation in Britain. On the day Casement's Report was published, the results were reported of a by-election in the St. Albans division of Hertfordshire. Formerly it had been regarded as a safe Conservative seat—so much so that in the elections of 1895 and 1900, the Conservative candidate had been returned unopposed. Now, a Liberal was elected. With a general election due that winter, ministers were anxious not to give the Opposition ammunition which would be useful in the coming campaign. An admission that they had known all about the Congo, and had neither disclosed what they knew nor taken any action, would certainly have been vigorously exploited by the reviving Liberal Party.

If Casement had known the reasons for the Foreign Secretary's decisions, he would at least have understood why they had been taken, even if he did not agree with them. But the editing of his Report, and the refusal to publish confirmatory extracts from the files, drove him to the conclusion not merely that he had been used by the Foreign Office for their own purposes, but that his reputation was now being deliberately sacrificed. It was time, he felt, to assert himself. He was still, in theory, British Consul in the Free State—Nightingale's appointment was only temporary. But the previous summer, while he was on the Upper Congo, he had heard that he was next in line for the Lisbon Consulship; and although he had noted the fact without comment in his diary, he must have been flattered, as it was considered one of the best posts in the Service. If the offer still held—he wrote to tell Sir Eric Barrington, Lansdowne's Private

Secretary—he would accept it. But in view of what had passed, he could not go back to the Congo; and 'it might relieve the Foreign Office of some embarrassment were I to resign from the Service.

CHAPTER FIVE

DISILLUSIONMENT

The Congo Reform Association   1904

> My dear Casement [Barrington replied on March 27th], Nobody wants you to resign. I never heard of such a thing. As to your temporary return to the Congo, I think it very unlikely; but it has always been intended to appoint you to Lisbon when the time came.

At first sight the letter might appear comforting; but the return to the Congo was described as 'very unlikely' rather than 'out of the question', and the Lisbon appointment remained in the indefinite future. It can have done little to mollify Casement, especially as by this time his indignation against the Foreign Office was being fanned by Morel.

Following their December meeting, Casement had gone to stay with Morel and his wife at their home in Gladstone's old village, Hawarden ('talked all night; wife a good woman'); and when he left for Ulster, they kept in touch by frequent letters. Morel insisted that he had been shamefully treated. It had been a fight between the rogues of the Free State and the gentlemen of the Foreign Office; and the gentlemen, by their reluctance to use the really damning material in the Congo files, had left Casement exposed to attacks of 'great malignity and virulence'. The only recourse was to rouse public opinion to his side. But how? The inept editing of his Report had deprived it of its expected impact; and his efforts to attract influential support had been unavailing. Conrad, in particular, had been a disappointment. He shared Casement's feelings; 'it is an extraordinary thing', he had written to him just before Christmas,

> that the conscience of Europe, which seventy years ago has put down the slave trade on humanitarian grounds, tolerates the Congo State today. It is as if the moral clock had been put back many hours. And yet nowadays if I were to over-

work my horse so as to destroy its happiness or physical well-being, I should be hauled before a magistrate. . . . In the old days, England had in her keeping the conscience of Europe. The initiative came from her. But I suppose we are busy with other things—too much involved in great affairs to take up the cudgels for humanity, decency and justice.

But as he was 'only a wretched novelist', Conrad felt, he was not the man Casement needed.

The more he thought about it—Casement wrote to Morel, while convalescing after his operations—the more important he felt it was to resort to a project he had outlined at their first meeting: the setting-up of 'a single organisation, having a single purpose, systematically and continuously to strive to enlighten public opinion in Britain about the conditions in the Congo'. The public, he felt sure, felt the same impulses of pity:

> I am confident that once any decent man or woman here in this country learns and appreciates the ghastly truth of the wrong done to the Congo man and woman—aye, and the poor hunted child!—they will not desert them. We shall grow in numbers day by day until there go up from the length and breadth of England one overwhelming Nay! to the continuance of a system which is a disgrace to our race and colour.

Fired by Casement's enthusiasm, Morel went to stay with him in Ulster, so that they could discuss how to launch the Congo Reform Association—as they decided it would be called. So long as he remained in the Foreign Service, Casement could not publicly identify himself with the Association; Morel would have to run it. But this would make it impossible for him to continue the freelance journalism with which he had been supporting himself and his wife. His wife, however, had been impressed by Casement; she insisted, when Morel put the idea to her on his return to Hawarden, that he must take the risk. 'You will need funds to start the things,' Casement wrote, on hearing the decision they had reached, 'and I give you something to start with.' The 'something', Morel found, was a cheque for £100. It represented a third of the annual salary which Casement, on his extended leave, was getting from the Foreign Office. 'The weapon which brought King Leopold to his knees,' as Morel was later to recall, 'was forged by two men in straitened circumstance who, so far as they could see into the future, had everything to lose and nothing to gain.'

Having persuaded Morel to found the Association, Casement characteristically grew worried. 'I have reproved myself often,' he wrote, 'for the passionate appeals I made to you when you were over here'; if the Association were going to jeopardise his future prospects, Morel must not go ahead with it. But Morel was already going ahead with it. He continued to do so even when he met with the opposition of Fox Bourne, whose Aborigines Protection Society had hitherto sustained the Congo campaign. Setting up a separate Congo Reform Association was bound to have unfortunate financial consequences, Dilke wrote in February to warn Casement; either it would fail or, if it succeeded, it would bleed the Aborigines Protection Society to death. Casement disagreed, and wrote to reassure Morel: 'all-round philanthropy doesn't meet the Congo evil at all.' He managed to secure some titled backers for the Association, to help establish its separate identity; and when its inaugural meeting was held in Liverpool on March 24th, with Lord Beauchamp as president and Morel as secretary, it had the support of a gratifyingly distinguished list of patrons, peers, bishops and M.P.s. Casement thought it would be unwise to attend, in view of his already strained relations with the Foreign Office. He contented himself with sending a letter of congratulation to Morel: 'the Congo Reform Association is *yours* . . .'

The Caudron Affair   1904

It would take time, though, for the Congo Reform Association to find ways to exercise effective pressure; and Casement, still in Ireland, continued to be disheartened by what he heard, and read, of the progress of the campaign. A further set-back came at the end of March, when Burrows was found guilty of libelling three Free State officers in his book. Although Casement had found the book's descriptions of the Congo 'horribly true' he mistrusted the author, whom he had met at Matadi in 1901, and he had warned Lansdowne that although Burrows's allegations were well-founded, the fact that his stay in the Congo 'was not distinguished by temperate habits' might be used against him. Burrows was unable to contest the charges, through lack of funds; and when the verdict went against him, it was exploited in the Belgian press as a vindication of the Free State —'The British campaign condemned by British Justice', as *Etoile Belge* described it.

Irritating though this was, Casement was more concerned about the failure of the Foreign Office to follow up the advantage which his Report had given them in their duel with Leopold. The most Britain could do, Salisbury had advised, was to lay the evidence before the signatories to the Berlin agreement: 'if nobody out of England takes any notice', he told Arthur Balfour, 'I do not see that we are called on to do any more.' Nobody did take any notice.

The only step which the British Government could have taken on its own account would have been to announce that it was going to protect its own subjects in the Congo by setting up consular courts—as Casement had suggested, and as Fox Bourne urged on behalf of the Aborigines Protection Society. But by this time Farnall had joined Percy in opposing it—and for reasons which were certain to carry weight. British subjects, he pointed out, were scattered all over the Congo. Jurisdiction could not be resumed without a very large increase in consular staff; and that would mean a very large increase in expenditure. So Lansdowne did nothing.

The only consolation for the reformers came in a report of a case heard in the Boma Court of Appeal. From time to time, since attention had been drawn to the illegalities practised in the Concessions, agents had been charged with exceeding their authority. Some of them had been sentenced to imprisonment —and then released. A Concession agent, Philippe Caudron, had been arrested for raising a force of native soldiers, members of the *Force Publique*, and destroying a number of villages, killing some of their inhabitants; but when he was found guilty and sentenced, he had elected to appeal. He made no attempt to deny the charges made against him, when his appeal was heard in the Boma Court. He did not even plead that what he had done was justified. 'It does not appear,' the court's judgment noted, almost incredulously, 'that the victims had committed any further fault than that of failing to furnish the company with the amount of labour required . . . on no occasion did the natives attack or commit any sort of hostile act.' Caudron's excuse was simply that he was obeying orders, which he was able to produce to show the Court. And the Court, though reducing his sentence because they felt he had believed he must carry the orders out, had to admit that they were flagrantly illegal.

For Casement and the Congo reformers, the judgment was important. It constituted the first official indictment of the system from within. On the evidence, too, all the Free State authorities were implicated, right up to the Governor-General, Wahis; and although an attempt by the defence to compel him to give evidence broke down—because, the Court ruled, he held a personal mandate from the sovereign—this itself meant, as the *Morning Post* pointed out on May 6th, that the man whom Leopold had given his mandate must personally have authorised the Concession companies to break the law. 'What does King Leopold propose to do?' the *Morning Post* asked. 'His Majesty must either disavow or dismiss his mandatory, or share with him his responsibility—in which case the final link in the chain will be completed.'

There was no longer any need—Casement told the Foreign Office, in a letter displaying some of his old confidence—to be concerned about the 'full refutation' of his Report, promised by the Free State authorities. He had now been amply vindicated by their Boma Court's own judgment. Surely, then, there could be no excuse for continued inaction? But Lansdowne had such an excuse. He was involved in the final stages of the erection of the Entente, and the security of Belgium was one of the tent-pegs. He was therefore less anxious to humble Leopold; and the fate of the Congo natives had sunk out of his mind. On the other hand, it would be useful to be able to appear to be taking action, in case the Liberals used the Caudron affair to resume their onslaught of the year before; and Leopold's 'Notes on Mr. Casement's Report', on re-examination, provided just what was needed. The 'Notes' had unguardedly mentioned that as the Free State authorities' attention had been drawn to a few cases of cruelty, whether true or not, they would 'of course look into the matter, and cause enquiries to be made'. On June 6th, Lansdowne instructed Phipps to say that although the announcement there was to be an inquiry was welcome, His Majesty's Government would like further details. In particular, they wanted to be sure that the inquiry really would be impartial and thorough. There should be a Commission 'composed of members of well-established reputation, and in part, at least, of persons unconnected with the Congo State, to whom the fullest powers should be entrusted both as regards the collection of evidence and the measures for the protection of witnesses'.

Too late, Leopold realised his mistake. Now, he could hardly avoid naming a Commission which had at least the outward appearance of impartiality. All he could do would be to exact a price. To do its work properly, the Commission must have a copy of Casement's original Report, with the names of witnesses. This left Lansdowne in a quandary. He had rejected an earlier request from Brussels that the names should be made available —actually using the Caudron affair as his excuse; he was not, he claimed, impugning the Free State administration, but could it now be sure it could trust its own agents? Having come so close, though, to securing a concession from Leopold which would not merely silence the Government critics in the forthcoming Commons debate, but would keep them quiet for months thereafter, he was unwilling to take the risk of Leopold using this excuse to refuse to proceed with an independent Commission of Inquiry. Phipps was instructed to say that he had agreed to the request for a copy of the original Report, provided the Free State administration gave an assurance that witnesses who had given evidence to Casement should be protected. But when Phipps replied that the administration declined to give it, Lansdowne did not press the point.

From Lansdowne's point of view, to have compelled Leopold to agree to an independent Commission of Inquiry was an achievement. To Casement, it seemed a further betrayal. He had always disliked the idea of an inquiry, because it would mean further delay before any positive steps could be taken on behalf of the Congo natives. He was convinced, too, that the Free State authorities would ensure that the Commission would hear only such evidence as they wanted it to hear. Only by returning himself to the Congo, he decided, could he ensure that the Commissioners, when they arrived, were adequately briefed. But obviously he could not go back as Consul. He had, in fact, just offered his resignation. 'So far,' he complained in a letter to Villiers—

The Congo State has got all the honours. Their lying 'Notes' hold the field, and have clearly produced a widespread impression—since they have not been answered—that there is no answer to the assertion that I was 'misled'—to put it politely—and that, therefore, *all* the statements in my Report should be dismissed as even more untrustworthy than the Epondo incident . . . I do not mind a bit so far as my reputation goes, but I do mind very much for the sake of the unfortunate people of the Congo, whose cause I know, so grievously, to be a right one. It is their cause which is being sacrificed—and I feel greatly depressed. It seems to me that my duty is to resign my post, and return to the Congo, and take my place with the people who are going to suffer through my attempt to help them, and my evident failure.

A debate on foreign affairs was due in the Commons on June 9th; it could have been embarrassing for the Government if Casement's resignation—and, still more, the reasons for it— became known. Somehow—perhaps with the reassurance that the Lisbon post would soon be his—he was smoothed down. But Morel had been at work; and in the debate Alfred Emmott, Liberal M.P. for Oldham, attacked the Foreign Office for leaving him in the lurch by refusing to back up his Report with evidence from the Congo Atrocity files. The reason, Emmott suggested, must be that some of the stories in the files were so bad 'that if they were published the Government could be asked why they had not taken measures at an earlier date'. And with what Sir Edward Grey described as 'gruesome unanimity', all the M.P.s who referred to the Congo in the course of the debate—including Lord Edmund Fitzmaurice, Lansdowne's brother, who had been a member of the Liberal Government when the Free State was set up—expressed their horror at the Congo revelations. Unlike the unfortunate Cranborne the year before, however, Lord Percy could face his Government's critics in the Commons with confidence—even with simulated gratitude. Their opinions, he claimed, accorded with his own. Shocked by Casement's Report, the Government had demanded an independent inquiry into the condition of the natives in the Congo. The Commons could rest assured that the Inquiry would be held, and would have the British Government's full co-operation.

The Commission of Inquiry 1904

Disappointed though he was over the debate's outcome, Casement could be satisfied with it so far as it had related to him personally. The references to his Report had been flattering; Percy as well as Dilke drew freely from it, and Herbert Samuel described him as 'a gentleman of the highest standing and reliability, whose good faith even the Congo Free State had not ventured to challenge'. Certainly there was no sign that the Foreign Office's refusal to publish material from the Atrocity files was damaging his reputation at home. But on the following morning, any pleasure which he had received from reading the accounts of the debate was obliterated by the contents of a letter in *The Times*, in which a traveller, James Harrison, describing a journey he had undertaken from the Nile to the mouth of the Congo, lavished praise on the Free State.

Although it printed the letter, *The Times* did not appear to take it seriously; an editorial bluntly dismissed the Free State's replies to critics as inadequate. And when the Foreign Office made inquiries about Harrison, they elicited that he was a big-game hunter who, in order to get permission to go to the Congo, had contrived to let Leopold know that he would testify in the Free State's favour. There was consequently no need for Casement to take the letter to heart. But it contained a reference to him which caused him intense irritation. 'Personally,' Harrison wrote, 'I think it was a great mistake that Mr. Casement was chosen to act. As a trader, whether he was biased or not, he got the reputation of being so.'

Casement had originally been employed by Elder Dempster, and later he had worked for the Sanford expedition, which had finished up as a trading concern. But he had never thought of himself as a trader. In the Irish social circles in which he had grown up, a gentleman could not be 'in trade'; and although the barriers had broken down sufficiently for men in such old established firms as Elder Dempster to attain social acceptability, to be identified with trade was still demeaning—particularly in the Foreign Office: as Ernest Hambloch, who was later to work with Casement in South America, recalled in his memoirs, the Foreign Office tradition was to have as little as possible to do with 'anything as commonplace as trade'. Casement, too, had the feeling that most traders were concerned with natives only to exploit them. When he had heard who had been chosen to stand in for him as Consul at Boma, he was depressed because—as he commented in his diary—Nightingale was 'not very pro-native and is, after all, a trader at heart'.

The accusation did not merely irritate him; for a time it so preyed on his mind that he could think of little else. He drafted and re-drafted a long, rambling, repetitive rebuttal; and when it was finished, realising that he would not be allowed to have it published in *The Times* over his own name, he sent it to Morel, to ask him to sign it and send it to *The Times*. But when he found Morel had already written to *The Times* in his defence, he was aggrieved. With his relish for nicknames, he had taken to writing to Morel as 'My dear Bulldog', and signing himself 'Tiger'. Now, he wrote to 'My dear Morel' to explain that if somebody disparaged him it was his own business, and nobody else's, to decide whether or not to defend himself publicly. As it was, he had half a mind to reply to Harrison in his own way, and under his own name, even though the Foreign Office would surely ask him to resign.

He did not write the letter—or, if he did, it was not published; but for the next few weeks, he held aloof from the Congo issue, leaving it to the Association, and to the Foreign Office. Lansdowne, having secured his Commission of Inquiry, was content. Leopold was not. He had planned, and was now financing, an organisation in Brussels, ostensibly a philanthropic foundation set up to collect and publish information about the Free State, but really to finance foreign writers and journalists who were willing to write articles, and get them published, in which the Free State was shown in a favourable light, and its critics—Casement in particular—disparaged. From this material, pamphlets were compiled, and distributed all over Europe and Britain: some sold for 1d., and others judiciously distributed free—as even Phipps was disconcerted to find: it was a matter of notoriety, he reported at the end of June, 'that the saloons and sleeping cars throughout Europe at this travelling season are full of pamphlets, amended periodically and entitled *La Vérité sur le Congo*, with which it is sought to influence the opinions of the travelling public with regard to the royal enterprise during the idle hours of a railway journey'.

If he could have discredited Casement's Report internationally, Leopold might have been able to avoid setting up the

Commission of Inquiry; but his propaganda machine overplayed his hand. In April, the *Washington Post* had treated his 'Notes on Mr. Casement's Report' as if they had been a complete vindication: under the heading 'Congo Charges False', it had said of Leopold's reply that it 'refutes all the point of the British Consul's Report, and is a most convincing testimony to the humanitarian work which King Leopold has accomplished in Africa'. It happened that a Congressman had a business partner whose son had gone to the Congo as a missionary, and died there. Enraged at the aspersions cast by implication on the Congo missionaries, Senator Morgan drew Casement's Report to the Senate's attention, insisting that it was 'entirely just and correct', and arranging that the *Congressional Record* should include some fifteen pages of material about atrocities to prove it; and some American newspapers began to take up the cause of reform. On June 15th, the *New York Tribune* remarked in an editorial that if the Free State authorities continued to resist the demand for an independent Commission of Inquiry any longer, the only conclusion which could be drawn was that there was something they wished to conceal.

Always sensitive to public opinion in the United States, Leopold must have realised that he could not delay setting up the Commission much longer. The final push, however, came unexpectedly from Italy. The Free State had made extensive use of Italian army officers as mercenaries—the Italian Government being relieved to have them off its payroll; and with good relations between the two governments, there had been a disposition in Italy to ignore Casement's findings. But on July 6th *La Tribuna* carried an article, 'The Congo and the Italians', describing how an Italian lieutenant had committed suicide rather than face trial on atrocity charges; questions were asked in the Italian Assembly, and demands made for an investigation. Leopold decided it was time to announce his own team; and its composition revealed that he had lost none of his tactical skill. It was to consist of Edmund de Schumacher, head of the Department of Justice in the Canton of Lucerne; Emile Janssens, a Brussels lawyer; and the judge of the Boma Court, Baron Nisco. Nisco was an astute choice, because he and Casement had been on very friendly social terms; yet Leopold knew he did not share Casement's views. Following a conversation with him in Brussels that spring, Phipps had reported that 'whilst entertaining the most friendly feelings towards Mr. Casement, with whom he had lived on terms of intimacy, Baron Nisco appears to have arrived at entirely the opposite conclusions as regards the results of Belgian rule'. With Janssens known to be of the same opinion, two of the three members—Leopold could feel confident—would be predisposed in his favour.

There was another serious defect in the Commission, as Fox Bourne—by this time reconciled to the existence of the Congo Reform Association, and working in harmony with Morel—pointed out to the Foreign Office. No provision had been made for British interests, or views, to be represented. Surely the British Government must insist that their Consul in the Congo, or some other accredited representative, should be allowed to accompany the Commission, with the right to attend its hearings? Lansdowne declined to press the point. He had a better idea—from his point of view. On September 28th he instructed Phipps to tell the Free State authorities that if the Commission did not permit a duly authorised British representative to attend their sessions, 'they cannot, in the opinion of His Majesty's Government, feel surprised or aggrieved if the result should be to destroy in advance all the moral authority which might otherwise attach to the Commission'. Whatever the outcome of its work, in other words, Lansdowne would be covered. If its report echoed Casement's, he could take the credit for having insisted on the inquiry. If it whitewashed the Free State authorities, he could, if necessary, cast doubt on its validity, for having been conducted in secret.

Lisbon   *1904*

Casement had been out of touch with the Congo Reform Association, since he had taken offence over the Harrison letter. He had also been ill, again; and he was feeling his age—he had just turned forty. But the news of the Commission of Inquiry roused him to write on September 8th to make it up with Morel. It would be no reflection on the members of the Commission, he insisted, if they found themselves unable to win the natives' confidence. But obviously they could not expect to, as they would be given only the corrupt evidence which Leopold would be sure to arrange for them. And in this, Leopold need not fear he would be let down by the Foreign Office who, Casement felt, were 'sincerely sorry I was born'. Phipps and Villiers, he believed, were personally vindictive towards him; and the Government must be hoping that the Commission's report would turn out to be favourable to the Free State, so that the whole issue could be decently buried.

Casement was right about Phipps. His despatches from Brussels were full of almost hysterical resentment at the Congo reform movement in general, and Casement's contribution in particular. Casement was also right in his assumption it was very much in the Government's interest that the Congo issue should be buried. He was determined it should not be: on September 12th, he wrote to explain he had been out of contact because he had been seriously ill, and enclosing another memorandum. The only purpose it served, however, was to reveal just how out of contact he had become; it was little more than a rehash of the now disposed-of Epondo affair. It would have been more to the point if he had concentrated on publicising the reports coming in at this time from the Congo missionaries, through Consul Nightingale (who was belying Casement's contemptuous judgment of him); notably from John Harris, who had been subjected to reprisals. But the Congo Reform Association happened to be in no position to exploit such incidents, that autumn. Morel had been invited to visit the United States, to help set up a Congo Reform Association there; and Casement himself, informed at the end of September that the Lisbon post was at last vacant, had to leave to take it up. In their absence Fox Bourne took on the campaign. Seeing a chance to make an impression, he urged that missionaries who had been in the Congo should be allowed to give evidence to Leopold's Commissioners before they left, and the Commissioners agreed—only for Fox Bourne to find, to his embarrassment, that no Congo missionaries were available to go to Brussels—a humiliation which Lansdowne regarded as 'really quite intolerable'. And no sooner was Morel back from America than he, too, ran into trouble. An Italian, Antonio Benedetti, who had worked for the Free State, had offered to write a book for the Congo Reform Association which would expose conditions there. From Lisbon, Casement warned against acceptance of the proposal. His disclosures might be genuine, but, 'I am awfully suspicious of him; he looks a rascal'. It was too late; a contract had been offered, which Benedetti promptly took to his employers in Brussels, giving *Indépendance Belge* the opportunity at the beginning of December to splash the story that the Association had tried to bribe him to give false evidence.

It was very typical of the Foreign Office that although they had known all about Benedetti—because he had first tried, without success, to extract money from them through Nightingale—they had not warned Morel; and when the story broke, they did not tell him what they knew. For a time, therefore, it looked as if Morel had been detected in a shady transaction.* For Casement, though, who heard of Benedetti's treachery the day after he had sounded the warning about Benedetti, it was just one more indication that he had been foolish to accept the Lisbon post. Writing to Morel to commiserate, he told him that he was leaving it for good. He was returning for an operation, which would mean a prolonged retirement from the Foreign Service.

Before he had left for Lisbon, he had warned his predecessor there that he might not be able to relieve him, as he might have to have two operations: for a fistula, and to remove his appendix. But he had also written to his cousin Gertrude to say that his doctors were idiots, in particular the one who said that he had appendicitis—'I don't believe him at all'. Appendicitis, however, was very fashionable, following the successful operation on Edward VII in 1902; and for Casement's purposes it might be convenient, as doctors who diagnosed it tended to say that an operation would be necessary if the symptoms did not disappear. The excuse to return was available, if he wanted it. It had taken him only two months to realise he did.

For most members of the consular service, Lisbon was one of the best posts the Foreign Office had to offer. For Casement, it was one of the worst. What he had enjoyed in Lourenço Marques and in Boma was not just the status—he was ambassador in all but name—but the fact that the work taxed his capabilities. Ordinary consular routine, as his correspondence showed, bored him. But in Lisbon, there was a legation as well as the consulate; and the consular routine consisted chiefly of the work he had come particularly to dislike—clearing all British vessels in and out of the port, settling disputes, getting drunks out of gaol, registering seamen's deaths, arranging for repatriations. It was certainly flattering that the Foreign Office,

---

* It was not until six months later that the full story came out, after Benedetti apologised to Morel (*Morning Post*, May 12th, 1905).

in spite of any irritation they may have felt with him, should
have given him one of the most sought-after of consular appointments, for which there must have been several members of the
service more eligible by seniority and—for that kind of work—
suitability. But the fact they had decided to send him there was
also an indication that though they recognised his talent, they
had no understanding of his temperament.

According to a committee appointed by Lord Lansdowne to
inquire into the Consular Service—the future Conservative
premier, Bonar Law, was one of its members—which had reported a few months earlier:

> the general Consular Service as it at present exists offers no
> attraction to capable young men. It is not a properly con-
> stituted or graded public Service, and offers no definite pros-
> pect of promotion to those who enter it, for men who are new
> to the Service may be given appointments over the heads of
> others who have been there for years before them.

This was what had happened to Casement; and it was flattering to have been promoted over the heads of other Consuls in
this way. But the Foreign Office had ignored the fact that simple
promotion was not what attracted him. He wanted a job that
exercised his abilities. Lisbon could have been looked after by
any competent clerk.

The return of the symptoms of 'appendicitis' gave him the
excuse he needed to leave. Ten years later, he was to claim that
the real reason he returned was to support Morel; and letters
which he was writing at the time on the subject of the Congo
confirm this was his aim. To Nightingale, in Boma, he denounced
the Foreign Office; particularly Villiers, 'the physical embodiment of vacillation', and Lansdowne, wanting 'this bogus commission' only to save face, and waiting for a reconciliation with
Leopold. 'My blood is boiling', he wrote to Morel from London
on December 12th, and he offered to see the editor of *The
Times*, to try to win his support for the campaign. But he was
quickly forced to realise that there was nothing he could do to
bring it back to life. 'Is there not some extraordinary fate,' he
wrote again on December 14th,

> which seems to protect Leopold, and ruin—or greatly injure—
> those who are trying to expose him? It sounds like a contract

with the Evil One, his extraordinary success. It has practically
ruined me, this Congo business; and here I am now, injured in
health, most depressed in spirit and nerves, and with a hard
struggle before me; and you up to the lips, nearly, in deep
waters. . . . But—it *must* end in a betterment of things out
there, even if we go under.

To make things worse, he went on, the British public were
now firmly under the impression that the Government had dealt
diplomatically with the Congo issue 'We know, or suspect, this
Government to be only playing with the matter'; but what was
the use of saying so? There was nothing for it but to wait. 'don't
keep on hitting the same blows to cold iron that you would to
hot.' The Conservative Government could not last forever; when
a change came, it would be time to launch a fresh attack. 'I
know how cold this counsel seems,' he concluded, 'but I am
certain that it is wise.'

The reference to being 'practically ruined' related to the fact
he had decided to leave the Foreign Service. Rather than formally
resign, he had decided, he would ask to be seconded for a while,
without pay, on the grounds of health. This meant, he explained,
that there need be no formal announcement of, or comment on,
his departure; 'it is sufficient to be gone'. But his income would
be gone, too. 'I am practically a thing of the past, and for the
next year I shall have a *very* hard struggle for existence. This is
the strict truth. Where, up to this, I had pounds to play with, I
shall not easily find sixpences.'

Casement had every reason to feel depressed. To all outward
appearances, the Congo campaign had collapsed in humiliating
failure. In fact, as events were soon to show, he was needlessly
pessimistic; his Report was having delayed action effects in
Britain, in the United States, and even in Belgium. But he could
not have known this, at the time. It looked as if what he had
hoped would be his decisive contribution to the toppling of
Leopold had produced no result except the one he had not
wanted—a Commission of Inquiry with all the delay that would
entail. And in the meantime, he was still being assailed by Leopold's propaganda machine. His reliability as a witness was
impugned again in a penny pamphlet, *Are they all liars?*, printed
in Brussels and circulated in Britain, presenting the views of
many eminent and worthy Britons, who had eulogised Leo-

pold's rule in the Congo—Stanley, Sir Harry Johnston, Grenfell.
Casement knew that most of the men quoted had long since
changed their minds; but the ordinary member of the public,
casually picking up a copy, might well begin to have doubts
about the Congo Reform Association, particularly if he happened to have read about the Benedetti affair.

The cause of the Congo natives, to which Casement had given
so much of his adult life, and of his health, appeared to be lost.
He had repudiated his only source of regular income; and he was
going to have an operation. And yet, through the despondency,
descending on occasion into almost maudlin self-pity—'you can
count on poor old broken me to the end'—there emerges a kind
of forlorn jauntiness. He was free again. And he was in love—
with an abstraction, admittedly, but none the less passionately
for that. During the summer, before he went to Lisbon, he had
revived an old emotional attachment to the country of his
birth. Now, he was going back to have his operation in Ireland;
and when he recovered, he proposed to stay there. He had returned from Lisbon to try to help Morel; but when he realised
how little he could do, for the time, he had another idea. He
would devote himself to Irish affairs. This was what he now
did, for the next eighteen months—and was, in fact, to continue
to do, wherever he might be, for the rest of his life.

PART TWO

JOHN BULL'S OTHER ISLAND
1905–1910

CHAPTER ONE

THE DREAM OF THE CELT

'Kitchen Kaffir' 1904

'I do not think it is possible', Sir Wyndham Childs—chief of the Criminal Investigation Department at the time Casement was captured in 1916—wrote in his autobiography, 'to form any proper conception of Roger Casement's character without getting back into the past pages of Irish history.' Casement would have whole-heartedly agreed. A boy brought up an Irish Protestant, as he had been, first in County Dublin and then in Ulster, would not normally have learned any Irish history, except when it was relevant to the history of Great Britain. But Casement's background had been unusual. According to his sister Nina, their father, whose memory he revered, had sympathised with the Fenians, when they had attempted to raise a rebellion in Ireland in 1867. His mother, too, was a Catholic; and although she allowed the children to be brought up as Protestants, she had them baptised 'conditionally' when Roger was four years old. Later, he was to find the library in his uncle's Antrim home well stocked with books on Irish history: and although he claimed that he learned nothing of Ireland at school—'I don't think the word was even mentioned there'—he was always conscious of his nationality. 'From my childhood,' he was to recall in 1908, 'I had been led to call myself, an "Irishman"; the word has a certain significance I was proud of as a boy, which I certainly could not easily have defined.'

It was the more difficult to define because the Casements were an Ulster family and, like most Ulster Protestants, Unionist in their politics. But devotion to King and United Kingdom did not preclude regional patriotism in Ulster—any more than it did in Scotland. Even the most rabid Orangeman did not think of himself as British, except in relation to foreigners: he would have shouted for a British football team (including Irishmen) playing France, but with conspicuously less fervour than he could be heard shouting for an Irish team (from all parts of the island) playing England. And if a boy from a background like Casement's became interested, as he did, in his country's past, he could immediately see that his province had played a central and exciting part in Irish history. Early Irish legend is full of sagas from Ulster—King Connor, Deirdre of the Sorrows. It was to Ulster that St. Patrick came to found his Church, and from Ulster that Columba sailed for Iona, to begin on the mission by which the Picts were converted to Christianity. And it was the men of Ulster, under the O'Neills and O'Donnells, who held out longest in the protracted, though in the end hopeless, Celtic resistance to English domination.

After their defeat, Ulster had admittedly taken a different course from the other provinces. Earlier attempts to colonise Ireland with British settlers had never been entirely successful; but in the north, the 'plantations' in the reign of James I were more systematic and efficient, so that a recognisably different species of Irishman developed, with few of the discernible traces of the old Celtic culture which remained elsewhere. As a result, families like the Casements tended to regard their province's history as dating only from the beginning of the seventeenth century. But to a minority, the legendary Ulster giants and the leaders of the last stand against the English were also part of their heritage—just as a patriotic British schoolchild learned from his history books to regard as British such diverse figures as Boadicea, Canute, William the Conqueror, Cromwell, William of Orange, and George of Hanover.

From an early age, Roger Casement took this larger view of his country's history. According to Gertrude Bannister, he covered the walls of his room, when he came as a schoolboy to stay with her family in Liverpool, with pictures of Irish heroes; and they figured prominently in the verses he wrote before leaving for Africa to join Stanley's men. In particular, he was stimulated and saddened by the story of the men of Ulster's last stand against the Tudors and Stuarts, as an epic showed which he began on his way out to Loanda in 1898. 'The Dream of the Celt', completed three years later, was a paean of praise for the strong, noble Irish, wickedly deceived by the unscrupulous mercenary English:

> Stout Henry's purpose wrought with bastard blow;
> The Celt too quick to trust . . .

> Elizabeth! — though England dare not name
> Those dead, how can an Irish heart forget
> The reddest jewel in your Crown of Fame
> Was Erin, wet with blood and rent with flame
> By your white hands thus deftly wrought and set.

He was touchy, too, when he felt the Irish were being patronised. On September 17th, 1898, just before he left for Loanda, the *Saturday Review* published a poem by Henry Newbolt.

> Down thy valleys, Ireland, Ireland
> Down thy valleys green and sad
> Still thy spirit wanders wailing
> Wailing, wailing, wailing, mad.
> Long ago that anguish took thee
> Ireland, Ireland, green and fair
> Spoilers strong in darkness took thee
> Broke thy heart and left thee there.
> Down thy valleys, Ireland, Ireland,
> Still thy spirit wanders mad
> All too late they love that wronged thee
> Ireland, Ireland, green and sad.

In a letter to Richard Morten — an Englishman, a friend of Herbert Ward's, who was to be his own closest friend in England — Casement two days later contributed his version:

> Up thy chimneys, England, England
> Up thy chimneys black and sad
> Goes thy smoke-wrapped spirit, paling
> Goes pale-aleing — feeling bad.
> Long ago that anguish took thee
> England, England, lost and sunk
> Manufacturing darkness took thee
> That and drink — and left thee drunk.
> Up those chimneys, England, England
> Still thy spirit spoiling goes
> All too late they love thy valleys
> They who wrong their green with *those*.

For all his ardent national feeling, Casement was not at this stage a rebel. Ireland, he felt, had been wronged by England, and was still being wronged; but this did not mean that Ireland should sever her ties—simply that the wrongs should be righted. On leave in Antrim that summer, he castigated his fellow-Ulstermen in a letter to his cousin Gertrude for being less interested in the, to him, exciting results of the battle of Omdurman, than in the North Down by-election, or 'the Revd McQuinzy Drivelbag's last Orange harangue'; and in the Boer War his loyalty was to the Empire. But he could not think of himself as British. If the British generals in South Africa had no clear idea what to do—he warned Richard Morten—that would spell disaster; 'and I'm sorry to say, my dear Dick, that with all my admiration for *your* race, they seem in their history to have persistently shown a remarkable aptitude, at the start of every crisis, for not knowing what they were going to do'.

At this stage, Casement's nationalism was still historical, rather than contemporary. It was nevertheless pervasive. To an Englishman, the French writer R. C. Escouflaire once remarked, the phrase 'that's ancient history' means it is no longer important; to an Irishman, it means precisely the reverse. Ireland's Golden Age, when she had been a nation with a highly developed culture of her own, had been a thousand years back in time. There were still some traces of it; and in 1884—the year Casement went to the Congo—an effort was made to prevent the old culture from disappearing altogether by the founding of the Gaelic Athletic Association, to encourage the cultivation of national sports and pastimes. It was followed nine years later by the Gaelic League, designed to foster the Irish language. Soon, it had over five hundred branches, including a very active one in Belfast. Belfast, though, was not a city where the Irish language was likely to be heard; the members liked to go out to the nearest district where it was still spoken—the Antrim glens, beside Casement's old family home. And when he came back from the Congo, he had become interested in the movement, and made up his mind to try to learn Irish.

By this time Casement had no close link with his family in Ulster—apart from his sister, Nina, when she was staying there. Even if he had, the Casements would have been unlikely to object to his new hobby. They might have regarded his getting mixed up in the language movement as cranky; but they would not, as yet, have thought it sinister. The League's first President,

Douglas Hyde—later to be the first President of Ireland—was a Protestant, the son of a clergyman. Its co-founder, Eoin Mac-Neill, was a member of a respected Catholic family, known to the Casements, from the Antrim glens. Among the patrons of the Belfast branch of the League was a Church of Ireland bishop, and the Moderator of the General Assembly of the Ulster Presbyterians. It even numbered among its members an Orangeman, Dr. Kane, who used to insist that though he might be a Protestant, he was not going to forget that he was also a member of the old Irish family, the O'Cahans. So Casement found no difficulty in linking up with the Gaelic Leaguers; and—as he was to recall—'all the old hopes and longings of my boyhood sprang to life again.'

During his protracted dispute with the Foreign Office that year, over their handling of the Congo Report, he began to identify more closely with Ireland—'I should like to stay in this beloved country till I die,' he wrote in March to Gertrude Bannister, 'I like it better every day'—and with Irish, which he begged her to learn, 'a lovely, glorious language'. He wrote a play on an Irish theme; it was something, he commented, 'to have an infant Irish stage' (the Irish Literary Theatre, founded by Lady Gregory, Edward Martyn, and W. B. Yeats, had just merged with the brothers Fay to form the company which the following year found a home in the Abbey Theatre). That spring of 1904 he went to what became an annual gathering of Ulster men and women who were interested in the language revival, the *Feis*—Festival—of the Glens, organised by F. J. Bigger, a Belfast solicitor, editor of the *Ulster Journal of Archaeology*, who believed that the language should be learned with the help of music, song and dance—'with kilts and pipes you can do anything'. And among those attending was the Ulster writer, Stephen Gwynn, whose article on the Free State in the *Fortnightly Review* had pleased the Congo campaigners. In his *Memoirs*, Gwynn described his meeting with Casement:

What remains now in my mind is chiefly the impression of his personal charm and beauty . . . Figure and face, he seemed to me to be one of the finest-looking creatures I had ever seen; and his countenance had charm, distinction, and a high chivalry. Knight-errant he was; clear-sighted, cool-headed, knowing as well as any that ever lived how to strengthen his case by temperate statement, yet always charged with passion.

That passion was now for a while devoted to the Irish language. As he admitted to Ada—'Ide'—MacNeill, one of the moving spirits at the *Feis*, he found it hard to learn; and she advised him to take a correspondence course. But it was the ability to speak Irish which he craved, and he preferred to go to the extreme tip of the Tawin peninsula, in the west, where only Irish was spoken—reporting proudly later to Douglas Hyde, whom he had met at the Sligo *Feis*, that he had been able to follow something of what was being said around him. He also mentioned that the local school was in disrepair, and had lost its teachers; and Hyde promptly issued an appeal for funds.

That summer, the *Morning Post* rebuked the Irish for wasting the time of the House of Commons by discussing the teaching of the Irish language which, it argued, 'had as much relevance to Imperial concerns as the teaching of "kitchen Kaffir" has with the administration of the War Office'. On reading the editorial, Casement decided not to renew his membership of his London club in order that—as he wrote to tell Hyde—he could devote the amount of the annual subscription thus saved to a training college in Munster, 'where Irish teachers are perfected in a fuller knowledge, and more scientific methods, of imparting "kitchen Kaffir".' Acknowledging the 'very generous subscription', Hyde asked if he might forward his letter to Patrick Pearse, who would find it useful for the Irish language magazine he was running; and it appeared in *Uladh* the following spring. Casement also sent subscriptions to various Irish causes, and offered a batch of Irish books to the headmaster of a school in Donegal, to be distributed as prizes for the best scholars in the subject. 'We will all be most grateful to you,' Hyde wrote, 'and everybody should be, for what you are doing.'

'Rubber, rubber'   1905

Early in the new year of 1905 Casement had his operations (for the fistula, presumably, rather than for the removal of his appendix, as he was again to be diagnosed as suffering from appendicitis some years later). Then, he went to Ballycastle to convalesce. During those weeks his new preoccupation with the Irish language had again to compete with his old concern

for the Congo natives, sporadically revived by information
about the Commission of Inquiry from Morel, from Nightingale
(who kept him up to date on what was happening from Boma),
and from the Foreign Office (Villiers, needing his help at the
time when Leopold was mocking them, had given orders that
he was to receive copies of all relevant material going into
the Congo files). The evidence suggested that Casement's pes-
simism had been justified. The Free State authorities in the
Congo were displaying a total lack of concern, which they
would hardly have done if they took the Commission seriously.
It was still the same old story, Nightingale feared: 'rubber,
rubber, rubber, that is the cry'. The only purpose that the
Commission was serving, Casement thought, was to give the
Free State more time to exploit the Congo's dwindling resources
—and to subject him to a sustained campaign of denigration.

Leopold was now exploiting a device which was later to
become more familiar: making propaganda out of reports from
travellers who were prepared to extol the virtues of the Free
State, in order to discredit its critics. One of them was the
young Lord Mountmorres, who sent back a glowing account of
his experiences in the Congo to Sir Alfred Jones. How regrettable
it was—Jones commented, forwarding it to the Foreign Office—
that the Free State should have been condemned 'on the statement of one man—Mr. Casement. I tell you again, Belgium
is making very remarkable progress in West Africa.' The eulogis-
tic tone of Mountmorres's account was too much even for
Clarke, in the African Department, who minuted that it
sounded as if Mountmorres 'was in heaven, and not the Congo';
and Mountmorres's claim that he had adopted tactics, with the
full concurrence of the authorities, 'which precluded the possibility of our path being specially prepared for us', amused Lord
Percy, who contented himself with sarcastically underlining
with the full concurrence of the authorities'. But Foreign Office
minutes were not published, and readers of those newspapers
which gave Mountmorres's views might well begin to doubt
whether Casement's report ought to be relied upon—particularly as another traveller, Mrs. French Sheldon, strongly supported Mountmorres when she returned from the Congo that
winter. She, too, claimed that her itinerary had been kept secret.
Morel knew that this was not true. The missionary John Weeks
had reported that as she was travelling on a river steamer pro-

vided by the authorities, advance notice was being given of her movements; at Bangala, the Free State's agent had actually 'pulled down an old prison, and levelled the ground, and made it all nice, because she was coming'. But the British public would not know this: it was 'increasingly confused'—*The Times* remarked in an editorial: 'when versions so entirely discrepant are forthcoming, both from those who claim to have studied the question here and from those who have investigated the conditions on the spot, the reader may well-nigh despair of reaching any satisfactory conclusion'.

The Times hoped—though not very confidently—that the Commission of Inquiry would clear things up. Casement was more than ever convinced it would not; for he found that the Foreign Office had let him down again. When Lansdowne had sent copies of Casement's original Report to the Commission in October, he had contented himself with a request—not a demand—that an observer should be permitted. The Free State's reply had been that this was a matter for the Commission; and, as the Commissioners had by this time left for the Congo, Consul Nightingale had been instructed to ask them, while they were in Boma, if either he or some other representative of His Majesty's Government could attend their sittings. They left him with the impression that their answer was no. Only when they had reached the Upper Congo, in mid-December, did they casually inform the Foreign Office that there was no need to request permission to send an observer, as they were holding their sessions in public. But Nightingale did not receive this information until shortly before Christmas, by which time the Commissioners were far up the river at Coquilhatville. It would be more useful, he felt, if he stayed where he was in Boma, where at least he would receive reports from the missionaries on their progress. Instead, Vice-Consul Mackie had to be sent, from Lisbon. He could not reach Boma until January 17th, and then had to pursue the Commissioners up river. By the time he found them, their inquiry into the rubber-producing regions had been completed.

Nightingale was certain that the Commissioners had intentionally deceived the Foreign Office by this 'adroit manipulation of their discretionary powers'. Casement was more inclined to blame the Foreign Office for allowing themselves to be deceived. 'They are not worth serving,' he complained to Morel from

Ballycastle, early in February, 'and what sickens me is that I must go back to them, hat in hand, despising them as I do, simply to be able to live.' Six weeks later, he had only £20 between him and the workhouse; 'they have practically handed me over defenceless,' he complained, 'their own agent, their own mouthpiece, to be the worldwide butt of the very man they publicly accused'. However, 'dirty, mean trick' though they had played him, he feared he must now swallow his scorn, 'and creep back to serve such effigies of men'.

The chiefs' twigs   1905

Later that same day, however—March 15th—Casement's gloom was totally dispelled. 'I hear the Commission will *have* to back my report up to the hilt,' he wrote exultantly to Gertrude Bannister; 'they have been convinced against their wills.' The good news came through Nightingale, from Mackie. After linking up with the Commissioners, he felt justified from his conversations with them in sending a message to Casement, 'you have won all along the line'.

According to Nightingale, the Free State authorities had told their agents how important it was that no evidence of atrocities should reach the Commissioners' ears. But the Commissioners had felt bound to visit the places Casement had visited; and there, they met the missionaries who had helped him with his Report, and who were able to convince them of the truth of its findings. There had been a moving moment when, following an arrangement made for the native chiefs to show how many murders there had been, one of them had placed 110 twigs on the table, of varying sizes, saying, 'these are chiefs' twigs, these are men's, these shorter are women's, these smaller still are children's, and one by one, natives had appeared to show their mutilated arms, until the Commissioners could stand it no longer. During the evidence given about the district under the control of the 'gentlemanly' Lejesme, the President of the Commission had wept. Lejesme attempted to justify himself by claiming that over a hundred soldiers had been killed by the natives; this only made the matter worse, he was told: 'how terrible must have been the wrongs that led to such desperate reprisals'. Asked if he had anything more to say, he could only shrug his shoulders.

In a double sense, therefore, the work of the Commission of Inquiry could be regarded as a triumph for Casement. It had been he who, on his tour in 1903, had finally persuaded the missionaries that they must speak out, even at the risk of reprisals. And it had been his Report, leading as it had to the setting up of the Commission, which had given them their opportunity. Transmitting their accounts to the Foreign Office, Nightingale expressed his conviction that the Commission would 'in all probability publish an even more grave report than Consul Casement'—Janssens having admitted to Mackie that the evidence collected agreed with his in all essential details. The Commissioners had planned to stay out for six months; they had seen and heard enough to convince them in three. By the middle of March, they were back in Belgium.

The news revived Casement's enthusiasm for the reform campaign, and at the beginning of April he returned to London, to throw himself into it once more. He avoided the Foreign Office, because it would have been a little difficult to explain that he now had a job; he was organiser of the forthcoming public meeting of the Congo Reform Association, to be held in the Holborn Town Hall in June, designed to make the public aware of what was being done—in the United States, as well as in Europe.

Morel's visit had led to the founding of an American Congo Reform Association: Lord Beauchamp, on a visit to America in the spring of 1901, wrote to tell Casement it was 'doing capital work'. It had attracted the support of, among others, Booker T. Washington, the respected Negro educator, and Mark Twain. When he had written his *Yankee at King Arthur's Court*, Twain had contrasted medieval hokum with nineteenth-century reality; but he had allowed two exceptions to his theme of the advance of civilisation—Imperial Russia and the Royal Palace of Belgium. That Palace, he now asserted in the introduction to his *King Leopold's Soliloquy*, was

> still what it has been for fourteen years, the den of a wild beast, King Leopold II, who for money's sake mutilates, murders and starves half a million of friendly and helpless poor natives in the Congo every year . . . It is curious that the most advanced and most enlightened century the sun has looked upon should have the ghastly distinction of having produced this moldy and piety-mouthing hypocrite, this bloody monster

whose mate is not findable in history anywhere, and whose personality will surely shame hell itself when he arrives there —which will be soon, we hope and trust.

The *Soliloquy* itself consisted of Leopold's saturnine musings on what he had done in the Congo; and Mark Twain made it clear that the information had been largely gleaned from Casement's Report. Casement was obviously flattered, although professing himself sorry that he had been named; as usual, he was chronically uneasy at being referred to in print.

He was working energetically as organiser: arranging for press notices, distributing handbills, having the programmes printed, sending out the tickets—prompted from time to time, by the explorer and colonial administrator, Sir Harry Johnston. Reviewing Morel's book the winter before, Johnston had admitted that it was a terrible indictment of the Free State, if true; and Casement wrote to try to convince him. Suspicious, he sent his brother to test Casement out, first. 'I confess I took an instant liking to him,' Alex Johnston was to recall. He was also 'struck by the contrast between his normally gentle and melancholy manner, and the fury which made his dark eyes blaze almost with madness when he talked of the Congo, in particular, and of oppression in general'. Sir Harry, too, was won over, agreeing to join the Association, and to take the chair at the Holborn meeting: and thereafter, 'Harry always believed in the absolute sincerity and unselfishness of both Sir Roger Casement and Morel'.

The meeting was held on June 7th. According to the *Morning Post* it was 'largely attended', and a resolution calling for the Free State to be taken from Leopold's control, and put into Belgium's, marked—an editorial suggested—a significant new phase in the reform movement. It had demonstrated the need for reforms; now, it was asking what form they should take— and not before it was time, as another story in the *Morning Post* revealed the same day. The Italian emigration authorities, alarmed by Casement's findings, had asked a respected senior naval surgeon to check on conditions in the Free State. Dr. Baccari was horrified by what he found, and ill-advised enough to say so while he was still there. One evening, finding his wine tasted odd, he sniffed it and realised that it had been laced with corrosive sublimate—whose effects, being a doctor, he

luckily knew how to counteract. The Free State's official explanation, which Phipps forwarded to the Foreign Office, was that a
native boy, having found a beetle in the wine, had decanted it
into another bottle which had happened to have previously
contained corrosive sublimate. It would have carried more
weight if Rabinek's last letter had not still been remembered,
in which he had referred to the rumour that Europeans who
knew too much were poisoned, 'so if I disappear without any
further news you may guess what has become of me'.

C.M.G.   *1905*

To Lansdowne, the success of the Holborn meeting was not
entirely unwelcome. True, the Congo reform campaign had been
exploited by the Liberal Opposition, and was still identified
with them. But if the Commissioners' report turned out to be as
critical as Mackie and Nightingale predicted, the Government
would be able to claim the credit for having insisted on the
inquiry in the first place. It was certainly now safe to take
a tougher line with the Free State Government. Three days after
the meeting, he instructed Phipps to express concern about the
news from Nightingale, that natives who had given evidence to
Casement were being subjected to reprisals. What did the Free
State Government propose to do?

The Free State Government—in effect, Leopold—by this time
had Lansdowne's measure. It proposed to do nothing, he was
told, until the Commission had reported. As it was now four
months since the Commissioners had returned, it was obvious
Leopold was delaying publication as long as he could, in the
hope of finding some way to absolve himself from blame. And
now that the euphoria temporarily engendered by the Holborn
meeting was ebbing away, Casement had to realise that the
publicity it had secured for the Association left the Congo
natives no better off: the Foreign Office had failed them. But
at this point, his services were given recognition; he was informed by Lansdowne that His Majesty was making him a
Commander of the Order of St. Michael and St. George.

Casement was no republican. On the contrary, he had shared
the prevailing veneration for Queen Victoria; when in 1902 he
collected £30 for her commemoration fund—mainly from
British West Africans in the Congo—he explained that he

thought it very creditable 'to the sense of loyalty of these men that they should, so willingly and gladly, have raised out of their hard-earned wages a sum, small though it may be, towards the proposed memorial'. But with the change in his attitude to England, he now found the honour an embarrassment. His immediate reaction was to justify himself, in a letter to his friend Dick Morten, by complaining that he had not been consulted: 'I will not tell you what I think of it, D., for I should only offend your honest old heart—but I'm sick! Why on earth these things can be done without a man's consent I don't know; it's quite childish; like giving a poor baby a name at the font it cannot resist or discard.' He even composed a letter to Barrington telling him that he shrank from accepting any honour, and asking if there was any way out, as he would like to take it. But there was no way out; so he wrote a formal letter to the Duke of Argyll, asking him to convey to the King 'the expression of my dutiful regard and gratitude at this most gracious mark of his Majesty's favour', but claiming that the state of his health would preclude him from appearing at an investiture. When the parcel arrived containing the insignia, he left it unopened.

The award of the C.M.G. had forced Casement to realise his conflict of loyalties. While convalescing at Ballycastle he had amused himself, as he recounted to Morel, with the compilation of 'a string of healthy arguments in favour of the capacity and character of the Irish nation', which were to be turned into an article on Irish commerce and trade in medieval times, 'an untouched and vastly interesting subject'. He had also used the period when he was organising the Holborn meeting to make contact with members of the Irish party in the Commons. 'I am up to my eyes in the Irish question', he wrote to tell John Holt, on his return to Ireland; and he confessed to William Cadbury—one of the Quaker family who, with Holt, was the Association's chief financial backer—that though the Congo was very near his heart, 'the Irish question is nearer'. To Clarke, at the Foreign Office, he made the admission he was worried about accepting the C.M.G. because it would mean he would be 'regarded askance in every reputable quarter of Ireland'. By 'reputable', he meant nationalist. He had become, he admitted, a 'confirmed Home Ruler'.

CHAPTER TWO

SINN FEIN

Home Ruler 1905

'Home Ruler' at that time had two meanings. In the narrower sense it meant somebody who was a supporter of the Irish Parliamentary Party, which under Parnell had acquired virtually a monopoly of the Irish seats in the House of Commons, apart from those occupied by the Unionists from constituencies with Protestant majorities in Ulster. In the looser sense, which Casement was using, it meant a believer in the general principle that the Irish had a distinctive nationality which could not thrive within the existing constitutional framework of the Irish kingdom. His conversion had been foreshadowed long before, in his fascination with Irish history. Now, it was completed by his encounter with a woman who was to have a decisive influence on him for the rest of his life.

Alice Green was from an Irish Protestant family, the Stopfords—her father was a Church of Ireland archdeacon in Meath. She had married the English historian, J. R. Green; on his death, she had completed the book on the Norman Conquest which he had been engaged on; and then she had proceeded to build a reputation as a historian in her own right, chiefly on early Irish history. But she was also interested in the problems created by colonisation in Africa; and in 1901, she had founded a society designed to stimulate greater concern in Britain about what was happening there, which had led to her making Morel's acquaintance. At the time he was founding the Congo Reform Association, he had asked her to become a member; and when she had hesitated—because, she explained, she wanted any spare time she had to devote to her study of Irish history—Casement had written to her, to introduce himself, and to beg her to change her mind. His letter led to an invitation to visit her, when he was next in London. There, Casement found himself a welcome guest in a salon celebrated for having included people as diverse as Lord Haldane, Florence Nightingale, Bishop Creighton, and the young Winston Churchill.

Casement, though, was chiefly interested in Alice Green herself. Although in her fifties, she shared his almost adolescent fervour about Ireland's remote past. And he found her thesis, which was later to appear in *The Making of Ireland and her Undoing*, very much to his taste. The Norsemen and the Anglo-Norman invaders, she insisted, had not brought civilisation to a backward country. They had imposed a destructive alien rule on a highly civilised community. The old Ireland, therefore, was not to be looked back on nostalgically, as something lost — as an Englishman might yearn for the chivalry of the Knights of the Round Table. It should be regarded as a working model.

This was just what Casement needed to transform his own interest in Irish history from a congenial hobby into an absorbing passion. As his articles and letters on the subject began to show, he was continually relating the lessons of the past to the needs of the present. The immediate need, as he and Alice Green — and Gertrude Bannister, still ready to share her cousin's enthusiasms — accepted, was to obtain Ireland's independence. The British were not going to restore the old Ireland. They must be persuaded, or compelled, to get out. But for this purpose, the vision of the old Ireland, awaiting restoration, was likely to be less immediately effective than remainders of injustices perpetrated by the English during their occupation of the country.

Providing these reminders presented no difficulty. 'The fortunate peoples of the world think little of their history,' J. L. Hammond observed in his study of Home Rule, 'those who have suffered are apt to think of little else.' Even a barely literate Irishman was apt to have a better knowledge of his country's past than most public-school-and-university Englishmen knew about theirs. The Irish, too, identified with their patriot heroes. Wolfe Tone, Lord Edward FitzGerald and Robert Emmet were still, a century after their death, part of the common currency of Irish life, their pictures on shebeen walls, in a way that no English historical figure was, or was likely to be.

Brought up as Casement had been in what the Irish derisively called a 'West British' environment, where it was taken for granted that children were to be given English accents and English manners, in preparation for the day when they would take a job in the British forces or the Civil Service, he would ordinarily have found it difficult to link up with the nationalist movement; but his knowledge of Irish history was his passport. Not merely could he talk about it (and on his special subject, Irish trade, he could have instructed most of the academic historians of the day): he also had the 'feel' of it, the same capacity to identify with, say, Wolfe Tone, some of whose quirks of prose style he adopted. His sense of the past also helped to make his Ulster Protestant background less of a barrier than it might have been. In the Antrim glens, where he was brought up, though there was little of the Protestant bigotry to be found in other parts of Ulster, there was little social contact with Catholics, outside a handful of 'good' (socially acceptable) Catholic families—so little contact, that it was only when he had been back in Ireland some time, after the Congo, that Casement came to realise Catholics did not use the prefix 'Roman'. But he knew how the Catholics had been treated under the notorious Penal Laws—and he knew that his mother's family, the Jephsons of Mallow, had been Catholic (he had arranged to meet one of the Jephsons in 1895, to find out more about them; the meeting had to be put off at the last moment when he was sent to Lourenço Marques). So, irritated though he frequently was with Catholic politicians who tried to stir up sectarian prejudices, Casement's Protestantism did not obstruct his growing nationalist feeling.

Among the influences actively impelling him towards separatist beliefs were his Congo experiences. Leopold's 'system', he felt, owed its existence to the fact that he had introduced ownership of land. In theory, the State owned it; in practice, Leopold did. As a result, natives who did not work for Leopold were left with the choice between emigrating or starving. This, Casement knew, was the choice which had confronted Irish families. Before the English conquest, there had been no private ownership of land. But the English had not merely parcelled it out, as property; they had distributed it among themselves and, like Leopold, appropriated most of its produce. So far as the natives were concerned, it had not made any difference whether the produce was taken from them in forced labour or in taxes by the state—as in the Congo—or in rents by the landlords—as in Ireland. Either way, the effect had been destructive. Millions of them had been carried off by undernourishment, disease or emigration—in Ireland, the catastrophe being even more sudden, and devastating: the Great Famine of the 1840s.

It was his knowledge of Irish history, Casement was often to claim, which had enabled him to understand what was happening in the Congo, at a time when the Foreign Office could not believe the evidence because it did not make sense to them. 'I knew that the Foreign Office would not understand the thing,' he recalled in a letter to Alice Green, 'for I realised that I was looking at this tragedy with the eyes of another race of people once hunted themselves, whose hearts were based on affection as the root principle of contact with their fellow men, and whose estimate of life was not of something eternally to be appraised at its market "price".' And in its turn, the Congo had given him insights into what had been happening in Ireland—the main reason why, when he returned to Ireland, he repudiated the Unionism of his family, in spite of what appeared to be conclusive evidence that it was at last bringing beneficial results.

It was a new style of Unionism, based on the principle which had come to be known as killing Home Rule by kindness: giving more state money for public works, and a greater say in how it was spent to local authorities. It brought greater prosperity, and relative tranquillity—as the French historian Elie Halévy, no stranger to the country's troubled history, was surprised to find when he visited Ireland in 1903; and this proved—the Unionists contended—how dependent Ireland, the poorer country, really was on British assistance. Casement disagreed. From his study of history, he felt certain that Ireland was like a man who has been knocked to the ground; all that his assailant, England, was doing was helping him to his knees—with the intention of keeping him there. So far from helping the Irish, he believed, England had long been exploiting them for her own economic benefit, just as Leopold had exploited the Congo natives. And as it happened, confirmation had been lent to this thesis by a commission of inquiry, set up in London at the end of the century to examine the financial relations between the two countries. It had reported that since the Union of 1800 the Irish, so far from being helped financially, had actually been overtaxed relative to the English at a rate of around £2·5 million a year—not a great sum in English budgetary terms, but a very substantial one in Ireland's. Even the Ulster Unionist leader, Colonel Saunderson, was moved to sarcasm: 'when

Englishmen set to work to wipe the tear out of Ireland's eye, they always buy the pocket handkerchief at Ireland's expense.'

Why had the English believing themselves to be the bringers of peace and prosperity to Ireland, systematically milked her for their own benefit? From his Congo experience, Casement felt sure it was 'the system' which was to blame. Given that the land of Ireland was owned by the English (and the Anglo-Irish, who were English rather than Irish in their basic loyalties) the profits from it *must* accrue to the English. They were not aware of this—how could they be? It was unusual for their political leaders even to have visited Ireland; Disraeli never did; Gladstone, only once. And the general impression the English had of an Irishman was of Paddy Murphy, with a thick brogue and a shillelagh, a figure of fun when sober and a fighting menace when drunk. What chance was there of Ireland recovering her lost soul, so long as she was ruled by people who were so ignorant of her, and who despised her? No chance: until the system—its foundations economic, but with the political structure resting on them, and protecting them—was overthrown.

Casement was still not, then, at this stage anti-English, except in the sense that Colonel Saunderson—who thought English politicians were interested in Ulster only for their own political ends, and who used to excuse the manners of English guests on the grounds that not being Irish, they knew no better—was anti-English. But whereas Saunderson knew that Ulster, —industrial Ulster, at least—benefited, on balance, from the British connection, Casement knew that Ireland as a whole was worse off, materially and spiritually, and must remain so until the connection was broken. And it was to Ireland, rather than to Ulster, that he now gave his loyalty.

The Irish Party   1905

In ordinary circumstances it would have been natural for Casement, at this time, to become a supporter of the Irish Party— even if, owing to his connection with the Foreign Service, he could not actually join it. The Party's policy was derived from the Home Rule platform of Charles Stewart Parnell; and Parnell had been his boyhood hero; when he died in 1891, Casement had composed an 'In Memoriam' beginning,

> Hush! Let no whisper of the cruel strife
> Wherein he fell so bravely fighting, fall
> Nigh these dead ears; fain would our hearts recall
> Naught but proud memories of a noble life

He also had a ready source of introductions to the leaders of the Irish Party through Lord ffrench, whom he had come to know well in Lourenço Marques. When he returned to Ireland from the Congo, ffrench had married; and his wife in her memoirs was to recall her first meeting with Casement, at this time:

> I had been told that he was extraordinarily good-looking, and at first sight I realised this was true. He had, without doubt, great charm. One's critical faculties are all awake when one meets someone who has been highly praised. Something contrary in me, anyway, makes me look out for faults, but though Roger Casement was far from being dull perfection, there was nothing ugly or ordinary about him. He had a most romantic personality and an ideality of mind which was expressed in the type of looks at once Spanish and Irish. He was the strangest person imaginable to come out of Ulster.

Casement could not convert ffrench to the Home Rule cause, but ffrench was willing to help him lobby the members of the Irish Party on the Congo, even taking him to call on the Party's leader, John Redmond, in Dublin—though Redmond was not there (discontented members of the party used to complain that he rarely was, preferring as he did to spend such time as he had in Ireland, during Parliamentary recesses, at his home in the country).

The possibility that Casement might link up with the Irish Party, though, evaporated through contact with its members. It was difficult to interest them in any but Irish issues, and then, only if they were useful politically. The fate of the Irish language, for example, concerned them only if it could be exploited for its nuisance value at Westminster. By this time, too, Casement was beginning to believe that the Irish Party's strategy was at fault. It had been based on the assumption that Home Rule could be won constitutionally at Westminster; but even if a majority of the Commons could be persuaded to vote for it, what hope could there be of obtaining a majority in the Lords, with its veto? The more radical policy which was being put forward by a Dublin journalist, Arthur Griffith, had begun to attract him.

Cumann na nGhaedhael   1905

Griffith had founded the *United Irishman*, to champion the Irish language, Irish sports, and Irish industries; and although its circulation was very small, it had met with an enthusiastic response from its readers: 'I see all around me'—W. B. Yeats, who was a contributor, wrote—'among the young men who hold the coming years in their hands, a newly-awakened inspiration and resolve.' An attempt was also made to attract a wider public to the cause by the forming of an association, *Cumann na nGhaedhael*—the Club of the Gael—under the presidency of the old Fenian, John O'Leary. But the movement, Griffith realised, needed a policy, if it was to become anything more than a debating society; and in November 1904 he began to promote his ideas in a series of articles in the *United Irishman*. The Irish, he suggested, should follow the example of Hungary. In the 1860s, the elected Hungarian representatives had decided to boycott the Imperial Parliament at Vienna, and to meet in Budapest as the representatives not of an Austrian province, but of the Hungarian nation; and the Imperial Government had eventually been forced to grant Hungary a measure of independence. This, Griffith urged, was the policy which the members of the Irish Party at Westminster should adopt. They should behave as if Ireland had a parliament of her own, again —the Hungarian precedent suggesting that this would be the best way to ensure that she would obtain it.

When Casement read Griffith's articles in the Belfast nursing home, recovering from his operation, his interest was immediately aroused—for two reasons. One was that he had become a devoted admirer of Michael Davitt, the founder of the Land League, by which the Irish tenants had banded themselves together to try to restore their rights. Davitt had insisted that real political independence could not be obtained until the people of Ireland were restored to possession of the land of Ireland; so long as it remained under alien ownership, the Irish would be effectively enslaved no matter what political concessions they might obtain. As Casement had come to similar conclusions about the Congo, he was naturally attracted to the idea. Davitt had earlier himself urged the withdrawal of the Irish M.P.s at Westminster, to form an assembly in Ireland. It at once struck Casement that Davitt would be the ideal leader for Griffith's proposed movement.

The other reason for his interest in the Hungarian precedent was that he happened to have a curious family link with the Hungarian independence movement; his father—also called Roger—had been briefly involved. When the Hungarian patriots rose under Kossuth against Austrian rule, his father had gone to join them, but arrived too late; they had been forced to escape across the border into Turkey, where he found them interned. It was only a matter of time, they told him, before the Turks would bow to Austrian pressure and extradite them— unless the British Government did something for them. He set off back to England on horseback, and managed to secure an interview with Lord Palmerston, whose intervention saved the Hungarians. Kossuth—who at the time had not even known who he was—described in his memoirs an occasion when he was visiting the Niagara Falls many years later, and a man there stretched out his hand to him to give him a card, and a scribbled note to the effect that it had been he who had taken the message to Palmerston. 'Thus I got to know the brave man's name. I have not heard another word from him since; may God's richest blessings follow him on his way.'

Apparently Casement's father had liked to tell his children this story; and Casement now made an article out of it, which he sent to Griffith, and which appeared in the *United Irishman*. But it was Kossuth's follower, Deak, whom Griffith wished to emulate. It was useless, Deak had argued, to challenge Austria's authority with force, as Kossuth had tried to do. There must be no conspiracy, no attempt at a violent revolution; simply passive resistance to the Austrian authorities, coupled with a determined effort by Hungarians to run their own affairs, and make their own goods (Griffith favoured the principles of Fried-rich List, with their emphasis on economic self-sufficiency), and settle their own differences, without reference to Vienna. This was Griffith's prescription for Ireland; and Casement en-thusiastically accepted it. England, he wrote to tell Gertrude Bannister, would now find that the Irish could begin to play a more dangerous game than any they had yet tried; passive resistance on a gigantic national scale—no payment of taxes; no recruits for the Imperial forces; no acceptance of outside services from any Westminster ministry if they could be done at home. 'Such shall be the reply of Ireland—and please God, this ancient people shall not go down to the grave.' So long as the Irish people were true to themselves, he felt, they could hold out, as Hungary had done. It might mean terrible privations but—as it would be 'a shameful thing that a whole race should be slowly and relentlessly starved to death'—public opinion in the United States would surely bring pressure to bear on England, and she would be forced to grant Ireland self-government.

At the *Feis* of the Glens the previous summer Casement had met a young Ulster Quaker, Bulmer Hobson, who had been active in the Gaelic League in Belfast, and who was also a member of Griffith's *Cumann na nGhaedhael*. The two men quickly became close friends, and began to consider how they could best help the new movement. 'Bulmer, *a chara*,' Casement wrote to him in August 1905 (adopting, as he now regularly did with anybody whom he knew to be in sympathy with the movement, the Irish salutation), 'I have been thinking of you and your plan of national government and national policy a good deal of late . . . if we could find any means of raising money to keep an organisation in Ireland, to fight the battle here on the spot, we should have the country come back to its senses.'

What was lacking, he suggested, was Irish men of leisure and means who could give the country the kind of service the English aristocracy were trained to give theirs: 'if we had only fifty men, not obliged to work for their living, who could meet together at times, and put their energies into the work of nationality, we should do far more than the parliamentary party in the end'. What they could do—Hobson proposed—was to imitate Deak by trying to discourage Irishmen in Ulster from enlisting in the British forces; and with that purpose, a leaflet was prepared, which Casement helped to write. Anybody—its message ran—

> joining England's army, navy or police force takes his stand in the camp of the garrison; he is a traitor to his country and an enemy to his people.
>
> Any man entering the service betrays his own land and goes over to her enemies. Let England fight her own battles —we have done it long enough.

Let her arm and drill the sickly population of her slums.
The men of the hills and country places in Ireland will go no
more. Let her fight for the extension of her Empire herself;
the men of the Gael are not going to be bribed into betraying
themselves and their country again at the bidding of England.

And when that summer a Ballycastle man was arrested and tried
for distributing one of the leaflets, Casement made himself
responsible for collecting the costs of the defence.

Stephen Gwynn, when he learned about Casement's anti-
recruiting activities, was shocked. In his memoirs, he reiterated
that they did not diminish his admiration for a man who had
done such 'real and conspicuous service to humanity', and was
'one of the most noble creatures I have known'; but he could
not understand how anybody who was himself in the service
of the Crown, and who had just accepted an honour, could have
allowed himself to be drawn into such a campaign. Logically,
Casement had a defence, which he was sometimes to use when
taxed with duplicity: that it was very much in England's, as
well as Ireland's, interest that Ireland should be given her independence; and that if, as he believed, Deak's was the right
programme to achieve it, then he must do what he could to
help those who were supporting Griffith. Nevertheless, Gwynn's
uneasiness was justified. There are some things, as John O'Leary
put it, that a man must not do for his country. For Casement
to seek to brand as traitors Irishmen who served the Crown,
while he himself remained in the Crown's service, was to
tarnish his own integrity.

He was also, though unaware of it, being used by more extreme separatists, whose views he did not yet share. The anti-
recruiting drive was masterminded from New York by the old
Fenian, John Devoy, as part of his strategy to disrupt the constitutional Home Rule movement, and substitute physical force,
when the time was ripe for liberation. 'What you trample on in
Ireland,' Henry Grattan had warned the English, 'will sting you
in America'; and although in Ireland the Irish Republican
Brotherhood, the secret society which had tried to carry on the
ideals of the Fenians, was almost moribund, in America Devoy's
Clan-na-Gael remained an active revolutionary organisation,
lending moral and financial support through the I.R.B. to any
movement or activity in Ireland which might advance the cause

of independence—such as the anti-recruiting drive. As a young man, Devoy himself had been a recruiting officer for the Fenians, seducing Irishmen in the British forces from their allegiance to the Crown. Now, Casement—without knowing it—was doing the same work for him.

So was Griffith. Devoy had no great sympathy with the Hungarian notion, but he was prepared to subsidise the *United Irishman*, and watch to see how the movement developed. When 20,000 copies of Griffith's Hungarian articles sold in pamphlet form, the prospects looked encouraging. The time had come, Griffith felt, to form an organisation to promote his policies; and at one of the meetings held to discuss it, the suggestion was made, and accepted, that it should be called *Sinn Fein*.

Sinn Fein—'Ourselves'—had been used as a slogan for many years by Irish speakers, to symbolise self-reliance. Outside help would not be repudiated; but the Irish must first themselves lay the foundations for their independence—as the new *Sinn Fein* organisation would help them to do. It was not difficult to find encouraging historical precedents—notably Swift's campaign against the introduction of Wood's ha'pence, and Grattan's volunteer movement; and the name gave the movement a recognisably Irish flavour. Casement could not formally join *Sinn Fein*; but he became an enthusiastic supporter, subscribing generously to Griffith's journalistic enterprises, and writing unsigned articles on *Sinn Fein* themes—two appeared that autumn in the *Freeman's Journal*, the organ of the Irish Party, attacking the anglicisation of Irish history, and praising the prowess of Irish fighting men (especially Ulstermen) when they were fighting for Irish causes. He also wrote a sonnet, 'To a lady who wondered why all Irish poetry was "rebel",' which appeared in *Dana*, a shortlived literary magazine:

> Who would commemorate in lasting song
> The triumph of the mighty o'er the weak?

And in his correspondence over the next few years, he was continually to express his agreement with Griffith's principles—if not always with his policies.

'It is the plain duty of every Irishman to dissociate himself from all memories of Ireland,' George Moore recommended, 'Ireland being a fatal disease, fatal to Englishmen and doubly fatal to Irishmen.' Casement had now succumbed; and he was never to recover, until it did indeed prove fatal. It had become a passion with him, exercising a force over him beyond his control; 'Ireland' ceased to be an abstraction, and became intensely personalised—as it was to Patrick Pearse, also the son of a Protestant father and a Catholic mother, though brought up a Catholic.

As a child, Pearse had believed there actually was a woman called 'Erin', so that if Yeats's *Cathleen ni Houlihan* had then been written, and he had been taken to see it, he would have regarded it not as an allegory, but as something which might happen at any moment; and this had developed into a belief that 'there is a mystical entity which is the soul of Ireland, which makes Ireland a living nation'. This was also Casement's feeling. He had read Yeats's *Cathleen* that winter, enthusing about it to Alice Green; and H. W. Nevinson, the most respected crusading journalist of the day, who met him at this time (and was greatly taken with his 'very very remarkable blue-grey eyes, and the gentle and persuasive voice') found him 'pervaded and obsessed' by Ireland:

> Unusually sensitive to any form of beauty, he was bewitched by the beauty of his own country; unusually compassionate of all who suffer cruelty and wrong, he was consumed with indignation at his own country's history . . . to him, the passion of Dark Rosaleen was not a romantic mockery, but an inspiring enchantment, emanating from an ever-present being, almost visible, almost incarnate.

CHAPTER THREE

THE COMMISSION'S REPORT

The scapegoats   1905

Absorbed though he now was, that summer, with the cause of Irish independence, Casement was still too deeply committed to the Congo reform campaign to lose touch with it; and as the months went by without the Commission disclosing its findings, his conviction grew that they were never going to appear. Probably, he thought, Leopold would try to do a deal with the British Government. Perhaps he would offer to hand over the Free State to the Belgian Government, if it would agree to let him suppress the Commission's report. He reiterated a warning he had given to Morel at the time of the Holborn meeting that Belgium should not be given more than a mandate; the Congo must be under effective international control.

Leopold, however, had a different scheme in mind. He was busy preparing public opinion, abroad as well as in Belgium, to accept what was to be his excuse—that all the blame should be put on the Concession Companies; a view sedulously echoed by Phipps.

Early in September, Sir Alfred Jones told the Foreign Office that Leopold, shocked by the revelations about the treatment of natives in the Concessions, had decided he must make an example of one of the companies concerned; and he was prepared to offer its Concession to Jones—to Britain. So delighted was Jones at the prospect, and so certain that it would be enthusiastically welcomed by the Foreign Office, that he did not even wait for their sanction before writing to members of the Congo Reform Association to confess, with what presumably he must have hoped would be disarming candour, that he had sponsored and paid for the Congo visits of Lord Mountmorres and Mrs. French Sheldon; but now, he argued, all grounds for dispute between him and the Congo reformers were removed.

It had been the reports of Lord Mountmorres and Mrs. French Sheldon, more even than the denials of the Free State Government, which had caused the confusion in the public mind which *The Times* had noticed, and which had helped to cast doubt upon Casement's veracity. And both of them had specifically denied that they had any connection with Jones, in order to present themselves as independent witnesses. Yet here was Jones admitting he had put up the money—£3,000—for their visits. Naturally Morel pounced on the admission: 'a more disgraceful incident could hardly be imagined'. And the Foreign Office's reception of Leopold's offer was cool; for a British subject to accept a Concession which the British Government had been denouncing as illegal would give Leopold just the opportunity he wanted to denounce British hypocrisy. But again, the revelation of Jones's payments to the two travellers attracted far less publicity than their accounts of the happy condition of the Congo natives had done earlier: and Leopold's propaganda machine was quick to launch a fresh attack on Casement, in a pamphlet circulated to members of the Congo Research Association. Did they know Casement's background? the writer asked; were they aware that he

was formerly in the employment of the Congo Free State; he then occupied a subordinate position in one of the Congo companies; AND WHEN ACTING AS BRITISH CONSUL, HE WAS A SUBSCRIBER TO THE FUNDS OF THIS VERY CONGO REFORM SOCIETY, while supposed to be an impartial person, representing the British Government, and investigating the truth of the charges made against the Congo State?

The writer claimed he had drawn the attention of the Foreign Office to these facts; and half a century later, his identity was disclosed. He was the editor of the *Catholic Herald*, who had been attacking the reformers in his newspaper and, at the same time, privately transmitting to Lansdowne information from Brussels designed to discredit them—some of it, a Foreign Office minute noted, 'extravagantly mendacious'.

The pamphlet aroused Casement to write to Lansdowne, early in October—the first direct contact he had had with the Foreign Office over the Congo, he claimed (not strictly accurately), for almost eighteen months. Insinuations of this kind, he argued, were only possible because of the Foreign Office's pusillanimity. Fifteen months had passed since the Commission of Inquiry had been set up; seven months since it had returned. 'We are still without the first published word of the result of its examination, but a systematic attack continues to be directed against the author of a Report which, seemingly, cannot be shaken by partial or impartial investigation.' What was the Foreign Office going to do about it?

Lansdowne would doubtless have had to make the stock reply that they were awaiting publication of the Commission's report; but hardly had Casement's letter reached him than a despatch from Phipps announced that the report really was coming out, at last. Jones's failure to interest the Foreign Office in the Concession may have contributed to Leopold's decision; but his hand was also being forced by the realisation that he was losing support in Europe. The Baccari case had been raised in the Italian Assembly, leading to a ban on the seconding of officers for service in the Free State; and there had also been some unwelcome publicity in France. It was time, Leopold realised, to move to the next stage of his plan.

The report appeared in the Congo *Bulletin Officiel* for November 7th. The Congo natives, it showed, had been cheated out of their land by the Free State's definition of the term 'unoccupied'; and out of their trade. The Commissioners agreed, too, that grave abuses had arisen in connection with native labour, because the State's agents were paid by a commission on what that labour produced; and that military expeditions had been used illegally for commercial ends by the Concession companies, over which the State had in general failed to exercise supervision. These were findings which ordinarily could have been expected to create an international sensation. The Commissioners—whom Leopold had himself appointed, and whose bias, if any, could be expected to be in his favour—had not merely substantiated the charges which had been made against the Free State; by implication, at least, they were saying that he had deliberately flouted the Berlin agreement, and systematically deceived the signatory powers. But Leopold had had most of the year to make his preparations. Now, he played what appeared to be a hopeless hand with consummate skill.

To the press, a concise summary of such a report is always welcome, and the West African Missionary Association provided one which was gratefully used by British newspapers as the basis for their stories. It was not until later that the Congo reformers found that the 'West African Missionary Association' was another of Leopold's propaganda outlets, set up for the occasion. Its 'summary' had discreetly toned down the report's criticisms, and high-lighted passages favourable to Leopold. The Brussels correspondents of foreign newspapers, too, had been carefully briefed. *The Times* correspondent there concluded his report not by expressing disgust at the revelations, but by emphasising the benefits Leopold had brought to the Congo. He had simply been unlucky: 'in every country the early annals of colonisation are more or less stained with acts such as those of which complaint is now made.' This was just what Leopold had planned. He could now step forward as the great reformer. 'King Leopold had signified to me personally,' *The Times*' correspondent claimed,

> on more than one occasion, his desire that the whole truth, and nothing but the truth, should be made known. It is significant that to the report itself is appended a Royal proclamation nominating a Commission to report as to the best means of carrying out the recommendations therein contained. This promptness in action is . . . evidence of King Leopold's desire that any stigma resting on his work in Africa should be removed.

Casement agreed; that was precisely what Leopold wanted. He was now certain that Leopold had found some way to tone down the report, before publication. 'A *very* queer production' had resulted; 'a series of half-truths, each followed by its qualifying whole untruth.' And soon, Phipps confirmed that this surmise was substantially correct. Though Nisco had assured him that none of their criticisms had actually been suppressed, he 'felt unable positively to state that the report came before the public quite in its original form'.

But the worst aspect of the report, for Casement, was its failure to put the blame on the system. The Commissioners even accepted the necessity of the labour tax. There could be no hope of reform in the Congo, he wrote to warn Clarke at the Foreign office, so long as 'that Holy of Holies in Congodom' remained. Above all, Casement argued, the Foreign Office should not accept the device by which Leopold was attempting to prove his determination to implement the report's findings—the 'Reform Commission'. One of its members, he pointed out, was Alexis Mols —the same Mols who had just won notoriety from a visit to Paris in which he had offered £4,000 to the editor of *Le Temps*, if *Le Temps* ceased to criticise the Free State. All but two of the members of the Commission, it soon transpired, were Leopold's men. 'Why, everyone of them is as guilty as man can be,' Casement complained,

> they are simply the jackals of the King of Beasts. Until I indicted the whole blackguard system they had never lifted a finger, and when my report brought out to the light of day what was going on they attacked me with virulent abuse; and now when their own Commission, in guarded terms, supports my indictment, they appoint as reformers the men responsible, under their Master's eye, for the whole abominable thing.

It was a long time since he had written in that strain to the Foreign Office, and he warmed to it. But these, he explained, were simply his preliminary impressions. His formal commentary on the report would follow. 'I suppose we must say we should be glad of his observations', Clarke minuted—adding, apprehensively, 'we might give him a hint not to make them too long.'

Long or short, they were of little concern to Lansdowne. It was enough for him that a Reform Commission had been appointed; it would serve to replace the earlier Commission of Inquiry as his excuse for continued inaction. As the refusal to publish material from the Congo Atrocity files had left Casement exposed to a protracted smear campaign, Lansdowne might at least have taken the opportunity of a speech which he made on foreign affairs, later in the week, to say that his Report had been vindicated by the Commission of Inquiry; but he made no mention of the subject.

Sir Edward Grey   1905–1906

For once, Lansdowne had some excuse for his insensitivity. The Conservative Government was on the verge of collapse. On December 4th Balfour resigned; and Edward VII called on Henry Campbell-Bannerman to form a Liberal administration.

Three months earlier, Casement had told Morel that he felt there was no hope of any effective action on the Congo under Balfour ('not straight on *anything*') and Lansdowne ('honest but weak and not very capable';) 'but when we have got rid of Balfour for a spell of years—and a healthy, honest body of Liberals (if they can be got together) are in charge, we may do something for real reform'. And the composition of Campbell-Bannerman's ministry was encouraging. It included a number of M.Ps who had spoken in favour of the Congo reform movement: Sir Edward Grey (a year before, Alfred Emmott had assured Morel that Grey was 'absolutely convinced of the shame of the thing') became Foreign Secretary, with Lord Edmund Fitzmaurice as his Under-Secretary of State; Herbert Samuel and Emmott received minor ministerial appointments—as did Lord Beauchamp, the Association's president.

For Casement personally, too, the prospects seemed brighter. That summer it had been suggested he might be given a post in the Colonial Office, but nothing had materialised; and although he had told Lansdowne he was ready to return to the Consular Service, his offer had not been taken up. It looked, he wrote despondently to Nightingale, as if the Foreign Office might never again employ him. He had begun to grow desperate; as he told Morel, he had 'other troubles *galore*'—though he did not specify them. With the Liberals in power, however, a consular vacancy would surely be found; and Morel was soon able to tell him that he was to get Rio—regarded as the best post in the service. 'If I could get anything to do *at all*,' Casement still maintained, 'I would never give the Foreign Office another thought.' But as nobody seemed to want to employ an out-of-work Consul, he wrote again to the Foreign Office making formal application for a post, adding that if none were available, he would like to remain seconded—thereby making it clear that he was not proposing to leave the service.

For a while, he had no reason to fear that his hopes of the Liberals were to be disappointed. Early in the new year Grey instructed Phipps to convey a protest to the Free State Government about its failure to publish the Commission's minutes of evidence, and also to make some criticisms of the Commission's report; and when Phipps transmitted a barely civil reply from Leopold's Secretary of State, he was retired on a pension.

The general election results, too, at the end of the month, gave the Liberals a substantial majority over all other parties combined. The way seemed clear for them to take the tougher line over the Congo which they had been advocating in opposition. Very soon, however, the Congo reformers found that though the Government had changed, policy remained unaltered. 'I am to remind you,' Sir Eric Barrington wrote to the Baptist Missionary Society on February 8th, in reply to their request for information about the Foreign Secretary's intentions, 'that a Commission, appointed by King Leopold, is now sitting in Brussels, to consider the nature of the reforms to be introduced by the Congo State, and I am to state that until the result of their debate is known, no useful purpose would, in Sir Edward Grey's opinion, be served by the reception of the proposed deputation.'

It happened that at the time the Liberals came into office, France and Germany were involved in a dispute over Morocco which might have led to war. When he briefed the new Ambassador to Brussels, Sir Arthur Hardinge, Grey's chief concern— as Hardinge was to recall in his memoirs—was not with the Congo, but with what the Belgian attitude would be in the event of a war between France and Germany. Hardinge agreed. As a Tory (although he was in the Diplomatic Service, he had canvassed for the Conservatives in his home constituency during the election campaign) he had a hearty contempt for the Liberal humanitarians. 'Always prone to sentimentalism,' he complained, 'about slavery and other local customs to which the native populations were attached.' It was left to the amiable Lord Fitzmaurice (he had become a peer in his own right early in the new year) to explain in some embarrassment to Dilke that the Government's policy would mean keeping on good terms with Leopold: 'as you know I am not a believer in the King, "at all, at all"; but one has to observe the forms of diplomacy'. The Reform Commission, he explained, had provided a useful excuse for not pursuing the attack on Leopold: 'it is not our interest to be having a row with Belgium also, if perchance we were having a row with Germany'.

Leopold naturally exploited his good fortune. When, in March, Grey sent a reminder of the British Government's wish that the Commission's minutes of evidence should be published, the reply was even more insolent than before; publication would benefit only hostile critics who wanted to twist the evidence against the Free State. 'He seemed to think,' Hardinge reported, 'that the renewed demand for publication had been suggested to you, with some sinister design, by the Congo Reform Association.' Grey meekly swallowed the insult; 'for the present, at any rate, it appears useless to press for the publication of the evidence'.

So Casement continued to be exposed to Leopold's propaganda campaign against him. By this time it had spread to the United States, with the publication of an impressively detailed history of the Congo Free State by a New York attorney, Henry Wellington Wack. Only an expert on the subject could have realised that it was a sustained exercise in distortion. Lothaire, for example, was mentioned only for his heroic part in the campaign against the slave trade; Stokes was dismissed as a 'so-called martyr' who had been 'caught red-handed bartering guns and ammunition with the native enemies of the Free State'; Rabinek was not mentioned; nor was Caudron. But Wack's main aim, inevitably, was to devalue Casement's Report. He departed, for this purpose, from his usual practice of extensive quotations, giving only one from the Report—the paragraph at the beginning in which there was praise for the Free State's communications system. The rest, Wack claimed, was too long to give in full; he would therefore content himself with a summary. The 'summary' ran to two sentences: 'the Report contains many paragraphs in praise of the wonderful changes wrought by the Belgians in the Congo during the last twenty years. There are other passages in the Report which condemn the land and Concessionary system of the State'. The Free State's reply, by contrast, was given in full, thirty-four pages in all. Many of Casement's findings which had been favourable to the Free State had been suppressed, Wack explained; and a complete answer to his criticisms, sent to the London newspapers, had also been suppressed, by all of them. Without wishing to impeach Casement's integrity, therefore, he felt compelled to say that the material he had provided had been inaccurate and parital; and that his Report, 'magnified, distorted, garbled, has afforded material for the enemies of the Congo Free State upon which they have not ceased to work'.

Lord Fitzmaurice 1906

After his brief period of euphoria following the publication of the Commission's report, Casement gradually sunk back into despondency. So little money had he left that he was unable even to afford to send out Christmas cards; and in the new year he fell ill again—something wrong with one of his legs, which left him limping. He wrote to ask Nevinson whether there might be some opening in journalism; Nevinson replied with the traditional warning that it was an overcrowded and discouraging profession—'stick to the public service if you can'. This was hardly tactful advice to give Casement, who had good reason to believe that the public service did not wish to stick to him. He had not been offered Rio; he had received no offer of any post. And in April, he found out why. A letter from Sir Eric Barrington informed him that the Foreign Secretary felt unable to offer him any of the existing vacancies in the Consular Service, and hinted broadly at the reason: 'it was in my opinion most unfortunate that you should have so hastily resigned Lisbon, which is one of the nicest posts in the service, and was given you in recognition of your work in Africa'.

It was too close to the truth for comfort; and that it should come from Barrington served only to infuriate him. He wrote to William Tyrrell—a fellow-Irishman two years his junior; one of the few men in the Foreign Office whom he liked and trusted—claiming that Barrington was prejudiced against him, and had been heard to describe him as 'a beggar who wishes to be a chooser'. Again, as after the Harrison letter in *The Times*, he suffered a spasm of persecution mania. Even Morel, sorry for him though he was, reported to Harris that 'his troubles have made him unreliable'—though without explaining what form his unreliability took. And when, with the help of his Irish interests, he recovered his equanimity, a slight but perceptible shift in his political attitude was noticeable. He was ceasing to be a Home Ruler, and becoming a separatist.

The Barrington letter was an excuse—much as the lack of a letter had been the excuse, over a century before, for Wolfe Tone's conversion to separatism. Tone had written to William Pitt the younger, offering to found a British colony on one of the islands which Captain Cook had discovered in the Pacific; his idea was that it would provide a base against the Spaniards.

When Pitt did not bother to reply, Tone had registered a vow to make him sorry—and, but for the persistent easterly gale which prevented the French expeditionary force from landing in Ireland in 1796, he might well have redeemed that pledge. Casement lacked Tone's insight into his motives, but the change in his attitude became perceptible in his correspondence. He still identified himself with Arthur Griffith's policies—as he showed in a letter that May to Gertrude Bannister, lamenting the death of Michael Davitt: 'we have no leader for *Sinn Fein* now'. But he was coming more under the influence of an earlier patriot figure. An essay—unpublished, undated, but written while the Conservatives were still in office—reveals his growing admiration for John Mitchel, the Ulster Protestant who in 1848 became convinced of the need for Irishmen to use force, to get rid of the English, and acquire total independence for Ireland.

For the moment, though—as he told Alice Green—he lacked the means to do anything active for the cause; all he could do was immerse himself in Irish history, and await events. And that summer, an unexpected development in the Congo campaign compelled the Foreign Office to recall him. Early in the year two books had been published in Belgium exposing the Free State system in detail: one by Professor Cattier, based largely on his Report and Morel's researches; the other by a Jesuit theologian, Father Vermeersch, revealing among other things how the Catholic as well as the Protestant missionaries in the Congo had been wheedled and bullied into silence. Informed public opinion in Belgium at last began to turn against Leopold. A motion in the assembly to annex the Free State, though it was not carried, attracted enough support for Hardinge to describe it as a humiliating defeat for the King.

With a general election due in May, Leopold had been in trouble. He eased himself out with a characteristic manoeuvre, letting it be known that he had come round to favour annexation—thereby ensuring that the Congo was not an eléction issue—and reasserting himself as soon as he found that the government had been re-elected: 'my rights over the Congo can be shared with no one'. But Grey, who had gratefully endorsed Leopold's acceptance of annexation, could hardly now support Leopold's repudiation. Nor would he be wise to, as the stability of Belgium—his main concern—might be jeopardised by encouraging Leopold to defy public opinion. Morel, too, had managed to get together a small group of Congo reformers in the Commons, under the chairmanship of a new Labour member, Ramsay MacDonald; and they were asking awkward parliamentary questions. In the circumstances, Tyrrell and Fitzmaurice realised, a hostile Casement could be a danger.

Tyrrell had direct access to Grey—he was the Foreign Secretary's précis writer. Fitzmaurice backed him: Casement, though 'a bit hotheaded and impetuous', was an Irishman of a very good type. To Casement himself, he wrote reassuringly to assert that Barrington was not his enemy; and if he wanted proof that the Foreign Office had nothing against him, all he had to do was come over and talk to Fitzmaurice. It proved an astute move, on Tyrrell's part; he introduced the two men, early in June, and they took to each other immediately. As a result, when the subject of the Congo was brought up in a debate on foreign affairs in the House of Lords on July 3rd, and reference was made to the part Casement had played there, Fitzmaurice was able to dispel suspicion that there was prejudice against him in the Foreign Office by delivering a eulogy of him. Casement, he said:

> had an exceedingly difficult task, and was subject to all those perils of flood and fire which a man who has work to do in the interior of Africa has to encounter. He had, moreover, to carry on an inquiry which could not fail to be more or less disagreeable to those concerned, and to make him an object of suspicion and dislike to them. It is, as has been pointed out, unfortunate that the Report of the first Commission was not accompanied by the evidence, but the Report is sufficient to vindicate Mr. Casement.

The fact that Leopold had just issued new Decrees, based on proposals made by his 'Reforms Commission', could also be used as evidence that the campaign was having its effect. Casement was not deceived: so long as Leopold controlled the Free State, he had always insisted, new regulations would be observed only when they suited him. Fitzmaurice, too, could not resist expressing his own scepticism about them; if they were implemented, he said, the position of the natives would become so idyllic that some of your lordships, on leaving this House, might almost be disposed to take a ticket immediately for the Congo'. But in the Commons, Grey actually took credit for the Decrees, implying they were the result of the Foreign Office's tactful but firm pressure. They should be given a trial, he recommended. Then they would see 'what the autumn may bring'.

With Parliament lulled, and soon to enjoy the summer recess, Casement might again have been forgotten; but Morel came to his rescue. He, too, was outraged by the Government's acceptance of Leopold's Decrees; but the public, he found, were prepared to accept Grey's policy of wait and see. The Congo Reform Association, he wrote to tell Casement a few days after the debate, was 'almost *in extremis*'. At least, though, some benefit could come to him out of the debate. 'I am sure,' Fitzmaurice had claimed, 'that I am giving utterance to the feelings of all here when I express the hope that Mr Casement, whom reasons of health have compelled to retire from an appointment which he held at Lisbon, will have an opportunity of adding further services to those with which his name is already associated.' Why, then—a Parliamentary questioner proposed to ask—had he been left without employment since the publication of his Report, over two years before? When notice of the question reached Grey, he asked Barrington why. Barrington, who could hardly contradict Fitzmaurice, admitted that it had been for health reasons. With Casement in the news again —*The Times* had called Fitzmaurice's tribute to him well deserved, because 'this gentleman has been the object of many unjust attacks'—a suitable answer was going to be difficult to compose.

Casement now had the chance to make it more difficult. He was about to be forced—he told the Foreign Office—against his inclination, to resign from the service. Even after the meeting with Fitzmaurice, he had remained unconvinced that there was any intention of finding a consular vacancy for him, and he had continued to look for work. He even seriously considered going back to the Congo for the Reform Association, to do another report on conditions there; 'they'll have to hang me', he wrote, but 'one couldn't do better than be hanged in order to end that den of devils'. But now, at long last, he had been offered the prospect of a job—through Thomas Lennox Gilmour, who had been responsible for getting the *Morning Post*'s backing for the Congo reformers. He was to look after the finances of a company which proposed to begin growing cotton in Portuguese East Africa. He had no choice, he felt, but to accept; because, as he explained in a self-exculpatory letter to Alfred Emmott, it was obvious there was no real wish in the Foreign Office to employ him.

Probably Emmott alerted the Foreign Office; perhaps Casement hoped he would. Grey acted quickly. Privately, he explained to the M.P. who had put down the question that Casement had not been offered a post only for health reasons. As these no longer applied, he could now be employed; so the question could be withdrawn. On July 25th Casement was offered the consulate at Bilbao. Five days later, he received another offer; Grey, pleased to hear that he had decided to return to active service, wanted to know whether he might prefer Santos, where there was also a vacancy.

There were a number of considerations which should have impelled him to refuse Grey's offers; one of them being that they were too obviously a species of hush-money. For over two years the Foreign Office had either exploited him or ignored him, for their own purposes. His aims and his work, he had been forced to realise, meant no more to Grey than they had to Lansdowne. The fate of the Congo natives had been his concern; it had never been theirs. With the British public apathetic, the Free State might survive for a few more years; from South America, there would be little chance of his exercising any influence over Grey's policies when the autumn revealed, as he was certain it would, that Leopold's Decrees had been a sham.

Casement knew, too, that his was not an isolated case. The Foreign Office regarded the Consular Service as a poor relation, and particularly resented outsiders who had come in without going through the usual channels. Alfred Parminter had done well as Casement's successor in Lourenço Marques; but when he had come back to England in 1904 to take the four months' leave which was due to him, he had been told by Barrington that he must leave for his next post, Panama, the following week. And when he left Panama, a year later, it was to be told the Foreign Office had no further use for him. Barrington, Parminter thought, had done this deliberately, because of his 'deeply-seated loathing of interlopers pushing themselves into the Service'—a view with which Casement was unlikely to disagree, particularly as he felt fierce protective loyalty towards those who had been Stanley's men. 'So long as I have a roof to shelter my own head,' he told Alice Green, 'he can share it as my guest and friend.'

But an even more important consideration, in any decision he had to make about his future, should have been recognition of his growing disloyalty to the Crown—and dislike of loyalism in others. In past years the Antrim Unionists had been quite tolerant of the antics of the Gaelic Leaguers at their annual *Feis* of the Glens; but in 1906 a landlord, Francis Turmley, threatened to take reprisals on one of his tenants who had offered to lend a field to the *Feis* committee for the sports—and the nervous tenant withdrew his offer. The only field they could obtain was overgrown with weeds and thistles; Casement had to take a scythe to clear it. Still, 'some evil-disposed person', he wrote gleefully to Gertrude Bannister, actually dared to print and circulate a ballad ridiculing Turmley; and 'several naughty young boys sang it among the crowd'. 'Loyalists,' Casement concluded, 'are the devil: it is enough to make anyone who is decent and kind-hearted declare himself a Fenian, just to differentiate himself from them.'

At this stage, Casement obviously did not regard himself as a Fenian. He set out his attitude in a letter to Richard Morten on July 10th:

Very few Protestants in Ireland are by education or temperament (the product largely of education and early influence) qualified to discuss any Irish question from an Irish standpoint. They are reversing the old Anglo-Norman saw of the 'degenerate' English–Irish aristocracy, who were said to have become 'more Irish than the Irish themselves'—*Ipsis Hibernis Hiberniores*—becoming more English than the English themselves; and I do not know of any official of the Crown of Ireland who is not far more anti-Irish than any Englishman in England. It is not merely 'patriotism' but place and profit they think is at stake, and in talking frankly to any Irish 'loyalist' (who is quite disloyal, really, for he cares only for himself), he will tell you he is not a Home Ruler or an Irish worker because *he thinks* (mistakenly, but he is taught from pulpit and press to believe it) that if any form of national government came to Ireland he and his jobs would go to the wall.

It was a perceptive analysis. The revival of loyalism in Ulster carried the seeds of disloyalty, in the last resort, to Britain, should she decide to give Ireland her independence. And this, Casement went on to urge, she must do, in her own interest.

> You know my view well. If the British Empire is to endure, it can only be by recognising Ireland's right, not by 'holding down' a 'sister country'. The British Empire must become a great Commonwealth of free states, bound together by love and interest and *fellow* feeling, not kept chained to heel.
>
> The liberty you are delighted to give Natal, or New Zealand, or Canada, must also be exported to Ireland. You will have a far closer Union, and a real one, when Ireland is free to develop nationally on national and independent lines of thought; to develop her own characteristics and elevate her own ideals of life as freely as a friend. But I cannot go on; it is hard to discuss these things with an Englishman, because there are fundamental issues at stake that he cannot well realise, since he inevitably thinks he is conferring an enormous benefit in 'anglicising' a people or a country, whereas he may be working a great wrong. Every people has the right to live its own life, provided that it works thereby no grievous wrong on its neighbours. England has that right; but she has no right to insist that another country shall adopt her mode of life, and to break them on the wheel if they resist.

By a coincidence—the two men had not met—Bernard Shaw was presenting a very similar case in the preface to *John Bull's Other Island*, published in 1906. Shaw's self-introduction exactly fitted Casement, too: 'I am a genuine typical Irishman, of the Danish, Norman, Cromwellian and (of course) Scottish invasions. I am violently and arrogantly Protestant by family tradition; but let no English government therefore count on my allegiance; I am English enough to be an inveterate Republican and Home Ruler'. And Shaw argued, as Casement did, that it was not his fault if, owing to the conquest of his country, he was a British citizen. He had a perfect right, as an Irishman, to be loyal to Ireland and disloyal—a traitor, even—to the Crown: a view Casement was coming to share. Because Morten was an Englishman, and one for whom he had so deep an affection, he did not give full play in his letter to his growing anti-English feelings. He did say, though, in his conclusion, 'I feel so strongly about some of the shameful things done (and done not longer ago than forty years, nay, twenty years) that I find words inadequate'; and to his Irish friends, he rarely found words inadequate to express more extreme opinions.

In the circumstances, he would have been wise to accept the job Gilmour offered. But to do so would have entailed going back to Portuguese East Africa, which he had come to loathe when he was Consul there; and it would have meant becoming, in effect, a trader, the species he despised. His friends, too, pointed out that he might still be able to do more for suffering humanity if he remained in the Foreign Service; and Morel reminded him that to leave the Foreign Service at this stage would mean the sacrifice of his pension rights. He decided to stay in the Foreign Service—to Morel's relief. Casement, he wrote to tell Cadbury, had been 'in a terrible state of mind, and I was really fearful of what he might do'.

The spirit in which his decision was made can be judged by the reason he gave Alice Green for deciding he would go to Santos, rather than Bilbao. The Bilbao salary was so low that he would have had 'no money to spare for Ireland'; whereas from Santos, though he had heard it was 'a hideous hole, and very expensive', he had hopes of being able 'to finance one or two small Irishisms of my own'. Chief among them was *Sinn Fein*. The King's speech at the opening of Parliament that autumn, outlining the Liberal Government's legislative intentions, expressed the desire that the people of Ireland might be more closely associated with the conduct of Irish affairs; but the Liberals had no intention of offering Home Rule. They were thinking only in terms of 'devolution'—hardly more than an extension of local authority powers. This, Casement felt, was useless.

In God's name, what Ireland wants is responsibility. Until the public here feel that they *must* tackle the state of their own country and abide by their own acts there can be no real improvement. We have to create a governing mind again after 106 years of abstraction of all mind from this outraged land.

Arthur Griffith's criticisms of the Liberals—and of the Irish Party, unable to exert much influence because of the Liberal

Government's overall majority—seemed to Casement to be entirely justified; and he was determined to give Griffith's journal all the help he could. Nor did he lose interest in the language movement. One of his first actions, when he knew his financial future was assured, was to send a subscription to a centre for Irish studies.

As the time approached for his departure, he became more determined to show he was not going to be any the less devoted to the cause of Irish independence. On the day he left for South America, September 21st, his farewell postcard to Gertrude Bannister—his letters to her were still often in the playful manner he had adopted when she was a child—depicted the Euston Hotel with the flag inked out. 'The "Union Jack", I am so sorry, got *blacked* out over Euston in early hours of this morning. Awful disaster! Many fainted!' On the voyage, he read A. M. Sullivan's *New Ireland*; the account of 'the Manchester Martyrs', executed for the accidental killing of a policeman while they were trying to rescue some Fenian prisoners, wrung the tears 'from eyes and heart'. And he also read Mitchel's *Jail Journal*. It was heady stuff, for anybody in his frame of mind, opening as it did with Mitchel's description of leaving Ireland in chains, sentenced to fourteen years' transportation, and arguing that the Liberal Government of the day had shown that for Ireland, 'there is but one and all-sufficient remedy, *the edge of the sword*'.

Casement was not yet ready to accept that remedy as the only solution; but he was much closer to acceptance than he himself realised—as he was to recall in the diary he kept while he was in Berlin, during the war. The months he had spent seconded from the Foreign Office in Ireland, he wrote, had been decisive. They 'moulded all my subsequent actions, and carried me so far on the road to Mitchel's aspirations that everything I have since done seems but the natural upgrowth from the seed then sown'.

CHAPTER FOUR

SANTOS

'A nation without faith'   1906-1907

Hopefully, Casement had told his cousin that his new post might be 'rather interesting'. From the day he arrived, he found it miserable. Always before, as Consul, he had had a consulate—though at Boma, it was necessary to build a new one. But in Santos, the Consul had to rent what accommodation he could; and his predecessors had tended to take the cheapest office available, to squeeze some additional income out of the Foreign Office's £600 a year. The office was located at the back of a coffee store. 'Everyone walks in, as the door is wide open,' Casement told his cousin; 'I expect *they* expect me to provide coffee and buns.' His predecessor had actually put up wire netting as far as the ceiling, to prevent angry British subjects, waiting for an interview, from lobbing missiles at him.

The work, too, was the kind that had so irritated Casement in Lourenço Marques. There was scarcely anything to be done, he told the Foreign Office, except to deal with sailors and beggars. The sailors

> cause infinite worry and trouble—more so than in any other port in South America I am told, and this place is indeed what Sir R. Burton called it in 1867—'the Wapping of the Far West' ... a nasty hole—but people are kind and obliging. The Board of Trade has no idea of the trouble of running a Consulate like this when drunken sailors and deserters come and go the whole day—and I lose hours of time each day over matters of no importance to anyone but which, nevertheless, as a public officer, I cannot refuse to attend to.

Richard Burton had been appointed Consul in Santos in the year Casement was born; and his wife's description of the town still applied forty years later: 'the climate is beastly, the people fluffy. The stinks, the vermin, the food, the niggers are all of a piece. There are no walks, and if you go one way you sink knee-deep in mangrove swamps; another, you are covered with sand-flies'. And by the time Casement arrived, he found Santos was also an exceedingly expensive place to live. The pound was worth a third of its value in England; 'the dock labourers, who go barefoot, are earning now rather more than the salary of this post'. It was not long before he had decided that the job had nothing but frustration to offer; 'of all the futile and absurd posts, none I have ever heard of, or read of, or dreamed of, equals Santos!' Africa, he had decided, was the only place for him, 'if it can't be Ireland'.

Ireland remained his constant preoccupation. 'Remember,' he had told Alice Green before he left, 'my address is the Consulate of Great Britain and IRELAND, Santos'; and he took pains always to add on the 'Ireland' himself. The high cost of living made it hard for him to send back money, as he had promised, for Irish causes; but he did what he could for Tawin, urging that Douglas Hyde should be brought down to give a lecture—'it might make the whole peninsula, of which Tawin is only the jutting-point, Irish-speaking'. And books which he read, such as a life of the novelist Charles Lever, continued to fan his growing animosity against England. Lever, like himself, had been a Protestant Irishman, and a British Consul—but a loyal one, who 'hobnobbed with ambassadors and cabinet members'—to all intents an Englishman. 'I have no belief in Englishmen', Casement commented, writing to Alice Green in the spring of 1907. He went on to quote with approval Michael Davitt's views on the subject:

The idea of being ruled by Englishmen is to me the chief agony of existence. They are a nation without faith, truth or conscience, enveloped in a panoplied Pharisaism and an incurable hypocrisy. Their normal appetite is fed on falsehood. They profess Christianity and believe only in Mammon. They talk of liberty while ruling India and Ireland against the principles of a Constitution professed as a political faith but prostituted to the interests of class and landlord rule.

It was a mistake, Casement went on, for an Irishman to mix himself up with the English; 'he is bound to do one of two things—either go to the wall, if he remains Irish, or become an

Englishman himself'—as he had so nearly done, at the time of the Boer War, when he accepted imperialism: 'I was on the high road to being a regular imperialist Jingo'. The war, though, had given him qualms, and his experience of Belgian rule in the Congo, reminding him as it did of English rule in Ireland, had completed the conversion. 'In those lonely Congo forests where I found Leopold, I found also myself, the incorrigible Irishman.'

So strong did his antipathy to all things English become that he at last began to admit to himself that it was odd, for somebody in his official position. 'I am a queer sort of British Consul, *alanna*,' he confided to his cousin; 'I really ought to be in jail instead of under the Lion and the Unicorn.' In the spring of 1907, the contradictions became too much for him; he must, he decided, find a way to leave the Foreign Service. In May, when he was again approached by Gilmour with a renewed offer of a job in Portuguese East Africa, he wrote saying he would accept it.

The decision, once taken, restored him to a more philosophical frame of mind. 'Have you ever felt,' he asked Alice Green, 'what I feel daily growing stronger; that the Irish character is a nobler heritage to claim than anything else on earth? ... You are the descendant of a Cromwellian invader, but your heart has gone to Ireland—just as Parnell's went—just as Grattan's went.' There was a soul, he felt, in every country, just as in every human being.

> It is something more than Race; more than 'Nationality'; more than any reason I have yet seen put forward. There is something in the soil, in the air, in the inherited mind of a country that is as real, nay more real, than the rocks, the hills and the streams. No historian defines the thing, yet it exists in all lands—and in Ireland, its influence has never failed.

'They offered me Para!'   1907

Casement sailed for Britain that summer imagining he would be taking his last leave as a member of the Foreign Service. When he reached London, he found that they did still not want to lose him. They had reacted to the threat of his resignation by finding a vacancy: Haiti. The climate was good; and as Haiti was a

Black Republic, it would provide an interesting sequel to his Congo career. He would also keep his pension.

Again, it was events relating to the Congo which were making the Foreign Office solicitous on his behalf. In his letters from Santos, he had begged to be kept in touch with developments: 'Ireland first and forever', he told his cousin, but 'poor old Congo too, for the sake of the dark skins and all they have suffered, and all that the brave, indomitable Morel has done to free them'. And that winter, the *New York American* took up the campaign with a devasting series of muck-raking articles exposing the lobbying methods used by Leopold's propaganda agency in the United States (one of its employees, it was now disclosed, being the 'historian' Wellington Wack). These included suborning State officials in Washington; and in the angry reaction, a resolution proposed in the Senate there, offering the President support in any measures he might take to redress the evils of the Free State, was passed without a dissentient vote.

The exposure could not have come at a more embarrassing time for Leopold. The Belgian Assembly was engaged in a protracted debate on the future of the Congo, and he had already been compelled to hush up one scandal—Lothaire, who had been relieved of his Concession post, had sued his employers for Fr. 500,000, which he alleged they owed him, at the same time discreetly letting it be known that if the money were paid he would agree to return certain incriminating documents, revealing among other things how his trial for murdering Stokes had been rigged in advance; and Leopold had found it advisable to come to terms. Hardly had he done so when the *New York American* ran its articles; and the news of the Senate resolution settled the issue. The Belgian Assembly authorised the Government, by an overwhelming majority, to draw up proposals for the annexation of the Free State.

At last, Leopold had been worsted; and in the process, Casement had again been vindicated. But from the time that annexation of the Congo by Belgium had been made the policy of the Congo reformers at the Holborn meeting two years before, he had insisted that annexation should only be allowed subject to stringent guarantees; and as soon as he read the Belgian Government's proposals, he denounced them to Alice Green as 'a monstrous sham'. Morel agreed; and when Casement returned they decided to rally the Association for a further campaign to compel the Belgians to accept the principles laid down in the Berlin agreement, and initially adopted by Stanley's men.

The summer before, Morel had feared that the Association was *in extremis*; but he had helped to revive it with his *Red Rubber*, published that winter. Unlike his earlier books, it was a best-seller. The feeling that the Association's work had been justified by events now gave its members an access of self-esteem; and disconcertingly for the Foreign Office, they had begun to attract influential new supporters, in and out of Parliament. It would be risky for Grey to have a hostile Casement on the loose against him—a risk of which Tyrrell, to whom Casement had confided his resentments about Santos, must have been aware. And Tyrrell, whom he still trusted, was now even better placed to help; he had been promoted in May to become Grey's private secretary. If, as seems probable, it was Tyrrell who thought of the Haiti post, to mollify him, the ruse had the desired effect. Casement urged Morel to pursue the campaign against simple annexation, and continued to encourage him—'the pen, in your case, in the hand of a very honest, very brave human being, has beaten the Principalities and Powers of Darkness out of all their Domains'. But he did not lend the campaign open support.

The offer of Haiti, too, was enough to keep him from leaving the service. He told the Foreign Office he would accept, and went back to Ireland for his leave in a markedly more contented frame of mind—the more so when he learned, in August, that although he was not required to go to Haiti until December, he need not return to Santos; he would be given leave of absence in the meantime. Gratefully, he took the opportunity to resume his study of the Irish language at a summer school in Gortahawk, in County Donegal—'a *grand* neighbourhood'—he wrote enthusiastically to Bulmer Hobson—'all Irish. English is scarcely heard—among themselves, never ... it makes me *mad* to think how Irish *could* have been saved over widespread districts—within my lifetime—if only there had been an effort'. He could also resume his links with *Sinn Fein*, though he was disappointed at its failure to attract wider support. 'Surely after *this*,' he had told Bulmer Hobson, referring to the Government's abortive devolution proposals that spring, 'after waiting fourteen years in pitiable subjection to the incoming Liberals, the Irish Party will reconsider their position, and set their sails for Ireland instead of for Westminster?' Instead, their reaction had been to disparage *Sinn Fein*, as a potential rival. The temptation had been to hit back. Casement advised against it—'I don't think we should attack any Irish man'. It was better, he thought, to leave them 'to come to their senses, as they will later on'; Parliamentarian and Unionist alike should be shown that *Sinn Fein* meant no more than it said, 'the material uplifting of our country by her own efforts'; and he put forward various ideas how this might be done, in ways calculated to appeal to Irishmen in general. Ireland, for example, should send her own team to the coming Olympic Games.

In mellow mood, he prepared to leave for Haiti. Just before he was due to depart, he was asked if he would relinquish the appointment, and go to Brazil instead. He was to describe what happened in a letter to Gertrude Bannister:

I came home from Santos last July, intending to leave the Foreign Office for good and all. I had been offered an excellent post out in East Africa by a big undertaking—good pay, and *most interesting* duties, far more useful than a consul's. The F.O. on my landing promoted me to be Consul-General for Haiti and San Domingo, one of the six first class, top-rank posts in the whole Consular Service. I accepted this after some hesitation, and declined the good African offer. Well, in November, when I went over from Ireland to London to get final instructions to go out to Haiti, and to be gazetted, they had the audacity to *appeal* to me and my good nature to make room for another man; to resign Haiti and wait for another Consulate General some time next year when a certain post (Rio de Janeiro) would be vacant.

The appeal to my generosity, on behalf of the other man, I met. I gave up Haiti for them to give to him, and then, when this had been accomplished, I told them nothing would induce me to go to Rio, or live in Brazil, and they might give Rio to anyone they pleased except me. I told them also, that if they made me Ambassador I should not live in Brazil. They offered me Para!!! They thanked me of course profusely and effusively for my generosity in surrendering Haiti, saying there was no other man in the service they could have appealed to, and so forth, but nonetheless they send me back to the country I told them I loathed and abominated. They first *do* me out of my East African appointment by offering me a post I liked (Haiti) and where I would save £500 a year clear out of my pay, and then calmly ask me to surrender it. I have told them pretty frankly what I think of them, their methods, and their Consular so-called 'Service'. It is no service at all, but only robbery and corruption, and an enormous fraud on the public.

Casement's bitterness was understandable. He had, in fact, been subjected to greater irritation even than his letter described. At first he had had some doubts about Haiti, but in October he had heard from the Consul whom he was to replace, telling him about the job, and it clearly would have suited him admirably. Haiti was in all but name a Diplomatic post. All he was required to do was look after the Jamaican colony—'there was *no routine work*, and *no shipping*'; and he could live comfortably on half his salary. This last was a vital consideration, for that October he had been forced—against his inclination, he told Hobson—to sacrifice a good deal of money (probably, to judge from later references he made, to come once again to the rescue of his brother Tom). He had been asked to give up Haiti, too, not for some fellow-member of the Consular Service (of whom several must have had a better claim, from seniority, than he had) but for an army officer, an Old Etonian, who had been a temporary Consul some years before, and who was being given the post by Grey as part of the Foreign Secretary's patronage. But Para ... when Casement made inquiries about the town from William Churchill, who had been Consul there, Churchill described it as 'a hideous nightmare' where the Foreign Office 'certainly do not deserve to have a man like you'. But Churchill could suggest no better alternative—'they are nearly all the same, damnable, and a Consul's life is a dog's life'. In any case, the Foreign Office had been adamant; he must choose between Santos and Para. He could not bear the thought of returning to Santos; and with his financial resources now so stretched, he dared not resign from the service. Para it had to be.

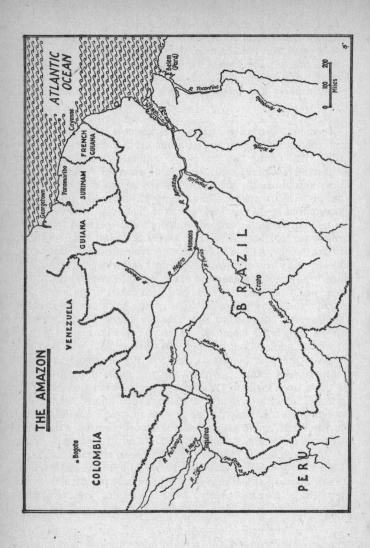

CHAPTER FIVE

PARA

'I am suffering horrors'   *1908*

Official notification of the new appointment reached Casement early in the new year of 1908, when he was recuperating—he had been ill again that winter—in Lucan, a spa where Dubliners took the waters. He had been trying, he wrote to tell Bulmer Hobson, to set up a co-operative in the Antrim glens; and he hoped it might become self-supporting before the year was out. He also sent £50 to Hobson for his projected new journal—a lump sum, he believed, being the most effective way to help a paper: 'driblets of money don't do this at all—merely keep it living, or rather dying, from hand to mouth'. But he was not happy about the progress of the Irish independence cause. 'I saw Griffith yesterday and he is cheerful of feeling and hopeful too —which is more than I am! The only hopeful thing is the Gaelic League and the *Sinn Fein* idea, between them; but they've a long ridge to hoe yet'. *Sinn Fein* was not collecting support fast enough. Only one member of the Irish Party at Westminster had joined, resigning his seat to contest a by-election against his old party. Casement left for Para before polling day; 'did Charles Dolan, the *Sinn Fein* man, poll a decent vote?' he wrote to ask Gertrude Bannister. Dolan did, but it was not big enough to defeat the Irish Party candidate.

After spending a couple of days with Herbert Ward and his family in Paris, Casement (who now preferred to take a train to Vigo, or Lisbon, and catch a ship there, to avoid the Bay of Biscay) sailed for Para, arriving before the end of February. Para, soon to be known as Belem, was becoming Brazil's chief commercial centre, with a population of over 100,000. Its cathedral, its theatre and its parks, at first attracted him; but it did not take him long to begin to find life there intolerable. The streets tended to peter out in forest, or swamp; and the fact that they were on a level only just above high water mark had left apparently insuperable drainage problems, with a consequent high mortality rate. Within a fortnight he was writing to Lord Dufferin at the Foreign Office to warn him that he would be compelled to resign. The chief trouble, he explained privately to Tyrrell, was financial; Para was extremely expensive. His predecessor had sold up the entire disposable contents of the office before he left; and the files were in a chaotic condition. There was no register of documents, state despatches were hopelessly mixed up with commercial, local and general correspondence; and he could not get them sorted out and filed without considerable cost. There was also the weather. 'I am stuck in this vile country and place and not able to do anything for it or you,' he wrote to tell Hobson. 'It rains here daily, and I am suffering horrors, I can assure you—in every way'. Once again, he wrote to Gilmour to say that he had weighed all the considerations and finally made up his mind that 'even with the loss of pension, I should prefer immediate retirement from the Foreign Service'. He was prepared to accept the Mozambique job, if it were still open, if necessary at less than the £1,200 salary which he had been offered.

It was a depressing period for him—made more depressing by the news from Morel of setbacks in the Congo campaign. For a while, Grey had appeared to be impressed by the weight of support the Association had collected. No external issue, he had to admit in the Commons, had so moved public opinion for thirty years; and he had actually warned that unless there was a change in the system on the Congo, he would instruct British merchants to refuse to pay duties, and send a gunboat to the lower part of the river. But Grey's new forcefulness—though it sounded as if he were at last implementing Casement's own proposals, made when he had been Consul in Boma; even to using his terminology, like 'the system'—was more in the nature of a final insult to the departing Leopold, than a serious threat to the Belgian Government. The Belgian Foreign Minister was not worried. His reply indicated that he was not prepared to be any more accommodating than Leopold had been: what the Belgian Government decided to do in its new colony would be none of Britain's business. And in the meantime, reports during 1908 from British missionaries and Consuls revealed that the conditions which Casement had described four years before continued unchanged.

During the summer, to add to his troubles, he came down

with a disorder which was endemic in Para: gastro-enteritis. It was serious enough to keep him in bed for a month. On the doctor's orders, he was then carried aboard a ship which was sailing for Barbados. But Barbados—'ghastly little Britannic Island', as he described it to Hobson, 'of princes and paupers'— brought little improvement; he had 'shrunk to a shadow', and could neither eat, nor walk, nor sleep. It was far worse, he complained, than the old familiar Congo fever, for at least when that left him, he immediately began to feel better. Eventually he applied for, and received, permission to return on leave to England. There, he was told that Rio would soon be vacant. As the Mozambique job had been filled he had no choice, he felt, but to accept.

RIO

'This ghastly strain city' 1909

Casement's promotion to be His Majesty's Consul-General in Rio was announced at the beginning of December 1908; but he was granted an extension of leave on the ground that he had been seriously ill. On his way, he caught a cold in Paris so bad that he feared he was getting 'the national complaint, consumption'; he did not arrive in Rio until March, and then had one of what he described as his Congolese attacks—a violent bout of fever, 'fierce come, soon go'. But when he had recovered sufficiently to resume work, he found he rather liked Rio. Certainly it was a pleasant change after Para. He had assistants, who could take care of most of the routine work; and his consular territory included a number of ports, up and down the coast, each with its Vice-Consul to be visited and supervised. The climate could be uncomfortably hot—one week the temperature never fell below 90 degrees in his Rio office, occasionally reaching 100 degrees. Still, he was able to go to live in Petropolis, a diplomatic settlement 2,700 feet up, and cool. The two-hour journey each way by boat and train was boring, but worth it.

Soon, he settled down to write much the same kind of despatches to the Foreign Office that he had written from Lourenço Marques; complaints about the cost of living and the inadequacy of consular expenses, and long tirades against the Brazilian authorities for wrongs done to British subjects. His work on one case was praised by Grey in almost the same terms as Salisbury had praised his earliest consular effort: the Foreign Secretary, he was told, 'is of the opinion that you have handled an awkward situation with tact and good judgment'. But although the occasional challenge of this kind could arouse him, for most of the time there was nothing to tax his capabilities, and he soon grew bored with 'this ghastly strain city'. Brazilian life, he wrote resignedly to Gertrude Bannister in September, was 'the most perverted, comfortless and dreary of any in the world. The country is beautiful beyond words and the people uninteresting, pretentious shams beyond conception'. Dress was their religion, vanity their high priest. The Monroe Doctrine protected them, but one day it would be challenged from Europe. The best outcome he felt, would be a German state 'with honest clean laws and institutions'.

Boredom with Brazil had the effect of concentrating his interest in Irish affairs. When Alice Green's *The Making of Ireland and her Undoing* was published, her conclusion—'Now, in recalling the way of sorrows they have traversed, their history will renew their confidence in the strength and vitality of a race which no ruin has destroyed, and no calamity has yet vanquished'—delighted him: 'isn't that a splendid ending?'; and he wrote a commentary on the book, published in the *Freeman's Journal*. He also wrote for *Homestead*, which George Russell—A.E.—had founded; and he became a £50 shareholder in the new daily *Sinn Fein* which Arthur Griffith had decided to bring out in Dublin—though he feared it would be money thrown away. The old weekly *Sinn Fein* had not been flourishing enough, he thought, to justify the change. Still, he'd promised to help; and he wished for Griffith's sake he could have afforded more.

How Ireland and Irish affairs obsessed Casement in the period while he was Consul-General in Rio was to be recalled by Ernest Hambloch, who went out there early in 1910 as his Vice-Consul —'a man of brains, intelligence, and a good honest nature', Casement described him. In his autobiography, Hambloch was to recall his Consul-General with less enthusiasm:

Tall, yellow-skinned, grey-eyed and black-bearded, Casement must have made a considerable impression on everybody who met him for the first time. His manners were elaborately courteous, but there was a good deal of pose about him, as though he were afraid of being caught off his guard. His conversation was not profound, and I never heard him probe any subject on which he spoke. He was an easy talker and a fluent writer. He could expound a case, but not argue it. His greatest charm was his voice, which was very musical. He must have been aware he had great powers of persuasion, yet I think he was quite unconscious of the charm of his voice.

Few men can be heroes to their Vice-Consuls, and Hambloch had been uniquely situated to appreciate Casement's weaknesses. Casement had not, before, had anybody of his own social standing working under him; and he appears not to have realised that Hambloch was keeping a cool eye on him, and finding him at times a bore. Hambloch, admittedly, wrote his recollections for a British audience, to whom his subject was a traitor. Nevertheless his comments sound as if they came from observation, not hindsight. Casement, he realised, was no egalitarian; he believed in a professional class, and his main objection to the Consular Service was that it did not enjoy the status of the Diplomatic. He sympathised with oppressed natives, but it did not occur to him that they could ever be regarded as the equals of whites. And his anti-English feelings amounted to monomania; Hambloch remembered him 'marching up and down the room with ungainly strides', pouring forth 'a torrent of violent abuse not only of the English, but of everything British'.

When Casement was in the grip of some powerful emotion, too, it sometimes carried him away. On a visit to one of the Vice-Consuls at some port north of Rio, he suddenly swept the flower vases off a table, took them out to the verandah, and hurled them into the garden below. The houseboy accepted this with equanimity, as if accustomed to such behaviour. Casement, Hambloch decided, was possessed.

'Never again . . .'   1910

Alone among those who knew Casement well, Hambloch also claimed to have been aware there was a suspicion that he was 'not normal'. This was on no very strong evidence; simply that on one occasion, he observed two English residents, father and son, exchanging smiles when the father hearing his good-looking son was to have lunch with Casement, advised him 'be careful'. It might easily have been dismissed as a misunderstanding of some private joke between the father and the son, were it not for the fact that two of the 'black' diaries discovered in London in 1916 happened to be for 1910 and 1911. The first of them consists mainly of jotted down impressions, along with afterthoughts. For January 13th:

Last time—'polpito' at Barca at 11.30. To Icarsby 'precisa

muito'. 15$ or 20. Also on Barca the young caboclo (thin) dark gentleman of Icarsby, eyed constantly and wanted, would have gone but Gabriel querido waiting at Barca gate. In *very* deep thrusts.

The descriptions of his sexual encounters were both more numerous than in 1903, and more explicit. During the early part of the year he hardly bothered to record anything else, except the names of the places where he was staying, the times when he was ill, and occasionally, people he met, like Alfred Parminter, for whom he had secured a job with a coffee firm in Santos. Experience, though, had not made him any less of a romantic; he still longed for love. At Buenos Aires, when he went there, he was able to enjoy a relationship with 'Ramon' that was less transient, and more intense, than usual. They saw each other frequently; when he departed in the beginning of April to take his home leave, the parting was sentimental—'To Tigre with Ramon from Belgrano, never again'; and while he was on his way back to England, and during his leave, he and Ramon exchanged letters and cards.

His sexual appetites, society's condemnation of them, and the cash transactions involved were conducive to promiscuity; but this only meant that he valued established relationships the more. When he got back to Belfast in May—after a chance encounter with John McGonegal—'huge and curved and he awfully keen. X 4/6'—he met his old love, Millar, and brought him to a hotel in Warrenpoint.

Turned in together at 10.30–11—after watching billiards. Not a word said till—'wait I'll untie it' and then 'Grand'. Told many tales and pulled it off on top grandly. First time after so many years and so deep mutual longing.
Rode gloriously, splendid steed. Huge, told of many. 'Grand'.

—and the next day, 'Millar, again. First time he turned his back, "Grand" back, voluntarily.'
The 'never again' reference when leaving Ramon in Buenos Aires suggested that Casement already had it in mind that he would not be returning to Rio; but, whatever his plans for the future might have been, he spent the leave much as he had its

predecessors—in London, where he saw Tyrrell at the Foreign Office, and went to *Tales of Hoffmann* (he found the Barcarolle 'heavenly'); in Dublin, where he preferred to go to the zoo rather than to King Edward's funeral service; and in Bally-castle, where he could be with his sister Nina, and go to see how the Irish language was faring on Rathlin Island. But on June 17th, he noted in his diary, 'Got letter from Anti-Slavery people about Putumayo River and the Amazon Rubber Company.' The writer was the former Congo missionary, John Harris, who had taken over the secretaryship of the now combined Anti-Slavery and Aborigines Protection Societies. He had been in Ireland earlier that summer; they had gone together to see Tara, where the High Kings had once held court. Now, he explained, he had suggested to the Foreign Secretary that Casement should be invited to join a Commission of Inquiry that was going to the Upper Amazon. Would he come over to discuss the idea with members of the Society, and some M.P.s who were taking an interest? Leaving £10 for the Rathlin school fund, and £2 for an Irish prize, he departed for London, and spent an exhilarating evening with the members of the Society and the M.P.s, including Dilke and Josiah Wedgwood: 'splendid talk'.

The Anti-Slavery Society, he learned, had been disturbed by stories of maltreatment of natives in the rubber-producing region named after one of the Amazon's tributaries. The territory was claimed both by Colombia and Peru; but the company accused of maltreating the Indians was British, and it employed British subjects from Barbados. The Society had been badgering the Foreign Office for an inquiry, and the Foreign Office had prevaricated. But eventually the company's shareholders, disturbed by the publicity, had insisted that the directors should nominate a Commission of Inquiry of their own, and the Society were trying to persuade the Foreign Office to send Casement along with it. The idea appealed to him. He had planned to go to his loved Donegal; but he stayed on in and around London, awaiting the Foreign Office's summons; seeing his cousin Gertrude, Mrs. Green, and Count Blücher (who had married an English girl); enjoying casual sexual encounters; and occupying himself in connection with the Congo reform campaign—the final service, as things turned out, that he was to render it.

In December 1908 there had appeared what was, in a sense,

the most remarkable of all the Congo Reform Association's achievements: a letter in *The Times* warning what would happen if the Belgian Government was allowed to annex the Free State without giving the required guarantees, signed by eleven peers, nineteen bishops, seventy-six M.P.s, thirteen editors of news-papers, and many other well-known citizens. It was a tactfully-phrased reminder to Grey that he still had to contend with the most formidable humanitarian pressure group since the days of the fight against the slave trade. Then, in 1909, the campaign had been taken a step further by the publication of Conan Doyle's *The Crime of the Congo*, which put the reformers' case more succinctly (and, at 6d., more cheaply) than Morel had been able to do, reminding readers of the full horror of Leo-pold's system, as exposed by Casement—'a man of the highest character, truthful, unselfish—one who is deeply respected by all who know him', and warning that so far from reforming the system, the Belgians were likely to allow it to continue. But although the Congo Reform Association had shown itself strong enough to deter Grey from formally recognising Belgium's sovereignty over the Congo, Casement and Morel had realised that he was only waiting for an excuse to do so; and it came in December 1909, with the death of Leopold. When the young King Albert promised a new era of humanity and progress in the Congo, Morel feared Grey would seize the opportunity to wash its hands of the whole business. Casement agreed. The Foreign Office, he wrote to tell William Cadbury—the Associa-tion's most generous backer—had been 'miserably weak'; somehow, pressure must continue to be applied until the Belgian Government complied with the demands of humanity. And he had thought of an idea which, he hoped, would not only give the Association fresh publicity, but also provide its founder with some reward for his services—a Morel Testimonial Fund. Conan Doyle agreed to be treasurer, and Lord Cromer con-sented to launch it. On Casement's suggestion, the fund was to be in trust for Mrs. Morel and the children. 'You will never know,' Mrs. Morel wrote to him when she heard, 'what your natural generosity of mind, and your unfailing sympathy, were to the Bulldog. Oh, magician, may you have much success in your new undertaking.'

The new undertaking had just materialised. Tiring of London life (which included a visit with Conan Doyle and Morel to a dramatised version of the Sherlock Holmes story, *The Speckled Band*), Casement had grown impatient. On July 11th—the day the Morel Testimonial Fund was launched in a letter to the newspapers—he wrote to Tyrrell at the Foreign Office to say he had heard he might be asked to go to the Putumayo. He was ready, if Grey wished it. Tyrrell sent for him, to meet Grey; they had a long talk; and the outcome was that he spent the best part of the next two days in the Foreign Office, examining the Putumayo files.

PART THREE

THE DEVIL'S PARADISE

1910—1913

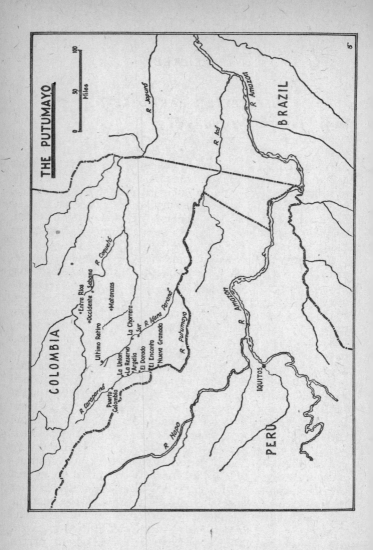

THE PUTUMAYO

100   50   0
       Miles

COLOMBIA

BRAZIL

PERU

R. Caquetá
R. Japurá
R. Içá
R. Amazon
R. Caraparaná
R. Igara Paraná
R. Putumayo
R. Napo
R. Amazon

Puerto Colombia
La Union
La Reserva
Argelia
El Dorado
El Encanto
Nuevo Granada
Ultimo Retiro
La Chorrera
Sur
Entre Rios
Occidente
Sabana
Matanzas

IQUITOS

CHAPTER ONE

JULIO CESAR ARANA

Truth   1909–1910

When Casement had sat down twelve years before to read the Congo Atrocity files, on his appointment to Loanda, he had had the benefit of his own experience in the Free State, and of what he had heard and read about conditions there since he had left. Although he had been Consul for some years in South America, he knew little about the Putumayo, apart from what he had heard since the controversy began. The story, as it unfolded, can only have seemed to him to be a grotesque parody of his Congo experience.

The Foreign Office had become involved, he found, the previous autumn, following the publication of articles describing the experiences of two young American explorers, W. E. Hardenburg and W. B. Perkins, in the magazine *Truth*. It had been Hardenburg's childhood ambition to follow the Amazon from its source in the Andes down to the Atlantic; partly with scientific aims, but chiefly for the adventure—the two men had undertaken the journey with few thoughts in their minds but to see all there was to see, and shoot at almost everything that moved. At one stage of their voyage, they had been entertained by a Colombian settler—the last, he claimed, to be left undisturbed there by the Peruvians, who had laid claim to the territory because of the wealth of indigenous rubber to be found there; and he had told them ugly stories of the methods that were being used to collect the rubber. Any doubts Hardenburg and his companion might have had about the truth of his account were dispelled when a Peruvian force turned up, evicted their host, and arrested them. While under arrest, they saw for themselves how rubber was collected; they saw, too, that the Peruvian forces in the region were operating not for the Lima Government, but for Julio César Arana, who claimed to have a title to the region—known, from the name of one of the Amazon's tributaries, as the Putumayo.

Researching into Arana's background later, Hardenburg discovered he had chosen to exploit the Putumayo's rubber resources because he could operate there without risk of interference. It was formally claimed both by Colombia and Peru; and the Peruvian Government had been delighted to give him a Concession, on much the same lines as Leopold's in the Congo, and a free hand. Like Leopold, though, he had needed men to act as 'sentries' and for this purpose he had sent a recruiting officer to Barbados, a British colony, in 1904. Four years later, he had decided to seek capital in England, to which most of his rubber found its way; and the Peruvian Amazon Company was founded. Realising that it might be dangerous to try to fight Arana in Iquitos, Hardenburg decided to seek to expose him in London.

It was difficult, he found when he arrived, to persuade any editor to publish his account, because of the risk of libel. Eventually John Harris suggested he should try the magazine *Truth*, which had won a reputation for publishing articles that other journals were afraid to accept. And on September 22nd, 1909, the first of a series of articles on the Putumayo appeared in *Truth* under the headline THE DEVIL'S PARADISE—a name, the writer claimed, which it had earned locally. It was to stick.

The article was subtitled 'A British-owned Congo'; the writer, Sidney Paternoster, was sufficiently familiar with the Free State's history to realise the similarities. And the reaction of the Peruvian authorities was similar to, but ruder than, that of the Belgians to Casement's charges. Before leaving Iquitos, they claimed, Hardenburg had attempted to blackmail the Aranas, unless he was more generously compensated by the company for the loss of his property. He had also, while in Iquitos, cashed a bill which he had forged. But the manager of the company in London was unwise enough to offer a reporter a bribe, which cast doubts on his trustworthiness; and at the Foreign Office, Grey was warned that M.P.s, disturbed by the allegations, were giving notice of questions they wished to ask about this British-owned company. Grey ordered that all the information available about it should be brought to him, so that he could prepare suitable replies. There was no information, he was told; the consular and commercial departments knew nothing. But an Englishman, Captain Whiffen, had recently been in the Putumayo; he might know about conditions there. Captain Whiffen, tracked down in Harrogate, confirmed Hardenburg's account.

Armed with Whiffen's evidence, the Foreign Office wrote to the company to ask what measures it had taken, and proposed to take, to remedy the state of affairs *Truth* had described. In their reply, the company expressed pained surprise that the Foreign Office should have given any credence to *Truth*'s allegations. One of their staff, H. L. Gielgud, had just returned from the Putumayo; he had reported that the Indians, who seemed to him to be simply children of a happy disposition, were well looked after by the company's kindly agents. As for Whiffen's evidence, he, like Hardenburg, had tried before he left Iquitos to blackmail Arana. Arana had a letter in which he had threatened, unless his 'expenses' were paid, to denounce the company when he returned to Britain—as he had now done.

Feeling in the Foreign Office, which had been hostile to the company, swung in its favour. Rowland Sperling recommended letting the matter drop; even if there were any Barbadians still in the Putumayo, their evidence would be worth little, 'all West Indian negroes being liars'. But Grey had the Commons to consider; and, like Lansdowne six years before, he saw an opening that Arana had unwittingly provided for him. When he had first heard of *Truth*'s attack, Arana had let it be known that he was writing to the President of Peru, asking for an inquiry to clear his name; and although President Leguia had replied that there was no need, as the allegations were so evidently circulated by blackmailers, Grey was able to tell the Commons that he felt the proposed inquiry would offer the best solution.

The Peruvian Amazon Company disagreed. The appointment of a Commission of Inquiry, its directors replied, was the responsibility of the Peruvian Government. Ordinarily, for Grey, this warning would have settled the matter. But in the spring of 1910, the stories circulating about the Devil's Paradise began to stir public opinion in Britain. Resolutions flowed in to the Foreign Office from philanthropic societies, demanding action, as formerly they had demanded action on the Congo. On May 30th the Dean of Hereford publicly denounced the Peruvian Amazon Company; and although the company's management replied with a solicitor's letter, which led the Dean to recant and apologise, the company's shareholders, worried both about their capital and the company's good name, began to grow alarmed at the adverse publicity. Why not have an inquiry, if that was what was being asked for? On June 8th, the company, which in its communications with the Foreign Office, had been, as Orme Sargent complained, 'somewhat truculent', suddenly capitulated. An inquiry would, after all, be held. 'The public interest which has been recently aroused by the "Putumayo atrocities" has had more effect upon the company', Sargent had to admit, 'than our former representations had!'

The team, the company announced, would consist of the Hon. R. H. Bertie, a former colonel of the Royal Welsh Fusiliers; an unnamed director of the company; H. L. Gielgud, who had become its secretary; and 'perhaps' others. Sargent at once realised that this would arouse suspicion; Bertie was the only independent member, 'and even he may have had some connection with the company, for all we know'. The Foreign Office, he thought, should ask the company to accept a British consul, to accompany the expedition; and Grey agreed. The Anti-Slavery Society, however, were still not satisfied. That Grey 'proposed to suggest' to the company that a British Consul should accompany the Commission was not enough—particularly as the other members had yet to be named. Resolutions again began to flow in to the Foreign Office, from such diverse sources as the No. 96 branch of the Steam Engine Makers Society in Coventry and the Congregational Men's Brotherhood in Hitchin ('I wonder how many of these signatories', a minute queried, 'know where the Peruvian Amazon is situated?'). On July 7th, the Society added its own demand for immediate action; 'To keep the Society quiet', Sargent advised, it should be told the issue was 'at present under consideration'; but the formula was too jaded to keep the Society quiet for long. So Casement had been sent for, and asked to read the Putumayo files, before undertaking the task for which Harris had proposed him.

Commission of Inquiry   1910

Casement received his formal briefing on July 21st. He was to proceed to the Putumayo to accompany the Commission of Inquiry—the Peruvian Amazon Company had named other members: in addition to Bertie and Gielgud, there were to be L. H. Barnes, an expert in tropical flora; W. Fox, an expert on rubber production; and Seymour Bell, a merchant. As a Consul accompanying them, his object was 'to ascertain whether any British subjects have suffered or are in distress, and if so from what causes, and whether they stand in need of relief' (on behalf of the company, Gielgud had tried to confine his inquiry to present conditions, but this the Foreign Office would not accept). Privately, Casement was told he would have complete freedom of action, and could use whatever methods he liked to elicit information, though he should be careful to avoid causing annoyance to the governments of any country he visited.

The voyage was uneventful, apart from a brief stay in Madeira:

> July 28. Hotel. Splendid testiminhos. Soft as silk and big and full. No bush to speak of. Good wine needs no bush.

Crossing the Atlantic, Casement felt very low; but he revived at the prospect of what he would do when the ship docked:

> August 8. Should arrive in Para and get on there by 6 p.m. will go Val de Peso and Cafe's first, then to theatre and then on to Cafe in Independencia and back to theatre about 10.30 and Val de Peso at 11.

—a programme which, when the ship berthed, he put into execution:

> . . . after dinner to Vero Peso, two types, also to gardens . . . then Senate Square and Caboclo (boy 16–17) seized hard. Young, stiff, thin. Others offered later.

Evidently he was little concerned about the age of any of the youths with whom he had his sexual encounters, so long as there was the physical equipment—not with small boys; and so long as they enjoyed it. He hoped that they 'wanted badly', as he did. And he was sentimental. 'Shall I see Joao, dear old soul! I'll get up early . . .' and he did. 'To cemetery, and lo! Joao coming along—blushed to roots of hair with joy.' When they met the next day, João brought roses.

After the four days in Para, Casement took the river steamer to Manaos, eight hundred miles up the Amazon; and river steamers offered opportunities only for fantasy. Colonel Bertie was with him, but Casement at once saw that he was not going to be well enough to carry on with the tour; when they reached Manaos on August 16th, he reported to the Foreign Office that on medical advice, Bertie would be returning to Britain. 'This greatly weakens, if it does not destroy, the prestige of the Commission,' Grey noted, 'it is as well we have preserved our independence of it, and given our Consul the latitude which he has.' Barnes now became the titular head of the Commission. Casement remained on good terms with him—and with all the members, though he was sometimes irritated by Gielgud, who had the presumption to call him 'Casement', as if they were social equals.

He spent only a night in Manaos, a 'horrid town', but it gave him time to visit the local pleasure gardens—'Several policemen wanting, I think. One lovely schoolboy, back and forward several times'—before catching the river steamer for Iquitos, a further 1,000 miles up the Amazon. They reached it on the eve of his forty-sixth birthday; a well-situated town, he observed, but 'horribly neglected and dirty'; the streets were atrocious, and the houses poor. And there, the home of the Aranas, the investigation began.

From the start, he made it clear that he was conducting a separate inquiry—though he took good care to pass on information which might be useful to the Commission; it would also be useful to him, later, to have their corroboration. His aim, now and throughout the tour, was to win the confidence of the score or so of Barbadians who were still in the company's employment, and to persuade them to describe what cruelties they had seen—and, all too often, they had perpetrated. The day after his arrival in Iquitos he found that one of them, Frederick Bishop, was willing to talk; and though he nearly backed out, afraid that what he said would get him into trouble, Casement persuaded him to repeat his account to the Commission.

Over the next few days, Bishop revealed more and more about his work for the company—Casement taking notes. He had been engaged with the other Barbadians—most of them were boys of fourteen or fifteen—to check that the Indians (who were not paid) brought in the stipulated quantity of rubber, and, if they did not, to flog them—on the orders of the agents he worked for: Andreas O'Donnell of the Entre Rios Station; Elias Martinengui, of Atenas; Innocente Fonseca, of Sabana; and Alfredo Montt, of Ultimo Retiro.

Some Indians would lie down of themselves and take the flogging, others would struggle and have to be held by the arms and legs, laid flat on the ground, and flogged.
The flogging would be given on their bare buttocks. They were often cut and bleeding, and healing washes would be rubbed into the wounds, such as vinegar or salt, so that they might be able to go into the forest for more rubber.

If the Barbadians did not give the agent satisfaction, he would order them to be put in the *Cepo*—stocks. Some agents, too, devised crueller punishments.

Martinengui had an Indian girl—one of several he kept; and one night when with her he discovered she was sick with venereal disease—so he said. So in the morning he had her tied up and flogged in the station yard, and then made one of the young Indians (Bishop called him 'an Indian boy') insert burning firebrands into her body. Bishop did not like to say where, but indicated with his hand. I said, 'did you actually see that?' and he replied, 'Yes, sir, I saw that done with my own eyes.'

The members of the Commission left Iquitos on September 14th, with Casement, for the Putumayo. On the way, a Barbadian who had worked in the Section controlled by one of the more notorious of the Peruvian Amazon Company's agents, Fonseca, described what had happened there; 'murders of girls, beheading of Indians and shooting of them after they had rotted from flogging'. But the Commission still knew of the atrocities only at second-hand, from the Barbadians' accounts. First-hand evidence was not available until on September 22nd they reached the company's base at La Chorrera, run by Victor Macedo, one of the agents Whiffen had denounced. Casement was immediately convinced he was 'a scoundrel'. Some of the Indians who came on board to carry off their luggage, and who were naked except for a strip around their loins, had broad scars on their buttocks —'weals for life . . . this is their welfare, their daily welfare. All slaves.'

The following morning he got hold of the five Barbadians who were working at La Chorrera and interrogated them. Three of them refused to talk, but two 'spoke out like men and told of dreadful things; they had flogged men and seen them flogged and killed too often, and said so and maintained it'. They were prepared to talk in front not only of Barnes, but of Señor Tizon, the company's representative who was travelling with the Commission. Tizon had believed that Hardenburg and Whiffen had simply been blackmailers; now, he began to be worried. The next evening proved decisive. One of the Barbadians, Dyall, admitted to having murdered five Indians after being put in the stocks for refusing to obey the order. The stocks had been too small for his ankles, when they tried to close the stocks on his legs, they could not shut them, and a man had to sit on them and press 'with all the weight of his body to make them shut'—so that for a time, afterwards, Dyall had been unable to walk. Bishop, who was with Casement as an interpreter, confirmed Dyall's account; and the marks, Casement observed, still remained. Dyall also described how Normand had compelled him to kill an Indian who had refused to carry his load. The Indian had been 'thrown on the ground by Normand and himself, his legs distended and apart, Normand holding the legs apart while he, Dyall, beat the man with a stick between the legs, and killed him.' At a full meeting of the Commission that afternoon Dyall's evidence was read over, and confirmed by Bishop. Tizon, who was present, 'practically chucked up the sponge and admitted things were very bad and must be changed'. Sweeping reforms, he promised Casement that evening, would be carried out; and he repeated his promise the following day to the Commission.

Casement felt he had probably done all he could do; but he had not forgotten how the fact that he had visited only certain regions of the Congo had been used to suggest that what he had seen was exceptional; so he went on. At the next station they visited, there was another echo of the Congo tour. The agent, Velarde, had laid on a dance, as Lejesme had done, to show how happy the Indians were. They were happy—at the dance; but many of them arrived naked enough to 'show clear marks of flogging; one small boy, a child, quite recent red weals unhealed'. And two days later, while the members of the Commission were off with Tizon at a demonstration of how rubber was tapped, Casement managed to persuade the Barbadians to talk. Stanley

Lewis, who had himself been flogged by Fonseca when he refused to flog Indians, recalled how he had often seen Indians die, as a result of their punishment: 'the wounds would get maggots in them and then fester, and the house even became fouler smelling for the number of people in the condition. They would then be taken away and shot'. And Stanley Sealy described how Augusto Jimenez had taken an Indian woman who had refused to disclose where her tribe were, and hung her up over a fire; 'big bladders (blisters) I see on her skin up here' (he pointed to his thighs). When she still refused to talk, he had her head cut off. 'I shall never forget the effect it produced on me,' Casement noted, about Sealy's evidence. 'It was told with a simple truthfulness, and even grace of simplicity, that would have convinced anyone in the English-speaking world of the man's absolute good faith.'

On hearing the evidence of Lewis and Sealy even Seymour Bell, the last member of the Commission to remain unconvinced, had to agree that the allegations had been justified. And at each station they visited, the story was the same. The worst section was Armando Normand's — 'a loathsome monster', Casement found; 'absolutely filthy' with his harem of seven squalid 'wives'. A Barbadian there, Westerman Leavine, claimed that Normand had killed many hundreds of Indians during the six years he had been in charge of a station: 'by many kinds of torture; cutting off their heads and limbs, and burying them alive. He more than once saw Normand have Indians' hands and legs tied together, and the men or women thus bound thrown alive on a fire . . . he saw Normand on one occasion take three native men and tie them together in a line, and then with his Mauser rifle shoot all of them with one bullet.' But he and the other Barbadians did not dare to protest, because there were no Peruvian officials or magistrates in the Putumayo to whom they could appeal.

It was hateful, Casement felt, to have to be the guest of the agents the Barbadians were denouncing; but there was no alternative accommodation. Their stations, too, were abominable, as was the weather, and the food. He began to suffer from severe eye trouble, as well as from the attentions of the sandflies. But so long as there remained sections to visit, and Barbadians to interview, he was determined to stay on with the Commission. The tour continued until October 28th, when he returned with the Commissioners to the company's Putumayo base at La

Chorrera; and there, he made up his mind to 'buy' a couple of young Indian boys, Ricardo and Omarino, and bring them back with him to England to give them their freedom, and an education. An Indian youth, Aredomi, also begged to be allowed to leave the Putumayo with him—'a very fine lad, would like to take him'; and the discovery, when they went swimming, that Aredomi had 'a big one' was a further inducement. The tour, like the steamer journeys, had provided him with only the pleasures of a voyeur ('saw Andokes bathing, big thick one, as I thought') and agreeable memories of João.

He had been briefed to concern himself with the fate of British subjects in the Putumayo; and at this point he received a tactful reminder from the Foreign Office that there was nothing to show from his despatches that British subjects had experienced any ill-treatment. Now the tour was over, he could devote more time to their grievances; and he put his knowledge of accountancy—acquired when he was working for Elder Dempster, and for the Sanford expedition—to effective use. The Barbadians had been brought over on two-year contracts; but as they were not permitted to leave until they had got out of the company's debt, the company had ingeniously arranged to keep them indebted. They had been encouraged to buy such supplies as they needed from the company, on credit, which was then set off against their pay; and the prices they had been charged, even compared with those which Casement had been charged when buying goods from the company in Iquitos, were extortionate, 'in some cases nearly 400 per cent on top'. Some of the men's chits, too, turned out to have been forged; 'the cheating has been colossal'.

Almost all the Barbadians, he was relieved to find, wanted to leave the Putumayo. It would have been difficult, if they had wished to stay, to make a convincing case that they had been maltreated. Leaving the other Commissioners in La Chorrera, he returned to Iquitos, expecting to have a fight on his hands to protect them; so fearful was he for their safety that he left those who wanted to leave Peru downstream, in Brazilian territory, before confronting the Iquitos authorities. But Tizon's reports had had their effect. The sub-Prefect of the Loreto province was there to meet him, to tell him that an inquiry had been ordered from Lima, and that Judge Valcarcel was on his way.

Waiting for the next boat, Casement was left with little to do except play dummy bridge with the British Consul, David Cazes, and his wife—'I am as sick of the Cazes as a man can be!'—and enjoy Ignacio, who had been one of the stewards on the boat coming down from La Chorrera. 'poor Ignacio', he noted sentimentally in his diary when he was about to leave on December 5th; 'never to see again'. The return journey to Para was much quicker, and more agreeable, than the voyage upstream had been; and in Para to meet him was João, with 'a big bunch of flowers, very nice indeed'. But it was very hot, and Casement was not feeling well. He was relieved to find there was a passage to England on a ship leaving only four days later, and he despatched the Indian boys to Barbados, to stay there in charge of a Catholic priest until he could send for them. It was so rough, for most of the way across the Atlantic, that there was nothing to do except play more bridge; and as the *Ambrose* was calling at Cherbourg, early on New Year's Eve, he decided to see in the new year in Paris:

> . . . to Grande Armée; Later, in Champs-Elysées, soldier, and then in B. des Capucines, green hat and small, two last no copper, but Denis 10s. Mild evening, great crowds . . . silly songs being sung, and pretended gaiety, without heart in it. Wrote F.O. life certificate, and so to bed at end of year. Already in 1911.

and with that, the second of the 'black' diaries which were later to be found in London in 1916 ended.

CHAPTER TWO

THE PUTUMAYO REPORT

'You are much to be congratulated'   *1911*

By the time Casement reported back to the Foreign Office, early in 1911, they had already heard through the Peruvian minister in London that his Government had decided to act 'with due energy' in the Putumayo. Louis Mallet, one of the under-secretaries, wrote formally to tell him how pleased Grey was that good had already come of his visit. 'You are much to be congratulated', Mallet added—his reserve having been broken down by hearing Casement's account of the Putumayo tour which, he admitted, haunted him. He asked for a short preliminary report which could be telegraphed to Lima, with a request for immediate action against the offenders; and Casement handed it in on January 7th, along with a warning that the appointment of Valcarcel as the examining judge should not be taken too seriously—it was for form's sake, 'and to keep us quiet'. He also warned that the company, knowing the Commission of Inquiry had got testimony which, if published, could not be upset, would now begin to do everything they could to delay publication. Why, Julio Arana himself had written to ask for a meeting, to get Casement's suggestions for 'the better development of the country's affairs'! This, Casement felt, was 'rather cheeky' and though it might do good 'to meet the rascal', he would not reply until he had heard from Mallet. Mallet replied that he did not feel there would be much to be gained from seeing Arana; and if Casement did, it should only be in the presence of witnesses.

While Casement went ahead with the report, Grey tactfully informed the Peruvian foreign minister about it, adding that the British Government would withhold publication to give the Peruvian authorities time to bring the chief criminals to justice; and when a reply came that the Peruvian Government was determined to enforce justice throughout its territory, he could feel that he had acted with firmness and discretion. But days, and then weeks, passed with no further news; and when eventually Consul Cazes reported, it was to say that the judicial inquiry had not even begun. Judge Valcarcel had returned from Iquitos to Lima, ostensibly because he was ill. Grey irritated, instructed the British Consul in Lima, Lucien Jerome, Chargé d'Affaires while the Ambassador was on leave, to remind the Peruvian authorities that of the criminals were not brought to justice, there would be demands that Casement's report should be published; and if it were published, it would create, for Peru, 'a very bad impression'.

The report was going ahead, but slowly, because Casement found he was not in the mood. 'I am "full up" with horrors at times,' he explained to the Foreign Office at the end of February, 'and it is only the thought of those poor, hunted, gentle beings up there in the forests that keeps me going.' He had gone to Dublin, only to come down with fever in a hotel; and it took time to throw off its effects. He was also depressed by the news from Iquitos. At the beginning of March, however, there was more encouraging news from Peru. The Peruvian Government was appointing a substitute for Judge Valcarcel; and peremptory instructions had been issued to the Iquitos Prefect that the Putumayo criminals should be arrested. When Casement returned to London, it was to receive once again the Foreign Office's warm congratulations on the success of his mission.

The satisfaction was short-lived. A copy of the Peruvian Government's organ *El Diario*, forwarded to the Foreign Office, was found to contain a eulogy of Arana, coupled with the announcement that he had been appointed the official Peruvian representative at the forthcoming International Rubber Exhibition, about to be held in London. The appointment, Mallet felt, was an outrage; and he was even angrier when he heard from the Foreign Office's commercial department that the patron of the exhibition was to be the Prince of Wales. 'Arana,' he wrote undiplomatically, 'is a criminal of the most appalling type and ought to be hanged.' He even asked the legal department whether Arana could be arrested, and charged with murder, if he arrived in England. As a Peruvian citizen, the department replied, Arana could not be charged with murder committed in Peru. But there was nothing to stop him being declared *persona non grata*, by the exhibition authorities; and Grey agreed that they should be instructed to inform him he would not be welcome—though without involving the Foreign Office.

On March 17th Casement delivered his report, followed four days later by a transcript of the evidence of the Barbadians. The report began with a brief survey of the topography of the Putumayo, and a description of the Indian tribes who lived there—he had been careful to read up all the available literature on the subject, which was not extensive—designed to show that the Indians were not (as the Peruvian Amazon Company had alleged) bloodthirsty—far from it: 'I believe it is a fact that the Amazon Indian is averse to bloodshed, and is thoughtless rather than cruel.' The Peruvian Amazon Company, in fact, had taken advantage of their docility to exploit them ruthlessly. The Indians were not paid for collecting rubber; or if they were, the payment was derisory. They worked because if the amount they collected was less than the amount they had been told to collect, they were flogged. The Amazon Indian had a natural timidity, Casement had found, an inherent dislike of being flogged that 'rendered this form of punishment one specially indicated for the end in view—namely, to terrorise him into compliance with his captors' wishes'. But this only encouraged the company's agents, whose salary was based on the amount collected, to push up the amount of rubber required for each Indian until only the most energetic, and the luckiest, could fulfil his quota. The consequences in the Putumayo had been the same as in the Free State. Casement then described what he had seen, and recorded in his diary; and concluded with the estimate that the methods adopted by the Peruvian Amazon Company had 'cut down the Indian population by possibly three fourths of its former total', and gravely injured the economic resources of the region.

'In the hollow of our hand'   1911

It must have been immediately obvious to anybody in the Foreign Office who read the report that it was not, strictly speaking, what Casement had been asked to provide. It told far more about the wrongs inflicted by British subjects on the Indians, than about the wrongs inflicted on British subjects by the Peruvian Amazon Company. Still, the company was British; and the account of the treatment of the Indians was so horrifying that it would have been difficult to say it was none of Bri-

tain's business. The Foreign Office were more concerned about
its tone, in places. The Congo Report had been written in studi-
ously moderate language. So, when it appeared, was the Putumayo Report; but this was only after some passages had been
removed. This time, Casement had been unable to resist indignant asides—'What lying there has been! And those scoun-
drels accuse Whiffen and Hardenburg of lying and
"blackmailing", forsooth!' This and similar passages were removed, making the report seem more objective than it had
really been.

Compared to the report on the Congo, too, it had one serious
limitation. Casement did not ignore the influence of 'the system',
but he concentrated so heavily on its cruel consequences that
his intention appeared to be to rouse indignation against the
immediate perpetrators, Macedo, Normand, and the rest. In
the Congo Report, he had begged for the names of the Free
State agents not to be disclosed, because they were the victims
of the system; in the Putumayo Report he named the Peruvian
Amazon Company agents and urged that they must be rounded
up and punished. Their activities, admittedly, had been more
vicious than that of the Free State's agents. But they were just
as much victims of the system.

With the report in hand, the Foreign Office felt renewed
confidence. Grey so far forgot his deference to business firms as
to send a sharp note to the Peruvian Amazon Company's
offices in London, rebuking them for their continued inaction.
The news, too, came in from Peru that Romulo Paredes, chosen
to replace Judge Valcarcel, was about to leave for the Putumayo,
and that warrants were out for six of the men Casement had
accused. But the effect was soon spoiled by a despatch from
Consul Cazes. Only one of the six, and not an important one, had
lingered in Iquitos long enough to be arrested; and he had been
released on bail. And in Lima, Consul Jerome was helpless. He
still believed in the good faith of the Peruvian Government: but
the rainy season had been disrupting their telegraphic communication with Iquitos. 'There always seems to be something',
Grey complained, 'to prevent them taking energetic action.'

He might have said, 'someone', for on April 18th another
issue of President Leguia's organ El Diairio reached the Foreign
Office, containing a denunciation of the British for their insult
to Arana over the International Rubber Exhibition, attributing

the Putumayo atrocity stories to the inventiveness of the Colombians, and saying that Peruvian affairs were no business of Britain's.

In similar circumstances over the Congo, Casement had been critical of the Foreign Office's willingness to believe the Free State excuses, and ready to tell them they were wasting their time if they hoped for any action. But now, he was becoming involved in a project which, he believed, might make it unnecessary to rely on the good faith of the Peruvian authorities. So long as the Aranas had a stake in the Peruvian Amazon Company, they must want it to remain profitable. 'We have the company in the hollow of our hand', he reminded Grey on April 17th: 'they must do what you indicate, I think.' The aim must therefore be not to destroy the company—which would simply allow Arana to start afresh in the Putumayo 'with as many of the old spirits of evil as he can gather round him', but to keep the company in being under the Foreign Office's control. Grey was not prepared to allow the Foreign Office to be directly involved, but he liked the idea; and when Casement came back to London in the middle of May, he was told that the Peruvian Amazon Company had been informed 'unofficially and privately' that his services were to be at their disposal.

He was duly asked to come to their next board meeting—which he would do, he told Mallet, only if there was a shorthand writer present. He was taking no chances 'with men in such a desperate hole'. When he turned up for the meeting, at the beginning of June, there was no note-taker of any kind. At his insistence, one was sent for; but she did not arrive until the meeting was nearly over, and her usefulness could be gauged, he observed, 'from the fact that she describes me as His Britannical Majesty's Consul'. And the meeting, which had been chaotic, convinced him that the board simply did not have the ability to carry out any scheme of reform. They were entirely in Arana's hands—for if they purged him, he could destroy the company. Such was Arana's confidence that he had actually written to Casement expressing his gratitude for the help, and his astonishment at the Putumayo revelations which, he claimed, had come as a complete surprise to him. 'Impudent!', Gerald Spicer commented, agreeing there was obviously no chance of reform while Arana remained. But Mallet was inclined to think that Arana might still be useful. The Peruvian Government must surely be disturbed, and they would work on him, if only to prevent publication of the report. As there was to be another board meeting later in the month, with the members of the Commission of Inquiry, which Casement could attend, it was decided to wait and see what happened then.

In the meantime, telegraphic communication between Lima and Iquitos had been restored; but the information Jerome had to transmit as a result was discouraging. Arana's chief agents, almost without exception, had been allowed to escape—some of them across the border into Brazil—taking several dozen Indians of both sexes which they would be able to sell, as slaves, for about £50 each. Soon after, Cazes wrote to say that the reforms recommended by the company's Commission of Inquiry before they left the Putumayo, which the company in Iquitos had agreed to introduce, were to be abandoned, because they had led to a falling off in the quantity of rubber collected. Still haunted by Casement's story, Mallet was furious. There was nothing for it, he argued, but to show what a formidable weapon the British Government still possessed—the report; and two copies of it, translated into Spanish, were sent to Lima. They should be showed to the Peruvian Foreign Minister, Jerome was instructed, with a broad hint that His Majesty's Government would be unable to resist parliamentary pressure for publication unless the Peruvian Government could give more definite assurances that they were taking action to end the abuses which the report described.

Sir Roger   *June 1911*

It was five months since the threat to publish had first been made, and they had been frustrating months for Casement. Now, he was to be compensated. On June 15th, 1911, he heard from Grey that he was to receive a knighthood.

When he had sent in accounts of his Putumayo expenses it had been decided, unprecedentedly, that he had not asked for enough. He should receive some extra emolument, Mallet thought, 'or be rewarded in another way for a most arduous and dangerous service'. Nicolson had replied that this was being considered; and a knighthood (which, as he already had a C.M.G., was the least he could be offered) was decided on—

perhaps because it would be easier to obtain than any extra emolument.

The news was less of an embarrassment to Casement than the C.M.G. had been. A knighthood was not just a routine token; it was a real honour—at least when given to somebody for services of the kind he had rendered; and he could easily be persuaded that it was very desirable that services of that kind, to humanity rather than to party, should be recognised. He was also, at this time, less directly involved with Irish affairs than he had been when he received the C.M.G., partly because of his absorption with the Putumayo, but also because during most of what little time he had spent in Ireland, since his return, he had been ill. Although he had lost none of his desire that Ireland should be independent, his separatism had, for the time, lost its edge. He expressed—or rationalised—what he felt in a letter to Alice Green:

My dear Woman of the Good Woods *
Your congrats have been the best, for you alone have seen that there was an Irish side to it all. What you say is true—although few will believe it, can possibly believe that I have not worked for this—for a 'distinction' and 'honour'—or whatever they call it, instead of, in reality, deeply desiring *not* to get it. In this case, it was like the C.M.G.—I couldn't help it at all—and could not possibly fling back something offered like that. Yes, it was Sir E. Grey—I had a charming letter from him telling me it was he who did it. But there are many in Ireland will think of me as a traitor—and when I think of that country, and of them, I feel I am.

Had Asquith's Home Rule bill, introduced that summer, gone through both Houses of Parliament without difficulty, and become law, Casement could have considered his knighthood as much of an honour to Ireland as Alice Green felt it was. Later,

---

* A variation on Casement's more usual salutation to her, 'Dear Woman of the Three Cows', taken from James Clarence Mangan's version of an old Irish ballad.

> O woman of three cows, agrah!
>   Don't let your tongue thus rattle,
> O don't be saucy, don't be stiff
>   Because you may have cattle.

when the resistance of Ulster and the Lords delayed it, his
loyalties began again to conflict to the point where he could
see that taking it had been a mistake. But at the time, he was
content to admit to being a traitor to Ireland—as, later, he was
content to admit to being a traitor to England. He went on:

> How I should have rejoiced if I could have said to the King
> what is really in my heart instead of the perfunctory words
> of thanks (cold and formal enough).

The words of thanks, as he put them in his letter to Grey,
were:

> I find it very hard to choose the words, in which to make
> acknowledgement of the honour done to me by the King.
> I am much moved at the proof of confidence and apprecia-
> tion of my services on the Putumayo, conveyed to me by your
> letter, wherein you tell me the King has been graciously
> pleased upon your recommendation to confer upon me the
> honour of knighthood.
> I am indeed grateful to you for this signal assurance of your
> personal esteem and support and very deeply sensible of the
> honour done me by His Majesty.
> I would beg that my humble duty might be presented to
> His Majesty, when you may do me the honour to convey to
> him my deep appreciation of the honour he has been so
> graciously pleased to confer on me.

Read in conjunction with his letter to Alice Green, the wording of the letter explains itself. He was uneasy about the award,
but he was moved by the fact it had been given to him. He
would have liked to express that emotion; but he considered
himself bound, as always throughout his official career, by the
formal diplomatic usages. 'Graciously pleased' and 'deeply
sensible' and 'humble duty' were obligatory phrases for him, on
such occasions. What he would have preferred to have done
would have been to write to King George as he wrote to Alice
Green, expressing his appreciation in his own words. But pro-
tocol did not allow him to. He must write through Grey, in the
prescribed formulae. At his trial, and frequently thereafter, the
wording of the letter was to be used against him, with the im-

plication being that it was sycophantic—too fulsome. One of the sadder ironies of his life was that when he wrote it, his only regret was that it did not sound grateful enough.

Ex-Officio   1911

There was little more Casement could do that July—though he was able to help the Anti-Slavery Society in their preparations for a Putumayo Reform Campaign by bringing to their meetings the two Indian boys, Ricardo and Omarino, who had arrived from Barbados. They entranced people with whom they came in contact, especially his London landlady—he was staying in lodgings in Philbeach Gardens—and William Rothenstein, who began to paint a portrait of them. But the attention they attracted, Casement was disappointed to find, was not of a kind to do much for the finances of the Putumayo cause. Perhaps it would have been better had they been less attractive— the battered victims of a Normand.

He still had hopes, though, that he would be able to achieve some results through the Peruvian Amazon Company, now that he had an *ex-officio* seat on the board. The report of its own Commission of Inquiry was completed in June, confirming his own in all respects; and he went to the board meeting at the end of the month determined to press for decisive action. The outcome was discouraging. Nothing was decided; none of the directors (Julio Arana was still absent) seemed to know what was happening; and the only information disclosed was that a director, Pablo Zumaeta, had secretly mortgaged £65,000 worth of company stock to his sister—Mrs. Julio Arana. Casement's suggestion that someone should be sent to report on the state of the company in Putumayo was considered difficult, because there were insufficient funds; and his suggestion that the British directors should dip into their own pockets for the purpose was not enthusiastically received (it also alarmed Grey, who minuted that he hoped it had been made clear this was a personal recommendation, 'involving the Secretary of State in no responsibility whatever').

Casement was not involving Grey. Gradually, he was coming round to the view that he himself would be the saviour of the company, and of the Indians. As he told Cadbury, the aim must be to set up a real commercial business within the company's present structure; and at the next board meeting, early in July, he began to take charge, persuading the reluctant directors that they must send some representative to Iquitos to look after their interests on the spot. When, a week later, he had an effusive letter from Arana congratulating him on his proposals, and suggesting the formation of a Trust to manage the company's remaining assets, he felt confident enough to reply curtly that he did not propose to discuss the subject. Working through the board, he was coming to believe, he could begin to handle the whole Putumayo situation himself.

But he was ignorant of the company's position, and innocent in financial dealings—as he was quickly to discover. At the next board meeting, he was informed that the company was on the verge of bankruptcy. If it went bankrupt, the Foreign Office would have no further excuse for intervention; nor would he. Only one man could save it, now: Arana. He was at the meeting. They had met once a few years before, Casement realised, at the captain's table on a liner. Arana was friendly, and apparently anxious to be co-operative. Only three days after having written to say he would have nothing further to do with Arana, Casement now told Grey that he must stay with the board—even adding that he thought Arana was 'sincere in his pledges'.

But at this stage, the Lima situation appeared suddenly to take a turn for the better. Prodded by a succession of questions in the Commons, Grey had said that the report would be published if the Peruvian Government failed to act. The Peruvian Government gave way. On July 14th President Leguia told Jerome that they were anxious to take whatever action His Majesty's Government might suggest. Perhaps the Foreign Office would be kind enough to furnish them with draft legislation for the Putumayo?

Encouraging news, too, arrived from Washington. Casement had heard that his report had been sent to the State Department, but he had not expected them to do anything. 'Some of their people care,' he told Cadbury, 'but far more don't care—especially where it is a question of "injuns".' There was also the Monroe Doctrine—and one of Grey's guiding rules as Foreign Secretary was not merely to accept it, but to allow that the doctrine was—as he once put it—'whatever the United States says it is'. But, on July 17th, a despatch arrived from Bryce to say that he had had an opportunity to discuss the Putumayo with the Secretary of State, Philander Knox; 'I trust now I have been able to arouse them to a sense of their duty to humanity'. A week later, Jerome cabled from Lima that Paredes had returned to Iquitos after his tour of the Putumayo, and his preliminary report fully corroborated Casement's. Two hundred further warrants had been issued for the arrest of the criminals concerned; among those who had actually been arrested was Arana's brother-in-law Zumaeta. Indictments would be heard before Judge Valcarcel, now back in Iquitos; and the only worry was whether the local gaol would be large enough to hold all the arrested men. 'This is by far the most satisfactory news we have had,' Campbell minuted. To Casement, it seemed 'almost too good to be true'.

Now was the time, he felt, for him to return to Iquitos. 'I am quite willing to go out at once', he told the Foreign Office, 'if it is thought I could be of service in this direction. I think I might be.' There was a suitable pretext; some of those for whom the warrants were out were Barbadians—British subjects. No additional expense would be incurred, except the cost of his return ticket, because he was still on full consular salary. Spicer thought the idea a good one. Casement's suggestion that there should be a full-time Consul in Iquitos had been accepted by the Treasury, and George Michell, who had for a while been Consul in Boma, had been selected. As he was not due to leave until the autumn, Casement could undertake the task until he arrived. Grey gave his authorisation.

CHAPTER THREE

IQUITOS REVISITED

Failure of a mission   1911

Once again Casement was both absorbed and happy. The Foreign Office had done all he had asked them to do; and in spite of setbacks and frustrations, it had really begun to look as if the strategy had been sound. He got on well with the men he had been dealing with—Spicer might be an 'awful ass' but at least they were on terms of amiable banter. 'If you even attempt to "Sir Roger" me again', Spicer was told after offering his congratulations, 'I'll enter into an alliance with the Aranas *and* Pablo Zumaeta to cut you off some day in the woods of St. James's Park, and convert you into a rubber worker for our joint profit!' And although his Putumayo report had not been published, everybody who had been shown it had been impressed, and moved.

His only cause for concern, before he left in mid-August, was about what should be done with the Indian boys. He had thought of sending one of them to St. Enda's, the Irish school which Patrick Pearse had founded near Dublin; and Pearse had written that he would be glad to take him, for £45 a year—which 'would cover *everything*'. But now that he was going back to Peru, Casement decided it would be wiser to take them with him, and find a good home for them in Iquitos. Cadbury, on whom he had come to rely—for financial assistance, in the case of the boys, as well as for advice—approved; the boys would be very lonely, if left behind in England. Rothenstein came to see them off, regretting that he had not had time to finish the portrait; and they left for Barbados, where Casement hoped to see some of the former Putumayo workers, before going on to Iquitos. He did— but not those he had hoped to see. He was greeted on landing by one of the criminals, Andreas O'Donnell—'the best of a bad lot, who had flogged and killed for rubber rather than for sport'. As the cheque for £2,000 with which O'Donnell had been paid off by the company had not been honoured, he was now 'perfectly miserable'; Casement even felt rather sorry for him.

When Casement reached Para early in September, it was to hear that some of the worst of the Putumayo criminals, including Fonseca and Montt, were still at large in Brazil, just across the frontier from Peru. They, at least—he suggested to the Foreign Office—could easily be dealt with. They need not be extradited; all that was needed was an expulsion order from Rio. And when he reached Iquitos, his good spirits were fully restored by a copy of Paredes's journal *Oriente*, which he enclosed in a letter to Spicer: ' By far the most interesting article,' he wrote—facetiously, but with evident self-satisfaction—'you will agree with me, is the one upon myself. This is one of Paredes's finest flights, I am told—it is the work of his own pen and speaks worlds for my reforming influence on the Putumayo—and elsewhere.' He also saw the Prefect of Loreto, who eulogised him to his face; and a few days later, he was introduced to Paredes himself, who was full of wrath against Arana, and 'really takes a very sensible view'. The brother-in-law, Pablo Zumaeta, was being proceeded against; though he was temporarily at liberty, on appeal, Paredes felt that he had no case.

All this was encouraging; but it was not connected with Casement's mission, which had been to keep an eye on the company. But the company was now, he heard, in liquidation; Arana was away; and Paredes advised him against going to the Putumayo, as the risk that he would be murdered was too great. Why, then, did he stay on? He had the excuse that he was awaiting the arrival of Consul Michell; but his 1911 diary suggests another answer. From January until he left for South America in August, he had not bothered to keep it up, using his cash accounts book, instead, for such comments on the days' or nights' events as he felt moved to make. But from his arrival at the mouth of the Amazon, the diary came into regular use again, in anticipation of what he was going to do when he reached Para. He would go to the park, 'when I hope almost at once to come across a good *big* one'. And for the next fortnight —the difficulty of getting his luggage out of the Customs providing an excuse for the delay—he pursued good big ones with a dedication that was almost obsessional—and wildly dangerous: 'Dinner at 8 p.m.', he noted on the 16th, 'and out to cemetery and met Friend who entered *at once*. Huge *testi-*

minhos. Police passing behind paling—but he laughed and went deeper. $10.' João was still around, and they met occasionally; but for Casement, absorbed in pursuit of physical sensation, the mechanics of the act and the dimensions of the actors had become the chief consideration.

In Manaos, where he stayed for five days, it was the same; and in Iquitos, once he had finished his round of calls. For much of the two months that he stayed there he was ill, with colds and indigestion and sciatica; but even when he was confined to his room, he watched avidly all that went on from his window— 'long and thick about 7″ wobbling down right thigh'—and began a protracted seduction of José, 'his lovely Indian face suffused with glorious Indian blood, and eyes glistening', in the hope that José could be induced to leave Iquitos, and come to Rio with him.

It would have been out of character for Casement to have decided to return to Iquitos simply because of the sexual opportunities the mission would provide him. He was not that calculating. But they may have provided the lure, which, even if he was unaware of it, had put the idea into his mind. He could not have known, before he left England, just how helpless he would be when he arrived there; but while he was there, the uselessness of his visit was brought home to him. On November 1st, he heard that Zumaeta had been released, and Judge Valcarcel dismissed—clear enough indication that his presence in Iquitos was not regarded as of any significance. Only eight of the Putumayo men were now left with charges against them, and none of them had been on his list of the chief criminals. His mission had been a failure. So long as the courts in Iquitos remained corrupt, there was nothing that he or anybody else could hope to achieve there. The only chance, he wrote to tell the Foreign Office, was for the Lima Government to send somebody there with powers to deal with the situation; 'and in all Peru I doubt if there is an honest or really capable official— Cazes says not—and he ought to know'.

On his way back down the Amazon, when he reached the place where it had been arranged that Fonseca and Montt would be arrested and put back over the frontier into Peru, he heard that they had been warned in time, and had escaped. In Para, there was depressing news of a different kind: a letter from Tyrrell to tell him that the consulate in Buenos Aires, where he might have gone, had been given to Mackie of the Congo—'alack, alack, so I am done out of that. What a shame!' After consoling himself in the park, he sailed for Barbados, spending Christmas on board.

Consul Jerome   1911

The Foreign Office for a time remained in ignorance of what was happening in Peru. Their hopes were actually raised, in Casement's absence, by the news from Consul Jerome, in Lima. 'Tell me what His Majesty's Government want me to do,' President Leguia had begged him. 'Telegraph at once my *personal assurance* to your Government that I will take any action His Majesty's Government think should be taken.' The State Department's criticisms, too, transmitted to Leguia by Clay Howard, the American minister in Lima, had had their effect, Jerome, who had briefed Howard on what to say, preened himself on his success: 'I need hardly point out to you the almost feminine relish of praise possessed by the Ibero–Americans, and how they can by careful coaxing be induced to take a line of action that all the logic, right and justice in the world would never persuade them to follow.'

Jerome's letter, however, was delayed. When it reached the Foreign Office at the beginning of October, it was accompanied by a later despatch in which the Consul, crestfallen, had to admit that he had over-estimated his powers as a coaxer. He had just heard that Judge Valcarcel had again left Iquitos, and that 'a more convenient magistrate' had been appointed in his place. He had also discovered, belatedly, that the Peruvian Government, without informing him, had imposed a punitive tax on exports of rubber from Peru, clearly designed to drive out British traders. The Government, he was now compelled to realise, had been fooling him; they were 'a set of very crooked, tricky gentlemen'.

The time had finally arrived, Grey decided, to tell the Peruvian Government that Casement's report must be published. It was, in fact, the fourth time in nine months that the time had arrived. But again, he changed his mind. Jerome was instructed merely to convey to the Peruvian Government that the news from Iquitos had come as 'a most painful surprise'.

What followed continued to be painful, though is ceased to

be surprising; a cable from Jerome on November 1st informing
the Foreign Office that Judge Valcarcel was in London. Far from
being run out of Iquitos, he had presumably accepted a substantial payment to leave, and, was now enjoying a holiday in
Europe on the proceeds. The Peruvian Government, Spicer
minuted, 'will never be got to take any vigorous action against
the Aranas'—a view confirmed when the Ambassador, des Graz,
arrived back in Lima early in December after his leave, and
cabled that not merely had the Government there taken no
action on Paredes's recommendations; they still, or so they
claimed, had 'no official cognizance' of his report. In the meantime, too, the Foreign Office had been subjected to yet another
humiliation by the Peruvian Amazon Company. When a liquidator was appointed in London, it was announced that he would
be—Julio Arana. Grey felt he had had no power to intervene; it
was a matter for the shareholders. All he could do, he felt, was
issue yet another warning:

> The release of Zumaeta, the neglect to send telegraphic orders
> for the arrest of Montt and Fonseca, the failure to arrest
> Zimenes and Macedo, and the futile pretext for disregarding
> Paredes's report convince me that the Peruvian Government
> intend to disregard their obligations to the Putumayo, and
> that they never had any intention of carrying out their assur-
> ances to His Majesty's Government.
>
> It will therefore become necessary, sooner or later, to pub-
> lish Casement's report, as well as the repeated referrals which
> I have made to the Peruvian Government and the manner in
> which they have been disregarded.

Still, it might be wise—Spicer suggested—to take no action
until Casement returned. Grey accepted his advice.

Washington   1912

When Casement left Iquitos he realised there was little to show
that the Putumayo Indians were any safer as a result of his
labours on their behalf. Pondering their future on his return
journey, he had one of his inspirations. If Britain could not
intervene successfully, the United States might. He would go

there on his journey back to England, and see what could be achieved.

He arrived early in the new year of 1912—to find himself fortunate in the composition of the British embassy in Washington, at the time. James Bryce was an Irishman—a Protestant Ulsterman, but a Liberal; he had been Chief Secretary for Ireland before his Washington appointment. And he was deeply concerned about South America. He was actually writing a book on the subject; when it appeared, later in the year, its description of the effect of the rubber traders was clearly derived from Casement's report. Under Bryce, there was Alfred Mitchell Innes. He and Casement took to each other immediately they met, and as their correspondence was to show, over the next few months, he was to feel as deeply about the Putumayo as the Ambassador did. And there was George Young, who was later to describe what happened:

> Peru appealed to Washington, then very pan-American. Casement had started home with a dossier that would have given out stunt press material for a month, while the shade of President Monroe began to loom large in the American yellow journals. 'Get Casement up here', said the Ambassador, and he was accordingly intercepted and brought north in a cruiser. President Taft was lured to dinner in the embassy and led away to a quiet corner where Casement was let loose on him. A queer picture they made—the tall Celt, haggard and livid from the Putumayo swamps, fixing with glittering black eyes the burly rubicund Anglo-Saxon. It was like a black snake fascinating a wombat. But Putumayo gave no further trouble in Washington.

The cruiser interception may have been memory's embellishment, on Young's part; but the immediate results of the visit were as he described them. Casement—Bryce wrote to tell Grey on January 12th—'was able to create a personal interest among the higher authorities, which gives strong grounds for believing that publication of the report will be welcomed by the United States Government'. This was the time, Bryce felt, for the two Governments to get together, so that they could begin to put joint pressure on Peru. A few days later, his optimism was shown to be justified. The Secretary of State informed him that a cable was being sent to the United States minister in Lima, telling him to draw the Peruvian Government's attention to the fact that corrupt local influences had led to the dropping of court actions against the Putumayo criminals, and to say informally that unless drastic action were taken, world opinion might be influenced by 'an account of that iniquitous system'—a reference to Casement's report—into believing that Peru 'had shown herself unable properly to exercise sovereign rights over disputed regions'—a broad hint that the United States might contemplate siding with Colombia on the boundary issue. This was all the more remarkable, Mitchell Innes wrote to tell Casement, because Peru had been considered America's great mainstay in the south; the only real friend the U.S. had among the Latin Americans. Gratefully, Grey decided to suggest to the State Department that the timing of the publication of Casement's report should be a joint British/United Sates decision.

CHAPTER FOUR

PUBLICATION

'Go for reform!'   1912

On his way back to London, Casement wrote a memorandum
setting out his views on future policy, now that the Americans
were ready to co-operate. The first step, he thought, should be
to arrange for a mixed commission of United States, British
and Brazilian consular representatives to go to Iquitos to begin
an inquiry. 'As we have quite failed to secure punishment let
us drop it, and go for reform! And let the first step to reform
be the publication of what it is we are seeking to have reformed.'
Paredes's report, he suggested, would provide ideas. He was
translating a copy Paredes had given him, and he would give
the Foreign Office a précis.

Paredes's report closely followed Casement's, but was even
more outspoken; and the Foreign Office accepted that it might
provide the basis for an agreed policy. But first, it would have
to be shown to the State Department. This raised a difficulty:
Paredes had given it to Casement in confidence, and he might
be embarrassed if it was found to have been seen both by the
Foreign Office and the State Department before it had been
published in Lima. And it had still not even arrived there—
though it was 'six months yesterday', Casement recalled, 'since
Paredes had handed it in to the Prefect at Iquitos'. Surely it was
incredible that Lima should still not have received a copy?

To the Foreign Office, nothing which happened in Iquitos or
Lima was any longer incredible; but the delay over Paredes's
report now appeared of little importance. To Grey, the great
thing was that since Casement's visit to Washington, the Putumayo was strengthening rather than, as he had feared, weakening Anglo-American accord. On March 7th, Louis Mallet wrote
to Casement to transmit a message from Grey that his proceedings throughout the second tour had been 'entirely approved'.
His request for reimbursement of the expenses of his Washington diversion, too, were accepted—the Foreign Office's recom-

mendation to the Treasury explaining that although he had not
been authorised to go there, 'the results of his visit, which was
of great advantage to the public service, had been highly commended by the Secretary of State'. The Lima Government,
admittedly, was inclined to prevaricate; when des Graz went
with Clay Howard to see the Peruvian foreign minister, he told
them confidentially that Paredes's honesty was not above suspicion—he was alleged to have been trying to blackmail Arana.
The Iquitos proceedings against the Putumayo criminals, too,
had been delayed because the relevant documents were being
forwarded to Lima via New York, 'for safety' (the actual trial,
Casement commented, could be expected to begin 'long after we
are dead, and the last Putumayo Indian has been gathered, in
fragments, to his fathers'). But this, Grey felt, no longer mattered, now that Washington was taking the Putumayo seriously;
and on March 24th Bryce cabled from Washington to say that
the Secretary of State had decided to leave it to His Majesty's
Government to decide when to publish, and broadly hinted that
he thought it would be in their interest to publish soon. Grey,
who had decided to make a 'Blue Book' out of all the relevant
material, including correspondence and memoranda, ordered
it to be prepared for the printers.

The Peruvian Government made one last bid to delay publication. At the beginning of April, they announced that they were
setting up a commission to investigate rubber production on
the Amazon; and Clay Howard reported his view that they were
sincere. According to Jerome, Howard was not himself sincere:
'he never goes to his office, but spends his time in the different
business houses in Lima trying to work up business for the
American exporters'; but the State Department was inclined to
listen to him. Mitchell Innes, who had just seen some of the
pictures of scarred native children taken on the Putumayo tour
('I nearly wept,' he wrote to tell Casement, 'and so did the
Ambassador'), gave Grey a chance to press on with publication
by informing the State Department that it was already being
proceeded with; but Grey warily ordered another postponement.

In the old days, Casement would have exerted himself to
dissuade the Foreign Office from delaying any longer. But he
was not in a fighting mood. He had been ill again, in April, for
nearly a fortnight, with a throat infection; and he was deter-

mined to take a holiday during May, to tour Germany. He told the Anti-Slavery Society before he left that he hoped his report would be published shortly, but that this would depend on the State Department. It can hardly have surprised him to find, when he returned, that no date had yet been fixed. By then, however, the Lima 'Commission of Inquiry' had proved to be a farce—four of the five members declined to serve on it. When a formal request for further delay reached the Foreign Office, the reason the Peruvian Government gave—that Paredes was going to the Putumayo to prepare a fresh report, which would be ready 'early next year'—had the opposite effect to the one intended; the device was too transparent. All that Grey now asked for was an excuse for publication. Casement provided it. If the Peruvian Government were sincere in their protestations that they wanted reforms, he pointed out, they ought to welcome publication of his report, as it would strengthen their hand when they came to introduce them. 'This is also my view,' Grey commented; and he ordered that it should be the line taken in the Government's reply. He hesitated once more, on the brink of publication, writing to Mitchell Innes at the end of June to say he would not go ahead with publication if the State Department had some compelling reason for delay; but the *New York Sun* contrived to put an end to his worries. It had somehow acquired a copy of the report, which gave it a welcome scoop. On July 13th, 1912, almost three years after the articles on the Devil's Paradise had appeared in *Truth*—the *Putumayo Blue Book* appeared.

'An appalling iniquity'   1912

The immediate impact of Casement's Congo report, at the time it appeared, had been small. The report on the Putumayo created a sensation. *The Times* gave it two columns, and a long editorial: the horrors revealed, it claimed, 'must stir the anger and compassion of all who are not utterly dead to the sense of humanity and of right . . . Sir Roger Casement has deserved well of his countrymen and of mankind by the ability and the zeal with which he has investigated under very difficult conditions an appalling iniquity.' The *Daily News*, nominating Casement as the 'man of the week', had an article on the 'Bayard of the Consular Service', by Morel.

To denounce crime at a distance is a relatively simple task. To track the criminal to his lair in the equatorial forest, to rub shoulders with him round camp fires, to realise he knows it is only you that stands between him and immunity—you, and a few inches of cold steel, which makes no noise . . . to be enervated by fever, and maddened by the bites of stinging flies; to run short of food—and what food! to parch in thirst, to experience the lassitude of damp, moist heat which makes exertion a misery—this is different. And to retain, through all, your clearness of vision, capacity to weigh evidence, self-control and moral strength—this is to pass through the highest test of mental and physical endurance, to attain the most conspicuous point of human achievement.

It was well for the nation, Morel concluded, that it should possess this type of public servant; 'it is even better that the nation should realise that it does, and realising it, be stirred to its inmost fibres by a great example'.

Casement was furious, or claimed to be, about the eulogy; he could still be embarrassed by personal publicity. But he was very satisfied with the press response to the *Putumayo Blue Book*—J. L. Garvin's article in the *Pall Mall Gazette* particularly pleased him. He was receiving offers to write a book on the subject—T. Fisher Unwin and Heinemann both approached him; and he felt that his objective at last had been achieved. 'I believe we have broken the neck of the evil on the Putumayo,' he claimed in a memorandum to the Foreign Office on July 23rd; 'we have broken up the organised band of murderers and torturers and, I hope, now that the horrid truth has been made so evidently public, nothing of the kind can possibly be set up again.' To Gertrude Bannister he wrote even more exultantly: 'I have blown up the Devil's Paradise in Peru. I told you I should—and I have done it. It's a great step forward in human things—the abodes of cruelty are not so secure as they were—and their tenants are getting very scared. Putumayo will be cleansed—although nothing can bring back the murdered tribes—poor souls!' And, as he had hoped, public opinion was stirred, as it had not been since the Congo reform campaign was at its height.

For Grey, however, the reaction was less satisfactory. M.P.s and newspaper editors demanded to know what he proposed to do about this shocking affair, as it was to some extent Britain's responsibility. The *Spectator*, the oldest-established and usually one of the most sober of the weekly journals of opinion, actually called for a blockade of the chief Peruvian ports—'Thank God! we have the power, and we must use it' (to use it would entail sending the fleet up the Amazon, Campbell sourly commented in a Foreign Office minute, to blockade the mouth of the Putumayo river).

Abroad, too, so far from his receiving credit for publishing the *Blue Book*, Grey found it was being exploited for anti-British propaganda. From the Berlin embassy, Lord Granville enclosed cuttings out of German newspapers about the Putumayo, their implication being that as the company responsible was British, Britain was responsible for the atrocities. 'These butcheries,' the organ of the Prussian Lutherans asserted, 'remain an indelible blot on the British name.'

The most awkward question, however, that faced the Government was why, even if nothing could be done in the Putumayo, there could not be proceedings against the Peruvian Amazon Company's directors in Britain? Surely they could be held liable? Grey defended the company: as soon as the matter had been brought to their attention, he told the Commons, they had appointed a Committee of Inquiry. Nobody knew better than Grey that this was untrue; that the directors of the Peruvian Amazon Company had contemptuously rejected his requests for information for almost a year after the *Truth* allegations had appeared. He had covered this up by omitting the correspondence from the *Blue Book*. Casement, who might have given him away, had retreated to Ireland to escape the publicity which he had guessed would follow publication. And when a suspicious M.P. asked why the correspondence had not been included, Grey blandly replied that he had felt it was not really material to the main point at issue.

Anger continued to mount, however, against the company. Early in August, Hensley Henson, a canon of Westminster Abbey, preached a sermon before a very large congregation in which he denounced the company's directors by name; and when he received a solicitor's letter (as the Dean of Hereford had done two years before) he replied that if they seriously meditated legal proceedings, 'they will not lack the requisite encouragement from me'. And in the debate on the Foreign Office estimates on August 1st, which gave M.P.s the chance to discuss the Putu-

mayo—as it had given them the chance, years before, to discuss
the Congo—a Liberal M.P., Joseph King, pointed out that whatever might be thought of Peru's failure to bring the criminals
to justice, many of the horrors had been perpetrated by British
subjects, recruited through a British Government agent, to serve
a British company, the product of whose operations had been
brought to Britain by British ships, to be the raw material of
British manufacturers. It was humiliating and intolerable, in
these circumstances, that the criminals could not be brought to
justice. And—final insult—now that the company was in
liquidation, who had been appointed liquidator? None other
than its manager, Arana!

Grey could find no convincing reply. 'Of all the things I have
ever read that have occurred in modern times', he admitted, 'in
or out of office, the accounts of the brutalities in Putumayo are
the most horrible'; and he went on to praise Casement, whose
presence, he had no doubt, had suspended the atrocities for the
time being, and ensured that they could not begin again without
becoming known. But all the Government could do, he reiterated, was reveal the facts. The reply did not satisfy Grey's critics;
and Asquith, who had succeeded Campbell-Bannerman as
Prime Minister, decided he would have to intervene. He resorted
to a device that Governments had so often utilised in the past to
disarm their critics—at least for a time. On August 6th he announced the setting up of a Select Committee of the House of
Commons to consider the implications of the Putumayo affair,
and to decide if any changes were necessary in the law. As it
would not begin its sessions until after the summer recess, the
move would provide welcome temporary relief.

Consuls on tour   *1912*

That summer of 1912, Casement was at the summit of his official
career. His name, if not quite a household word, was familiar in
Europe and America, as well as in Britain. All that was needed
to crown his work for humanity was that his report should produce a salutary effect—which United States pressure on the
Peruvian Government should help it to do. Then, he could
reasonably hope to be allowed to finish his career in the Consular Service in some healthy and unexacting post, and later
enjoy a well-earned retirement. And in the meantime, he could

occupy himself with a project for which he had secured the Foreign Office's sanction—provided he did not involve them in it: the setting up, in the Putumayo, of a mission.

The difficulty was that in Peruvian law, it had to be a Catholic mission; and the Archbishop of Canterbury, who had warmly congratulated him on the report—'nothing could be better than your marshalling of the appalling facts'—was cool.to the idea. 'Old shifter', Casement commented; but even so sympathetic a friend as Conan Doyle had now become was sceptical; he sent £5, but added 'give me a half-educated flat-foot Baptist for such work'. And when, after the publication of the *Blue Book*, an appeal was launched for £15,000—sponsored by Conan Doyle, the Duke of Norfolk, a member of the Rothschild banking family, and Count Blücher—it promptly encountered Protestant suspicion. 'I think there is mighty little Christianity in any of these "Churches",' Casement complained to Morel; 'a good dose of severe heathenism would be good for mankind.' The sectarian uproar provided an excuse for individuals and institutions whose names would ordinarily have been expected to appear on the list of contributors to a fund of this kind to withhold their cheques. Although £2,000 came in in the first few days, the flow soon became a trickle, and the fund raisers realised they would be lucky if they could get a fifth of the sum they had asked for.

Casement's hopes that his visit to the State Department would have a decisive effect in the United States were also soon disappointed. Canon Hensley Henson, who took the opportunity of a visit to the United States that summer to lecture and preach on the Putumayo, found that his congregations' self-esteem made them reluctant to admit that what was happening in an American sphere of influence could be as bad as what had happened in the Congo; and they also feared that Casement's report might bring commercial free enterprise into disrepute. Without any strong push from public opinion, the House of Representatives was content simply to ask the State Department for more information about the Putumayo; and by then—Mitchell Innes wrote to warn Casement—it was in any case too late to expect any action before the vacation began. Knox contented himself with appropriating the excuse British foreign secretaries had so often used; as the newly-appointed American Consul in Iquitos,

Stewart Fuller, was going on a tour of the Putumayo, judgment should be withheld until he had returned.

From the start, the tour—on which he was accompanied by Consul Michell—was a farce; hilarious, from Arana's point of view. The Consuls had arranged to set off in a Peruvian Government launch in July; but as no launch arrived, they accepted Arana's generous offer of the use of one of his own steamboats. This meant, they found, that they were to be accompanied by a strong force of Peruvian police, under the command of Señor Rey de Castro, the Peruvian Consul-General at Manaos. The excuse given was that the force was needed to protect them, and also, if necessary, to arrest offenders. But Castro had been named by Casement, Michell recalled, as being in Arana's pay. Castro's real function, the Foreign Office immediately realised, was to keep the Consuls from seeing anything Arana did not wish them to see.

Hearing this news, Casement wrote to Spicer light-heartedly to say he would not be surprised to hear that Arana himself was accompanying them. He was. So was his brother-in-law, Zumaeta, and between them they rarely let the Consuls out of their sight. Arana exuded benevolence; his only desire, Michell reported was 'to be called Papa Arana by the women and children'. The Indians were invited to feasts, and dances; but whenever he and Fuller tried to talk privately to them, they would not talk freely, because of their fear of spies. There were also endless delays, on various pretexts, to prevent the Consuls from moving on when they wanted to; and as they were travelling on Arana's steamboat, there was nothing they could do.

As Casement had expressed scepticism about the value of the Consuls' tour, he could not be criticised for its failure. On the contrary, it reflected credit on him for having refused, on his own Putumayo visit, to be beholden to the Aranas. By the time Michell's report came in he was on holiday in Donegal, and he could ordinarily have relaxed there, sending replies only to urgent messages. But he was suffering from lumbago, which had left him so crippled that he could do nothing except read and write; as a result, letters, memoranda and enclosures on the Putumayo continued to flow from him daily to the Foreign Office, the quantity actually increasing while he lay in bed, though forced to scribble uncomfortably with a pencil. His output became prodigious, even by his own standards; up to four or five thousand words a day, in early September. It was largely energy wasted. Many of the people he ordinarily corresponded with were on holiday; the letters were read by Foreign Office clerks who had little knowledge of the background. 'Sir Roger Casement's despatches make one's head go round', one of them commented, though he had to admit they were 'full of incident' —as they were. But they did nothing to suggest a way by which the Foreign Office could begin to exert more effective pressure. His counsels, when he gave them, were of despair. 'the right action, of course, would be to evict the Aranas and Peru together from the Putumayo and get it administered by civilised men, but this, I fear, is impossible'.

It was a drepressing autumn for him, offering only one consolation. An article he had written on the Putumayo was accepted by the *Contemporary Review*. He had originally been asked to write it for the *Daily Mail*, and, in the hope of securing some publicity for his Putumayo fund, had agreed to do so—as the *Mail*'s owner, Lord Northcliffe, wrote angrily to remind him. He had indeed said he would write for the *Mail*, he replied; but it had been drawn to his attention that as he was still in the Foreign Service, to write the kind of controversial piece they wanted would be improper. An article for the respected *Contemporary Review* was a different matter; it would not be controversial. In fact, it was; but the controversial aspects were judiciously masked by a display of erudition, historical and sociological. His aim was to prove that the Putumayo Indians were not savages, in the sense Arana had claimed, but more highly developed, morally speaking, than their white oppressors. The tribes, he claimed, 'preserved a gentleness of mind and docility of temperament in singular contrast with the vigorous savagery of the far abler African'. That had been the trouble with the Putumayo Indian; lacking a competitive streak, he was 'a Socialist by temperament, habit, and possibly, an age-long memory of Inca and pre-Inca precept'. 'Is it too late,' he asked in his conclusion, 'to hope that by means of the same humane and brotherly agency, something of the goodwill and kindness of Christian life may be imparted to the remote, friendless, and lost children of the forest?'

CHAPTER FIVE

THE SELECT COMMITTEE

In Session 1912

At the end of October, Casement was restored to a better humour by a letter from Charles Roberts, the Liberal M.P. who was to be chairman of the Select Committee into the affairs of the Peruvian Amazon Company. 'I wish to lose no time in getting in touch with you', Roberts wrote; the Committee, he was sure, would want to have Casement's evidence at an early date. Pleased, Casement wrote back at once to place himself at the Committee's disposal.

Roberts proved a very efficient chairman. When the Foreign Office tried to prevent the Committee from seeing the original correspondence between them and the company, he demolished the excuse they gave—that some of it, notably in connection with Whiffen, had been given in confidence—by promising that the sessions relating to it would be held, if necessary, *in camera*. With the company, he was more forthright. Under the pretext of asking for some missing papers, he authorised what amounted to a raid of its offices, to seize them. And his handling of Casement was masterly, compounded of the deference due to his knowledge and experience with the realisation that Casement could be persuaded to do a great deal of the Committee's work for it, without having to be paid.

Casement gave evidence twice to the Committee, on November 13th and December 11th, recounting what had happened since he was asked to go out to the Putumayo, and answering the questions of individual members of the Committee and of counsel for the Peruvian Amazon Co.—Raymond Asquith, the Prime Minister's son, who was shrewd enough to concentrate on eliciting information from him which would show the English company directors had been fools, rather than knaves. 'I think we all feel, Sir Roger,' he was eventually assured, 'that you did a great public service in laying bare this state of things and, we trust, in bringing it to an end.' But his main usefulness to the

Committee was as prompter. Kept informed by Roberts which witnesses were next to be examined, he suggested the questions they should be asked to elicit the required information. He also gave a running commentary on the proceedings, letting Roberts know when the Committee had failed to make some essential point, or had allowed itself to be misled.

It would have been easy for Casement, had he so wished, to make it appear that the British directors of the company and those who had worked for it were conspirators. Instead, he did all he could to show they had been Arana's dupes. When the London papers (which gave quite extensive coverage to the sittings) quoted him as saying in his evidence that the company's directors had been cognisant of what had been happening in the Putumayo, he begged Roberts to make it clear that this referred only to the Peruvian directors. Although appearances were against Gielgud who, it was found, had allowed his report on the Putumayo to be altered by Zumaeta, Casement insisted he had been 'made a fool of', and attributed his failure to see any evidence of atrocities when he was in the Putumayo in 1910 to the fact that 'he went out to look at the books, not at the backs of Indians'. As for Consul Cazes, who had failed to see what was happening from his post in Iquitos, 'I hope,' he told Roberts:

> poor Cazes may not be harassed too much at his public examination. He was in a very difficult position as a local trader, and could not quarrel with his bread and butter. The F.O. are almost as much to blame, for leaving such posts in the hands of local traders, 'Consulates' only in name, until the avalanche fell. Another trouble is that they never will wake up till the avalanche falls.

The jibe at the end reflected a new mood of disillusionment with the Foreign Office, caused by their decision that he must return to his post as Consul-General in Rio. He had hoped that his reports on the state of his health would convince them that he should not be sent back there; his attack of lumbago in September had been followed, in October, by what Richard Morten's doctor at Denham diagnosed as a kidney complaint; and during his stay in London, working for the Select Committee, he was in continuous pain. On December 12th, he applied for two months' sick leave, which he proposed to spend in a warmer climate. The following day, he was told that he must return to Rio, and that he must leave the following week. 'It would be throwing your life away,' Lord ffrench advised him, offering to find out if the Mozambique post was still available; but it was not.

Having no intention of going back to Rio, Casement resorted to the expedient he had used successfully before: a medical opinion. To be on the safe side, he saw two eminent specialists. On December 20th, Dr. J. W. Thompson Walker traced his arthritic pains to an inflammatory condition in the spine (a few years later, he would have called it a slipped disk): and on the same day Sir Lauder Brunton, after examining him, wrote (for the benefit of the Foreign Office): 'I found him suffering from congestion of the liver, feeble circulation, gastro-intestinal catarrh, and so much irritation and tenderness over the appendix as to render it questionable whether he ought not to have the appendix removed.'

The only trouble with Sir Lauder's diagnosis (which also, incidentally, revealed the reason for at least one of Casement's operations: piles) was that Casement was determined to go somewhere he could get the sun. 'I am full of rheumatism,' he had written to Morel that autumn, 'and feel "quare and old" indeed, and "terrible failed" . . . the Sun, the Vital Sun, is the only thing will get me straight', and in mid-winter the nearest place he could hope to find it was the Canary Islands—a prescription which Sir Lauder, fearing there would be no surgeon there to operate on him if the need arose, refused to endorse. Both specialists, however, vetoed Rio; and their combined testimony was too high-powered for the Foreign Office to defy. Three months' sick leave was granted, and before the end of January 1913, Casement was back on Teneriffe.

South Africa   *1913*

Casement's self-prognosis proved to have been justified. From Teneriffe, he wrote to Alice Green to say he was beginning to recover; soon, he felt robust enough to contemplate going on to South Africa, to stay with his brother Tom. He would ask the Foreign Office for a further month's leave, to make this possible. If they refused, he would retire. Whatever happened, he was not going to return to Rio.

He now had, as he liked to have, an excuse for indignation with his employers. They had taken £400 off his Consul-General's salary and allowances when he went to the Putumayo; and, since July, they had put him on half that reduced pay. 'They never said a word to me, either!' he told his cousin. 'I only found out from my bank! Aren't they beauties!' But there was gaiety in his wrath. He was enjoying himself on Teneriffe. Writing to sympathise with him on his illness, Nevinson remarked that he had thought him case-hardened to both the tropics and London, 'but I suppose it is indignation kills you, as it kills us all . . . if we could cease from cruel rage we should all be well'. The rage had abated; and his health was returning. To complete his cure, he decided, he would carry out his project of a visit to his brother.

'I wish Tom would either grow up or revert to infancy,' he had told Gertrude Bannister a few months before, 'in the one case you could reason with him, in the other smack him.' Approaching Cadbury for some capital for Tom's hotel, he had described his brother as 'not a waster, or ne'er do well, but an extraordinarily unbusinesslike human being'—hardly an inducement to part with the required £400. Now, when he got to South Africa—though he found Tom as engaging as ever, and liked his new wife—it was to find that although the hotel was attractive, not enough people were coming to it to make it pay. Had the enterprise been thriving, he might have been tempted to stay on in South Africa; but it was money, not help, that his brother required, and there was nothing for him to do. When his leave ran out, although the thought of London, 'with its noise and worry and strain', did not appeal to him, he had no choice. By mid-May he was back in England.

The Committee's Report   1913

After Casement had left England, that January, he had continued to keep in touch with Roberts—'I seem fated,' he had written from Teneriffe, 'to write to you every day.' But in South Africa, he had been too far away to continue to influence the course of the proceedings; and when he returned, it was to find that they had ended—and that he had missed the most absorbing part of them.

The January sessions had been chiefly devoted to a systematic evisceration, by the Committee, of the Peruvian Amazon Company's British directors, for their failure to investigate the Putumayo atrocity stories, and for the delaying tactics with which they had held off the Foreign Office. By the end of January, there was little more to be done; but Roberts, hearing that Arana was on his way to England, had decided to keep the Committee going, in the hope of persuading him to give evidence. He would have liked, he wrote to tell Casement, to have had the 'dramatic moment of your confronting Arana before us'; but he had not thought it proper to summon him back and 'perhaps interfere with the cure'. When Arana arrived in England at the beginning of April, however, and presented himself for questioning, Roberts had an even more dramatic confrontation awaiting him.

Arana had chosen to come to England because it was temporarily inconvenient for him to remain in Peru. In Lima, a new President, Guillermo Billinghurst, had decided that it was time for action. 'I am taking up the subject of the Putumayo,' he told the Foreign Office, 'with the keenest personal interest.' On his instructions, Paredes was told to undertake a second tour of the Putumayo forthwith; Valcarcel was reinstated as examining judge in Iquitos; and he celebrated his appointment by ordering Arana's arrest. Arana, explaining that much though he would have liked to face his accusers in Iquitos, it was necessary for the prestige of Peru that he should face them first in London, had sailed for Europe. Any of his countrymen who doubted him, he hoped, would suspend judgment until he had put his case. It would 'produce a world-wide reaction in favour of Peru, and leave my name unblemished'.

Questioning Arana through an interpreter, the Select Committee elicited that he was not prepared to deny there had been atrocities in the Putumayo. He merely insisted that they had been greatly exaggerated. But when taken through Casement's charges, one by one, he was unable to point to exaggeration in any of them. Where the Committee hoped to catch him out, though, was over his accusations against Hardenburg. Did he still believe, he was asked, that Hardenburg had forged a bill? Something—or someone—must have forewarned Arana. The bill had certainly been forged, he replied; but whether Hardenburg (to whom it had been endorsed) or by the endorser, he could not tell. Unable, even with judicious prompting, to make him repeat his earlier more forthright accusation, the Committee sprung its trap. 'Turn round,' one of his questioners told him, 'and see Hardenburg before you!' And there, indeed, was Hardenburg.

The confrontation, however, was more dramatic than significant. Arana had his reply ready: 'Yes, and I am very pleased to see him here, because we can enter into details.' But this was just what they could not do—not, at least, during the court's sittings. The procedure did not permit them to spar together in front of their questioners.

Hardenburg revealed to the Committee how he had been duped. He had cashed a bill for a sick man who had worked for him (and also, it had later transpired, for Arana) and who—he later found—was a forger. The Whiffen affair was also explained. Arana had managed to get him drunk, and talked him into accepting payment of his 'expenses' in the Putumayo, on condition he did not disclose certain 'irregularities', by which Whiffen had taken him to mean customs evasions. He had agreed to write a letter to this effect, to Arana's dictation, in Spanish—a language with which he was not very familiar. Sobering, he realised this was foolish, and had torn up the letter. But he had not destroyed it; Arana had recovered the pieces, and pasted them together again to use as evidence of blackmail.

The Committee had no hesitation in accepting both Hardenburg's and Whiffen's versions, and rejecting Arana's. Their report, which was being printed at the time Casement returned from South Africa, was a sustained indictment of the Peruvian Amazon Company. The company's British directors, it conceded, were not aware of what was happening; but in their anxiety to avoid harmful publicity, they had seized on anything which might discredit the witnesses against them; and 'while they wrote leisurely debating replies to the Foreign Office, the killing and torture of the helpless Indians was going on all the time, and some of the worst atrocities were being perpetrated'. Later, they had protected not the Indians, but the very men who had been responsible for the atrocities. 'The British directors had been urged by Sir Roger Casement to make personal efforts and sacrifices to secure just treatment for the Indians, whom their agents had abominably oppressed'; their reply had been to authorise payment to those agents of the sums they had earned on commission, in spite of the fact that the amount involved — between £10,000 and £20,000 — would have been sufficient to save the company from having to go into liquidation. And after all that, they had named Arana as liquidator. But as he had just been removed from that post, following a court order in March for the company to be compulsorily wound up, the Committee contented itself with echoing the judge's comment on that occasion: Arana was 'the last person in the world to whom the winding-up of the company should have been entrusted'.

The Committee then gave its views on the implications of the affair. Company directors, it argued, 'who merely attend board meetings and sign cheques, or limit themselves to a special branch of the business, cannot escape their share of the collective moral responsibility when gross abuses under their company are revealed'; the directors should have realised this, and 'not lightly have exposed to risk the good name of England'. As for Arana, the report found simply that he 'together with other partners in the vendor firm, had knowledge of and was responsible for the atrocities perpetrated by his agents and employees in the Putumayo'.

Damning though the report was, it attracted little attention. On the morning of the day it was due to be presented to the House of Commons — which traditionally was supposed to have first look — The Times, which had been 'leaked' a copy, published an account of its contents. Knowing that it would be criticised — there were in fact to be mutterings about the possibility of proceedings for contempt of Parliament — The Times would ordinarily have anticipated the publicity and spread itself on the story, to discomfit its rivals. It happened, though, that the previous afternoon, the suffragette Emily Davidson had flung herself under the King's horse in the Derby; and this — coupled with the fact that the horse first past the post had been disqualified, letting in an outsider as the winner — made it unlikely that the misdeeds of the Peruvian Amazon Company would be the day's talking-point in clubs and pubs. When the report was formally released, too, apart from the fact that The Times's rivals had little relish for rehashing it, it was overshadowed — as Casement, writing to congratulate Roberts on the Committee's efforts, sadly observed — by the inquiry into the Marconi shares scandal, which was threatening to drive two prominent ministers, Lloyd George and Sir Rufus Isaacs, out of public life.

As public opinion was not roused, Asquith was able to reject Roberts's request for a debate on the subject; he was able to bring it up only in the debate on the Foreign Office Estimates, in August. There was evidence, he said, that 'a system practically akin to slavery' was rampant in many parts of South America, and that British capital was heavily engaged. British subjects who were involved should be brought to trial; if the law did not cover their activities, then the law should be changed. In any case, the Foreign Office must begin to exercise more effective guardianship. They were excusing themselves by claiming that the Consular Service was not an investigating body; but they had used it for that purpose when they sent Casement to the Putumayo, and they must continue to use it in that way whenever the need arose. But Roberts was unable to attract support. The only response he obtained from his speech was an invitation to come to the Foreign Office, some time, and talk the subject over.

So although Casement could feel that the Select Committee's report was a further testimonial—and the references to him personally were in glowing terms—he could not regard it as likely to be of much service to the Putumayo Indians. True, he had heard from Dr. H. S. Dickey, whom he had been with on his last visit to Iquitos, that Tizon really had been working wonders; but this would not help for long if Arana regained control of the area. And by the time the Committee reported, Arana had routed his enemies in Iquitos. While he was away, demonstrations had been mounted in Iquitos by his supporters against Paredes and Valcarcel. Threatened with lynching, they had both precipitately fled; and the Iquitos 'High Court' had promptly quashed the order for Arana's arrest.

The *Voz del Oriente*, the journal which looked after the interests of the Loreto province in Lima, drew its conclusions: the attacks on Arana had been the work of Roger Casement, blackmailer. After his visit to Iquitos, *Voz* explained, Casement had presented himself to the directors of the company in London, which by his machinations he had put into debt, and proposed a deal: 'Gentlemen, I will pay you the sum of £300,000, the amount of your debt; but in exchange I will take shares in the company to the value of £700,000, thus becoming one of its principal shareholders'. As the company had disdainfully re-

jected the offer, he had published his hostile Putumayo report.
'Is there not a close connection,' *Voz* asked, 'between these acts
and unbridled and clamorous vengeance? Casement, the would-
be shareholder, becomes subsequently the man whose report
has discredited Peru and brought about the ruin of an undertaking which, before that, was rich and powerful.'

In one of the letters by which he kept Casement informed of
what was happening while he was in South Africa, Spicer had
remarked that it was 'a hopeless game'. Now, its full hopeless-
ness was finally revealed. The two Consuls, Michell and Fuller,
had put in their reports on their visit to the Putumayo to their
respective ministers; and the way appeared open for joint action
by the British and United States Governments. But in the spring
of 1914, the Foreign Office heard the views of the American
Secretary of State. Owing to the vigour apparently animating the
new Peruvian administration, Knox wrote, as well as

the remoteness of the district, and attendant obstacles in the
way of effective reform, I am of the opinion that any further
action on the part of His Majesty's Government or of the
American Government would appear inopportune, at least
for the time being, in as much as it might be instrumental
in stirring up public sentiment in Peru to such an extent as
to hinder whatever real desire now exists there for bettering
the conditions under which the Indians labour.

Knox had become worried that the United States might lose a
valuable friend in South America if he pressed the Peruvian
Government too hard—just as Lansdowne and Grey had been
worried they might lose a valuable ally in Europe over the
Congo. So the last opportunity for joint action had been lost.

The winding-up   *1913*

Repeatedly, Casement and others who had been concerned with
the Putumayo had drawn attention to the parallels with the
Congo. Now, by a coincidence, at the time his connection with
the Putumayo was being severed, the Congo Reform Association
was winding itself up.

The Association had hoped to end its work sooner, after
Casement's launching of the Morel testimonial fund. It had not

had the success he had expected because—he found, on a visit to Liverpool—there was a widespread impression that Morel had made a good thing out of the Association—a malicious lie, he felt, which had been deliberately circulated by Leopold's supporters, who had suffered from Morel's exposures. Still, he had been able to double the sum collected; and the testimonial had duly been presented.

The Association, however, had been kept in being to try to ensure that the Belgian Congo was not formally recognised by the British Government until the Belgian Government fulfilled the last of its pledges: to return the land of the Congo, or at least a substantial part of it, to the natives. This, the Belgians refused to do; but so great was the improvement of conditions generally that eventually the members of the Association felt they had done all that could reasonably have been expected of them. In April 1913, shortly before Casement returned from Africa, the executive held its last meeting. Morel recalled what it had achieved:

First and foremost the entire Leopoldian policy, so long and so persistently defended, not only by the Congo State Government but by successive Belgian Governments, has been completely abandoned. The false economies, the vicious principles and attitudes of mind which we denounced remorselessly, and which we were derided for denouncing, have been recognised as false and vicious. The atrocities have disappeared or been reduced to impotence, and with their disappearance swarms of irregular levies which terrorised the countryside have also disappeared. The revenues are no longer supplied by forced or slave labour. The rubber tax has gone. The native is free to gather the produce of his soil and dispose of it in trade. He can buy and sell—the primal essential of human liberty. A responsible government has replaced an irresponsible despotism. Money is no longer flowing from the Congo into a Brussels exchequer. Belgium is sinking money in the Congo. She is running the Congo at a loss.

At a final meeting, praise was lavished on Morel for what he had done; but in his reply, he insisted on giving credit to his absent friend:

while I was listening to all that was being said, I had a vision. The vision of a small steamer ploughing its way up the Congo just ten years ago this month, and on its decks a man that some of you know; a man of great heart, great experience, great knowledge of African races; a man of great insight. You know the man I refer to—Roger Casement. If he had been another kind of man than the man he was ... I shudder to think what might have happened.

If Casement had been another kind of man, the sufferings of the Indians in the Putumayo, too, would have been even more protracted. But he could not feel as satisfied with his achievement there as he could about the course events had taken in the Congo. True, the Congo campaign had taken ten years to bring to a reasonably satisfactory conclusion; but at least the indications were that the natives there could in future look forward to some protection by the colonial government from the worst exactions of the commercial exploiters. No such protection could be expected by the Putumayo Indians, if Tizon was replaced—as, with Arana back in triumph, he was likely to be.

What Casement ruefully described as 'the last string to our bow', too—the Putumayo mission—had also almost broken even before it had been drawn. Sectarian malice had kept the Putumayo mission fund from reaching even £3,000 of the £15,000 aimed for; only the generosity of an acquaintance of his, who preferred to remain anonymous, eventually sufficed to guarantee the expenses of sending four priests to the Putumayo. 'It is you who have done everything,' Percy Brown, the fund organiser, told Casement: 'without you, nothing would have been done.' But there could be no certainty yet that the four missioners would be able to establish themselves; and even if they did, the region would be too large for them to supervise.

It was not Casement's fault that he had failed to secure any real safeguards for the Putumayo Indians. Much of the responsibility lay with the Monroe Doctrine, which had held Grey back from more decisive intervention. Grey, though, could have acted more decisively without risk of giving offence to the State Department. He had not wanted to, because of a convention which had first begun to establish itself a century before; that the Government should not interfere with business enterprises, however dubious, so long as they kept within the letter of the law.

The Select Committee had now recommended that the law should be reviewed. Company directors, they felt, should be held responsible for the consequences of their actions. Had such a law been in existence, the Peruvian Amazon Company's directors would unquestionably have been convicted, and heavily punished. But, more important, had there been such a law they would never have allowed the situation to have developed in the way it did—for, the moment they had heard rumours of atrocities there, they would for their own safety have been prompted to investigate the charges, and to take immediate action to punish offenders, so that should they ultimately be taken to court, they could face a jury with confidence. The law, however, was not changed. There was no guarantee that what had happened in the Putumayo would not happen again, given similar commercial opportunities, in some other region.

Casement had pointed out this risk in a thoughtful letter to Grey, shortly after receiving his knighthood. Arana, he reminded Grey, had been able to introduce what amounted to slave labour simply by securing a title to the land, thereby making sure that every native who lived on it was effectively in his power. Surely no British company ought to be allowed to operate on such a principle? When Grey showed reluctance to intervene, Casement had decided that the only way to secure a change in the law would be to launch what he described, in letters to Alice Green and Morel, as 'a movement of human liberation' designed to rouse people to the evils of allowing primitive peoples to be 'civilised' for the benefit of commercial enterprises, without control. And he found a sympathetic listener in Mitchell Innes, who had come independently from his experience in the Foreign Service to believe that the kind of civilisation which commercial interests introduced into primitive communities usually debased, and sometimes destroyed them. The difficulty, Mitchell Innes pointed out, was that too often the commercial foundations were laid before the colonial power stepped in; and if it tried to stop the process there was an outcry—the firms complained they were being ruined, and that the employment they gave would have to be withdrawn. Still, he liked Casement's project. But Casement did not follow it up. If it had attracted Morel, or someone of Morel's bulldog quality, he would have been free to absorb himself in it; and his subsequent career would have been very different. But that summer of 1913, another cause beckoned, even closer to his heart: Ireland.

PART FOUR

CRAIG'S ULSTER

1913–1914

CHAPTER ONE

RETIREMENT

Connemara   *May 1913*

It had been Casement's intention to retire and devote his years in retirement to Ireland even before he left for the Putumayo. 'This is my last external effort on behalf of others,' he had written to tell Morel; 'henceforth and for aye I shall concentrate on Ireland alone.' But he was disconcerted to find, when he returned in the summer of 1913 to await the Foreign Office's decision about his future, that neither of the two causes—the Irish language and *Sinn Fein*—closest to his heart had been flourishing. The causes themselves had not lost their hold over him, but he found them ill-served, as he believed, by the organisations which had grown to sustain them.

This was no sudden disenchantment. There had been earlier intimations of discontent with the way both organisations were being run. In the case of the language movement, they can be traced back to a correspondence he had had just before leaving for Santos with a young teacher of Irish, Seamus O'Goffin, whom he had written to reproach for giving up his post in a school in the west. O'Goffin had replied giving very much the same excuses that he was himself using, at the time, to justify his decision to leave Ireland, and take up his consular career again. 'The plain facts,' O'Goffin told him, 'are that my people are depending on me, and I have no money, and there is none to be had where I am.' He went on to warn Casement against being too sanguine about the language revival:

> You have no idea of the wretchedness of living on a starvation salary in a poor country district, and with that you undoubtedly degenerate ... you don't know how rotten the country is; were it not for the few noble characters the Gaelic League has brought forth, the rest of the people are not worth thinking about. You have not experienced the corruption and jobbing, the total lack of self-respect or national spirit that

exists among them. And amongst the biggest offenders are the Catholic clergy.

The local politician, using the patronage which Unionist subsidies had provided for him to dispense; the parish priest, alarmed at the prospect of his flock being educated in a language he did not understand, and, perhaps indoctrinated with revolutionary sentiments of which he disapproved; these were greater threats, Casement gradually began to realise, than the contempt of the loyalists. And the Gaelic League had not grasped this fact. It had concentrated too much on trying to revive the language among those who had ceased to speak it; too little on saving it where it was still spoken.

His leave in Ireland in the summer of 1911, between his two visits to Peru, had finally extinguished his former optimism. 'I have *really* in my heart no hope for the language', he wrote sadly to Alice Green. It was Irish spoken as a matter of course, in the home, rather than from affection or a sense of duty—he now felt certain—that 'was the one, sole hope of the tongue of the Gael surviving'. The Gaelic League had thought 'that by chanting nouns and verbs in Dublin streets they would revive Irish as a spoken tongue—chopping turnips would revive it as well! The one and *only* thing was to keep it a *living* tongue, from mother to child, in its last home by the Irish peninsulas of the west'.

Whether Casement realised it or not, he was himself an example of the limitations of the League's policies. Try as he would, he could not master the spoken language himself. Other languages had come easily to him: he spoke French fluently, and had picked up some Spanish and Portuguese during his career, but Irish continued to elude him. His cousin Gertrude did better, and he urged her wistfully to become a really proficient speaker: 'I wish I were one.'

Neither his difficulty in mastering Irish, nor his uneasiness about the Gaelic League's policies, had diminished his desire to be able to speak the language and to help others to do so. In the spring of 1912 the headmaster of Ballymena Academy, as his former school now called itself, wrote to the now famous Old Boy to ask for a subscription for the school's endowment fund; Casement replied that he preferred to help educational establishments 'of a distinctively *national* character', such as a

Alice Green

sement in his thirties

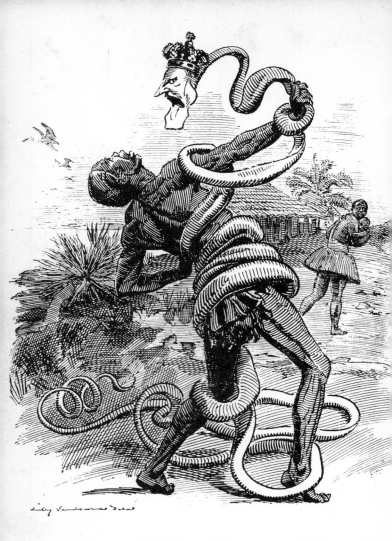

The Royal Python: *Punch* (November 28th, 1906) attacks the 'Rubber System'

Chained Indian rubber gatherers in the stocks on the Putumayo River

Leopold II, King of the Belg[ians]

Julio César Arana

Roger Casement talking to Irish prisoners in a German prison camp, by W. Hatherell

Roger Casement, 1916

Casement in court, May 16th, 1916

Casement leaving the Law Courts after his appeal had been dismissed

Teachers' Training College in Donegal, an Irish school in Galway, and Patrick Pearse's school, St. Enda's, 'where the course of teaching is Irish throughout—that is, a course primarily to interest boys in their own country and make them good and useful citizens of it'. He liked a school which 'trained its youth to know, love and respect their own land, before all others—and St. Enda's was the only one he knew in Ireland that was doing this'. He continued to give all the help he could to the summer schools in the west, where Irish was being spoken; in August, he visited the summer school which had been started at Tawin, of which he was patron, and sent a cheque for £5 to Eamon de Valera, who was running it, to be awarded in prizes—asking that 'all competitions be in Irish not English—the judgments in Irish—and so far as practicable the prizes of Irish make'. And later, when his work delayed his departure for Donegal, he wrote to Gertrude Bannister, who had gone on ahead of him, to express his envy of her for being able to pursue the language, 'which disappeared from the more civilised parts of Ireland, along with the Potato, Brogue, Fine Legs and High Spirits, some eighty years ago', but which he hoped she would find 'a garb to be worn without blushing'. But by this time, the language was becoming identified in his mind with agreeable holidays in the west, among friends. He no longer had any illusions that it could be revived throughout the country.

In much the same way, and during the same period, although his enthusiasm for *Sinn Fein* as a principle and a policy remained undiminished, he had begun to lose faith in the organisation. In the letter Arthur Griffith had sent to him while he was Consul-General in Rio, appealing for funds for the new daily *Sinn Fein*, Griffith had shown petulance about some potential allies, in particular the Gaelic League; and writing to Bulmer Hobson, Casement expressed concern about this aspect of his character.

I've never felt confidence in him as a leader, I may tell you, but I did not like to say a word to anyone that might weaken their faith. The meeting I attended in Dublin in December last convinced me of his narrowness—and that we cannot stand, in our far too narrow Ireland. Had *Sinn Fein* been properly handled at the start, we'd have had the three Johns on their knees to it today.

—the 'three Johns' being John Redmond, his second-in-command John Dillon, and John Bull.

After the General Election of 1910—which left Redmond and the Irish Party holding the balance of power—the prospects for Home Rule appéared to improve; the two Johns, Redmond and Dillon, had consequently recovered authority and popularity, and the *Sinn Fein* organisation had begun to crumble. Casement remained convinced that it would be required again: there could be no Home Rule, he told his cousin; 'not by this means, I am sure. The Lords will throw it out. Home Rule will come only when the English people feel the necessity of it, and that won't be until Ireland goes *Sinn Fein*, and gets another Parnell.'

But the Liberal Government's decision to introduce a Home Rule bill encouraged many members of *Sinn Fein* in the hope that perhaps after all independence might be won at Westminster; and when Casement returned to Ireland after his visit to South Africa, he would have been hard put to find a branch of the organisation anywhere in Ireland, outside the capital.

For a while he was at a loss to know what to do with himself. He was even tempted to go back to South Africa, as Tom was in dire straits again: he would never be able to forgive himself if he did not 'try to save that sinking home'. But Cadbury had commissioned the young Irish artist Sarah Purser to paint his portrait, which required him to complete the necessary sittings; and while he was still undecided about his next move, his humanitarian urge was roused by accounts in the *Irish Independent*, in May, of epidemics of typhoid and typhus in some islands off Connemara, along with pictures of the rural slum conditions in which the peasants lived. The *Independent* opened a relief fund; and a letter appeared supporting it from his sister, Nina. Probably she drew it to her brother's attention, for on May 20th the *Independent* published a letter from him enclosing a cheque, and saying that he hoped soon to visit the area, to 'see whether something lasting cannot be done to remove the stain of this enduring Irish Putumayo from our native land'.

The editor felt it necessary to explain that apart from his consular career, Casement was 'an Irish gentleman who takes a deep interest in the Gaelic speaking districts of Ireland'—of which Connemara was one of the largest, and poorest. Early in June he went down there, returning with the feeling that the 'white Indians'—as he described them—of Ireland were heavier on his heart 'than all the Indians of the rest of the earth'; and at the end of the month he wrote to the *Independent* to say that in addition to the amount they had been able to collect (by that time approaching £2,000) he had secured a sufficient sum, through the generosity of friends in England, to ensure that all the children who attended the infant school on one of the islands would have a free meal every day for a year.

What he had seen in Connemara helped to confirm him in his decision finally to break with the Foreign Service. Alarmed by the rage in which he found his 'dear Tiger', Morel tried to calm him down—though not very tactfully. It would be madness, he agreed, for Casement to go back to Rio; 'but you are a difficult man to help. You are very proud, for which I admire you, in the first place. Also, forgive me for saying so, it is a little difficult sometimes to know how exactly anything can be done that would fall in with your exact wishes'. Ordinarily Casement did not relish such candid advice; but Morel's reference to him at the last meeting of the Congo Reform Association, which came four days later, may have soothed him. In any case, Tyrrell once again intervened. The difficulty had been that Casement had still not served long enough to qualify for a pension, if he retired; but with the help of a medical report to say that his health might be permanently impaired if he stayed on in the service, Tyrrell thought Grey would recommend him to the Treasury for the highest pension that his 'long, valuable and distinguished services made to the Crown, and the Regulations, allow'. He could quite understand the way Casement felt, he went on; but he felt sure 'it could not make any difference to those happy relations which you have established with everybody you have had to deal with from my chief downwards'. 'I have indeed to express a very keen regret,' Casement replied, 'at severing my connection with a Service I have for so long been associated with, and still more at severing ties with persons from whom I have so often and continuously received marks of much friendship and esteem.'

It was formal; it was stilted; but as Casement ordinarily used such phrases in such circumstances, it might have passed for sincerity if he had not told Morel it had been composed with a view to animating the soul of the Treasury, when they came to settle how much to award him as a pension. By this time, he was thoroughly disillusioned with the Foreign Office. For a while, under Grey's spell, he had believed that they had the interests of the Putumayo Indians as much at heart as he had; but this had only made the final disillusionment, when it came, more bitter. It had become obvious to him that the humanitarian side of Grey emerged only when it did not conflict with more important interests—the Entente, the Monroe Doctrine, the sanctity of commercial operations. And now, Casement had begun to feel that Grey was taking Britain on a course likely to lead, in the near future, into war with Germany.

The Germans

'I like the Germans,' Casement had written, 'and believe in them.' He had come to like them as individuals when he began meeting them in Lourenço Marques: Count Blücher, and a merchant, Fritz Pincus, on whose behalf he was later to send an impassioned plea to the Foreign Office, when he heard that Pincus was in trouble with the authorities in South Africa. He admired the Germans as colonists, frequently expressing the wish that Germany, rather than the United States, could be the dominant force in South America. While in South America, in 1908, he had even sketched a novel in light-hearted outline in which a German force landed in Ireland, to be 'received everywhere as deliverers and friends', which they showed they intended to be by allowing the Irish to hold a plebiscite, to decide on whatever form of government they wanted.

Before the days of the Entente, there had been nothing eccentric in being a Germanophile. Joseph Chamberlain and the Duke of Devonshire had hoped to establish an Anglo-Teutonic movement for world leadership; and of the men with whom Casement had been involved over the Congo, both Dilke and Morel shared his pro-German feelings. In his *Great Britain and the Congo*, published in 1909, Morel had included a chapter on 'the German Bogey', in which he argued that Grey, by allowing Leopold to exploit British fears of Germany in order to retain his hold on the Congo, was actually creating mistrust in Germany, both of Belgium and Britain, of a kind which was bound to lead to trouble, later; and this was a theme that was to recur in Casement's letters. 'Instead of trying to arrive at a general friendly arrangement,' he explained to Morel from Rio in the autumn of 1909,

we have gone out of our way now for several years to eliminate Germany from our councils, and as far as we could from
the councils of others. ... Now, things have reached so evil a
pass that peace between the two great powers can hardly be
kept. Both are preparing for war, and faster than the world
suspects—but the fault lies far more with England than with
Germany. It has been a wretchedly stupid business—based
first on jealousy, trade ill-will and greed of commerce, and
now resting very largely on fear, too. The English have become
afraid of the Germans.

Casement's visit to Germany in the spring of 1912 further
impressed him. He did not like the look of the Prussians, with
their 'thin pork chops of cheeks, criss-crossed as if for cook-
ing'; but he admired their efficiency. The Bavarian education
system also greatly impressed him. He returned convinced—
according to Hambloch, who met him at the time—that the
Germans were 'magnificent organisers', and he was more certain
than ever that they were being shamefully treated by the
Foreign Office.

Inevitably, the growing rift between Britain and Germany
had been observed in Ireland; and the separatists had begun to
remind each other how John Mitchel had forecast that in the
event of a European war, a strong nationalist party could grasp
the opportunity to win Ireland her independence.

Casement's contribution was an article on 'Ireland and the
German Menace', which appeared in the *Irish Review*, over the
pseudonym 'Batha MacCrainn', in September 1912. England, he
argued, was granting Home Rule to Ireland only to secure her
as an ally against the Germans. 'The question arises: could we
not secure better terms? Would Germany offer us better? The
more we value our own worth, the more others are likely to
value it. Ireland, if she only knew, holds a winning hand between
England and Germany. If she—or her leaders for her—play it
well, they can secure a measure of freedom for the old land that
Thomas Davis may not have dreamed of.'

He was not looking at the question simply from an Irish
nationalist standpoint. From England's own point of view, he
was also convinced, the policy of ganging up against Germany
with France and, worse, Russia was madness. As he put it in a
letter to Cadbury, written on his way out to South Africa,

I think Grey's tenure of the Foreign Office will be regarded in history as a national disaster to England. He has leagued the country with the reactionary powers of the Continent—especially Russia—and has failed abjectly to import any element of Liberalism into the conduct and outlook on foreign affairs. He has been in almost all things the tool and engine of the clique who run foreign affairs at the Foreign Office, and has served them better than probably anyone else could have done. Under the shield of Liberalism they have been able to advance the autocracy of their hold on foreign affairs and more and more to remove the conduct (and criticism even) of these from the control and supervision of Parliament. This Government deserves to be rejected by Liberals more on the ground of Grey than of all other things combined.

But although England might be to blame, if war broke out, would it not be better for Ireland to cast in her lot with her? This was the line Conan Doyle took, in an article he wrote for the *Fortnightly Review* in February 1913. By Casement's account, which he gave Theodor Schiemann in Germany after war broke out, he had converted Doyle from Unionism to Home Rule; but the proofs of the article, which he sent to Casement at Las Palmas, showed that he continued to take it for granted that Ireland, whether or not she left the United Kingdom, must share whatever fate overtook England at Germany's hands. Disagreeing, Casement wrote a reply, 'Ireland, Germany and the next world war', in which he suggested that the Germans would realise, if they defeated Britain, that it was very much in their interest 'not to impoverish and depress that new-won possession, but to enhance its strategic importance by vigorous and wise administration, so as to make it the main counterpoise to any possible recovery of British maritime supremacy'. By keeping Ireland in subjection the Germans would only offend the rest of the world, and particularly the United States. By liberating her, they would destroy England's naval stranglehold for all time; 'a free Ireland, restored to Europe, is the key to unlock the western ocean, and open the seaways of the world'. He sent the reply to the *Fortnightly Review*, which agreed to print it, but only if he signed it; which, being still in the Foreign Service—and still involved in the Putumayo, as the Select Committee had not finished its inquiry—he could not do. But he was able to have it published in the *Irish Review*, over the pseudonym 'Shan van Vocht', in July.

There was a further reason, though—he believed—why Ireland should detach herself from England and put her trust in Germany. If war broke out, he was convinced Germany would win. In an article he had composed in 1912, he had likened England to Carthage, relying on wealth; just as Roman men had beaten Carthaginian mercenaries, so must 'German manhood, in the end, triumph over British finance'. He relied upon what he described as 'the honesty and integrity of the German mind, the strength of the German intellect, the skill of the German hand and brain, the justice and vigour of German law, the intensity of German culture, science, education and social development'; he believed, too, that the Germans could be trusted to give Ireland her freedom. But even had he been less confident about them, he could still have argued that if Mitchel's advice— that a European war in which England became involved would give Ireland her opportunity—was sound, it was all the more essential to be prepared to seize it if England was going to be defeated.

Belfast

It might seem devious, even dishonest, that Casement should have come to hold such views while he was still working for the Crown. But he was not alone in holding them. Very few of the Irish separatists shared his enthusiasm for Germany; but it was widely shared, though for different reasons, by Ulster Protestants. For all their fervent loyalism, they were prepared, as he was, to enlist Germany's support, should the need arise.

The Ulster Protestants did not think of themselves as British. They were Irish, and intensely proud of it (the fact that the Celts had been in Ireland before them no more inhibited them from regarding themselves as Irish than the presence of Red Indians before the arrival of the Mayflower inhibited a Californian from regarding himself as an American). They did not even much like the English—whom they found patronising. But they greatly admired England as an abstraction, and English institutions, and the Empire. Home Rule, they felt, would deprive them of two assets which, in the United Kingdom, they enjoyed; access to British markets, and protection for the Protestant faith. It had not been Gladstone's intention, when he tried to introduce Home Rule, to deprive the Irish of access to British markets; but that might come. And in an all-Ireland Parliament, Protestants would be in a minority. Catholic teaching was explicit: the Church could not tolerate Protestantism, because that would be tolerating error; it might have to be tolerant from expediency—as in England, where Catholics were in a minority —but it need not be tolerant when it could dictate. The Ulster Protestants were understandably determined that it should not be able to dictate.

So long as the House of Lords, with its built-in Unionist majority, could veto legislation, they had little to worry about. But in 1910 they were confronted with a dual threat from the Liberal Government, kept in power by the Irish Party; curtailment of that veto power, and a new Home Rule bill. When the Ulster Protestant leaders found that some English Unionists were actually negotiating with the Liberals to try to reach agreement on Ireland—agreement which would inevitably have meant a measure of Home Rule—they reacted by making it clear that they would, if necessary, look to the Continent for help.

If Ulster were deserted by Great Britain, Thomas Andrews, the Secretary of the Ulster Unionist Council, was reported by the *Morning Post* of December 19th, 1910, as saying, 'I would rather be governed by Germany'. Three weeks later, the *Morning Post* carried an echo of that sentiment from James Craig, leader of the Ulster Unionists at Westminster: 'there is a spirit spreading abroad, which I can testify to from my personal knowledge, that Germany and the German Emperor would be preferred to the rule of John Redmond, Patrick Ford, and the Molly Maguires' (the Southern Irish, the Irish Americans, and the Ancient Order of Hibernians—the most powerful Catholic organisation in Ulster). And on April 30th, 1912, the *Belfast Newsletter*—like the *Morning Post*, a Unionist newspaper—described how Colonel Sharman Crawford had been rapturously applauded at Bangor when he told an audience that Irish Protestants had nothing to thank England for: if they were to be put out of the United Kingdom, 'he would prefer to change his allegiance right over to the Emperor of Germany, or anyone else who had got a proper and stable Government'.

It was not hypocritical of the Ulster 'loyalists' to utter such threats. It would, in fact, have been hypocritical if they had held any other view, considering that they believed they owed their survival to their ancestors' repudiation of James II—when he acted, as they believed, in bad faith—in order to replace him with their hero-figure, William of Orange. An Ulster Catholic, giving loyalty to his Church, felt it was unconditional; he might disagree with its rulings, but he accepted them, or confessed himself a sinner if he did not. To the Ulster Protestant, this was precisely what he disliked and feared about the Catholics: that they were willing to act against belief and conscience at the will of a parish priest. He preferred to give his loyalty to men and institutions only so long as they deserved it. The British Crown would continue to deserve it only so long as it fulfilled its ancient pledge to preserve the integrity of the United Kingdom.

The Kaiser was naturally aware of this feeling, and looked forward to being able to exploit it. He had gone out of his way to cultivate Colonel Saunderson, when he was staying in Wiesbaden in 1902; and when the leader of the Irish (as distinct from Ulster) Unionists at Westminster, Sir Edward Carson, went to Hamburg in the summer of 1913, the Kaiser invited him to lunch, and tried to draw him out on the Irish issues. Carson refused to be drawn, but the meeting naturally attracted considerable publicity, and was greeted with high glee in Ulster—Carson's supporters, according to St. John Ervine, 'openly bragged of the fact that a powerful foreign monarch, whose name began with a "W" had offered to help Ulster in the event of the Home Rule Bill becoming law'.

It was later to be argued that the threat was bluff; and James Good, perhaps the shrewdest of the political correspondents covering Ulster at the time, agreed that the prospect of becoming the Kaiser's subjects was not seriously contemplated. Yet nobody who mixed with the Ulster Protestants at the time, he recalled, 'would question the assertion that Germany shone in their eyes as a radiant example of what the attitude of Great Britain should be, but unfortunately was not. Their appeal to her practice ran like a *leit motif* through their speeches; and her belief in "resolute government" as the right medicine for small nationalities was the final proof of the superiority of her imperialism over the decadent Liberals that had corrupted English life.'

The Parliament Act, limiting the Lords' power to veto bills to three years, duly went through in 1911; and a Home Rule bill was introduced and passed the following year, which meant that unless the Ulster Protestants found some way to prevent it, they could expect to find themselves under an all-Ireland Parliament in 1914. They continued to threaten secession. As James Chambers, a Unionist M.P., put it on May 24th, 1913, the day Home Rule became law he would act as he had a right to act. 'I shall sing no longer, God Save the King!'; more than that, he would say, 'England, I laugh at your calamity. I will mock you when your hour cometh'. So freely were such sentiments being expressed that Winston Churchill, First Lord of the Admiralty, referred to them in the Commons: 'This, then, is the latest Tory threat. Ulster will secede to Germany . . .' And though he was shouted down, it was from embarrassment, rather than from conviction.

Casement, however, had been involved with the Putumayo during the period when the Ulster Protestants were beginning to agitate against Home Rule; and by the time he began to involve himself in Irish affairs again the secession threat was being heard less often. The Ulster Protestants' leader, James Craig, was trying a different approach.

Craig, who looked like a retired army officer (which he was) quietly going to seed as a country gentleman, was younger than he appeared—he was seven years Casement's junior—and a man of imperturbable resolution. He was also a shrewd judge of the political situation. If the Ulster Protestants stood on the narrow ground of their minority self-interest, he realised, they would not attract support in Britain. It would be wiser to campaign against Home Rule for Ireland generally. Craig had little confidence in the Southern Irish Protestants, but he knew how influential they were at Westminster—the former Foreign Secretary, Lord Lansdowne, in particular. And he had been fortunate enough to find, in their leader in the House of Commons, a man on whom he could rely: Sir Edward Carson. Not only was he influential; he was also—from Craig's point of view—trustworthy. Unlike so many Conservative M.Ps he really was a Unionist. 'It is, I think, a passion with me,' he had told his friend Lady Londonderry, 'as I hate the degradation of Ireland being turned into a province, and our own splendid folk being put under in the race for progress.' By 'our own splendid folk',

Carson meant the Protestant Anglo-Irish, whom he felt were a superior breed to the Celtic, Catholic stock. He did not care for the Northern Orangemen, either; their speeches, he said, reminded him of 'the unrolling of a mummy—all old bones and rotten rags'. But he needed them for the Unionist cause, and Craig needed him, for Ulster's.

The chief danger, to both Craig and Carson, was that sectarian strife in Ulster would forfeit English sympathy. During the summer of 1912, relations between Catholics and Protestants in the North deteriorated, culminating in September in a bloody clash between the supporters of two rival football clubs in Belfast. It was time, Craig realised, to impose discipline; and for this purpose he used the Ulster Volunteers, a force which had begun to grow earlier in the year. He also had drawn up, for all who agreed with it to sign, a covenant based on the earlier Scots model; to 'stand by one another in defending for ourselves and our children our cherished position of equal citizenship in the United Kingdom, and in using all means which may be necessary to defeat the present conspiracy to set up a Home Rule Parliament in Ireland'.

The covenant was ready for signature in the autumn of 1912. Casement, knowing little of the background, had happened to be in Belfast at this time, after his Donegal holiday; when he saw a Volunteer parade, it was Carson who led it, and he assumed that it must be Carson who had organised it (Craig, as usual, remained discreetly in the background). The idea of Carson arriving to stir up sectarian strife in Ulster—which was how it appeared—infuriated Casement: 'how truly *awfully* ugly he is', he wrote to tell Gertrude Bannister. And the Volunteers repelled him:

> How appalling they look with their grim Ulster Hall faces, all going down to curse the Pope and damn Home Rule in kirk and meeting house, and let their God out for one day of the week—poor old Man, with his teeth broke with the cursing. I presume you read the Covenant? You see He is trotted out there. They are confident He will 'defend the Right'. Supposing he doesn't! How awful if God should turn out to be a disloyalist!

Casement's reaction, then, was the stock reaction of the

Home Ruler to Ulster intransigence. Mitchell Innes, to whom he had poured out his resentment, had to tell him, 'Steady on!'; to attribute dishonesty to Carson, he pointed out, was simply to say what in all probability Carson was saying about him, equally ignorantly—'you lash yourselves with your own eloquence, till the pain makes you forget everything else'. Whether owing to Mitchell Innes's advice, or the calming effect of the voyage south to the sun, he had taken the hint: a letter he wrote to Alice Green on the subject on his way to South Africa, showed a better appreciation of the position. 'Until these men are convinced that they *can't* prevent Home Rule,' he wrote, 'they will fight; and now they are really convinced that they *can* prevent it.' He still believed that in the end they would abandon their resistance, but they would not do so lightly. 'I think the Ulster men are the best part of Ireland in many ways —and they should be convinced by appeals to their sense of justice, affection, and at bottom, love of Ireland.'

For a while, when he returned to Ireland, he was kept away from Antrim by the embarrassing fact that Ada ('Ide') MacNeill, his early mentor in the Irish language, had fallen passionately in love with him. 'I wish, poor old soul, she would leave me alone,' he had written—when he realised—to tell his cousin, enclosing one of Ide's letters: 'these repeated invitations to go to "meet her" are a bit out of place . . . I have very strong feelings of friendship for her, and goodwill, and brotherly Irish affection—and I wish she could leave other things out of her reckoning.' But he paid occasional visits to Belfast, and one of them happened to coincide with July 12th. What he saw revived his feelings about the Covenant. 'Ulster day is come and gone,' he told his cousin.

The poor duped, sincere multitude of honest boys has paraded before Carson, Smith and the God of our Fathers . . . I *love* the Antrim Presbyterians—Antrim and Down—they are good, kind warm-hearted souls—and to see them now, *exploited*, by that damned Church of Ireland—that Orange ascendancy gang who hate Presbyterians only less than Papishes, and to see them delirious before a *Smith*, a Carson (a cross between a badly raised bloodhound and an underfed hyena, sniffing for Irish blood in the track) and whooping

'Rule Britannia' through the streets, is a wound to my soul. For they are Irish right through, really.

If Casement had paused to work it out, he might have wondered whether the Ulstermen really were the dupes of the English Unionists, or whether it might be the other way around. Yet his mistake was understandable. The real leader of the Covenanters, Craig, so far from having to set the pace—as he had had to do in the early stages of the campaign against the Home Rule bill—had found the English Unionists setting it for him.

In the event of a parliamentary battle with the Liberals over Home Rule, Lord Randolph Churchill had suggested at the time of Gladstone's bill, 'the Orange card will be the one to play!' Now, Craig had realised he could persuade the Unionists to play it again, to serve his purposes. And he was lucky; Bonar Law—who had succeeded Balfour as the leader of the Unionist Party —though by birth a Canadian, was descended from Ulster Protestant stock, and he had been brought up in a family atmosphere steeped in that tradition—except that, as J. L. Hammond noted, 'the most ardent Orangeman has an Irishman beneath the skin: Mr. Bonar Law is an Orangeman without an Irishman beneath the skin'. Where Lord Randolph Churchill had said, 'Ulster will fight, and Ulster will be right', Bonar Law had taken the occasion of Ulster Day to say that if Ulster fought, she would not fight alone; 'I can imagine no length of resistance to which Ulster will go in which I shall not be ready to support them'.

F. E. Smith was even more provocative. At forty, he remained something of an *enfant terrible* in the Unionist Party, but his contemporaries were so lacking in personality that he had established himself as one of its chief spokesmen. He would not shrink from the consequences of Ulster's resistance to Home Rule, 'not though the whole fabric of the Commonwealth be convulsed'. Not to be outdone, Carson replied on September 21st to a charge that what the Unionists were advocating amounted to treason by saying: 'I do not care twopence whether it is treason or not. It is what we are going to do.'

The Ulstermen had little faith in the English Unionist leaders. According to Carson's biographer, Ian Colvin, Law was regarded as more zealous than discreet; and it was not forgotten that Smith had been one of the Unionists who had tried to do the

Home Rule deal with the Liberals in 1910. When he performed as a general's galloper at a Volunteer Review, 'Galloper' became, and remained, his derisive nickname. Still, it was useful for Craig to have political support in England for his contention that Ulster had a right to reject Home Rule. And here, though they were not aware of it, Craig and Casement held a very similar point of view. Both were claiming that the Union had validity only so long as its constituent parts were united in spirit, as well as by a common administration—an attitude very different from Lansdowne's 'We have Ireland, and we mean to keep her'.

It was also, though for obvious reasons Craig did not care to make the point, different from Carson's—as Casement realised. In an article he wrote in the autumn of 1913 for the *Nation* magazine, on 'Ulster and Ireland', he pointed out that the logic of the Unionist campaign must be that Unionism was a failure. The aim of the men who had imposed the Union in 1800—as its name implied—had been to unite the people of the two countries. Not merely, however, had the Union failed in this 'its primary function, and sole justification for the means employed'; but the Unionists themselves were claiming that Ulster had a right to secede. Their main argument against Home Rule, therefore, 'seems, to my Ulster mind, to constitute the chief argument in its favour'.

If Protestant Ulstermen were even to contemplate seceding from the United Kingdom, with or without Germany's help, they could not logically object to the Catholics of the South taking the same step. And the fact that secession was in contemplation by both might even, he argued, serve to bring them together, if there was somebody who could be the go-between. Now, he found himself cast in that role. He was asked to speak in favour of Home Rule at a meeting on October 24th in Ballymoney, near his old Ulster home.

Ballymoney   *October 1913*

The invitation came at a time when he needed it: the summer had been dispiriting. The tendency among most of his old associates, he found—MacNeill, Griffith, even Pearse—had been to fall in behind Redmond in support of Home Rule. But Asquith's Bill, in Casement's eyes, was utterly inadequate. It did not even give the Irish Parliament power to choose its own executive; foreign affairs, the armed forces, trade, tariffs, customs, even patents and trade marks, were to remain under the control of Whitehall. So limited a measure of independence, he felt, represented little more than an extension of local government powers; and when they had last been extended—by the Unionists, in the killing-Home-Rule-by-kindness period—the consequences, he knew, had been saddening for anybody imbued with Alice Green's ideals. They had merely given more power to the local politicians and the priests. Home Rule would further increase their pickings; Irish-speaking areas, which resisted their influence, would be left to rot.

Yeats's 'September 1913' reflected Casement's feelings, too. He greatly admired Yeats's poems: his favourite, he had told Alice Green two years earlier, was 'The Lover tells of the Rose in his Heart', particularly the last verse:

> The wrong of unshapely things is a wrong too great to be told
> I hunger to build them anew, and sit on a green knoll apart
> With the earth and the sky and the water, remade, like a
>   casket of gold
> For my dreams of your image that blossoms a rose in the
>   deeps of my heart.

But 'September 1913' revealed a new Yeats:

> What need you, being come to sense
> But fumble in a greasy till
> And add the halfpence to the pence
> And prayer to shivering prayer, until
> You have dried the marrow from the bone?
> For men were born to pray and save,
> Romantic Ireland's dead and gone,
> It's with O'Leary in the grave.

In England H. W. Nevinson, reading the poem, told himself: 'It is not for an Englishman like me to speak of Ireland, but Roger Casement remains alive.' But Casement, though not yet fifty, felt his age; and there was no longer any Irish movement into which he could throw himself, with *Sinn Fein* moribund, and the Irish language everywhere losing ground. And as an additional mortification, he found two causes he admired, the Co-operative movement and the Gaelic League, at loggerheads.

Writing for A. E.'s *Homestead*, and helping to found a Co-operative in Antrim, Casement had already shown his interest; and he was an admirer of Sir Horace Plunkett, who had been mainly responsible for the introduction of Co-operatives into Ireland: 'I have a very high feeling for him,' he told Cadbury, 'for his goodness of heart and love for Ireland no less than for his intellectual capacity'. He was consequently irritated to hear that Patrick Gallagher, a stalwart peasant who had founded a Co-op. society in his district of Donegal becoming locally, and eventually nationally, known as 'Paddy the Cope'—had said he had enough on his hands fighting the local storekeepers and gombeen men without having to try to keep alive a dying language, too—'an appalling illustration', Casement felt, 'of the wholly commercial and non-national side of the Co-operative movement'. When Gallagher came on a visit to London in November he and Alice Green met him, and tried to argue him round to their side. They did not succeed—rather the reverse; Gallagher, though he professed to feel it was presumption on his part 'to disagree with such a brilliant man', was able to produce convincing evidence that if the money he had obtained had been spent on the language, rather than on introducing his Co-op., the poor in his district would have been some £8,000 a year poorer than they now were. Casement could not bring himself to look at the figures that way. There should, he felt, be funds enough for both causes. But he could hardly deny that the funds available would not stretch to both. If Home Rule went through in the form now awaiting ratification by the House of Lords, the language was likely to be the first casualty.

All Casement had been able to do, for the time being, was write for the *Irish Review*—founded by, among others, the poet Padraic Colum, who was to recall him at this time as having 'the appearance and manner of a hidalgo', and talking 'in a low unforgettable voice, of impending crises'. As it happened, Casement was here in the company of many of the men who were later to be the leaders of the 1916 Rising—Sean MacDermott, Thomas MacDonagh, Joseph Plunkett, and James Connolly, as well as Pearse. But at the time, the pleasure of seeing his work in print was poor compensation for the lack of more active work to occupy him, in the cause of Irish independence.

The invitation to speak at the Ballymoney meeting trans-

formed his life. He had continued to keep his distance from the
glens that summer, because he was dodging Ide MacNeill—he
even felt unable to go to an Irish summer school in Donegal, as
he liked to do if he could, because she would be there; and early
in September, when he heard she was back in Antrim, he begged
his cousin not to let her know that he was going to be in Belfast.
But at Ballymoney, Alice Green was also to be on the platform;
the prospect was too good to resist; and the objective—to show
that some Antrim Protestants, at least, were 'standing out to
fight Carsonism, and proclaim their faith in a United Ireland'—
delighted him. He had never before appeared on a political
platform, rarely on a platform of any kind; and it would be his
first attempt at a public speech.

His host was the local Presbyterian minister, the Reverend J.
B. Armour. 'Armour of Ballymoney' was already a legendary
figure, one of the leaders of the campaign for tenants' rights,
years before, and a Home Ruler. He combined great Christian
charity with a shrewd notion of how to deal with the local
Unionists; when he heard there was to be an Orange counter-
demonstration with drums, on the day of the Home Rule meeting, he announced that the cost of bringing in a force of police,
should that be necessary, would be defrayed from the rates—
'the only way', as he put it, of allowing 'a tolerant spirit to
enter the brains of those anxious for interruptions'. He found
Casement 'a very charming guest'; and Casement was delighted
with his organisation—'everybody says it was the finest meeting
ever held in the Town Hall'. Not even the fact that Ide came
could spoil it for him.

In his speech, which was reported almost in full by both the
Unionist *Irish Times* and the Nationalist *Freeman's Journal*, he
argued that the exclusion of Ulster would not be a solution to
the Home Rule crisis—and the fact that the Town Hall was filled
with local Protestants, applauding such sentiments, could be
taken as one indication why. The London *Times*' special correspondent, however, dismissed Ballymoney as only 'a small
and isolated pocket of dissident Protestants'—the last of the
Irish Gladstonian Liberals; and what the meeting in fact did, he
felt, was 'reveal the scantiness of their numbers'. Casement
disagreed. There were other places nearby, he claimed in a letter
to the editor, where a similar meeting could be held. But he was
mainly concerned to rebut the *Times*' correspondent's implica-

tion that he had been asked to speak because of the fame he had won on his travels, rather than as an Ulsterman. 'My father and grandfather were both citizens of Belfast,' he pointed out, 'and my family for generations have been closely associated with County Antrim life'—which was more than Carson or F. E. Smith could claim; 'I have lived amongst Ulster people many years of my life, and in quiet and daily contact with them I have learned to know them well.'

The Ballymoney meeting introduced Casement to the role he was best fitted to undertake in the independence movement: persuading his fellow Ulster Protestants that they need not fear Home Rule. There were others who shared his view— Stephen Gwynn, Bulmer Hobson, Herbert Pim—whose *Unconquerable Ulster* was to have a foreword by Carson, but who was a member of *Sinn Fein*—and St. John Ervine, the Abbey Theatre playwright, who insisted there was no more difference between a Southern Catholic and an Ulster Protestant than between a Manchester Dissenter and a Tunbridge Wells Anglican, and who argued that Home Rule would give Ulster the chance to run the entire country. 'What Ireland needs is not Home Rule, but Ulster rule; and when Ulster has recovered from her sulks, she will take care that Ireland gets it.' But none of them were in as good a position as Casement to put this view across—as Ervine obliquely recognised, when he said that if the Ulster Covenanters had wished to rebel 'they would not have sent for Sir Edward Carson; they would have sent for Sir Roger Casement'.

In a second article on 'Ulster and Ireland', Casement proposed the aim should be to revive the Presbyterian tradition—still alive, as the Ballymoney meeting showed. In 1798 some Ulster Presbyterians had joined in the rebellion against the Crown, and the Ulster Anglicans had flogged and hanged them, along with the Catholics. Since then, out of self-interest, the Anglicans had stopped persecuting the Presbyterians, in order to win their support against the Catholics. If the Presbyterians could be made to show how they had been duped, and persuaded once again to regard the Catholics as their natural allies, there would be no more Ulster problem.

Written under some such pseudonym as 'An Ulster Protestant' the article would have attracted little attention; but Casement was able to put his name to it. During October, the negotiations over his pension were finally brought to their con-

clusion. 'Yes, I'm finally finished with the Foreign Office for
good and all—thank goodness', he wrote to tell his cousin.
They had not been generous with his pension (he was to get
£421 13s. 6d. a year) but he did not mind that, 'freedom at any
price is a blessed thing'; and one of the earliest uses to which
he put it was to tell the *Fortnightly* editor that he could use his
name. Congratulatory messages about it came from people
whose opinions he respected, like Alice Green. Erskine Childers
—the author of *The Riddle of the Sands*, and one of the group
of what Conan Doyle described as 'Imperialist Home Rulers'—
also wrote to pay his respects, and to invite him, when next he
came to London, to stay.

But these tributes, though flattering, represented a reminder
that he was still in an equivocal position. As he was no longer
in the Foreign Office, he could in theory write as he pleased. But
to continue to impress Childers—or even Alice Green, who for
all her nationalism continued to believe in the need for close ties
between England and Ireland—he could not safely avow his
pro-German sentiments; certainly not in the form he had expressed them in his unsigned articles. If he wished to become a
unifying force in the independence movement, he must proceed
warily.

But he was not disposed to be wary. He knew what he wanted
for Ireland, and was becoming impatient to get it. At the Ballymoney meeting one of the speakers had been another Antrim
Protestant, James White; a complex character, the son of the
general who had defended Ladysmith, himself a former captain
in the army, but a convert to Tolstoy's ideas. They had a row,
at their first meeting; and although White came to admire his
dedication, he thought his character was flawed; 'do all diplomats think they can wangle anything? Casement did'. Other
friends had begun to find him the prey to his obsessions. Even
Alice Green at times found him hard to bear: 'sometimes when
I listen to that man,' she complained, 'I feel that I never want
to hear the subject of Ireland mentioned again'. To the staff of
the *Irish Review*, when it printed one of his poems incorrectly,
he appeared as 'an Etna vomiting a most devastating lava of
boiling hot abuse'. The young Cork nationalist, J. J. Horgan,
introduced to him that winter, admired and liked him, but felt
he gave an impression of instability and restlessness; and Erskine Childers's young wife, when they met, thought him crazed.

CHAPTER TWO

THE VOLUNTEERS

Rise, men of Ireland!   *November 1913*

Casement had hoped that—as he told Alice Green early in
November—Carsonism 'might open the eyes of all that is best
in John Bull and stiffen his resolution'. But now,

> I feel I have no heart to try and plead: I feel far more disposed
> to go to Athlone, to Dublin, to Galway, and plead there, and
> say, 'Rise, men of Ireland, and arm, too. Arm yourselves to
> defend your land, your homes, and assert your freedom as
> men—that is the task that Ulster sets you. Follow her lead,
> and in this day of trial Ireland shall win her freedom by her
> own strong heart and arm.'

The Volunteer movement in the North, he felt, was fine; 'it is
the act of men, and I like it'. Within days, he was to be given
the opportunity—two, as it happened—to fulfil his ambition,
and work for the introduction of the Volunteer movement in the
South.

One of them was offered by Captain White. Just as Casement
had been appalled by the conditions he had found in Connemara,
White had been horrified by what he saw in the Dublin slums,
where—an official inquiry revealed in 1913—6,000 families of
seven or more lived in single rooms. 1913, too, was the year in
which the Dublin employers, led and held together by William
Martin Murphy, fought and eventually won a protracted battle
against the workers of James Larkin's trade union. 'Blind Sam-
sons', A.E. described the employers in October, 'pulling down
the pillars of the social order'; and he warned that 'the men
whose manhood you have broken will loathe you, and will
always be brooding and scheming to strike a fresh blow'. They
had not brooded long. Larkin advised them to take a leaf out
of Carson's book; when he was arrested and imprisoned for
seditious language of the kind Carson was using with impunity,

James Connolly took up the idea—'Why should we not drill and train our men in Dublin as they are doing in Ulster?'; and Captain White undertook to do the training of the new Citizen Army.

His immediate aim, as he wrote to tell Casement, was to give the workers some discipline, through drill; his ultimate ambition, to fuse the Socialist and Nationalist causes in Ireland on the prescription which Fintan Lalor had first provided in the later 1840s. This was very much to Casement's taste; Lalor's prescription had been Davitt's, too. Like Davitt, Casement did not call himself a Socialist, but he was not offended when described as one—as he had been in 1905 by a friend who thought an article he had written on Tzarist Russia was 'red-hot socialism'. When he described the Putumayo Indians' tribal society as Socialist, he clearly meant it as a compliment. Disparaging the English political parties, he dismissed their different labels on one occasion as of no significance; all were playing the same game—self-interest; 'until a real Socialist upheaval comes to sweep the whole building nothing can really be changed'. But he thought of 'a real Socialist upheaval' much as a Christian might think of the Second Coming: not as practical politics. Although he wrote back, expressing his warm approval of White's plans, he did not follow up his letter, as he ordinarily did when his imagination was fired.

It was fired, without qualification, by the news that a Volunteer force on the same line as Craig's was about to be formed in the South of Ireland. During the summer a few groups had formed locally; Hobson had suggested that they ought to be welded into a national force; and on November 1st, an article by Eoin MacNeill appeared in the Gaelic League's journal, taking up the idea. Hobson thereupon visited him, along with the journal's business manager, The O'Rahilly (his 'The' representing a claim to be head of the clan), to ask whether he would be prepared to set up a Volunteer organisation with their help; and MacNeill agreed.

It proved to be an unlucky choice. The estimable MacNeill was a scholar by training and temperament. 'I have seldom seen a man more unfitted for action', Alice Green said of him; 'less fit to lead others in a difficult crisis, and less wise in his judgment of men.' A Home Ruler rather than a separatist, he saw the Volunteers' function much as Grattan had seen it. They were there to make sure that Home Rule, now promised, was not unconstitutionally blocked. But Hobson and the other members of the Irish Republican Brotherhood who were on the provisional committee were content temporarily to accept this line, hoping recruits would be attracted who would not join an overtly separatist organisation.

With MacNeill and Hobson both friends of long standing, Casement was naturally drawn to the Volunteers: he became a member of the Provisional Committee, and was despatched to London to explain to the English press what was afoot. On November 20th the Liberal *Daily Chronicle* devoted a column on its main news page to an interview with him under the headline 'Why he is organising National Volunteers'; and the point he was chiefly concerned to make was that they were not directed against the Ulster Volunteers. To the Ulstermen, Casement said, he would say:

> You are arming and drilling to suppress crime and disorder or an attack on your liberties. There we shall be with you. We believe it is our right equally with yours to arm and drill in the same cause, and should any attack be made upon your liberties from any quarter, we shall be the first to come to your assistance.

He also emphasised that the Volunteers were not going to be used to try to coerce Ulster. On the contrary, he insisted, Catholic Ireland 'would shrink at no sacrifice, short of the principle of self-government, in order to secure the goodwill and co-operation of the Irish Protestants as a whole'.

He was still in England when the new Volunteers were launched on November 25th, at a meeting at the Rotunda in Dublin; but when he returned, he helped MacNeill to compose their manifesto—an over-long and stilted document, with only one pithy sentiment, 'they have rights who dare maintain them'. The Volunteers' objective would be:

> to secure and maintain the rights and liberties common to all the people of Ireland. Their duties will be defensive and protective, and they will not contemplate either aggression or domination. The ranks are open to all able-bodied Irishmen without distinction of race, creed, politics or social grade.

Means will be found whereby Irishmen unable to serve as ordinary Volunteers will be enabled to aid the Volunteer forces in various capacities. There will also be work for women to do.

'She knows we are slaves'   *December 1913–January 1914*

As he was the best known—to the general public—of the members of the Volunteer executive, and as his time was his own, Casement was an obvious choice to tour the country on a recruiting campaign; and for the next six months, this was to be his main activity. It happened that the first meeting which he went to address, along with MacNeill, was in Cork; and this was to lead to a development which was to have a decisive influence on him—the first, in fact, of a series which were eventually to carry him over the border between constitutional action and treason.

The Cork meeting itself was almost a disaster. The attitude of the Home Rulers to the Ulster Volunteers had been hostile; Casement at this time was almost alone in his approval. But he found an ally in MacNeill; and at the end of his speech, MacNeill actually called for three cheers for Carson. As he had failed to explain why, there was an ugly riot, some of the audience trying to rush the platform. The newspapers—which, if they were not Unionist, tended to support the Irish Party—reported that the meeting had ended in disorder. Not so, Casement claimed in a letter written to his sister and his cousin:

The Cork meeting was a *great success*; the press report lies. I had a grand reception, a hurricane of cheers and embraces too from workmen, and 700 men enrolled as Volunteers! The reporters bolted when the row began, and we held our place, and then when the tumult died the O'Scodge * called the sea back from its bed, and the Cork men said yes, they wanted to hear me; and so it all ended splendidly.

As he went on to explain, Casement had another reason for his visit: he was 'fighting hell and all its angels over the Cork and Queenstown route to the U.S.A.'. The Cunard company,

* Casement usually signed himsef 'Scodge', or some variant, in his letters to his sister and cousin.

which had long called to take on passengers at Queenstown (as Cobh was then called), had announced that autumn that it was not sufficiently safe for its new large liners. Why not, then— Casement had suggested in a letter to the *Irish Times*—invite one of the German lines to call instead? Finding the Cork nationalists were interested—especially the young J. J. Horgan, a follower of Redmond's—he decided to approach the company through a German intermediary; and he persuaded it to try the experiment—putting the English, he told his cousin just before Christmas, 'in a blue funk, a regular panic'; they were 'trying every dodge they can to keep the German line off'. The Hamburg–Amerika line duly announced that one of its eastbound liners would call at Queenstown in January; a date was fixed; and the Lord Mayor of Cork prepared to give a civic reception. 'There may be strange sights in Cork harbour on the 20th,' Casement wrote gaily to Alice Green: 'Irish flags and German joined—and other strange things.' It was from that harbour, he recalled, that John Mitchel had 'sailed a convict in H.M.S. *Scourge* (well-named).' He would himself, he had decided, charter a tug, to bring out the Cork Volunteers, along with a band, to welcome the liner.

The following day, there was the first indication that all was not going smoothly with the project: a letter to say that although the Hamburg–Amerika line would welcome the Lord Mayor on board the *Rhaetia*, they felt that the proposed civic (and musical) welcome was going too far: it might offend British susceptibilities. As for demonstrations, if there were going to be any, they would give up the idea of calling at Queenstown altogether. Casement had to go again to Cork to explain why the plans must be changed. 'I am in despair,' he wrote to Alice Green. '*Sean Buide* * has won! The *Rhaetia*, due on the 20th at Cork, may not call!' It did not call. The pretext was that no passengers had made bookings; but this, he felt sure, was just an excuse. He was momentarily heartened when told that the company had only postponed the call—'it was the demonstration they feared—at least so they say'. But when it was announced that the *Fürst Bismarck* was not going to call, either, he guessed that the Company had been frightened off. They had. At the end of January it was formally announced that the liners would call in future at Southampton, rather than at Cork.

* John Bull.

Casement's involvement in the affair was no sudden whim. He wrote in a letter to the *Irish Times* on February 3rd (he had been keeping both the *Irish Times* and the *Independent* supplied with information on what was happening behind the scenes) that it would 'make a chapter in commercial history that I venture to think should turn many Irishmen at home into Home Rulers—and those abroad into something more'. The episode had touched on an issue he felt deeply about: the exploitation of the Irish, throughout Irish history, by English governments in the interests of English merchants. From his study of Irish commerce in the Middle Ages, Casement knew how English merchants had made it impossible for the Irish to trade with other nations, except through Britain. Now, through his study of trade statistics, he knew that the English merchants were still at the game. In an article which he had been composing, he estimated that of the £63 millions-worth of exports from Ireland in 1910, Britain had taken more than £52 millions; and of the £11m-worth of exports from Ireland shipped to other countries, only £700,000-worth was sent from Irish ports. More than £10 millions-worth of Irish exports, in other words, had to be sent to England, 'to pay a heavy transit toll to that country for discharge, handling, agency commission, and reloading on British vessels in British ports, to steam back past the shores of the Ireland it had just left'.

So long as there had been hordes of Irish emigrants compelled by the threat of starvation to leave for America, it had been worth Cunard's while to pick them up at Cork, in order to discourage anybody else from trying to capture the business. But now that it was mostly wealthier Irishmen and women who were travelling across the Atlantic, 'why trouble to delay in Irish ports when you can get the Irish all the same by making them go to your ports?' This plan would have been spoiled if the Hamburg–Amerika liners had begun to call at Cobh. So, the Post Office (which disliked the delay that a call in Ireland necessitated) and the Board of Trade (which was concerned about the need for faster times for Atlantic crossing, enabling British liners to compete with European rivals) must have agreed to put pressure on the Hamburg–Amerika line, presumably by the threat of withdrawing facilities the line enjoyed in British ports.

This was the explanation Casement gave to the *Irish Times* and, at greater length, in a series of three articles in the *Irish*

Review. The *Irish Times* expressed the opinion that he had said either too little or too much. If, as he claimed, diplomatic pressure really had been brought to bear on the German line, 'Irish Unionists will be the first to protest'; but was this really true? The public was entitled to know what had happened. Neither the Hamburg–Amerika line nor the British Government cared to explain; and the mystery has never been resolved.

For Casement, the episode was decisive. Writing to Colonel Maurice Moore—a former British army officer who had undertaken to train the Volunteers—he had emphasised the need for funds to equip them, but admitted he could see no hope of collecting them locally. The only possible source was America. According to the census of 1910, there were over 4,500,000 people in the United States who were Irish-born, or had one Irish parent; the memory of the circumstances which had forced their families into exile—the famine, and evictions—made them sympathetic to the cause of Irish independence, and ready, if their feelings were touched, to contribute to funds for this and for related causes (Patrick Pearse had been over that winter, to get money to keep St. Enda's going). For some years, Casement had been in casual correspondence with John Devoy, still in control of *Clan-na-Gael*—which meant, though Casement did not know it, that he was virtually in control of the Irish Republican Brotherhood. As the best-known name in the independence movement, Casement felt, Devoy should welcome him. And he had more to offer Devoy. When Bulmer Hobson went to the United States early in 1914, he took with him a memorandum from Casement on relations between Ireland and Germany in the event of a war in Europe, which Devoy described as 'an able document'; and also, the promise of a manuscript which, Casement believed, would devastatingly expose the ugly truth about the British administration in Ireland. It had been written by William Henry Joyce, who had worked as a secret agent for the British Government, and who had decided to reveal what this had entailed. 'The evidence is there,' Casement wrote to Alice Green on January 30th,

the corruption is there, the shamelessness is there, the debauchery of the 'public service' by the higher servants of the State is there; all for political ends against Ireland. It is an

epitome of English dealing with Ireland, and might walk
straight out of the Calendar of State Papers of Tudor days.

Better still, it showed how deeply Balfour had been involved
in the manipulation of spies and *agents provocateurs* to try to
discredit Parnell and the whole nationalist movement. Now, the
Hamburg-Amerika affair finally determined Casement to go to
America; 'the whole centre of the game is the "Anglo-Saxon
alliance" and it is in the U.S.A. we must hold up the hand of
Ireland';

> I am going, Please God!, to carry this fight much further than
> they think in Downing Street—to an arbitrament they dread
> very much. They will pay dearly for their 'diplomacy', and
> our whole people, I hope, will begin to *think* on these things
> —and think as freemen, not as slaves. For the solution lies
> always in our hands. The day we *will* our freedom, we can
> achieve it. Rest assured of that. It is not England now enslaves
> us. She simply deals with us as slaves because she knows we
> are slaves.

If John Bull betrayed Ireland again, Casement concluded, 'as
I'm quite sure he means to do, then with the help of God and
some Irishmen, he'll learn that all Irishmen are not slaves, and
there is fight in us still'.

The Curragh 'Mutiny' *February—March 1914*

While he was involved in the negotiations with the Hamburg—
Amerika line, Casement had continued with his recruiting
activities for the Volunteers, visiting town after town around
Ireland, and addressing rallies. Without exception the meetings
had been crowded and enthusiastic. In Galway, he wrote to tell
his cousin, young men had filled the town hall almost to the
roof. Trying to speak without notes, he forgot what he was
going to say, but it made no difference; at the end, they stormed
the platform to sign on. The Limerick meeting in January was
also splendid; 'the faces were handsome, strong and good'.
Although he had been billed as the chief speaker, when he found
that Pearse was to be there he handed the honour over to him,
as an accomplished orator; and Pearse had spoken very impres-

sively. So, Casement had contented himself with talking to the audience, rather than trying to make a speech, and they had cheered him—cheered even his praise of the Ulstermen.

He still believed that there was a chance of bringing the Ulstermen round to see that their real interest lay in allying themselves with the Southerners; and on February 10th, 1914, Carson dropped a broad hint that he himself contemplated that possibility. There were only two ways to make Ulster accept Home Rule, he told the Commons: she must either be coerced, or won over to the Home Rule cause. Did Redmond really want to coerce the North into obedience? 'You have never tried to understand the position . . . if you want Ulster, go and take her, or go and win her.' To Casement, here was the opportunity he had been looking for. Although by this time he no longer believed that any solution for the Irish problem could be found at Westminster—'what loyalty can any Irishman with brains and heart have for *any* English Government?' he asked Alice Green, 'I have none'—he was still prepared to argue that independent Ireland 'could and would be loyal to a true Imperialism—or, as I hate the word, to a true Common Weal of Federated Irish and British States'. Carson's speech seemed at last to hold out hope that a way could be found to bring this about. Now was his chance, as he wrote to tell Horgan on February 16th:

> I've a good mind to write to Carson tonight, and ask him to come to Cork with me. My God! I wonder what would happen if he said, 'yes' . . . He could save Ireland, and make Ireland. But it is a dream to think of him doing it—if he really loved Ireland, as I do, he'd come. Shall I ask him? I don't know him at all, and I've blackguarded him openly in the Holy of Holies (County Antrim), but he knows I'm honest, and sincere, and fearless—qualities he himself, I think, possesses. I like him far better than those craven, scheming, plotting Englishmen, whose one aim is to see how *little* freedom they can give Ireland.

But it was a dream, Casement feared; and a dream it turned out to be. Redmond threw away the opportunity; and Carson was soon jeering again at the Home Rulers, who wanted 'not Ulster's affections but her taxes'. Casement was despondent. 'I feel it in my bones I am going to have an awful time of it,' he told Alice Green. 'But it must be—Fate drives me on', and he begged her not to blame him if he now appeared to be consumed with hatred of John Bull: 'it is wholly impersonal, just as we are told to hate *Sin*'. But Casement was deceiving himself. He could no longer love the sinner. And in March 1914, there came the blow which seemed to him to demonstrate conclusively that he had been right not to trust John Bull.

During the parliamentary recess in the autumn of 1913, the British Unionists had calmed down a little over Ulster; and with Asquith's consent King George had seized the opportunity to open consultations with the party leaders, to look for some compromise solution. One had already been put forward, in an amendment to the Home Rule bill: a partition of Ireland, leaving the North in the United Kingdom, and giving the South Home Rule. Redmond was put under steady and skilful pressure to accept a compromise whereby Ulster, or part of Ulster, would be temporarily excluded from the terms of the Home Rule bill, to avoid the risk of bloody conflict. Early in March, he accepted —on condition that this really was the last compromise that he would be asked to make—'that on the rejection of the proposal by the Opposition, the Government should pass the bill as it stands', and face whatever consequences might ensue—including the inevitable rejection by Carson.

This, Asquith felt, was reasonable; and the Government prepared for enforcement by ordering troops stationed in the Curragh camp, near Dublin, to the North. On March 30th the War Office was informed that the great majority of officers in the regiments involved would resign their commissions, or accept dismissal, rather than obey the order to move North; and they secured a pledge that they would not be used, under the pretext of maintaining law and order, to enforce the provisions of the Home Rule bill. Although Asquith repudiated the pledge in the form it had been given, the damage had been done. Home Rule might become law, but would the law be obeyed by the military? Technically, the officers concerned had not been guilty of mutiny. Asked what they would do in certain circumstances, they had given their reply; but as the circumstances had not arisen, they had not felt called upon to risk facing the consequences. To the Irish nationalists, however, this was a quibble —just one more indication that English governments could not be trusted. It was also suspected—rightly, it was soon to be known—that the plot had been hatched in the War Office. If the British Government could not control its own government departments, there could be no certainty that Home Rule could be introduced even in the South.

'What a mess!' Casement wrote to Alice Green. 'Well,—you know what I have always told you! I've said to you, dear and priceless woman of the Gael, that *this* Government would not do it. And you see that I'm right.' As Carson had said at a meeting at Dungannon—Casement and Erskine Childers had both been there, and heard him—'all government rests on force; all law rests on force'. This, Casement felt, could now be regarded as proved, so far as Ireland was concerned. He wrote a joint letter with MacNeill to the *Irish Independent*, which was published on March 28th, claiming that the Curragh affair had finally made clear what ought not to have been in doubt; the 'Union' meant no more than the military occupation of Ireland as a conquered country, and 'the real headquarters of the Irish Government on the Unionist principle is the Curragh camp, to which the offices of Dublin Castle are a sort of vermiform appendix'. The important point, Casement and MacNeill emphasised, was not simply that the Curragh officers had successfully dictated the course of policy to the British Government, but that their action had been wholeheartedly endorsed 'by leaders and spokesmen of the British governing class'. It was consequently as well, they concluded, that the Curragh affair had happened. The Irish people would now have to face the fact that they could not hope to get their independence from England. They would have to take it, and they must now realise the duty this 'imposed upon their honour and patriotism'.

Running the guns   *March–April 1914*

The recruiting campaign for the Volunteers was continuing to bring gratifying results; and for this Casement, as the recruiter-in-chief, could claim much of the credit. Colonel Maurice Moore, whatever his abilities as a director of training, found himself hopelessly confused when trying to deal with what he described to him, early in January, as 'heads of factions'—Foresters, Hibernians, Gaelic League, Labourers' Association, Temperance Association, Drapers Association, Celtic Literary Society, Town Tenants Associations (all these, Moore complained, existed in

one small town, Ballyglass in County Mayo, which wanted to
have a meeting; and all wanted to have their say). Casement
had sensed that what was important was not organisation, but
spirit. He refused to have anything to do with 'heads of factions',
addressing himself simply to potential Volunteers.

But it was not enough, he realised, to secure recruits. They
must have arms. 'Had we only rifles and officers', he wrote to
tell Moore early in April, 'we could have 150,000 splendid men
in six months.' To Moore, a constitutionalist, the proposal was
shocking: Casement had hastily to reassure him that he was
not anxious for a rebellion. Nor, at this point, was he; it was
simply that the Curragh affair had convinced him that independence would not be obtained without at least the threat of
force.

Redmond was slowly coming round to the same view. As he
had convinced himself that Home Rule would become law that
summer, he had regarded the volunteer movement with mistrust; they might get involved in some clash which would jeopardise the bill. But now that it was gaining recruits so rapidly,
many of them members of the Irish Party, he could no longer
afford to ignore it; and he summoned MacNeill to a meeting in
London. Nothing came of it, but MacNeill could see that
eventually Redmond would feel compelled to intervene; and the
following day, he went with Casement to have lunch with Alice
Green—whose faith in the Liberal Government's intentions had
been shaken by their handling of the Curragh affair—to discuss
what could be done to prevent him from securing control of the
Volunteers.

Also at the lunch was Darrell Figgis, an English author who
had spent many years in the west of Ireland, and had become
attracted to *Sinn Fein*. He had not seen Casement before. 'Of
all the men I have ever met,' he was to claim in his *Recollections*,
'in a wayfaring life, men of every sort and description, I have
never met a man of so single and selfless a mind, or of so natural
and noble a gesture of soul, as he.' The best way to keep Redmond from taking control of the Volunteers, Casement suggested, would be to ensure that any Volunteer corps which could
be relied upon should be armed: but how? Figgis—by his own
account—thereupon offered his services. MacNeill was returning
to Dublin that night. Figgis proposed that he should ask
O'Rahilly to come over with whatever money he could collect,

and with addresses of possible contacts on the Continent; and Figgis himself would then go and buy the arms:

> Never while I live will I forget the effect of my offer on one of the company present. The picture is indelibly written to the last detail . . . Looking outward before the window curtains, stood Roger Casement, a figure of perplexity, and the apparent dejection which he always wore so proudly, as though he had assumed the sorrows of the world. His face was in profile to me, his handsome head and noble outline cut out against the lattice-work of the curtain and the grey sky. His height seemed more than usually commanding, his black hair and beard longer than usual. His left leg was thrown forward, and the boot was torn in a great hole—for he gave his substance away always, and left himself thus in need, he who could so little afford to take these risks with his health. But as I spoke he left his place by the window and came forward towards me, his face alight with battle. 'That's talking,' he said, throwing his hand on the table between us; and I remember the whimsical thought crossing my mind that language had wandered far from its meanings when one man could say to another that he was talking, when his appreciation and brevity betokened an end of talking.

This decision, Figgis was to claim, was taken before the news that twenty thousand rifles and three million rounds of ammunition had been brought from Hamburg to Larne, where on April 24th they were unloaded and efficiently distributed throughout Ulster, while the authorities stood by helpless—or applauding. Logically, Casement might have been expected to be pleased by this further evidence of the North's determination to defy the British Government. And up to a point, he was. But Larne also destroyed the hope he had clung to that he might be able to do a deal with Carson. Early in April, he had tried to see Carson in Belfast, with a view to persuading him that there should be some link-up between the two Volunteer organisations—not as improbable as it might sound; in some places in Ulster they used the same halls for drill, and had established amicable relations. Carson, too, had wryly expressed admiration for the movement in the South; he actually said that if Home Rule were introduced he hoped it would succeed and, if it did, 'it might even be for the interest of Ulster itself to move towards that Government, and come in under it and form one unit in relation to Ireland'. Ultimately, he envisaged Ireland as a federal unit—which was not far off Casement's ideal of an independent Ireland linked by ties of affection to Britain—or St. John Ervine's idea of an independent Ireland run by the richer, more talented, and more industrious Ulstermen. But Carson was no longer in control. His value to Craig had been his influence at Westminster; now, Westminster mattered less to Craig. The Curragh and Larne had left his position so strong that Carson was almost expendable. Personally, Craig might have accepted Carson's and Ervine's view. A united Ireland dominated by Ulster would be an attractive proposition. But he would hardly be able to put it across to the Covenanters, conditioned as they had been so believe that they would be at the mercy of the Catholic majority in the South.

There was a further danger, which Casement realised; that the British Government, unable to coerce the North, would find some excuse to deny Home Rule to the South—and to do so, they could put the Curragh force to a purpose to which its officers would not object. This could only be prevented, he could now claim, by arming the Volunteers; 'when you are challenged in the field of force, it is upon that field you must reply'. O'Rahilly had not been able to raise the money; but Casement persuaded Alice Green and some of her English friends to put up a loan, to be paid back out of the proceeds of the sale of the rifles and ammunition to individual Volunteers. The difficulty would be transporting them: funds would not rise to the chartering of a ship. Private yachts, he decided, would have to suffice; and Erskine Childers, who was in London, offered his services, with his *Asgard*.

Although an Englishman, Childers had been brought up in Ireland; and like Alice Green, he was disgusted by what he felt was the spinelessness of the Asquith government over the Curragh and Larne. To be certain of securing Home Rule, he agreed, the Irish must have a force capable of frightening the British into giving it. Casement took him and Figgis to see the London agent for a Belgian arms firm; they also looked at samples which had been sent by O'Rahilly's Hamburg contact; and Childers and Figgis set off to make their purchases. The project was kept secret even from MacNeill. As things turned out, this was a sensible precaution. At a further meeting on May 7th, Redmond told MacNeill that the last thing he wanted was for the Volunteers to be armed—which would have worried MacNeill, had he known they were going to be.

Postscript   *May 1914*

While he was in London, Casement gave evidence to a Royal Commission on the Civil Service which was inquiring into, among other things, the Diplomatic and Consular Services. He had intended to sever all connection with his past, but this was an opportunity too good to be forgone. It paid his travel and living expenses (£1 a day); and it enabled him to make publicly all the criticisms of the Foreign Office that he had made privately (sometimes not very privately) during the twenty years he had been in its employment.

His own career, as he pointed out to the Commission on May 8th, was a striking example of the almost lunatic lack of any system of selection, promotion and employment. He had been brought in by a back door—from the Niger Coast Protectorate; there had been no examination. There ought, he suggested, to be open competition for entry as there was for other branches of the Civil Service. Once in the service, too, promotion and payment were not related to work or responsibility, but simply to status, a Vice-Consul might have far more responsibility than a Consul-General, yet he would be paid less. Perquisites varied ludicrously; at Lourenço Marques he had a consulate, at Santos, the office behind a coffee shop. The Consul was supposed to act as relieving officer, for British subjects who were in need; but he was not allowed to advance them money (if he did, he had to do it out of his own pocket, and hope to get it back later). He was supposed to fulfil many of the responsibilities of an Ambassador; yet if he had to leave his post, he might have to lay his hands on 'a publican or a nigger' (he might have added, a clergyman) to be his substitute. And he was supposed to represent, and to promote, his country's trading interests, in his spare time—after an exhausting day at the office. At the recollection, Casement's contempt for trade again erupted. How, he asked, could that be expected of a Consul?

If you are in a very hot and unhealthy climate the first thing you want to do is get home and take a bath and change your clothes—they are wet through—and get some food—and then you are not going out to rummage round the town and push British commerce in bootlaces.

The remedy, he urged, was simple: merge the Consular and Diplomatic Services, as they were merged in Germany. The trouble with the Consular Service was that it was controlled by the Foreign Office, and 'nobody in the Foreign Office has ever been a Consul, or knows anything about the duties of a Consul'. Men who would otherwise have been tempted to make a career in the service became discouraged: 'as now constituted, it offers no inducement to a man of intelligence or commercial ability, because there is no promotion in it'.

The chairman of the Royal Commission thanked him politely for coming over 'at considerable personal inconvenience'; but it was unlikely that any attention would have been paid to his advice, even if the war had not intervened to close the debate on the future of the two Services. Diplomats in the Foreign Office shared his repugnance at being involved in trade; a merger would not have commended itself. Besides, it would have meant the end of the social exclusivity of 'the Diplomatic'. Consuls could hardly be expected to put up the minimum requirement of £400 a year, the sum which Duff Cooper, who had just entered the Foreign Office, found to be the obligatory minimum of private means—twice as much being needed for a post in any important capital.

Before going back to Ireland, Casement wanted to see Wilfrid Scawen Blunt, a veteran fighter in Irish and other causes, to get his views on the Volunteer movement. He wrote to introduce himself by saying how much he had enjoyed Blunt's *Land War in Ireland*, and went down for the day. Blunt was impressed: 'an interesting man of the same type as Michael Davitt', he noted in his journal, 'only much bigger and better looking; still, very like him'—a compliment which he would greatly have valued. Blunt did not feel the prospects for the Volunteer movement were encouraging. 'All the same, I wish it well, and if anyone can manage it, Casement seems to be the man. He is well-bred, well-educated, altogether vigorous, and a good talker.'

Then, Casement set off back for Ireland, bringing an airgun with him—hoping, he wrote to tell Blunt, that it would be confiscated on his arrival, so that he could point to the contrast of arms flowing in to Ulster 'unchecked, unchallenged and unpunished'. The only solution, he was sure, was that arms should flow in to the Volunteers in the South, too.

Redmond intervenes   May–June 1914

At the end of May, Casement was exhilarated. His gun-running project was satisfactorily under way, and recruits were pouring in to the Volunteers in ever greater numbers—in Ulster, as well as in the other provinces. On his return, he addressed a succession of meetings in County Tyrone—three in a day, on one occasion; and he was delighted to find that the Ulster Catholics were prepared to cheer him, and other Protestant speakers. This, he believed, was greatly improving the prospects for Irish unity, because it meant that Southern Protestants were losing their suspicions of the Volunteer movement. A number of Protestant peers had publicly identified themselves with it. And that this was not unwarranted optimism was confirmed by a writer in the *Contemporary Review*, that summer; 'the broad spirit of the National Volunteers has given a message of hope to many Irish Unionists. These men in North and South have begun to respect each other; in an unexpected way, the shadow of the sword has become a presage of understanding and reconciliation.'

But, just as it looked as if Casement's hopes for the Volunteers were going to be fulfilled, Redmond at last intervened. His negotiations with MacNeill had continued, but without result; and he realised that time was running out for him. The Larne gun-running made it certain that Home Rule could no longer be introduced peacefully; and the Curragh affair suggested that it might have to be won by a show of force. If so, he must have the Volunteers—there was by this time over 100,000 of them —under his control. In a statement issued to the press on June 9th, he criticised the leaders of the Volunteer movement as unrepresentative, and demanded that twenty-five of his own nominees should be brought on to the provisional committee. Otherwise, he said, he would feel compelled to set up an independent executive, to which those Volunteers who supported the Irish Party would be asked to give their allegiance.

Casement had been ill, in Belfast, at the beginning of June.

Withdrawn from the recruiting rallies, he had been pondering the course the Volunteers should take. The success of the recruiting campaign, he realised, had left the provisional committee in an anomalous position; it was essentially a Dublin body, and the great mass of new recruits were from the country. On the evening of Monday, June 8th, he had come to the conclusion that it was time for each county to be represented on the committee by a delegate; and he went to Dublin the following day to put this proposal. It was agreed to call a special meeting of the provisional committee to discuss it; but before it could be held, Redmond delivered his ultimatum.

The provisional committee met again that evening, to decide what to do; and at the meeting—an unusually large one, with over twenty of the thirty members present—it was agreed to present Casement's proposal as an alternative to Redmond's. Being the more democratic of the two, he felt it would be difficult for Redmond to reject it, particularly as his chief criticism of the provisional committee had been that it was not sufficiently representative of the country as a whole; and he wrote long flattering letters to Redmond, to explain. But Redmond was not susceptible to flattery; nor was he interested in making the committee more democratic, only in gaining control of it. On June 12th, in a further statement to the newspapers, he intimated bluntly he did not intend to compromise.

Casement had gone back to the North, feeling so ill—he had told Redmond—that he would not be able to return to Dublin for a long time. When he heard of Redmond's intransigence, however, he sent him a telegram pleading for a compromise, and returned to once to Dublin to discuss with the other members of the committee what could be done. As he was too ill to get up, MacNeill, Hobson and Moore came to his room in Buswell's Hotel; and they reached the conclusion that they had no alternative but to resign. They could not in honour, they felt, meekly accept Redmond's dictation; but to reject it would split the nationalist movement irrevocably, and give the British the excuse they needed to say that Ireland was not yet fit for self-government.

That night, however, Hobson had second thoughts. If they resigned—he told Casement, the following morning—they would leave the Volunteers under Redmond's control. What, then, would happen to the arms, due to arrive a few weeks later?

Hobson had been in the United States when Casement was making the original arrangements; but after his return, Casement had taken him into his confidence about them, so that he could arrange for their distribution. To make use of the arms, Hobson pointed out, some representation must be kept on the committee. Casement had to agree. So, when they arrived, did MacNeill and Moore; and a statement was prepared to lay before the full committee, accepting Redmond's demand.

It was a tragic committee meeting—Casement told Alice Green, in his letter describing the course events had taken. The statement had been accepted; but the size of the minority opposing it—it passed by eighteen votes to nine—indicated that the unity of the nationalist movement had been preserved only on the surface:

> I am thoroughly wretched in many ways. I know we did the right thing. But it has caused me despair. The cause of Ireland seems so hopeless in the hands of such men. How can any freedom arise in the land with such a narrow-minded intolerant bigot as John Dillon, tool and agent of English Liberalism—and Joe Devlin—ignorant, forceful, greedy, ambitious. . . . I really think I'll join the Orangemen. They are better *men*—even better Irishmen than this gang of tricky schemers and place hunters.

The only hope for the future, Casement concluded, lay with the Protestants: 'if they will come in and raise a national standard of revolt—the people will rally to it'. He would therefore go to no more meetings of the provisional committee. In his place, he would send an ex-convict Fenian, with his proxy vote.

The 'ex-convict Fenian' Casement had in mind was Tom Clarke; and it was typical of both the strength and the weakness of the Irish Republican Brotherhood that Casement had no idea that Clarke was one of its members, let alone that he was the most influential of them. Clarke had been fifteen years a convict, for his revolutionary activities; then, after working for Devoy for a while in New York, he had come back to Ireland after O'Leary's death to run a small newsagent's shop, which was to be the nerve centre of Irish republicanism. Casement had visited him at the suggestion of another ex-convict Fenian, John Daly, following the meeting to launch the Limerick Volunteers; and

Clarke, though suspicious, was impressed by the results of Casement's recruiting campaign—'young fellows who had been regarded as something like wastrels', he wrote to tell Devoy in May, were 'now changed to energetic soldiers . . . it's good to be abroad in Ireland, these times!' But he had been horrified when he heard that Hobson and Casement proposed to give way to Redmond. On the morning of June 15th he went to Buswells with Sean MacDermott to try to persuade them to change their minds; and he never forgave Hobson for refusing to do so. 'How much,' he asked him, 'did they pay you?' He felt sure that Casement, too, must be in English pay.

But of this, Casement remained for a while in ignorance. He had only a few more days before he was to sail for America; and he wanted to spend them, he told his cousin, staying in the North 'for peace and quiet and retrenchment (I am ruined financially)'. Before he left Dublin, he made the final arrangement with Hobson and Childers for bringing in the guns in a month's time. On the last day of June he had intended to go to a Volunteer meeting, but felt too ill. Instead, he climbed to a point where a cairn had been raised to Shane O'Neill, one of the heroes of Ulster's resistance to Elizabeth I, and there harangued the open spaces 'in a cracked voice'. The following day, he set off for Glasgow, to catch a ship—as no liners now called at any Irish port—to cross the Atlantic.

PART FIVE

WAR
1914–1916

CHAPTER ONE

AMERICA

Running the guns   *July–August 1914*

Hobson had written to John Devoy to tell him that Casement was coming out to the United States; but when Devoy heard from Clarke about the betrayal—as Clarke thought it—of the Volunteers, putting the blame on Hobson and Casement, Devoy had promptly written to tell Hobson he had been sacked from his job as Irish correspondent of the *Gaelic American*, and added that in view of the prevailing irritation among Irish Americans, 'it would be useless for your friend about whom you wrote to come here'.

Devoy's letter, however, was sent too late: Casement was already on his way across the Atlantic in the *Cassandra*, which was taking him to Canada. When he arrived, on July 14th—still in ignorance of what had been happening since the capitulation to Redmond—he wrote from Montreal to Devoy to say that their 'mutual friend', Hobson, would have told him of his impending arrival and that he hoped to see him soon. And on the 18th, he set off for New York—musing, as the train took him along the shores of Lake Champlain, on the fate of the American Indians—'you had *life*—your white destroyers only possess *things*. That is the vital distinction, I take it, between the "savage" and the civilised man. The savage is, the white man has. The one lives and moves to be, the other toils and dies to have'.

Devoy had not met Casement before; but he had followed his career since his Congo days, assuming him to be an Englishman; it was not until Casement had written to him from South America, enclosing a subscription for the *Gaelic American*, that he learned of his background. Although he knew Casement had done good work for the Gaelic League and other Irish causes, he was not disposed lightly to forgive him for the surrender to Redmond. As he had voted in favour of it—Devoy told him when they met on July 20th—the chances of his being able to help the cause by raising funds in the United States were poor. Formidable though Devoy was, Casement remaining unabashed. He 'listened attentively to all I said', Devoy recalled, 'and then, in a calm and very friendly manner, undertook to persuade me that I was mistaken—which he proceeded to do the following day in a letter giving his version of the events which had led Hobson to recommend that they should accept Redmond's ultimatum, and concluding 'the *only* thought influencing Hobson was that which swayed me—to save the Volunteers from disruption and Ireland from a disgraceful faction fight, in which all original issues would have gone by the board'.

Whether or not it had been a mistake for Casement to give way, as Devoy still believed it was, he and his *Clan-na-Gael* colleagues were impressed with 'the sincerity of the man'. And Casement had a further argument: the balance of power within the Volunteers would be dramatically shifted, he pointed out, when the rifles and ammunition which were at that moment being transported from Germany were landed, and distributed to Volunteers whose loyalty would be to the cause of Ireland—not to Redmond.

Casement also confided the gun-running project to Joe McGarrity, an Ulster Catholic who had emigrated in 1890 to the United States, where he had made and lost a couple of fortunes, and become one of the three-man executive of *Clan-na-Gael*. On the Sunday that the *Asgard* was due off Howth, Casement was staying with McGarrity in Philadelphia, in a state of great anxiety, expecting hourly (as he wrote to tell Alice Green) that a telegram would arrive to say 'the picnic' had been prevented or broken up. At nine on Sunday evening, a journalist working on a Philadelphia newspaper rang McGarrity to tell him a message had just come through from Dublin; a cargo of arms had been intercepted and seized by British troops. The picnic had, after all, been ruined. ... But McGarrity, investigating, found that though British troops had tried to intervene, they had not captured the arms. Casement was ecstatic. 'How can I tell you all I have felt since Sunday?' he wrote later in the week to Alice Green:

I can never tell you! I was in anguish first—then filled with joy—and now with a resolute pride in you all. We have done what we set out to do! And done it well. ... Old J. D. says with a glow of joy 'the greatest deed done in Ireland for 100 years' — and keeps on repeating it.

The landing of the arms from the *Asgard* and two other small yachts involved in the gun-running hardly compared with Larne. The Irish Volunteers only obtained 1,500 rifles — of an antiquated type, Pearse wrote to tell McGarrity, inferior to Carson's. Pearse might grumble, but the psychological boost to the cause was considerable — particularly in the United States: the Irish there, Casement now found, were 'mad with pride, joy, and hope'. He could not have arrived at a better moment, it seemed, to embark on his fund-raising campaign. So far from his being the liability Devoy had feared, he became overnight the popular hero; 'the Irish' he told Alice Green, 'would make me into a demi-God if I let them'. To McGarrity, he was 'a reincarnated Tone'. As the man who had planned the gun-running, he could attract big audiences; and being by this time quite a practised platform orator, he could also rouse them. The first public meeting at which he spoke brought in two thousand dollars to the *Clan*'s fund for the Volunteers.

The day after the Howth landings, however, Austria declared war on Serbia; within a week, Russia, Germany, France and Britain were at war; and the immediate beneficiary, in Irish political terms, was John Redmond. As the summer went on, the chances of the Home Rule bill coming into operation had been receding. If the Government tried to bring it into operation, Asquith knew, the Northern Protestants would set up a Provisional Government. But by July 30th, the international scene was sufficiently menacing for Craig to see a way out. Home Rule, he suggested to Carson, should be set aside for the duration of the crisis. If it was, Ulster would offer her Volunteers 'to see the matter through'. The Redmondites, he thought, 'would find it extremely awkward to follow on with a similar offer from their side'. Carson, agreeing, presented the proposal, and Asquith gratefully accepted it. For once, though, Craig had miscalculated. Redmond promptly offered the services of the Irish Volunteers to the Government. 'If it is allowed to us, in comradeship with our brothers in the North, we will ourselves defend the shores of Ireland.' The gesture won general praise in the Commons — except from the mortified Ulster Unionists. It also put Redmond back into a strong bargaining position. For

Irish, and Irish-American, consumption he could now claim to be following Grattan's policy. As a result, he recovered the popularity he had lost. By the end of August, Devoy was noting with dismay 'the almost universal approval of John's pledge'; and the expectations Devoy had placed on Casement as a fund-raiser, after his first meetings, were not fulfilled. Instead of collecting fifty thousand dollars, as had been hoped, he was able to bring in only about seven thousand. But his mind, in any case, was turning to other projects; chief among them, how Germany could be enlisted in the cause of Irish independence.

God Save Germany   *August–September* 1914

From the moment war broke out, Casement's sympathies lay with Germany. 'My heart bleeds for those poor people, beset by a world of hatred', he wrote to Alice Green, in August; 'their crime is their efficiency.' The course of events leading up to Britain's entry into the war served to confirm him in his long-standing belief that the British Government, and in particular the Foreign Secretary, had been waiting for the opportunity; and the use of 'little Belgium' as the pretext was calculated to infuriate him, feeling as he did about the Belgians after his Congo experience. A letter which he wrote to his cousin on the subject was Messianic in its tone; Britain and Russia, he claimed, had joined in a new Holy Alliance to rob and plunder the Old World.

> England's crime in this war is the most flagrant of all—she made it inevitable—she leagued herself with the Powers of Darkness against Teutonic commerce and industry. May the Sword of the Just destroy and annihilate the League of Enmity—the conspiracy of assassins formed against them. I pray for the Salvation of Germany night and day—and God Save Ireland now is another form of God Save Germany!

Devoy cared little for Germany, but he was a believer in Mitchel's idea that a European war could be exploited for Ireland's benefit, and when the war broke out, he and some other *Clan* members went to see the German Ambassador in Washington, Count von Bernstorff, and his military attaché, Franz von Papen. The *Clan*'s 'friends' in Ireland, Devoy explained, were prepared to raise a rebellion but they lacked arms and trained officers. If Germany could supply them, they could create a diversion which would take British troops from the Continent. It would therefore be in Germany's interests, as well as Ireland's, to provide the necessary help.

Bernstorff said he would consider the proposal; but as he was temperamentally Anglophile, Devoy thought it might help to convince the Germans if Casement added his persuasion. He already knew and approved Casement's views, set out in the memorandum which Hobson had brought over earlier in the year. If Casement could not bring in money by making speeches, he might do something even more useful for the cause. Casement thought so too. In an address to the Kaiser, which he now composed, he claimed that the Irish Americans felt 'sympathy and admiration for the heroic people of Germany, assailed at all points by an unnatural league of enmity, having only one thing in common, a hatred of German prosperity and efficiency'. The British claim to control the seas of the world, he went on — harking back to the theme of his earlier articles —

rests chiefly on an unnamed factor. That factor is Ireland. It is solely by the possession of Ireland that Great Britain has been able for two centuries to maintain an unchallengeable mastery of the seas ... there cannot be peace in Europe until Great Britain's claim to the mastery of the seas, that great highway of the nations, has been finally disposed of.

The address concluded with the hope that His Majesty would have the power, wisdom and strength of purpose to impose a lasting peace 'by effecting the independence of Ireland, and securing its recognition as a fixed condition of final settlement between the great maritime powers'. Although *Clan-na-Gael*, Devoy was to recall, would have 'worded some portions of it differently' (he did not say which portions), there was nothing in the address at which they actually took offence; they decided to accept it, and it was duly despatched.

For a time, Casement did not formally embrace the German side; his memoranda were published in the name of the *Clan*. But he was growing increasingly impatient of his own equivocation. John Butler Yeats — the poet's father, who was in New York — noted that although he was 'afraid of no one, and is the soul of honour', he was maudlin about the Germans; 'he would mutter to himself, "poor Kaiser, poor Kaiser", almost with tears in his voice'. And while he was staying in Philadelphia in early September, Casement set out his views in a survey of the causes of the war, designed to prove it had been rendered inevitable not by the faults or the temper of the Kaiser, 'but because certain powers, and one power in particular, nourished ambitions and asserted claims that involved not only ever-increasing armaments, but ensured ever-increasing animosities'. Russia craved the dismemberment of the Austro-Hungarian empire, so that she could dominate the Slavs; France hungered for the return of Alsace-Lorraine; and this had given England— shaken by the discovery that in the first half of 1914 German exports had almost caught up with British—the chance to carry out her aim: 'the destruction of German sea power, and along with it the permanent crippling of German competition in the markets of the world'.

Moved by his own eloquence, he decided he must make his position clear. On September 17th he wrote a letter to the *Irish Independent* protesting against Ireland being involved in the war on Britain's side and summarising his reasons.

Ireland has no blood to give to any land to any cause but that of Ireland. Our duty as a Christian people is to abstain from bloodshed; and our duty as Irishmen is to give our lives for Ireland. Ireland needs all her sons. ... Were the Home Rule Bill all that is claimed for it, and were it freely given today, to come into operation tomorrow instead of being offered for sale on terms of exchange that only a fool would accept, it would still be the duty of Irishmen to save their strength and manhood for the trying tasks before them, to build up from a depleted population the fabric of a ruined national life.

No Irishman, he asserted, fit enough to bear arms in the cause of his own country's freedom, 'can join the allied millions now attacking Germany in a war that, at best, concerned Ireland not at all'. He did not go so far as to recommend Irish support for Germany; but in a memorandum to the Ambassador, Bernstorff, he made some practical suggestions how Germany could support nationalist movements in India and Egypt, as well as

Ireland. Then, at the end of September, he went to the German embassy to meet Papen, to discuss the possibility that Irish troops who had been captured in the German advance might be persuaded to change their allegiance. Papen, he was gratified to find, was interested in the idea. If Germany could promise to give freedom to oppressed peoples such as the Poles and the Irish, Bernstorff eventually conceded in a despatch, she would find friends in the United States. The essential issue, he suggested, was whether there was now any prospect of an understanding being reached with England, or whether it was to be a life and death struggle; if the latter, 'I recommend falling in with Irish wishes, provided that there are really Irishmen prepared to help us. The formation of an Irish legion from Irish prisoners would be a grand idea, if it could only be carried out.'

The man who would be best fitted to carry it out, in his own opinion, was Casement. It was, after all, his idea. And the publication of his letter in the *Irish Independent*, on October 5th, meant that it would be difficult and perhaps dangerous for him to return to Ireland—the more so because of the course events had been taking there.

For a time, after the outbreak of war, Redmond had kept his strong bargaining position. But when, on September 18th, Home Rule was put on the statute book (though its coming into operation was to be suspended for a year, or for the duration of the war, whichever should be the longer) he felt that his objective had been achieved. The Volunteers should no longer regard themselves as existing simply to defend their country—he told a parade two days later. 'It would be a disgrace forever to our country, a reproach to her manhood, and a denial of the lessons of history, if young Irishmen confined their efforts to remaining at home to defend the shores of Ireland from an unlikely invasion'; they must be prepared to go 'wherever the firing line extends'.

It was a fateful speech. Twenty members of the provisional committee, headed by MacNeill and O'Rahilly, repudiated Redmond's pledge, adding that they regretted that the absence of Sir Roger Casement in America prevented him from being a signatory with them; 'Ireland cannot, with honour or safety, take part in foreign quarrels otherwise than through the free action of a National Government of her own.' The Home Rule and Independence movements had once again split apart; and the two

wings of the independence movement, republican and *Sinn Fein*,
came together again, in alliance if not in unison, to oppose
Ireland's participation in the war.

Had Casement not sent his letter to the *Independent*, he
might have come back to help MacNeill rebuild the Irish Volunteers—or that small section of the force which followed him;
the great majority stayed with Redmond. But the letter had
attracted attention. Copies had been sent to the Foreign Office;
and Sir Arthur Nicolson, the Permanent Under-Secretary, wrote
to tell him that it had been passed to Sir Edward Grey. 'The
letter urges that Irish sympathies should be with Germany rather
than Great Britain and that Irishmen should not join the British
army. As you are still liable, in certain circumstances, to be
called up to serve under the Crown, I am to request you to state
whether you are the author of the letter in question'. Whether
or not Casement received it, he must have known of the hold
the Foreign Office had over him. If he returned to Ireland, he
could not expect to be allowed to resume life there as if nothing had happened.

He could have stayed on in the United States, but there would
have been little for him to do, apart from addressing the occasional meeting and writing the occasional article—as he did,
for the *Gaelic American*. In any case, he was no longer happy
there. The ecstatic reception given to him by the Irish Americans
at the end of July had raised his expectations to a level which
America no longer satisfied. Even before he left Ireland, people
had been suggesting that he might take over the leadership of
the independence movement; he would have liked to do so, his
reply had been, if he were twenty years younger. 'I am too old,
dear youth', he wrote to one admirer, 'and besides, I have no
personal ambitions.' Shortly before he sailed for America,
though, the tone of a letter he wrote to Richard Morten suggests
that the idea was beginning to attract him: 'I've been appealed
to again and again to come out and be a new leader—a sort of
aged Parnell! And thousands would have followed me.' When
the Irish Americans rose to him, 'I can see from the way they all
greet me', he told Alice Green, 'that they are setting their hearts
on a Protestant leader, and they think, poor brave souls, I may
be the man'; and again, a few days later, 'they are mad for a
Protestant leader'. And the history of the Irish independence
movement provided plenty of encouragement for him; almost all

the patriot hero-figures had been Protestant. But the sudden
collapse of interest in him, after war broke out in Europe, was
disillusioning; and he did not care for American materialism.
He liked individual Americans—and they him: Theodore Roose-
velt found him 'charming'. But American society's values
appalled him. 'It is all self, self, self, all the time,' he wrote to
tell his cousin, 'and intrigue in place of principle.' At the beginning of September, writing to Alice Green, he told her that
though the U.S.A. was a great country, 'the more I see it, the
less I like it'; and a month later an Englishman who met him in
Chicago, and was treated to one of his anti-English, pro-German
harangues, wrote to tell Tyrrell he thought Casement was profoundly unhappy, and out of touch; 'he is a fanatic of the type
of Mazzini ... great in the beginning of Italy's *risorgimento*, and
so greatly mistaken at the end'.

His solution to his troubles was simple: he would go to
Germany. He put the idea to John Quinn, with whom he stayed
when he was in New York, and received some sound advice.
Quinn's parents had been born in Ireland, and he had paid regular visits there before the war, becoming a close friend of
Yeats, A.E., and Douglas Hyde; when he heard Casement was
in America, he had offered to put him up. The two men liked
each other; Casement was much closer to him in general sympathies than to Devoy or even McGarrity. But Quinn, who was
an art collector, had become a passionate Francophile in the
course of his expeditions to Europe, and supported the Allied
cause. For a while, Casement had been tactful—suggesting to
him, for example, that the arming of the Volunteers was simply
to strengthen Ireland's bargaining position; 'Bull will want our
help, and it should be given only on terms'. But after the war
broke out, and he could no longer conceal his pro-German sentiments, Quinn found his guest less welcome, and at times a
nuisance. He 'seemed to get more and more excited as the war
went on', Quinn told Hyde, and eventually he became mentally
unbalanced. Nevertheless Casement had continued to consult
him, as 'a good staunch Irishman'; and when Quinn advised him
not to go to Germany, he might have listened, had the *Clan* also
opposed the project. Devoy, however, though fearing that Casement might be temperamentally unsuited to the task, was not
sorry to see him leave the United States. Casement, he had
found, could not be persuaded to work only through the *Clan*.

He had even shown one of his memoranda to Quinn, who was not a member (Devoy would have been even more irritated had he known that Casement intended to publish it, had Quinn not dissuaded him). After some hesitation, the *Clan* executive decided to let Casement go, and to pay his expenses—Devoy having found that Casement was both meticulous in his accounting and frugal in his habits; although short of money, he always insisted on paying for his own meals ('he was very sensitive on this point') and on washing his underclothes, which few people of his background would have thought of doing.

On his first evening in New York, Casement had been accosted by a young Norwegian sailor, Adler Christensen, with whom he had established an agreeable relationship; and Christensen, he decided, would be just the person to come with him to Berlin, as his 'servant'. Somebody who spoke German, as well as Norwegian—as Christensen boasted he could—would obviously be useful. Their passages were consequently booked to Christiania —as Oslo was then called—on the *Oskar II*. Casement did not even tell Alice Green of his decision. In his last letter to her from New York, he said he was likely to end his days in America —'as an editor. I have already been offered the direction of a paper to be founded, and shall probably accept.' He dropped a hint, however, that he had other intentions: 'I see no way out —save one, and that so removed, far off and improbable that it need not be discussed. And yet it is the only way.' Three days later, on October 15th, he took that only way. He had been staying again with the kindly McGarrity—'a most single-minded unselfish Irish patriot', Casement described him to his cousin, 'with only one thought in his mind and heart'. Before the final leave-taking, Devoy took McGarrity aside and asked him, had he absolute confidence in Casement? 'I will trust him with my life,' McGarrity replied. The two men went out to have supper together. Casement had a feeling he was going to get over safely: he had travelled on a Pullman car on his last two trips and he had found the name of the car was Christiania. They went to a café on 42nd Street; then— McGarrity wrote—'he shook my hand in a firm grip and took a stand on the rear platform of the trolley car, and as he waved his hat and kerchief, I watched him and waved back until the trolley disappeared in the darkness, and I saw him no more.'

Before he sailed, Casement sent a last message to Devoy:

I cannot go without a farewell word and a grip of the hand.
Without you there would be nothing, and if success comes, or
even a greater hope for the future, it will be due to you and
your life of unceasing devotion to the most unselfish cause on
earth.

From Casement's point of view, there was a logic, almost an
inevitability, about the decision he had taken. He had left himself little freedom of choice to do anything else. He could still
have gone back to Ireland; but he would certainly have been
told to report for duty, and when he refused, dismissed the
service, and thereafter kept under surveillance. It was inconceivable that he would be allowed to put his pro-German views
without immediately landing himself in gaol. In Germany, he
would at least be free to try to gain support for the cause.

But although, in logic, this must have seemed the right course,
Devoy had judged correctly; he was not well fitted for the task
he had now set himself. To begin with, there was his Foreign
Service background, and his decorations. In spite of all he had
done for the language, and later for the Volunteers, he had not
managed to impress on the general public that he was anything
but British; to Germans, as well as to Britons, he appeared a
traitor.

This, he could argue, was something he would have to bear
with until events, or posterity, made his true position clear.
What was more serious was that by going to Germany, he cut
himself off from Ireland. Irish attitudes to Germany were varied,
and complex. Among his own Irish friends there were many men
who believed that Germany could not be trusted. 'On the face
of it,' Conan Doyle argued, 'would any sane man accept an
assurance about Ireland which obviously has been already
broken about Belgium?' And there were other Irishmen, whom
Casement respected, who shared Conan Doyle's view—Erskine
Childers for one; although he had brought the *Asgard* into
Howth with its cargo of rifles, when war broke out he joined
the British forces. Childers's attitude had been that if the
Volunteers were not armed the Irish might be deprived of Home
Rule, which he felt sure was in Britain's interest as well as theirs.
But because he visualised Ireland continuing as a dominion, he
saw no inconsistency in fighting to preserve the Commonwealth.

Sinn Fein's policy came closer to Casement's; but Griffith did not believe the Germans would care about Irish independence—if they came, they would 'come to stay and rule the Atlantic from our shores'. 'We are Irish nationalists', he claimed, 'and the only duty we have is to stand for Ireland's interests, irrespective of England or Germany or any foreign country.' James Connolly held the Irish Labour movement on a similar line. If a German army landed in Ireland, the readers of his *Irish Worker* were told at the outbreak of war, they should be supported, provided they gave adequate guarantees for Irish independence. But his headquarters at Liberty Hall were draped with a banner. 'We serve neither King, nor Kaiser, but Ireland'; and privately, he was to confide in Pearse and Clarke that he thought the Germans as bad as the British; 'do the job yourselves!' And Pearse and Clarke had already decided to do the job themselves. If the Germans did send a force to Ireland, they agreed, it would be the signal for a rising. But they were not going to rely on German help.

If Casement had been able to return to Ireland before proceeding to the Continent, he could hardly have failed to realise how few people shared his enthusiasm for the Germans. He might still have decided it was worth going to Germany, to try to persuade the Government to send help; but at least he would not have gone with such high expectations. In particular, he would have been warned not to expect to recruit many Irish prisoners of war to fight England. If the great majority of the Irish Volunteers had preferred to stay with Redmond, even when he asked them to go to fight for the British in Flanders, it was inconceivable that Casement would find many recruits for his cause among the old sweats who had volunteered for service in the British army even before war broke out.

CHAPTER TWO

NORWAY

The Oskar II   *October 1914*

If the British had heard that Casement was on his way to Europe, they would presumably try to intercept him; so elaborate pains had been taken to keep his departure secret. A hotel room was taken for him in Chicago; and his passage to Norway was booked in the name of James Landy, a New York citizen, who duly boarded *Oskar II* — Casement, who had shaved off his beard and washed his face in buttermilk to get a fair complexion, coming with him 'to see him off'. He and Landy then switched roles, and it was Casement who stayed on board as 'Mr. Landy of New York' when the ship sailed; along with his servant, Adler Christensen.

If Casement had wanted to draw attention to himself, he could hardly have done so more effectively. As soon as he spoke, it was obvious he was British (like most Irishmen of his class, he had only a trace of an Irish accent). And yet, curiously, this may have saved him when a British cruiser, the *Hibernia* ('when I saw that on the caps of the men', he wrote to tell his sister, 'I nearly kissed them'), ordered the *Oskar II* to Stornaway, where six Germans were taken off to be interned. The passengers had formed the impression that Casement was a British spy — responsible, probably, for their ship's interception. One of them — Walter Muller, who was returning to Germany to join the forces — had realised that 'Landy' was Casement, and was to alert the German authorities to his arrival in Norway. But he assumed the British must know, too. So Casement was ignored, and the *Oskar II* allowed to continue on its way.

Casement and Christensen reached Christiania at the end of October, booking in at the Grand Hotel. After visiting the German legation to present his credentials from Bernstorff, Casement went back there to wait until arrangements had been made for him to proceed to Berlin. That afternoon, Christensen came back to the hotel, very excited, to say that he had been accosted by an Englishman in the hotel lobby, who had taken him in a chauffeur-driven limousine to 79 Drammensveien, where he had been interrogated about his employer. He had refused to give Casement away. They looked up 79 Drammensveien; it was the British legation.

For all his precautions, Casement realised, his identity must have been disclosed. The British minister could hardly have him arrested in Norway, but if doubts were thrown upon the validity of his passport, there might be trouble and there would certainly be delay. It would be as well—he told the German minister, Von Oberndorff, the next day—if he could depart for Germany immediately; and Oberndorff made the necessary arrangements. In the meantime, however, Christensen had again been accosted, on his way to breakfast, and informed that if he were to pay a further visit to the British legation, he could expect to learn something to his advantage. This time, he had met 'a very tall man, clean shaven except for a very short greyish moustache', wearing a tweed suit: the minister, Mansfeldt Findlay. Findlay made it clear that the identities of both Christensen and his master were known. As Casement was travelling on a false passport, Findlay pointed out, his disappearance would not be noticed; 'if someone knocked Casement on the head, he would get well-paid'. With that, Christensen was given twenty-five kroner—about six dollars—for taxi fares, and told that if he was interested in qualifying for a more substantial reward, he should return that afternoon.

As they were going to leave that evening, Casement judged it wise for Christensen to return to the legation, and pretend to be interested in the plot, while he tried to throw the British off the trail by making ostentatious arrangements to go to Denmark. Christensen reappeared only just before they were due to catch the train. He had driven a hard bargain, he said, with Findlay ('I smoked a cigarette in his face without asking his leave, and I filled my pipe before him. I used bad language several times, and swore that I was not going to do anything against Sir Roger for a small sum'). Eventually, Findlay had agreed to pay him five thousand dollars if he could lure Casement to some place where he could be kidnapped; he would also be paid for any useful information he could get out of Germany; and as an advance, he could have a hundred kroner.

Casement had found, to his relief, that he was to have a

German, Richard Meyer—the brother of Kuno Meyer, a professor
of Celtic studies, and an old friend of Alice Green—as a travelling companion. By this time he had begun to see British agents
in every doorway. When he went to the station with Meyer and
Christensen, and ostentatiously boarded a sleeping car for
Copenhagen, they were shadowed, he was certain, by a member
of the British legation staff. In the middle of the night they
eluded their pursuer by switching to a different part of the train,
leaving him to sleep on undisturbed, while they headed in a
different direction, and eventually reached the German frontier
at Sassnitz.

The circumstantial detail of Christensen's story led to Casement accepting it as true even after he had begun to have doubts
about Christensen. When the Foreign Office's files on the subject
were eventually opened for inspection, they told a different
story. On October 29th, 1914, a young Norwegian with a strong
American accent had called at the legation, asking to see the
minister; as the minister was out, he had been shown in to one
of the junior legation officials, Francis Lindley. It was Christensen, who explained that he had come from the United States
with an English nobleman who had been decorated by the King
('I understood,' Lindley noted in his memorandum, 'that his
relations with the Englishman were of an improper character.'
It was the first recorded occasion before his capture in 1916 that
his homosexuality was even hinted at; 'it is just possible I may
have been wrong in this, but I don't think so', Lindley wrote;
then, on reflection, crossed the qualifying sentence out). Christensen said he had steamed open some of his master's letters
from the German embassy in Washington, which he had been
given for safe-keeping when the ship was intercepted; they included a German cypher, which he had copied out. He showed
them to Lindley, but would not at this point give his employer's name, or reveal anything about him beyond that he
was coming to Europe to stir up trouble in Ireland. 'The man
did not say why he gave me this information,' Lindley concluded, 'and did not ask for money. He was very serious. It
struck me his story was true.'

When he returned the following day, Christensen was brought
in to see the British minister. 'Age 24'—Findlay described him
—'about six feet, strongly made, clean shaven, fair hair, blue or
grey eyes very small and close together, gap in front teeth ...

speaks English fluently, but with Norwegian-American accent. Says he is a naturalised American, but retains Norwegian nationality in Norway. Has a fleshy, dissipated appearance.' Inquiries which had been made in Christiania revealed he had been described by the police in New York as 'a dangerous type of a Norwegian-American criminal'. For Findlay, Christensen produced an article which his master (whom he at first still did not name) had written, urging the Germans to invade Ireland rather than England; and a pamphlet, 'The Elsewhere Empire', a tirade against everything British, written for American consumption. Eventually, Christensen disclosed Casement's identity; and Findlay gave him twenty-five kroner, assuring him that this was the normal price for such transactions and promising he would be paid more if he could provide additional information.

That afternoon, Christensen returned with a copy of the cypher, and a specimen of Casement's handwriting, for which he asked a hundred dollars, and was given a hundred kroner. The British naval attaché was despatched to the train on which, Christensen had revealed, he and Casement were travelling — but not to shadow them; only to warn a King's Messenger, who happened to be travelling to Denmark in the same *wagon-lit*, that 'these two men were dangerous rascals'. The term suggests that Findlay did not, as yet, take them seriously. But he transmitted Christensen's information to Whitehall, enclosing the material Christensen had handed over. It included a letter in which Casement described his servant. 'I am glad I brought him, indeed — he is a treasure.'

CHAPTER THREE

GERMANY

'At last in Berlin', Casement wrote on October 31st in his diary —preserved by a friend he made in Germany, so that it did not fall into the hands of the Home Office (it contained no references to homosexual activities—presumably because Casement realised it would be risky, in the situation in which he now found himself, to include them)?

> the journey done—the effort perhaps only begun! Shall I succeed? Will they see the great cause aright and understand all it may mean to them, no less than to Ireland? Tomorrow will show the beginning.

It did. Casement had three main tasks, so far as Devoy was concerned—and, as paymaster, Devoy regarded him as the *Clan*'s emissary, sent to carry them out: to secure German military help for Ireland, when the opportunity offered; to educate German public opinion on Ireland, so that the German people would support their Government in such action; and if possible, to organise Irish prisoners of war into a military unit, which could take part in the fight for Irish freedom.

To carry out this programme, though, Casement had first to persuade the German foreign ministry that he could be accepted as the envoy—even if as yet there could be no formal accreditation—not simply of the *Clan*, but of Ireland; and Richard Meyer offered to introduce him to members of the German Government. On Meyer's advice, he spent the first day discreetly in his hotel, awaiting news; 'here I am in the heart of the enemy's country—a State guest and almost a State prisoner'. Theobald von Bethmann-Hollweg, the Chancellor, and Gottlieb von Jägow, the Secretary of State—Meyer reported that evening —were both on a visit to the front with the Kaiser; but Count Artur von Zimmermann, the Under-Secretary of State, had agreed to see him the following day. Waiting for the interview in an ante-room at the Foreign Office, he surveyed his position, recording his reflections that night in his diary.

I thought of Ireland, the land I should almost fatally never see again. Only a miracle could bring me to her shores. That I do not expect—cannot in truth hope for. But victory or defeat, it is all for Ireland. And she cannot suffer from what I do. I may, I must suffer—and even those near and dear to me—but my country can only gain from my treason. Whatever comes that must be so. If I win it is a national resurrection—a free Ireland, a world nation after centuries of slavery. A people lost in the Middle Ages refound, and returned to Europe. If I fail—if Germany be defeated—still the blow struck today for Ireland must change the course of British policy towards that country. Things will never be quite the same. The 'Irish Question' will have been lifted from the mire and mud and petty, false strife of British domestic politics into an international atmosphere. That, at least, I shall have achieved.

And almost immediately, he was able to accomplish the first step towards its achievement. He liked Zimmermann, with his 'very good-natured face', which was a good start, and following their talk, went back to his hotel to draft a memorandum setting out what he thought the German Government should do. British propaganda against Germany had been largely based on the theme that Britain was fighting the war to protect the rights of small nations; one of the most effective ways Germany could combat it, surely, would be to declare her own sympathy with a small nation which was denied her independence by Britain: Ireland. Attracted by the idea, Zimmermann brought Casement in to meet Count Georg von Wedel, the head of the English Department at the German Foreign Office; 'a man of upright build, frank, with straight brown eyes and a perfect English accent'; and they discussed how Germany might show that she really wanted to help the Irish regain their independence. Wedel was evidently impressed. After leaving Casement back at his hotel, he went to the headquarters of the Secret Police and obtained a special identity card for 'Mr. Hammond of New York', which would protect him from molestation if his English caused suspicion—he could speak no German.

Wedel's report of the meeting, which he prepared for the Chancellor, was favourable. The Irish nationalist leader, he felt, made 'a reasonable and trustworthy impression'; and his proposals—the formation of an Irish legion from British prisoners of war, and a public proclamation by the German Government favouring the independence of Ireland—seemed sensible. 'My personal impression of Sir Roger Casement', Wedel wrote, 'inclines me to give them serious consideration.' If Bethmann-Hollweg agreed, the preliminary step would be to remove Irish prisoners of war from the various camps they were in, and bring them together somewhere 'to make it possible for Irish Catholic priests and Sir Roger Casement to exert their influence upon them'.

There was little more Casement could do until Bethmann-Hollweg returned; and he passed the time by planning how to trap Findlay. Christensen had been given a simple code for use when communicating with the British legation in Christiania; and Casement amused himself making up elaborate messages promising information from Germany. Occasionally he had qualms about what he was doing. 'It is not every day,' he wrote in his diary on November 7th, 'that even an Irishman commits high treason—especially one who has been in the service of the Sovereign he discards, and not without honour and some fame in that service.' But he had made his choice. It would only be a matter of time before his whereabouts were made known. And on November 20th the German Government formally announced that 'the well-known Irish Nationalist, Sir Roger Casement' was in Berlin, and had been received at the Foreign Office. He had asked to be told of Germany's intentions towards Ireland: and the acting Secretary of State at the Foreign Office, by order of the Chancellor, had been authorised to make an official statement:

> The Imperial Government formally declares that under no circumstances would Germany invade Ireland with a view to its conquest or the overthrow of any native institutions in that country.
>
> Should the fortune of this great war, which was not of Germany's seeking, ever bring in its course German troops to

the shores of Ireland, they would land there, not as an army of invaders to pillage and destroy, but as the forces of a Government that is inspired by goodwill towards a country and a people for whom Germany desires only *national prosperity* and *national freedom*.

To have secured this formal statement of intent, and to have secured it so quickly, was a triumph for Casement, as Devoy—who had not, by his own account, been optimistic—had to concede. The *Clan* passed a message through the German embassy in Washington to say it had made 'an excellent impression'; and the *Gaelic American* praised Casement for securing a pledge 'which will remove any doubt which may have existed regarding German goodwill by a section of the Irish people'. Casement had told nobody in Ireland of his project (though without his knowing, it had been sanctioned by the I.R.B.); now, he could write exultantly to MacNeill saying he was entirely assured of the goodwill of the German Government to Ireland, and begging him to proclaim it far and wide.

Tell all to trust the Germans—and trust me. We shall win everything if you are brave and faithful to the old cause ... the Germans will surely, under God, defeat both Russia and France and compel a peace that will leave Germany stronger than before ... we may win everything by this war if we are true to Germany; if we do not win today, we ensure international recognition of Irish nationality and hand on an uplifted cause for our sons.

MacNeill did not receive the letter: it went, thanks to Christensen, to the Foreign Office—as did letters to Alice Green; it was fortunate for her that the Chief Secretary for Ireland, Augustine Birrell, knew her. 'I don't know where she stands in the hierarchy of treason,' he wrote to the Under Secretary, Sir Matthew Nathan, 'but I should put her *low down*.' (She in fact ceased all communication with Casement when she heard what he had done.) Nathan added, though, as an afterthought, 'Still, there *is* or was a *Casement* movement.' By going to Berlin, Casement had made it easier for the authorities to believe that he was the leader of the separatists.

The Findlay affair

Hardly had Casement written to MacNeill telling him to trust the Germans than he began himself to be disillusioned with them. Not with the German people; he remained devoted to them. Looking at them—he wrote in his diary early in December —'at their manliness of brow and bearing, their calm front and resolute strong chests, turned to a world of enemies, and then reading the English columns of trash about Prussian barbarism and English heroism, I regret I am not a German'; and in a letter to his cousin he assured her that allied stories of German atrocities were lies. He even claimed that he had been to Louvain, and could prove that the stories of German atrocities there had been fabricated; though of all people, he should have known how easy it was to cover up the traces of past atrocities sufficiently to convince anybody who did not wish to believe in them. His disillusionment was with the German authorities. They were strangely reluctant, he found, to bother about the machinations of the British minister in Christiania. And if the Germans had had an inkling of the concern in Whitehall about the information which Findlay was forwarding from Adler Christensen, they would have shown a keener interest than they did.

The Foreign Office's initial reaction to the news of Casement's attitude had been characteristic. When his *Independent* letter appeared, Grey ordered: 'Stop his pension, if that can be legally done.' The law officers, however, were of the opinion that the Secretary of State had no power to withhold a pension. The Treasury agreed; whatever Casement's views might be, forfeiture of his pension would be 'quite out of the question, i.e. it would in our opinion neither be justifiable nor politic'—unless he was formally prosecuted; and the Foreign Office's legal advisers felt it was not wise to prosecute him on the evidence so far available. Only when it was learned that he was in Germany were the papers sent to the Attorney-General. The Foreign Office informed the Treasury that as they had taken the appropriate preliminary steps, payment of the pension could be suspended; and on December 8th, the Lords Commissioners of the Treasury formally directed that payments should cease, until further notice.

Officially, however, the Foreign Office pretended to be ignorant of his whereabouts. Gradually the news got around—provoking puzzlement, for a while, rather than anger. Alice Green expressed her 'profound and heartfelt sorrow' at what he had done, in a letter to Kuno Meyer in December; but she clearly felt he had been more misguided than treacherous. When the *Daily Chronicle* described his German adventure as 'an infatuation', Conan Doyle praised them for not having fallen a victim to the temptation to use a stronger term. Conan Doyle had greatly admired him: 'you have done so much good in your life', he had written to him prophetically in 1912, 'that no shadow should in justice come near you'. But wild letters Casement had written him from Belfast had made him uneasy; and in the *Chronicle*, Conan Doyle argued that as anyone who knew him would know it was inconceivable that he should be a traitor to the country which had employed and honoured him, he could not be in his right mind.

Whatever the reasons for his defection, it caused the Foreign Office so little concern that when Findlay wrote, early in November, to ask how much he could pay Christensen for getting him into British hands again, Nicolson authorised only up to a hundred pounds. But with the publication of the German Government's statement about Ireland, the Foreign Office's attitude changed. That he had managed to persuade the Germans to recognise Ireland's right to independence mattered little in itself; but it might turn out to be very useful to them in the propaganda war—particularly in the United States, where it could be exploited to show up the hollowness of the British claim to be fighting the war on behalf of small nations. Nothing could be done about the statement; but Casement himself might be caught if, as was expected, he decided to return to the United States. On November 24th, instructions were sent out to His Majesty's representatives in neutral European capitals to keep a watch out for him—on the assumption that he would have to leave, as he had arrived, through a neutral port.

Two days later, Nicolson heard from Findlay to say that Casement was still in Berlin. 'The Informer'—Christensen's name was kept out of the correspondence—had arrived in Norway with letters from him to friends in the United States, including one to Joe McGarrity, saying how useful his servant had been to him—he 'is absolutely faithful to me', and boasting of the benefits that his business trip to Germany was going to

provide for Ireland; 'the *sanitary pipes* will be furnished on a big
scale with plentiful stock of *disinfectant*. Enough for 50,000
health officers at least.' As Christensen also told Findlay that
there was a rich American involved, who was sympathetic to
the Irish cause and had a yacht, the Foreign Office assumed that
another gun-running was planned—and perhaps a German landing in Ireland. The affair could no longer be regarded, Grey
noted, 'as a personal matter affecting Casement'. Copies of
Findlay's despatch, and the enclosures, were sent to Lord Kitchener at the War Office, and to Winston Churchill at the Admiralty; and with Kitchener's concurrence, Findlay was
authorised to pay Christensen up to five thousand pounds—the
sum he had demanded—for information leading to capture. In
the meantime, a massive operation was mounted to intercept
Casement, should he leave Germany with the ship carrying the
'sanitary pipes'.

At the beginning of December, a message came from the
former Ambassador in Brussels, Sir Arthur Hardinge—by this
time, Ambassador in Madrid—saying that he believed Casement
was on the *Manuel Calvo*, bound for New York. The internal
memos flew; what could be done? It would be unwise to take
him off the ship, on the high seas; he had not been charged
with any extraditable offence, and even if he were, the United
States would probably insist that his was a political crime. Two
days later, it was found that the man who was sailing on the
Manuel Calvo, whoever he might be, was not Casement.

The Foreign Office was more concerned, by this time, with the
possibility that Casement would go to Ireland, there to be the
harbinger of rebellion. Basil Thomson, head of the Criminal
Investigation Department at Scotland Yard, had been alerted,
but he had been sceptical about the chances of catching him—
'if we knew the ship', he commented resignedly, 'the Admiralty
might be able to deal with the situation'. But if his destination was going to be Ireland, the Admiralty's chances were improved. Thomson conferred with Captain Reginald Hall, Chief
of Naval Intelligence, on how best to trap him; and they hatched
an elaborate plot. They would find a yacht, and charter her to an
American owner (who must be German-speaking). The captain
would be British, but would pretend to be American; and the
yacht would take a cruise off the west of Ireland, her captain
pretending to be an emissary from Casement, come to give his

plans to *Sinn Fein*—but he would really be collecting information from *Sinn Fein* about Casement's plans. It sounded like a parody of *The Riddle of the Sands*—except that Childers's plot was by contrast credible. A suitable yacht was found (she belonged to the American sportsman, Anthony Drexel), along with an 'owner' (a soldier of fortune, who spoke German like a native), and a captain (a young naval officer who had a flair for imitating American accents), and in mid-December, the *Sayonara* sailed for the west of Ireland. When Findlay wrote anxiously to the Foreign Office to ask whether the necessary measures had been made to deal with the 'advance party', Nicolson was able to reassure him. Everything possible or advisable had been done.

The German Foreign Office, however, had no inkling of the effect Christensen's information had had in Whitehall. They believed that Christensen was a rogue; that his story about Findlay was an invention; and that Casement was making a fool of himself. The scheme which he proposed only confirmed this diagnosis. Christensen was to tell Findlay that Casement was going to his rendezvous with a rich American's yacht; Findlay would tell the Admiralty; the Admiralty would send a cruiser squadron to intercept the yacht; and the German navy would intercept and annihilate the cruiser squadron. To Casement, it seemed a bold, imaginative design. The German authorities showed what they thought of it when Christensen, on his way to Norway at the end of November, was held up for two days at Sassnitz, and the 'evidence' which he and Casement had manufactured for Findlay was taken from him. And though he was allowed to proceed to Norway, a German official came a few days later to tell Casement that his servant was under suspicion.

This explained why the German authorities were unwilling to support Casement in his plans to trap Findlay. But there was another reason, he found, following a meeting with Count Blücher. He himself was mistrusted.

The Blüchers had returned to Germany before war broke out; and in her *An English Wife in Berlin* Princess Blücher (as she was to become later on in the war, on the death of her father-in-law) claimed that her husband, on meeting Casement there, had tried to show him what a false position he had put himself in, 'but it was no use. So after that we refused to see him or have anything more to do with him.' Casement's diary shows that this was not true; Blücher was very friendly, and his wife at least pretended to be, telling him that a rebellion in Ireland might help to bring the British Government to its senses. Why, then— Casement asked—were the German authorities so cool to him? There were still influential men in Germany, Blücher explained, of whom Jägow was one, who had not wanted war with England, and who still did not want all-out war because it would jeopardise the prospects of reaching a settlement with her. Jägow, too, did not like men who were traitors to their country—even if, as in Casement's case, they were working for Germany. 'In my heart,' he wrote disconsolately in his diary on December 12th,

> I am very sorry I came. I do not think the German Government has any soul for great enterprises—it lacks the divine spark of imagination that has ennobled British piracy. The seas may be freed by these people—but I doubt it.

The Irish Brigade   *December 1914–January 1915*

There remained, however, the project of recruiting from the Irish prisoners of war; and on this, Blücher could give Casement some encouragement. The German military machine, he said, desired only to get at England; and Irish prisoners of war were being collected into a separate camp of their own.

Of all Casement's projects, the Irish Brigade—as he decided to call it, after its Boer War predecessor—was to be the most destructive of his reputation, among sympathisers as well as enemies. One reason he should have sensed; the uneasiness which people felt about tampering with men's loyalty—which he had felt himself about the brigade which Major John Mac-Bride had raised to fight for the Boers. But in 1913 he had met MacBride, who turned out to be yet another Antrim glens Protestant, and congenial character (Yeats might have found it hard to forgive the 'drunken vain-glorious lout' who had married, and then separated from, Maud Gonne, but MacBride had impressed both O'Leary, who thought him the best sort of young Irishman, and Devoy). MacBride's account of the Irish Brigade had intrigued him; 'he did splendid work there', Casement reported to Alice Green; 'I begged him to *write* the story—to have on record the fight that little band of Irishmen (three hundred strong) made for Boer freedom. It was a fine fight and should be told.'

He was therefore delighted when the project found favour in Germany. As Richard Meyer put it, if he could undermine the loyalty of the Irish troops, it would be worth ten army corps. Wedel was also enthusiastic. 'It is this step that appeals most to the Germans, I can see,' Casement had written in his diary after their first meeting; 'they perceive its full moral value to the cause.' They also saw it as a test of his usefulness to them. If he succeeded in raising an Irish force, it would be humiliating to Britain; if he failed, the humiliation would be his, not theirs. They had arranged for the Irish prisoners of war to be assembled in a camp at Limburg; and the services of two Irish priests had been secured, through the Irish College in Rome, to help instil confidence in the men—one of them, he was delighted to find, being 'a raging Fenian'.

But soon, there was an indication that the task was not going to be easy. After a German bishop told the men at Sennelager, the prison camp where there had been the largest Irish contingent, that he hoped they would find their new camp more comfortable, the camp commandant received a message from the senior N.C.O.s of the Irish regiments saying that although they appreciated the efforts which were being made on their behalf, they wanted no concessions unless they were shared by all prisoners; 'in addition to being Irish Catholics, we have the honour to be British soldiers.'

Casement had made a fundamental miscalculation. The Boer War had not been generally popular in Britain; and in South Africa, it had been relatively easy for the Boers to persuade a captured Irishman that he, like them, was a victim of Britain's imperialistic greed. But to the Irish involved on the retreat from Mons, it was the Germans who had appeared to be the imperialist aggressors—despoilers of little Belgium; and the conditions which they had met in captivity had done nothing to endear the Germans to them. When Casement arrived at Limburg on December 4th, and addressed an assembly of N.C.O.s, most of whom had been in the British army for years, he found them uncompromisingly hostile. After two days, when he retired to bed with a throat infection, he had secured only a couple of volunteers, Sergeant MacMurrough and Corporal Timothy Quinlisk; and both of them, he thought, looked rogues.

This first visit, though, had been designed only as a preliminary inspection. 'I will not accept the responsibility for putting

a couple of thousand Irish soldiers into the high treason pot,'
he wrote in his diary on December 6th, 'unless I get very precise
and secure promises both in their regard, and for the political
future of Ireland.' And for this purpose, he told Blücher, he must
see either Jägow, or the Chancellor. Otherwise, he might have
to abandon the project. The threat was sufficient; on December
18th, he was received by Bethmann-Hollweg. They talked in
French, and the outcome was satisfactory. Bethmann-Hollweg
told him that the German Government liked his idea of an independent Irish nation, to secure the freedom of the seas; and
hoped his Irish Brigade would strike an immediate blow at
British recruiting in Ireland.

Casement had prepared a draft agreement on the Brigade,
emphasising that it was to be formed solely to achieve the independence of Ireland. The Germans were to train the men and
equip them, under his supervision, and to provide them with a
distinctive Irish uniform; but eventually they would fight under
their own Irish, or Irish-American officers. He now set out his
terms in the form of a draft treaty, and sent it to the Chancellor
on December 23rd. Five days later, Zimmermann told him that
they had been accepted, and handed him the agreement, which
bore the imperial seal.

Casement could now return to Limburg with more confidence.
The camp, by this time, had filled up; but the men, Casement
found, were suspicious. A few were actively hostile. At his trial,
witnesses who had been there as prisoners of war, and had later
been repatriated, were to describe his reception. 'On one occasion', Corporal John Robinson recalled, 'he was struck, and on
another occasion I saw him get pushed. When he was struck he
swung his umbrella round to keep the prisoners off him, and
when he was pushed, he walked out of the camp!' It was later
to be suggested that such stories were inventions, designed to
discredit Casement; but they were to be confirmed by the evidence of an eye-witness who was not unsympathetic to him,
Bryan Kelly, an Irish student who was in Germany when war
broke out, and had been in the civilian internment camp in
Ruhleben. Casement had heard about him—probably through
Kuno Meyer—and had persuaded the German authorities to
release him, in the hope he might co-operate in recruiting the
Irish Brigade. Kelly was in Limburg when Casement arrived on
his second visit, and heard him greeted by cheers for Redmond,

and shouts of 'how much are the Germans paying you?', which had led to his leaving the camp in disgust.

On January 9th Casement wrote a despairing letter to Wedel, admitting defeat. A sham corps of sorts might be collected, if sufficient inducements were offered; but any thought of getting the men to join from patriotic motives would have to be abandoned. 'They are mercenaries pure and simple, and even had I the means to bribe them, I should not attempt to do so.'

A letter to Sir Edward Grey   *January–February 1915*

Casement returned to Berlin despondent—only to find his prospects dramatically transformed, as he thought, by developments in Christiania, which had revealed that the Germans' suspicion of Adler Christensen had been unfounded.

For a time, he had been inclined to share them. It disturbed him that he made his Adler tell lies on his behalf, and he had used his diary to chastise himself, as a lover does: 'I hate what I am doing'. After the Sassnitz episode, he had begun to fear he might actually have been doing harm:

> I am *not* sure of Adler. His air and manner have greatly changed since he came back—or rather since he went away. He confesses that he now 'admires Findlay'! Findlay 'is a man'—'he would roll those d——d Germans up'.

It must be Adler's hurt pride, Casement decided. But he never doubted that Adler was loyal to him. It was simply that 'with myself out of the issue', he might be tempted to prefer Findlay to the Germans; 'knowing *now* all I do of his character, of its extraordinary complexity, I should feel gravely disposed to mistrust his fidelity in a matter where German ships were the issue as against British ships. I should even, now, be indisposed to trust myself to his schemes!' The emclamation mark gave Casement away. He was still so fondly sure of his hold over his Adler—which he attributed to the trust which had been reposed on him on the voyage over: 'his honour (or what corresponds to it) came to the top, and he determined to be as true as steel to me'—that he let him go to Norway at Christmas, and paid his expenses out of the funds Devoy was providing.

By Findlay's account to Nicolson, on December 27th ('very

urgent, most private and secret'), Christensen brought with him
tracings of two charts of minefields off the Irish and British
coasts, which he claimed to have found in a drawer in Casement's room. His instructions, he told Findlay, were to wait in
Christiania until he heard where he was to join Casement and
his party, who were now planning to leave for Ireland early in
January, from either Sweden or Norway. The Foreign Office sent
copies to Asquith, Kitchener, Churchill, the Irish Department,
and the Intelligence Services; and all was put in readiness for
immediate action as soon as the American yacht, which, it was
assumed, must now be on its way to collect him, could be
traced.

On January 3rd, 1915, Christensen came to Findlay with more
information. Casement was going to arrive in Christiansand on
the *Mjölnir*, from Gothenburg; and Christensen proposed to go
to Gothenburg himself, to join Casement there, so that in the
event of the *Mjölnir* being intercepted, he could prevent Casement from destroying his papers. Finding that Christensen
wanted a large advance for that purpose, Findlay demurred, and
Christensen left the legation in a rage, saying he would warn his
master. But he was soon back, 'evidently afraid of losing his
price'. Findlay gave him two thousand kroner, and repeated his
earlier promises of the £5,000 reward, if Casement should be
caught.

Christensen, however, had a new request. If, as he believed,
Casement had large sums of American money with him, could
this be added to the reward? Findlay told him that he would
have to consult the Foreign Office; and, writing to them, he
recommended acceptance, if only to stop Christensen murdering
his employer simply for the money, and then bolting which he
might otherwise be tempted to do. Nicolson agreed, provided
that no harm or injury was done to Casement. But nothing must
be put in writing; 'pray be careful on this most important point'.

The warning came too late. Persuaded that Christensen would
not deliver up Casement unless he had the British Government's
promise in writing, Findlay had given it to him; and he had gone
back to Germany. 'I would never have done it,' Findlay explained, 'in time of peace. I submit that the fact we are at war
modifies the importance of the rule in question, as we have
nothing to fear from publicity. As the promise given explicitly
mentioned the informer by name, he will never dare to show it

except in claiming payment, when it should be recovered.' But Nicolson was alarmed.

The *Mjölnir* arrived at Christiansand on January 9th. As Casement was not among the passengers, Findlay would have again become suspicious; but on the same day, a German U-boat was seen cruising outside that port. 'It must have some connection with Casement's expedition', he told the Foreign Office, 'either scouting to see of the road is clear, or watching for British ships attempting to intercept Casement.' And Christensen, when he returned to Norway, had a plausible explanation why things had gone wrong. Because Findlay had refused his request for an advance, he had been unable to see Casement, who was not in Berlin (he was, in fact, in Limburg at the time). The story that he was going to be on the *Mjölnir*, Christensen suggested, must have been put out by the German Intelligence. This, Findlay felt, was the explanation for the U-boat's appearance off Christiania; the Germans must have been hoping to find out whether their plans were being made known to the British.

Meanwhile, the crew of the *Sayonara* had been on their midwinter cruise, off the west of Ireland, seeking information; and the Irish—Captain Hall was later to claim—provided it. But he did not specify what the information was. If what they provided about Casement was a fair sample, all they had in fact done was feed back, in traditional Irish fashion, the kind of report that the crew of the *Sayonara* appeared anxious to hear: that Casement was expected to land in Connemara, possibly with German officers, and certainly with German gold. When the news reached the Admiralty that Casement had left Germany on the *Mjölnir*, Hall could congratulate himself that the trap was ready for him, as soon as he arrived off the west of Ireland in the American yacht. But with the news that Casement had not even left Germany—and, worse, that German Intelligence had been responsible for the *Mjölnir* story—there was no further purpose in keeping the *Sayonara* on her cruise. She was recalled.

The Germans must have suspected Christensen, Findlay now realised, or he was in their pay; either way, he was no further use to them. He still believed that the earlier information Christensen had given him was correct; but he could no longer disguise from himself that Christensen might have been playing a double game. In a penitent apologia which he sent to the Foreign Office on January 14th, he admitted that he had not been well-equipped to handle 'a mind unregulated by any rules of morality or intelligence' and 'guided by low cunning ... he is a most loathsome beast'. All he could now hope for was that Christensen's low cunning would keep him from making Findlay's written offer public. Even if it did, 'I cannot see how it can be used against us. It is simply an offer of reward for the capture of a self-confessed traitor, as might be posted on every police office in Britain.'

This was, in fact, how the German Foreign Office saw it. When Christensen returned to Berlin and found Casement was away, he had shown it to them, and they had simply filed it. Casement only heard about it from Richard Meyer when he arrived back in Berlin on January 23rd. It was, he felt, of vital importance. Whatever suspicions he or the Germans might have had of Christensen, they had now been shown to be unfounded. The British minister had confirmed Christensen's story in the most convincing way possible—in writing. At last, he had the evidence he needed if he was to do what he had planned to do; use the story to discedit not only Findlay, but also the Foreign Office and the British Government. He had told the German Chancellor about Findlay when they met in December; and when Bethmann-Hollweg had said he felt the story was incredible, Casement had explained that though individually the Englishman might be a gentleman, he had 'no conscience when it comes to collective dealing'. Collectively, the English were 'a most dangerous compound, and form a national type that has no parallel in humanity'. Now, he could show not only the Germans, but the world, how he had caught the British Government —as he wrote in his diary— 'in flagrante delicto'.

But the German Foreign Ministry, he found, were not merely reluctant to allow him to make use of the note; they did not even want to let it out of their hands. He was furious. 'They have wilfully kept me in ignorance of a fact of supreme importance to myself and the cause of Ireland, and have taken possession of a document they have no more right to than my purse.' He had only one course open to him, he decided. He must return to Norway, 'convict Findlay up to the hilt, get H.M. Government exposed, and if necessary return to Germany' (the return would become necessary, he thought, only if the Irish Brigade, against all the indications, began to attract recruits; a new priest was expected from America, who might be a help).

The best way to expose the British Government, he decided, was to write an open letter to Sir Edward Grey, relating the whole nefarious plot, and then to take it personally to Christiania. And when the German authorities warned that the British might take him off the mail steamer from Sassnitz, he would not listen. He would set off, he announced, on January 31st, by the morning train from Berlin, which connected with the Sassnitz ferry. When he reached the station, he found he had consulted an out-of-date time-table; the train did not connect with the ferry. He had to return to his hotel, and hang around until the evening train. In the course of the day he began to wonder whether he was wise to go to Norway; and although he eventually decided to take the train, during the night doubts again assailed him—not from fear of interception, he claimed in his diary, but simply from the realisation of what he was doing:

> To go out, single-handed, to thus challenge the mightiest Government in the world and to charge them publicly with infamous criminal conspiracy through their accredited representative, is a desperate act. I have no money; no friends; no support; no Government, save that of the one bent on destroying me, to appeal to. They are all-potent and will not sacrifice Findlay without a fight; and in that fight they must win.

The following morning, waiting at Sassnitz for the boat, he discussed the venture with Christensen, who did his best to dissuade him—presumably because he did not relish the idea of being in Christiania when the full story of his double treachery came out. Casement decided to return to Berlin. By this time, he was in a state of emotional turmoil. All he could think about was his letter to Sir Edward Grey. Dated February 1st, 1915, it was partly an apologia—as his pension and his honours had been referred to in Parliament, he wanted to make it clear that he had voluntarily given up the one, and now wished to divest himself of the others; partly an explanation of what he had done—and partly an apologia. He had deliberately decided to take all the risks, and to accept all the penalties which might attach to his action. What he had not bargained for were risks and penalties which lay outside the accepted legal procedure, in such cases; in other words, while he was prepared to face charges in a court of Law, he was not prepared to meet way-laying, kidnapping, suborning of dependents or 'knocking on the head'. Findlay had tried to suborn his servant; 'that this man was faithful to me and the law of his country was a triumph of Norwegian integrity over the ignoble inducement, proffered him by the richest and most powerful Government in the world, to be false to both.' As proof, Casement proposed to enclose, with his letter to Grey, a copy of Findlay's promise to pay. He concluded:

> At a date compatible with my own security against the clan-destine guarantees and immunities of the British Minsiter in Norway, I shall proceed to lay before the legitimate authori-ties in that country the original document and the evidence in my possession that throws light on the proceedings of His Majesty's Government.
>
> To that Government, through you, Sir, I now beg to return the insignia of the Most Distinguished Order of St. Michael and St. George, the Coronation Medal of His Majesty King George V, and any other medal, honour or distinction con-ferred upon me by His Majesty's Government, of which it is possible for me to divest myself;
>
>   I am, Sir,
>   Your most obedient, humble
>   servant,
>
>   Roger Casement

Writing the letter had failed to bring Casement peace of mind. Suffering from what in such circumstances used to be described as nervous prostration, he retreated to a sanatorium at Grune-wald, a prey to depression—and to paranoia. 'I am in my room,' he wrote, 'writing up my diary and eating my heart out. An agent of the secret police has just called (11.20 a.m.) to ask for my "military pass"—I have none.' Casement had given him his old police card, in the name of Hammond, and referred him to the authorities; 'it is highly possible they will bungle things there, and I may be hauled off to jail'. It was to be his last entry in that diary.

Over the next twelve months, Casement was beset by chronic, sometimes acute, depression. When he resumed his diary, he was to explain that he had stopped it 'when it became clear that I was being played with, fooled and used by a most selfish and unscrupulous Government for its own sole petty interests'; but he came nearer to the truth when he added, 'I did not wish to record the misery I felt, or to say the things my heart prompted'. Even this did not give quite the full picture, for he was in fact writing all the time—but as prompted by the overtaxed mind, rather than the heart.

He had lucid intervals; sometimes he could write with sense, even with irony. When he received a circular from the 'Patriotic League of Britons Overseas', asking him to help in raising enough money to present a warship to the Admiralty, or some other gift to the nation which would be 'unmistakably identified with the patriotism and loyalty of Britons abroad', his suggestion was, 'Say, a new gaol in Ireland, for treason-felony prisoners?' But much of the time he was producing the kind of memoranda and letters that are familiar to editors and members of parliament, as well as to doctors, and which usually turn out to have come from patients in, or about to enter, mental hospitals. He wrote drafts of tirades against 'the Downing Street Lie Factory'; and of letters—like one he began to Grey, but did not finish,

> Sir,
>   You have not answered my letter. I did not think you would. How could you? To answer was either to lie or to admit the truth. . . .

going on to liken Grey's conduct to Leopold's.

He also became morbidly sensitive to criticism, making it difficult for *Clan-na-Gael*, whose paid emissary he still was, to handle him. At first, Devoy had been very pleased with Casement's efforts in Germany. 'I must congratulate you on the splendid way you have done your work,' he wrote to tell him on New Year's Day, 1915; 'In this I speak for all your friends here. The Declaration was all that could be expected in the present military and naval situation.' But as the weeks went by, Devoy became more and more dissatisfied. The Findlay affair struck him as an unimportant side-issue; and from his own experience recruiting for the Fenians, he felt that Casement was going the wrong way about getting men for the Irish Brigade:

> instead of approaching the men individually, he had them all assembled at a meeting at which he delivered an address which went over their heads. The good and the bad, the Orangeman and the Catholic, the half-decent fellow and the blackguard, were all there to listen to his high patriotic sentiments, and, what was still worse, old Reserve men—whose wives were receiving subsistence money from the British Government and who naturally would think of the interests of their families before and above all else—were present. To step out of the ranks and volunteer for service against England under such circumstances required a degree of moral courage that is rare among Irishmen of that class.

When a copy of the Irish Brigade 'Treaty' with the German Government reached Devoy, he was further shocked by one of its clauses. Casement had agreed that if the German navy were unable to land the Irish Brigade in Ireland, they might be employed to assist the Egyptian people to recover their freedom; 'short of directly fighting to free Ireland from British rule, a blow struck at the British invaders of Egypt, to aid Egyptian national freedom, is a blow struck for a kindred cause to that of Ireland'. To Casement, this was a logical extension of Davitt's creed that the Irish, the Indians and the Egyptians should regard themselves as allies in the struggle against imperialism. He had also for years been convinced that the Turks were being shamefully used by the Western powers. The way in which Christianity was being used 'for a cloak to unbridled action against them', he had written to tell C. P. Scott of the *Guardian* in 1912, 'fills me with disgust. ... I fancy Europe may yet bitterly regret the destruction of Turkey.' Nevinson, who knew the Turks much better than he did, had tried to persuade him that they had brought retribution on themselves, and that there was no conspiracy among the Western powers to destroy them; but he had refused to listen. Now, the idea of the Irish Brigade fighting alongside them to liberate Egypt appealed to him.

It did not appeal to Devoy. 'We in America strongly object to any such proposal,' he wrote, 'and our friends in Dublin are unalterably opposed to it.' The only place for Irish troops to fight, he insisted, was in Ireland. But Casement, though the *Clan* were employing him, refused to accept their dictation. And he had no Irish friends in Germany to point out to him how inconsistent it must look to others—even if it seemed logical to him—that he should allow the Irish Brigade to fight alongside the Turks in the Middle East, while refusing to allow them to fight alongside the Germans on the Western Front.

Patrick Pearse

The result was that Devoy lost confidence in Casement; and this was unfortunate, because it tended to cut him off from his only source of information about the movement in Ireland, and at a crucial time.

Redmond's authority was gradually being eroded. To keep it, he had to be able to convince his countrymen that Home Rule was secure, even though it was not to be put into operation until the war ended; and this he could best do by showing that he and his National Volunteers had the complete confidence of the British Government. Kitchener, however, had no confidence in them. 'The Ulster division,' J. L. Hammond observed— chronicling the events which, he believed, were to lead to the rising of 1916—'had its badge: the Irish division was not allowed a badge. The officers of the Ulster Volunteers were given commissions; the officers of the Irish Volunteers were compelled to take further training. The Ulster division was treated as an Ulster army; the Irish division as a unit of the British army.' Sir Francis Vane, then recruiting officer for the British army in Ireland, claimed the War Office's attitude helped to promote the 1916 Rising: a view shared both by the Chief Secretary, Birrell, and by one of the most dedicated opponents of Home Rule, Walter Long.

A still more serious blow to Redmond's authority was Asquith's decision in the early summer of 1915 to form a Coalition Government, bringing in the Unionists, including all the most vehement anti-Home-Rulers—Bonar Law, Carson and F. E. Smith, as well as Long. To the world in general, the new Government might appear an impressive sign of political solidarity; to the Irish, it could only be interpreted as a warning that the Home Rule Act was, as Carson had described it, 'a scrap of paper', which would be torn up as soon as the Unionists were in power. To have included the Unionists in the Government without getting any pledge from them about Home Rule was the decisive step, John Dillon came to believe, in the destruction of the Irish Parliamentary Party.

The coalition was just what the Irish republicans needed, Devoy realised, to help persuade the more moderate separatists to regard Germany as an ally; and much use was therefore made by the I.R.B. of Casement's views. His articles had already been reprinted in Griffith's wartime journals—and in the *Irish Volunteer*, run by Bulmer Hobson; and when in 1915 police raided the house of a republican suspect, Laurence de Lacy, they found stacks of the pamphlets containing what he had written on Ireland and Germany, awaiting circulation not only to sympathisers, but to parish priests, members of public bodies, and other prominent citizens—much to their irritation; the pamphlets came through the post disguised as seed catalogues, in the name of a well-known Unionist firm, which later offered £100 reward for anybody who could provide evidence leading to the conviction of the miscreants responsible.

That summer, it became possible for the I.R.B. to begin to plan seriously for a rising, with German help. They no longer need worry about being accused of jeopardising Home Rule; the coalition had done their work for them. Redmond also helped them, by identifying all forms of separatism with *Sinn Fein*— a 'temporary cohesion of isolated cranks', as he described the movement in July; 'they have no policy, and no leader, and do not amount to a row of pins as far as the future of Ireland is concerned.' Republicans did not like to be identified with *Sinn Fein*; but the fact that they were, encouraged hopes of wider support for a rising when the time came; and the I.R.B. set up a Military Council, to make the necessary preparations.

Casement would have been surprised to hear that Patrick Pearse, whom he had known when he was a 'harmless literary man' (as he had wryly described himself), had become director of organisation of the Irish Volunteers. He was much more than that. As James Stephens described it, he had a power which made men who came into contact with him 'begin to act differently to their own desires and interests'; and he began to envisage a rising which would conform to his own desires, rather

than to those of MacNeill, Hobson, and the other Volunteer
leaders. That summer, Pearse let fall a hint of what he had in
mind in his funeral oration for the Fenian Jeremiah O'Donovan
Rossa, whose remains had been brought back from the United
States for burial in Ireland. The Volunteers, he claimed, did not
exist simply for the negative purpose of holding the British
Government to Home Rule. Theirs was the positive goal of the
freedom of Ireland; 'and we know only one definition; it is
Mitchel's definition; it is Rossa's definition'.

It was also Casement's—an Ireland separated altogether from
Britain, and from the British Empire, except in so far as she
voluntarily chose association. But what he could not know was
the plan which Pearse was evolving to secure that separation. If
the Germans sent arms, he would be willing to accept them;
but he did not rely on getting them, as Casement assumed the
separatists would. Still less did he rely on an Irish Brigade. 'How
can we defend such men,' a Connaught Volunteer asked him,
'who take an oath to fight in the British army, of their own free
will, and then break it?' Pearse felt the same way. Whether or
not help came there must, he felt, be a rising, even if it was
certain to be crushed. The Volunteers could achieve by their
blood sacrifice what the United Irishmen and the Fenians had
failed to achieve; a national spirit which would make continued
English domination impossible.

In Pearse's play *The King*, produced in 1912, the hero was a
child 'whose innocent readiness to give his life for his people
frees them when the efforts of the adult king have failed'; and in
his poetry, as well as in speeches, the theme was the need for
self-sacrifice, if necessary through death. Casement had come
close, at times, to expressing the same feeling—notably in his
letter from America to the *Independent*: 'if Irish blood is to be
"the seal that will bring all Ireland together in one nation and
in liberties equal and common to all", then let that blood be
shed in Ireland, where alone it can be righteously shed to secure
those liberties ... let our graves be that patriot grass whence
alone the corpse of Irish nationality can spring to life.' If Casement had known Pearse's design, he would have accepted it.
But he did not know. He remained under the impression that
the Irish Volunteers were in MacNeill's cautious charge.

So did MacNeill. Hobson knew that MacNeill was being deceived; that the I.R.B., of which MacNeill was not a member,

would make the decision when they should fight. But Hobson himself was unaware that the decision was going to be made not by the I.R.B., but by its Military Council, which was composed only of men of Pearse's persuasion; Joseph Plunkett—the poet who had worked on the *Irish Review*, when Casement had been writing for it; Eamonn Ceannt; and men they trusted sufficiently to co-opt, Sean MacDermott, Tom Clarke, Thomas MacDonagh. The Military Council became a junta, preserving secrecy about the plans for the rising ostensibly because it was safer to do so, to reduce the risk of betrayal, but also because their plans were different from the I.R.B.'s and from MacNeill's. Even Devoy was not fully aware of this development—and if he had been, he would have been unlikely to tell Casement.

The only man who was in a position that summer of 1915 to warn Casement what was in contemplation was Joseph Plunkett. Because he was consumptive, he had an excuse for travelling denied to his colleagues; and as 'James Malcolm' he was to get to Germany, through Switzerland, and to meet Casement there. But on the way, he had seen Devoy; and Devoy had advised him to deal direct with the German Government, rather than to rely upon Casement. Even with his close associates, in the junta, Plunkett could be conspiratorially devious; and he deliberately misled Casement into thinking that much depended on getting recruits for the Irish Brigade—'we'll get them,' he urged, 'if we have to kidnap them.' In fact, having been to Limburg and seen the 'Brigade', he realised it was a failure. He may have given a hint that there might be a rising with or without German support. Casement told him that if that happened, he would wish to be there. But he could not believe that what he regarded as an act of idiocy was really in contemplation.

Libel   1915

Not that Casement was in any condition rationally to assess the rising's prospects—or his own. The year 1915, which had started so badly with the collapse of his hopes for the Irish Brigade, the failure of the Germans to exploit the Findlay affair, and his breakdown, was to continue to harass him.

His hopes that the 'Open Letter to Sir Edward Grey' would cause an international sensation were not fulfilled. A copy had been sent to German representatives throughout Europe and

America; none of them did more than send perfunctory acknow-
ledgments. The German minister in Portugal actually returned
his copy, saying it was no concern of his. Nothing appeared in
the American press until six weeks later, when the *New York
American* published what Casement felt was a mangled version
—a retranslation from the German. The rest of the New York
papers either ignored it, or attributed it to the German propaganda machine. Devoy claimed he had not published the letter
because he was away when it came in, which gave him the excuse to wait until he received the full English text; but he was
also irritated that Casement should have so entirely lost his
sense of proportion as to imagine that, with a world war on,
people would be shocked by Findlay's offer.

Only in Norway did the story attract more than passing
attention. 'You made a great mistake in giving it', Nicolson
wrote to tell Findlay, 'and although there is nothing really compromising in the document itself, I have no doubt that Casement and his friends will make the most of it.' When the story
broke on February 15th, some Norwegian papers suggested that
Findlay had tried to suborn an innocent Norwegian lad. Naturally Findlay wanted to publish his version; but the Foreign
Office felt that it would not be necessary. They were right; a
week later, Findlay admitted that the matter had 'practically
died a natural death'. His only worry was that he had received
a cable from Casement—'evidently unaware that the informer
had stated the unnatural character of their relations'—threatening to come over with Christensen to charge him with conspiracy. A statement from Grey, Findlay felt, might be salutary, if
the Foreign Office thought it advisable. But the Foreign Office
thought it advisable to leave the matter alone; and when the
Norwegian Foreign Minister—who could foresee possible
trouble with Germany, as well as with Britain, if the controversy continued—gave the Norwegian editors what Findlay described as 'a strong hint' to let the subject drop, they did.

To Casement, the lack of interest in his exposure was a
humiliation. He had believed that the indictment of Findlay
would be more telling even than the raising of an Irish Brigade;
now, he had to realise that the German Foreign Office had not
been as stupid as they had seemed. From New York von Papen
wrote to congratulate him—'a long time since I saw you last ...
I hope you are well-off in my beloved country'—on the help his

disclosure had given to the cause, by enlightening neutrals on the method the English were capable of using. But this can have been small consolation for the general lack of interest; Casement was not an admirer of Papen.

By this time, Casement was immersed in another equally unprofitable and frustrating enterprise. An allegation had appeared in the *New York World* — placed there, in all probability, by the British agency which was busy feeding such material to the press in America — that he was in Germany, in hiding, and in the pay of the German Government. The cutting had reached him on March 15th — the day he made his last entry in his diary; and he at once cabled to John Quinn in New York to bring proceedings against the *World*. In a letter, he explained how he had never taken a cent from the German Government, even over Findlay.

> They offered to pay *all* my expenses ... I refused. I have refused every form of 'assistance'. I have never been 'in hiding' but staying in the principal hotels in Germany and visited by scores. My name is a household word through Germany today. At the moment I am the guest of the Baron and Baroness von Nordenflycht — he is the German minister at Montevideo, and my former colleague at Rio de Janeiro.

He had actually turned down attractive offers from German publishers, Casement went on, and from lecture agencies, for fear acceptance might be misconstrued.

A libel action on such grounds, Quinn told the German Ambassador (through whom he had received Casement's instructions) was not to be thought of. For a variety of reasons Casement would run the risk of losing it. He would not be there to testify in person, and although the Court might be persuaded that the allegation that he had received money from the Germans was false, they would not necessarily regard it as defamatory. All things considered, Quinn concluded, he could probably talk the case out of Court before it had begun, 'if I were counsel for the *World*'. 'Which you probably are,' Casement noted venomously in the margin, when the letter reached him. He handed the case over to another lawyer, and in a letter to McGarrity, described Quinn's attitude as contemptible.

He was later to admit that he had been guilty of hasty and

ill-considered judgments; and on re-reading the draft of what he had written on this occasion to McGarrity, he scrawled across the top of it, 'I much regret this letter. It is unjust and I withdraw'. But this may have referred to an imputation that the *Clan* was not doing enough for him—a charge which he put more strongly in a letter to Kuno Meyer. When he recovered from one of his black moods, he was apt to banish from his mind what he had written while he was in them, and to become optimistic again. 'With regard to the "Poor Brothers" ', he wrote about the Irish Brigade to Devoy in April,

> things are improving. So far as Ireland is concerned everything, almost, depends on this effort. If *this* cannot be done, nothing is done. The view here (in official circles) is that we must show some spirit of patriotism and sincere belief in our cause to get help from this country. If *we* do nothing, they say, how can they do anything? If Irishmen themselves care so little for Ireland that they will risk nothing, what proof is there that there is any national cause at all in Ireland on which Germany can count?

But the improvement which he spoke of was in his own mind, not in the prospects for the 'Poor Brothers', which had changed not at all—they did not change even when the fifty-odd men who had been recruited to the Irish Brigade were removed to a camp of their own, and given 'Irish' uniforms. The letter could only serve to irritate Devoy, who had been willing to let the experiment be tried, but wanted to abandon it the moment it failed—particularly when he heard the British and Redmondite newspapers were beginning to find the Brigade valuable for their own propaganda purposes. Their stories, he found, 'all represented Sir Roger Casement as offering bribes of "German money" to the men to volunteer to fight for Germany'; bribes which had been rejected with scorn even when the men who refused to join were put, as punishment, into unhealthy, vermininfested cells; and the guards who had charge of the Irish prisoners were having 'a hard time to keep the indignant Irishmen from tearing Sir Roger Casement to pieces'.

On May 28th, Devoy set out his views in a long letter to Casement. He should waste no more time on the Irish Brigade; instead, he should occupy himself wholly with winning recognition

for Ireland's cause—'the higher task for which you are so
eminently fitted, and in which you have achieved splendid success—a success which will go down in history as a splendid
achievement.' He must also learn to obey instructions: 'isolated
individual action can only tend towards disarrangement of plans
... we and our system have many shortcomings and limitations,
but we form between us the only *machine* with which the work
we have set out to do can be done. We may be unequal to the
task, but if we are, it cannot be done in our time.'

The kindly McGarrity was relieved when Casement's reply
turned out to be conciliatory. 'I am glad you have heard from
our friend,' he wrote to tell Devoy.

> and that he is in a better mood. We must make an endeavour
> to answer his letters promptly and, of course, his personal
> wants should be taken care of promptly. Let there be no
> room for complaint later that we handicapped him in any
> way. Of course, he is an idealist and it is well that he is one,
> even if we cannot live up to his ideals. You must take into
> consideration his situation, away from friends, and getting
> such a keen disappointment with the 'Poor Brothers' and
> other things that were even more discouraging. ... Don't
> write anything that would hurt his feelings, as of course the
> enemy would be delighted to see a break. My feeling is that he
> should be allowed sufficient to move in certain circles neces-
> sary to carry on the work in which he is assigned.

Devoy might have felt the same; but he had been shown the
angry letter which Casement had written while in the grip of
depression to Kuno Meyer. Again, he wrote to warn him that he
was in no position to know what was happening in the United
States, or in Ireland; and, as he had been sent $6,500 since he
left for Germany, he could hardly complain about having been
let down financially. Casement immediately came to the conclusion that he was being charged with misappropriating *Clan*
funds; and he compiled an elaborate statement of accounts
showing in detail how the money had been spent, adding that it
was his intention, 'should it be in my power, at any time, to
refund all the moneys received from Messrs. J. McGarrity and
John Devoy, whether used by me·for my personal needs and
requirements' or expended in the public cause I have been sus-

taining'. It was the kind of a letter a schoolboy might have written to a friend after a tiff over the division of a locker-full of mutually-held belongings; and McGarrity had to write to assure him that nobody was accusing him of anything. He was not for a moment to feel he was not appreciated; the failure of the Irish Brigade was not his fault; 'now brace up and don't be downhearted—all will come right.'

All did not come right. A further indignity awaited him, when the German Foreign Office showed him a letter received from a member of the staff of the *Gaelic American* telling them that he no longer had the confidence of the *Clan*. Only Devoy, he protested, had authority to speak for the *Gaelic American*, or the *Clan*. Devoy himself, when he heard, promptly repudiated the writer, and insisted that he had the fullest confidence in Casement; but communication between Germany and the United States took time, and in the meanwhile, Casement felt that he himself had been repudiated. Robert Monteith—a former officer in the Irish Volunteers, sent by the *Clan* to Germany to help train the Irish Brigade—found him in despair; 'he turned his face to the wall and cried'.

Monteith had been smuggled over to Norway, as a stowaway, with the help of Adler Christensen. In their anxiety to prevent the Findlay affair from becoming a *cause célèbre*, the Foreign Office had made no accusation against Christensen; and Casement had continued fondly to assume that the Germans had unjustly suspected him. Still, there had been no point in his staying on in Germany; and he had set off in March for the United States, where Casement begged the *Clan* to help him. 'We will welcome our Norwegian friend when he arrives,' Devoy promised, 'and do all we can for him. He is certainly a trump'; and in September, McGarrity was able to report that the *Clan* had found him a good job; 'he likes it, and is grateful; he would, as he says, die for you'. Christensen won the *Clan*'s confidence by getting Monteith to Norway; and Devoy then employed him in a more ambitious project, to bring some Irish-American Volunteers to Europe. By Devoy's account, in his memoirs, fifty 'dependable and partially trained men' were to go to Germany, where 'their presence might have induced a larger number of Irish soldiers in the British army to join the Brigade'. But at this point Christensen revealed himself 'as a trickster and a fraud, with the result that we had to abandon the project and to sum-marily dismiss him'.

The *Clan* also found Christensen had been systematically swindling them by getting money from them for the mainten-ance of his 'wife'—a girl friend, they found, from Berlin, whom he had managed to bring over with him. For Casement—who had just had a letter from his Adler, from Jersey City, full of unctuous flattery—the news must have been the final blow of a wretched year. 'I very much hope that peace would come,' he wrote from the Irish Brigade headquarters, where he was stay-ing, 'it is dreadful to think of all the world beginning the New Year with nothing but Death—killing and murdering wholesale, and destroying all that makes life happy ... I feel very sad, and it has been the most unhappy Christmas I have ever spent.'

Four men   1915–1916

In that black period, Monteith was one of four men who helped to preserve Casement's sanity, because he inspired their affec-tion and trust. Another was Father Crotty, at Limburg. Crotty had won the confidence of the Irish soldiers there, but he had done so in a way that made him of little value to the Irish Brigade, because he insisted that, as a priest, he could not allow national or political considerations to influence him. But Case-ment found solace with him; and Crotty, for his part, found Casement 'a most fascinating personality—one who was every inch a gentleman, upright, honest, sincere. In all things Ireland, his country, was first and last—her security and prosperity and her religion he loved.'

There was also St. John Gaffney, the United States Consul in Munich; an ebullient character of a kind that the Irish describe as a chancer (as he reminded Casement, he had been decorated in 1905 for defending Leopold against the Congo reformers). He was hospitable and amusing; but he was so passionately Anglophobe that, following complaints that he had publicly entertained Casement and uttered anti-English sentiments, he was dismissed. 'I wept at G's departure,' Casement noted, 'a true staunch friend and a faithful Irishman.'

Also in Munich, he had met another Irish-American, Dr. Charles Curry; and when Curry and his family went on their summer holiday to the Ammersee, he went with them. 'He was so happy and contented in his new environment'—Curry recalled in the preface to the edition he prepared to the diaries Casement kept while in Germany—'away from the noise and bustle of the city'. But though relieved to find somewhere to retreat to, Casement was not really happy. 'We have nothing to do,' he wrote on September 11th, 'only to eat out our hearts in sheer, deliberate idleness—and that is killing.'

From this mood, he was temporarily rescued by the arrival, in October, of Monteith. As a young man, Monteith had been a loyalist, and he had served in the British forces in the Boer War; but 'in the smoke and red flame of the first Boer farmhouse I saw burned', he was to recall in his *Casement's Last Adventure*, 'there appeared to me the grisly head and naked ribs of the imperialist monster'. On his return to Ireland he had found a job in the Ordnance Department in Dublin, from which he was sacked in 1914 because of his connection with the Volunteers. With his military experience, Tom Clarke felt he might be the man Casement had been asking for to come out and train the Irish Brigade. He had managed to get to New York, and then, with Christensen's help, to Germany, where he at once sought out Casement:

He was straight as a ramrod, deeply tanned by tropical suns, and his black hair and beard were touched by silver. Vigorous in every fibre of his body, if ever a man looked a knight, Roger Casement did. One would unconsciously associate shining armour with this resolute, courtly champion of the oppressed. I have known no eyes more beautiful than Casement's. In his case they were truly the windows of his soul. Blazing when he spoke of man's inhumanity to man; soft and wistful when pleading the cause so dear to his heart; mournful when telling the story of Ireland's centuries' old martyrdom. Eyes that seemed to search the heart and read one's very soul. At times when speaking of Irish children, particularly those of the west, whom he knew so well, his smile would transfigure his face in a manner that defied power of description. A man is indeed fortunate, who can say that he clasped Casement's hand, and received his kindly smile of welcome.

Reserved, almost shy—Monteith continued—Casement was ever ready to help the distressed; 'the sight of hunger or want cut him to the heart. For himself he had little thought; frugal in all things, his living expenses were kept to the lowest penny.' According to Pearse's biographer Le Roux, Clarke had sent Monteith out to work with Casement, but 'if necessary, to replace him'. But when he arrived, he was impressed by the way Casement roused himself to help—even going on route marches with the Irish Brigade. And Monteith found he could hardly keep up with him. 'Slowly, almost imperceptibly, we gained speed; forgetting all in the charm of his conversation, I would awake to the fact that we were almost a mile ahead of the column.'

Early in the new year of 1916, he fell ill again. Monteith found him prostrate, 'his nerves had gone to pieces and his general breakdown was complete. He presented a deathlike appearance. His bronzed face had turned almost ashen colour, his features were pinched and haggard, and he lay so still his breathing was scarcely perceptible.' He refused to see a doctor —because of the expense, Monteith found; he thought medical charges in Germany exorbitant. But a doctor was called, and ordered him to a Munich sanatorium. He had no doubt what was the matter with him; as he was to recall in his diary, when he resumed it, he was 'sick at heart and soul, with mind and nerves threatening a complete collapse. No man was ever in such a false position.' He did not wish to stay any longer in Germany; his loathing for the German Government had become pathological—'swine and cads', he told Monteith, 'of the first order'. But the only alternative, the United States, had little attraction for him. Writing out the words of 'The Wearing of the Green', early in January, he included a verse added, he believed, in 1848, which spoke of emigrating to a country:

> That lies beyond the sea
> Where rich and poor stand equal
> in the light of Freedom's day

But now, Casement commented, 'freedom had perished, and the most cowardly tyranny—that of money—slays again the founder of our Faith, and sells humanity for a handful of gold'. So anxious was he to get out of Germany, though, that he would have gone to America—with the help of Gaffney, who had returned to Germany in another job—if he had not heard from Monteith, early in March, that at last there was a 'move on' in Ireland. It was not a move Casement would welcome, but it settled his mind. At all costs, he decided, he must return there.

CHAPTER FOUR

IRELAND

A summons, Monteith explained, had come from the German General Staff: he had gone to Berlin, to be told that there was to be a rising in Ireland at Easter. Through the German embassy in Washington, Devoy had asked for a shipload of arms to reach Limerick a day or two before; and the Germans had agreed to send 20,000 rifles and ammunition.

If there was to be so small a consignment, with no officers accompanying it, Casement felt that the rising was doomed. His first assumption was that Devoy had been tricked by 'that ass von Papen'. The Germans, Casement felt, would prefer an unsuccessful rising to no rising at all; Papen must have encouraged Devoy to believe that they were going to receive more help than they were prepared to give. His suspicions were increased by the fact that the Germans had chosen to confide in Monteith, not him. Their excuse was that he had been ill; but he no longer believed what they told him. 'They always lie,' he wrote.

> They may or may not keep faith today; but I have no reason to believe that in anything they do they ever think of us, or of others, but only of themselves ... they have shown me repeatedly that they cannot keep faith and have no feeling about Ireland at all, that in anything they promise now, they seek only what ends of their own they are after.

However, as they were offering help, 'let us get what we can'. Von Papen was later to protest that the *Clan* had not been deceived. It was very much in Germany's interest, he pointed out, that the rising should succeed; but her commitments on various fronts made it impossible to send more help. And Devoy's memoirs confirm that if he was deceived, it was self-deception. Believing the Volunteers to be very much stronger than they actually were, he thought the rifles the Germans proposed to land would enable them to fight the occupying forces almost on equal terms. Devoy was also deceived by Pearse and the junta. He did not know that the plan which they had confided to him for a rising at Easter had not been confided even to the Council of the I.R.B.

Having found that Connolly shared their belief in the need for a rising whether or not it stood a chance of success, they had taken him into their confidence; but not Hobson, or MacNeill, who could be expected to oppose their plan as madness. In Germany, Casement—who knew MacNeill and Hobson well enough to sense that they would not plan a rising which had no chance of success—could only assume that they had been promised far more assistance than the Germans were proposing to give; and the thought made him desperate. He tried to send a warning, but the bearer, he realised, might never reach his destination. The *Clan's* specific instructions were that he should stay in Germany, as Ireland's accredited envoy; but this, he felt, would be the coward's way out. He must go to Ireland, with the ship which was to bring the arms.

The Irish Brigade, on the other hand, must not be allowed to go, when their inevitable fate would be to face treason charges, and a firing squad; and on their behalf, he engaged in acrimonious discussions with the German authorities. But he himself, he wrote to tell Dr. Curry, 'must be sacrificed'. All he begged of Curry was that he should 'show clearly later on—but *much* later—or when the proofs can be put in the hands of friends—how innocent he is—and how his action throughout, if mistaken, was based on unselfish regard for what he thought to be the welfare of his country'. And he wrote in the same strain to Alice Green:

I don't suppose, dear Woman of the Three Cows, we shall meet again—so I send you this little line of farewell and eternal remembrance. You know the truth. Some day it will all be made clear and I shall be judged with open eyes, and a true chapter written.

When he went to say goodbye to the Blüchers, it was to beg them, too, to make it clear that he had been loyal to Ireland, though it might not appear so. The Countess described him as beside himself with terror and grief; but the terror was not—

according to an American journalist, Gilbert Hirsch, who was in Berlin at the time, and met him—for himself:

> Everything about him—his tall, thin figure; his incredibly long thin face, with the deeply lined forehead and the sensitive lips and nostrils; something shy about his manner; something abstracted, half-apologetic about his way of speaking— all indicated a man extremely susceptible to suffering. But the perpetual sparkle of humour and intrepidity in the clear grey eyes made it clear that it was the suffering of others to which he was quivering, rather than his own.

On April 5th, Casement went to bid farewell to the Irish Brigade—'It was dreadful. I could not tell them the truth'— and to Father Crotty. The Brigade, he now admitted, had been a 'ghastly folly'; and he did not like to think of the men's fate once he and Monteith had left. The following day, a message reached him through Switzerland from 'a friend of James Malcolm' (transmitted by Joseph Plunkett's father, Count Plunkett, who was able to leave it in Berne on his way to see the Pope), telling him that the 'large consignment of arms' must arrive not later than dawn on Easter Saturday; that German officers would be necessary ('this is imperative'); and that a German submarine would also be required, in Dublin harbour. Casement knew that the consignment would not be large: that there were not going to be any German officers: and that the Germans could not send a U-boat into Dublin harbour—it was too shallow to be safe for the type of U-boat which would be needed for that length of voyage. To arrive with the arms ship, he realised, would be leaving it too late to give his warning. To prevent the rising, he must try to get to Ireland earlier. And the German authorities, though they delayed his warning cable, agreed to send him, with Monteith and a member of the Irish Brigade, to the west of Ireland on a U-boat.

During his last months in Germany, Casement had given the German Foreign Office little cause to remember him with affection; but Zimmermann—who was shortly to be made Foreign Minister—was saddened by his decision to leave. 'It was never my lot,' he was to write on hearing of Casement's execution,

> to know a man of loftier mind, of higher honour, or of more burning love of home. It was a matter of personal grief to me

when I heard he had made up his mind to accompany the expedition, which I greatly feared was fantastic. So I urged him, so far as I could in propriety, to remain with us and to do work among the prisoners. I felt sure Casement could not escape capture, and I knew what that meant. But he only shook his head, saying: 'I must go—I must be with the boys'.

On April 10th, the evening before they were due to leave, Casement had a farewell dinner with Gaffney, who tried to cheer him up with the aid of a bottle of champagne. But he remained depressed—particularly about the Irish Brigade: he begged Gaffney to help them, and ask their forgiveness for his desertion of them. In the final entry in his German diary, he wrote:

> The last days are all a nightmare, and I have only a confused memory of them, and some periods are quite blank in my mind, only a sense of horror and repugnance to life. But I daresay the clouds will break and brighter skies dawn, at least for old Ireland.
>
> I go tonight with Monteith and one man only of the 'boys', and I am quite sure it is the most desperate piece of folly ever committed; but I go gladly . . . if those poor lads at home are to be in the fire, then my place is with them.

On Banna Strand
April 1916

The U-boat was to leave Emden on April 12th; unless they were intercepted, there would be plenty of time to get a warning to MacNeill. But U-20 broke down; and that meant going back to Germany, and starting again. What Casement did not know was that even if the breakdown was an accident, the delay was deliberate. The commander had been told that in no circumstances was he to allow them to land before April 20th, even if they arrived earlier. The German Admiralty were taking no chances that Casement, or somebody in whom he confided, would give away the approach of the ship carrying the arms, which was due to arrive off Fenit, near Tralee, that day.

For Casement, it was an agonising voyage. The U-boat travelled most of the way on the surface, and Monteith was able to clamber up through the manhole to the conning tower, to take the air; but Casement was too ill to care to move from his bunk. The meals consisted largely of tinned ham and tinned salmon; 'anyone who has been to sea', Monteith observed, 'will know how such food appeals to a seasick man'.

When they reached the west coast of Ireland, Casement recovered a little, and they reflected on earlier attempts that had been made to bring help to the Irish from the Continent—all ill-fated. So was theirs. When they reached Tralee Bay on the evening of April 20th—Maundy Thursday—there was no sign of the *Aud*, the trawler which, under the Norwegian flag, was running the guns from Germany; and no signals greeted them from the shore. What had happened, it later transpired, was that a message had reached Devoy from the junta, less than a week before, telling him that the arms must not be landed before the night of Sunday 23rd; 'this is vital'. On the assumption that the instruction would be obeyed, the local Volunteers leaders were told to be ready for the *Aud* and the U-boat on that date. But by the time the message reached Germany, they had left; and they could not be contacted by radio, to warn them of the changed plans. As it happened, too, the captain of the *Aud*, after an audacious run through the British Atlantic patrols, made a navigational error which left him several miles from the rendezvous point on the night of the 20th; and the U-boat captain, unable to find either the *Aud* or signals from the land, felt that he had no choice but to put Casement—'a truly noble man', he was to recall—and his companions ashore, in time for the U-boat to reach the open sea before daylight.

The three men were provided with a dinghy—a cockleshell, Monteith described it. On their way to the shore, a wave overturned them and when they managed to clamber in again, they grounded on a sandbank. By the time they reached the shore, Casement was exhausted. Monteith, who had pulled the dinghy back out into deeper water and tried to sink it, without success, came back to find him unconscious, 'lying below the high-water mark, the sea lapping his body from head to foot, the bigger waves splashing all over him. His eyes were closed, and in the dim moonlight, his face resembled that of a sleeping child.'

But Casement was not unconscious; on Banna Strand, he was in a state of trance. 'When I landed in Ireland,' he was to tell his sister in a letter written while he was awaiting execution,

swamped and swimming ashore on an unknown strand, I was happy for the first time for over a year. Although I knew that this fate waited on me, I was for one brief spell happy and smiling once more. I cannot tell you what I felt. The sand-hills were full of skylarks rising in the dawn, the first I had heard for years — the first sound I heard through the surf was their song, as I waded through the breakers, and they kept rising all the time up to the old rath at Currsahone, where I stayed and sent the others on, and all around were primroses and wild violets and the singing of the skylarks in the air, and I was back in Ireland again.

Monteith had noticed the rath — the remains of a fortification from Viking times — marked on a map from the U-boat; and they had decided to make for it. To get there, they had to wade waist-deep through a slimy, evil-smelling inlet; and by the time they arrived, Casement was so exhausted it was decided that the other two would go on to Tralee, find help, and come back with a car to collect him. But the dinghy, still tumbling in the breakers, gave him away. A police constable found him in the rath, and — declining to accept his story that he was an English author out for a stroll — took him into custody. He had shaved off his beard, and was not immediately recognised; but he was found to be carrying a sleeping-berth ticket from Berlin to Emden; a cypher — which he attempted without success to tear up and throw away; and a diary, composed of jottings in an easily translatable code ('April 12th: left Wicklow in Willie's yacht'). He could not expect to conceal his identity for long. And as Pearse had given strict instructions that nothing should be done which might give warning to the authorities of the rising, no rescue attempt was made.

Casement's main concern was to transmit a warning to Mac-Neill that the German help, if it arrived, was going to be in-sufficient. When he was visited in Tralee gaol that evening by Father F. M. Ryan, a Dominican, he disclosed his identity, asking Ryan to keep it a secret (in case it should provoke an attempt to rescue him) but to pass his warning on — which, after some hesitation, Ryan agreed to do. And when, the following day, Easter Saturday, Casement was being taken under escort to London, he could have congratulated himself, if he had known, that his purpose had somehow been fulfilled. The parade of Volunteers due to be held on Easter Sunday had been cancelled, on MacNeill's instructions.

PART SIX

ON TRIAL
1916

CHAPTER ONE

EXAMINATION

The Tower   *April–May 1916*

Casement was brought overnight from Dublin to London, arriving on Easter Sunday morning. From Euston, he was taken under escort to Scotland Yard, where the two men who had hoped to catch him earlier, with the help of the yacht *Sayonara*, were waiting to interrogate him: Basil Thomson, head of the C.I.D., and Captain Reginald Hall, chief of naval intelligence. As soon as Casement realised it was useless to try to cover up his movements, which had been given away by the diary and the sleeping berth ticket, he ceased to feel any constraint, though what he was saying was being taken down by a shorthand writer. Thomson found him 'very vivacious and at times histrionic in his manner', anxious to explain what had happened, and why:

> I am not endeavouring to shield myself at all. I face all the consequences. All I ask you is to believe I have done nothing dishonourable, which you will one day learn. I have done nothing treacherous to my country ... knowing all the circumstances, I came from a sense of duty, in which, if I dared to tell you the facts, you would be the first to agree with me

—his hesitation about telling them all the facts, he added, coming from fear that he might involve other people.

He was taken off to Brixton prison, and brought back to Scotland Yard for further interrogation on Easter Monday—still ready to talk freely, except where he might implicate others. He was vain, Thomson thought, but an idealist, not a self-seeker. And the interrogation might have continued, with Thomson and Hall hoping to elicit more information about what was going on in Germany, if the news had not come through of the rising that day in Dublin. Would the Government give an assurance—a maverick M.P., Pemberton Billing, asked Asquith when the Commons reassembled in the afternoon—that 'this traitor will be shot forthwith?', and loud cheers indicated that it was a popular proposal. The Government had not yet decided how to proceed, whether by trial for treason, or by court martial; Casement was transferred from Brixton prison to the Tower of London, while they were making up their minds.

For the next fortnight, he was kept in the Tower *incommunicado*. Even the soldiers who guarded him were not allowed to converse with him. The only news he had, in that time, was from a Welsh corporal, who whispered to him that there had been a rising in Dublin, and that its leaders had been captured and executed. So his mission had failed, after all.

What had happened was not to be satisfactorily pieced together until many years later, because the members of the junta, having affixed their signatures to their proclamation of an Irish Republic, had signed their own death warrants. They had hoped to keep their plans for the rising secret until they could present MacNeill, Hobson and the Volunteers with what they would agree was a legitimate excuse for it: the impending arrival of German arms. But Hobson, becoming suspicious, had warned MacNeill what was afoot; and MacNeill, after some hesitation, called off the Easter Sunday parade. The junta decided to go ahead without him; such Volunteers and Citizen Army men who could be contacted were instructed to parade on Easter Monday. Ironically, Casement's arrest facilitated their plans. Hearing that MacNeill had called off the parade, the Under-Secretary, Nathan, assumed that the arrest and the loss of the arms had averted a crisis; he told a lunch party on Sunday that they could safely go to the fashionable Fairyhouse Races the following day. The Lord Lieutenant, Lord Wimborne, who had been an advocate of tougher measures against the Volunteer movement, agreed that the arrest would render it temporarily harmless; 'a stroke of luck'. Birrell, in London, was also reassured. Even when it became known that a parade was after all to be held on the Monday, it was not considered necessary to take it any more seriously than its innumerable predecessors. So the Volunteers and the Citizen Army had been able to march to their positions, while senior officials and army officers were on their way to Fairyhouse.

By a further irony, the course which events had taken prompted the authorities to assume that Casement had been the instigator of the rising. No other explanation fitted the facts. The signatories of the rebel proclamation were barely known in Ireland and, except Connolly, unknown in England. Only Clarke was older than Casement; most of the others were much younger. If MacNeill had been involved, he might have been held responsible; but he had clearly been repudiated by the rebels. No: obviously the Germans had employed Casement to foment the rebellion in Ireland—doubtless through the *Clan*, in America; and then sent him to Ireland, to lead it.

Until the rising began, Casement could be regarded in England as a curiosity—as Thomson clearly thought him, during his interrogation. By the time the rising was over, he appeared the foulest of traitors. Not that it had been a success: outside Dublin, there had been only a few isolated actions. But in Dublin, the rebel force of fewer than two thousand men had held on throughout the week, just long enough to lift the rising out of the dismal category of farcical earlier failures, and quite long enough to give the impression to loyalists, in Ireland as well as in England, that it was a stab in the back, with Casement's hand on the dagger. 'Germany plotted it', Redmond claimed, 'Germany organised it, Germany paid for it'; and although, as Casement was in custody, Redmond refrained from mentioning him by name, he clearly had him in mind when he referred to those men who had tried to make Ireland Germany's cat's-paw.

So it had come about that Casement, who had come to Ireland to try to prevent the rising, was regarded as responsible for it. And as the evidence appeared to build up against him, the Government began to be attracted to the idea of a civil trial for treason. The Government's first instinct, presumably prompted by the fact that the leaders of the rising in Ireland were being tried by court martial, had been to deal with Casement in the same way; it would be quicker. But on April 27th Asquith reported to King George that the Cabinet favoured civil proceedings, provided they could be 'carried through as promptly as those by court martial'. Soon, they ceased to be concerned with the speed of the outcome: on the contrary, they came down in favour of a leisurely show trial, because—or so Wyndham Childs, the War Office official who had the responsibility for Casement at the time, believed—'a greater impression would be made on the neutral countries'.

While the procedure was being discussed, Casement remained in the Tower. In Brixton, as he was to acknowledge, he had been treated with scrupulous fairness. In the Tower—perhaps because of a futile suicide attempt, with some curare which he carried around—two soldiers were always in his cell, 'never to leave me, and looking at me all the time'; and a sentry outside looking in, 'three men with eyes never off me, night and day, changed every hour, and electric light full on at night, so that sleep became impossible and thought became a page of Hell'. Nobody came to visit him. His friends, he could only assume, must have deserted him, appalled by his treachery or fearful of being identified with it.

They had not deserted him. As soon as Gertrude Bannister heard that he had been captured, she had come up to London to see what she could do to help him—though she must have known it would ruin her career as a teacher. Wilfred Blunt was to describe her, after a meeting a few weeks later, as 'a very superior woman, in mind and somewhat in looks like Charlotte Brontë, to me most attractive'. For the next few weeks she was to use all her attraction, and her powers of persuasion to help her cousin. Her first step was to call on Alice Green, in despair over the rising and Casement's part in it, but willing to write a letter to the Home Secretary—Herbert Samuel, Casement's old ally in the Congo campaign. Gertrude Bannister took it around to the Home Office the next morning. But until the decision was taken whether to hold a military or a civil trial, Casement was in a kind of administrative limbo; and the result was days of frustration. The Home Office told her it was a matter for the Secretary for War. The War Office said she should apply to the Home Office and, when told that she had already done so, suggested she should try Scotland Yard. 'Thus passed day after day of weary trudging from Public Office to Public Office, always refused with absolutely blank, stony indifference.'

On May 1st, George Gavan Duffy—the son of one of the leaders of the Young Ireland movement, and himself a *Sinn Fein* sympathiser—offered to arrange for Casement's defence; but it was not until over a week later that the authorities allowed him to see the prisoner. Gavan Duffy had known him; now, he found it hard to believe that this really was Casement, standing before him. 'Terribly changed', he reported to Gertrude Bannister. His beard had not yet grown again. His eyes were bloodshot, his manner hesitant; he found difficulty in remembering names and words. His clothes were filthy; he was still wearing the trousers which had been soaked in the landing, and covered with slime when he waded through the inlet; his braces had been taken away, so he had to hold them up. He had not been allowed to take any exercise: and as his cell was verminous, he was covered with bites, for which he had been given no treatment.

As soon as Alice Green heard of these conditions, she wrote to Asquith to describe them, with a hint that if he took no action she would pass her information to American newspaper correspondents. Asquith acted. Casement, it was announced, would stand trial in the civil courts. In the Commons, Dillon raised an objection: why should he be allowed a civil trial, when the Dublin rebels had been sentenced and executed by a secret military tribunal — though they were 'comparatively obscure men whom he has been largely responsible for seducing into rebellion'? Casement would have agreed; he had no wish to be treated differently from them. In a memorandum he prepared in the Tower (after Gavan Duffy's visit, he was allowed writing material) he expressed the wish to be tried by a military tribunal 'like my friends in Dublin'. But at least the decision meant that he would be removed from the Tower. On May 15th he was transferred back to Brixton prison, where he was allowed to put on some ill-fitting civilian clothes his cousin bought for him, to have books and newspapers, and to see visitors. He could also write letters. The first was to Inspector Sandercock, who had become his escort when he reached Euston, and had remained in charge of him, whenever he was being moved.

> You showed the best side of an Englishman's character — his native good heart. Whatever you think of my attitude towards your Government and the Realm, I would ask you to keep only one thing in that good heart of yours — and that is that a man may fight a country and its policy, and yet not hate any individual of that country.

Brixton

From the newspapers, and from his visitors, Casement now began to realise that the rising had not been a failure. The initial reaction of the great majority of the people of Ireland, admittedly, had been anger with the rebels. In Dublin, James Stephens found, the men were at best indifferent, and the women, from the best-dressed to the worst, were unanimous that the rebels deserved to be shot. But as the week drew on, a measure of pride began to insinuate itself over the fact that a small body of men were withstanding the might of the British army; and the news that Francis Sheehy Skeffington had been arrested and shot caused a revulsion of popular feeling, against the British.

'A very honest man', Casement wrote of Skeffington, when he heard of his death, 'trustworthy in every way'; and, 'he *was* a pro-German'. He was—as he was in favour of so many unpopular minority causes; socialism, pacificism, vegetarianism, women's suffrage. 'There are multitudes of men in Dublin,' James Stephens observed, 'who can boast that they kicked Sheehy Skeffington, or that they struck him on the head with walking sticks and umbrellas, or that they smashed their fists into his face, and jumped on him when he fell.' But whatever they may have thought of him, Dubliners *knew* him, in a way they knew none of the leaders of the rising. They knew that (again, in Stephen's words) 'his tongue, his pen, his body, all that he had and hoped for were at the immediate service of whoever was bewildered and oppressed'. He had, in fact, been shot on the orders of a British officer who was later found to have been insane; but this was not known at the time. And so Skeffington, who had been concerned only to help those who had been wounded or rendered homeless, had become the first martyr of 1916—the first of the blood sacrifices which Casement, and Pearse, had believed would be necessary to rouse the Irish people.

The authorities, however, took no heed of the public reaction to Skeffington's death. General Maxwell, who had spent much of his life keeping order in the colonies with what he regarded as a firm but fair hand, insisted that the forms must be observed. The rebel leaders, when they surrendered, were not immediately shot; they were tried individually, and condemned to death by a court martial. But not merely did this mean that Pearse and Connolly met the fate they had expected, and were prepared to suffer, for the cause; it also meant that the executions were carried out in batches, spaced out over several days; and—as the trials were held in secret, the only announcements being of the executions—nobody knew how many more of the prisoners would have to die. Even loyalists who had agreed with the Protestant Archbishop of Dublin when he advocated 'punish-

ment, swift and stern', found it not swift enough. In a phrase
which stuck in the mind of the Countess of Fingall, it was like
watching 'a stream of blood coming from beneath a closed door'.
'You took care that no pleas for mercy should interpose', the
Catholic Bishop of Limerick wrote, rebuking the authorities;
'I regard your action with horror, and I believe that it has outraged the conscience of the country.'

When Casement left the Tower, he found another of his hopes
was being fulfilled. The rising was identified with *Sinn Fein*—the
cause closest to his heart. This had not been Pearse's design,
and certainly not Connolly's; but to the public it was the *Sinn
Fein* rebellion—as it was even to more knowledgeable ob-
servers: 'the heroic, tragic lunacy of *Sinn Fein*', Yeats described
it to Lady Gregory. And the different factions of the independence movement were being drawn together under the *Sinn Fein*
banner, united by their horror over the excutions. 'I am not hot-
blooded or emotional,' Arthur Griffith (who had good cause to
be resentful at the way the junta had deceived him) wrote, 'but
something of the primeval man woke in me, I clenched my fists
and ground my teeth and longed for vengeance on the murderers.'

Casement's only cause for regret, then, was that he had been
unable to join the rebels, and die with them—as he would have
done. A year before, he had told Joseph Plunkett—one of the
executed leaders—that he could not approve of the idea of a
rising which did not have enough German support to have a
chance of success; but:

If you do it, if you are bent upon this act of idiocy, I will come
and join you (if the Germans will send me over) and stand or
fall beside you. Only I deprecate it wholly, and regard it as the
wildest form of boyish folly. I am not responsible for it, and
while I strongly disapprove of it, if these boys break out I
could not, in honour, refuse to stand beside them, since however vain and futile their fight may be, it would be a fight—
an act, a deed—and not talk, talk, talk. I, who have always
stood for action (but not this action and not in these circumstances) could not stay in safety in this land while those
living in Ireland who have cherished a manly soul were laying
down their lives for an ideal.

To Nevinson, who came to visit him in Brixton, Casement explained that although he would have supported MacNeill's attempt to stop the rising, he would have joined in as soon as it started. 'Since those there were bent on it,' he was to claim, 'I too, like O'Rahilly, would have gone with it.' O'Rahilly had been deceived by the junta, but—as Yeats quoted him—

> Because I helped to wind the clock
> I come to hear it strike

And Casement would have died as O'Rahilly did, in action—or as MacBride did, before the firing squad; not on the scaffold.

Bow Street   *May 1916*

The fact that he had not been killed in action, or executed after a court martial, at least gave Casement an opportunity denied to the leaders of the rising. He would be able to use his trial to justify their actions, as well as his. But first, a barrister had to be briefed to conduct his defence, and Gavan Duffy was finding it difficult to obtain one. John Hartman Morgan, who had helped Casement over the Putumayo, offered his services; but he was a professor of law, who did not ordinarily appear in the defence role. And none of the senior Counsel Gavan Duffy approached, including Sir John Simon and Tim Healy, would touch the case for fear that they might become identified in the public mind with the traitor.

For the preliminary police court hearing at Bow Street, however, a junior would suffice. The one Gavan Duffy found had already qualified for a niche in legal history—as a plaintiff. A few years before, the Paris correspondent of an English Sunday newspaper had been asked by his editor to look at high life in what were then fashionable resorts, for the English, in northern France; and he had vividly described the double lives of some of the respectable citizens he had observed there. 'Up on the terrace marches the world'—he wrote about Dieppe. 'Why, there is Artemus Jones with a woman who is not his wife; who must be ... you know ... the other thing. Who would suppose by his goings-on that he was a churchwarden at Peckham?' There was, it transpired, a barrister—Thomas Artemus Jones; and he decided to sue the newspaper. It was pointed out by the defence that he did not live in Peckham, and was not a church-warden; but although it was not disputed that the writer of the article had deliberately chosen the name of Artemus for its improbability, Jones was awarded the sum of £1,750 damages, which was upheld on appeal (one of the judges unkindly remarking that if the writer of the article had only stuck to Tom Jones, he would have been safe). The brief for Casement presented him with his first real opportunity.

In Bow Street police court, on May 15th, Jones found himself up against F. E. Smith—by this time, Sir Frederick Smith, Attorney-General; Archibald Bodkin, an experienced senior Counsel, later to be Director of Public Prosecutions; and Travers Humphreys, who, though he had chosen to remain a junior, had already a formidable reputation. The hearing itself was concerned mainly with satisfying the court that Casement really had been in Germany—former prisoners of war from Limburg who had been repatriated were called upon to identify him—and that he really had been landed in Ireland; witnesses were brought over from the Banna Strand district to testify, their Irish brogues entertaining the court.

The hearing lasted three days, with Casement—*The Times* reported—restless and ill-at-ease, continually passing notes to Gavan Duffy. The notes, which were preserved, show that he was absorbed in the trivia of the trial. Why, he wanted to know, had the police sergeant from Tralee not been asked to give evidence? And when one of the Limburg witnesses said he had seen Casement at the camp about the end of December, Casement noted 'coudn't have—at camp 6 January'—which was hardly going to help his case. But the Prosecution did give some clues about the line they were going to take in the Old Bailey. Clearly, Casement's connection with the Irish Brigade was going to be the chief count against him.

Artemus Jones had one further task. On May 20th, the *Daily Graphic* carried a feature 'The Traitor in the Dock', which enabled him to begin proceedings against the proprietors and editors responsible for contempt of court. But it was unthinkable that he, a junior, should represent Casement at the Old Bailey. If a big enough fee were offered, Gavan Duffy knew, some briefless King's Counsel could doubtless be found to risk the obloquy of defending a traitor. But where was the money to come from? They must try to find some rich backer; and one

possibility was Bernard Shaw, whose wife Charlotte was re-
putedly a millionaire.

Charlotte described the approach in a letter to T. E. Lawrence
in 1927.

When Casement was arrested and brought to England, we
were, of course, much moved, but really did not pay exceptional attention to the matter, as we only knew him in a
general way, our paths never having run together. But very
shortly there appeared at Adelphi Terrace a Miss Gertrude
Bannister, who asked for an interview. She was an Irish-
woman of a fine type: sensible, shrewd, capable, responsible;
at that moment teacher in a girl's school near London. ...
She came to us in the first place for some money help, and in
the second, to ask if we would work with her to get together
a little group of people to attempt to work up some real defence for him.

Shaw had been the first to warn the British public, in a letter
to the *Daily News*, that the inevitable consequence of the executions would be to hand Ireland over to *Sinn Fein*. He himself,
he explained, had been a consistent critic of *Sinn Fein*—one of
his attacks on the movement had appeared in the *Irish Times*
only two days before the rising. And he had disagreed even more
strongly with those nationalists who looked to Germany as a
liberator. But the news of the executions appalled him. They
had done what the rising itself had failed to do:

it is absolutely impossible to slaughter a man in this position
without making him a martyr and a hero, even though the day
before the rising he may have been only a minor poet. The
shot Irishmen will now take their places beside Emmet and
the Manchester Martyrs in Ireland, and beside the heroes of
Poland and Serbia and Belgium in Europe; and nothing in
heaven or earth can prevent it.

And although to name Casement might have landed him in
trouble for contempt of court, he made an oblique reference to
the case: 'I remain an Irishman; and I am bound to contradict
any implication that I can regard as a traitor any Irishman

taken in a fight for Irish independence against the British Government.'

At the same time, Alice Green had approached Beatrice Webb who, with the same idea in mind, brought her together with the Shaws for lunch. Charlotte, Beatrice observed, was sympathetic. When Casement's treason was mentioned 'her eyes had flashed defiance'. But Shaw would not allow her to contribute to the defence fund. According to Beatrice Webb:

> He as usual had his own plan. Casement was to defend his own case; he was to make a great oration of defiance which would 'bring down the house'. To this Mrs. Green retorted tearfully that the man was desperately ill; that he was quite incapable of handling a court full of lawyers; the most he could do was the final speech after the verdict. 'Then we had better get out our suit of mourning,' Shaw remarked with an almost gay laugh. 'I will write him a speech which will thunder down the ages.'

And off he went, to write it. It was to be published, after the war; and in a prefatory note, he explained its aim. The essential need, as he had seen it, was to explain why Casement, having worked for so long in the Consular Services, and having accepted a knighthood, should have gone to seek German assistance for Ireland against England when war broke out. What he must show, therefore, was what he had long believed in the need for an independent Ireland (as had a great many loyal Irishmen — and some Englishmen); but he had been driven to the conclusion that the only way to achieve it was through a guarantee by the great powers of her independence, and her neutrality — a theory he had propounded in articles of the kind that might have been expected 'from an educated professional diplomatist'. And because, when war broke out, he had believed Germany was going to win he had naturally concentrated on obtaining German support for his scheme — 'any trained diplomatist would have speculated in this way. Indeed, he could not have speculated in any other way, because there was no other possible move on the diplomatic board.' And although Shaw happened to disagree — because he believed that Prussian junkerism was more sinister than English imperialism, and because he did not believe Germany was going to win the war — this, for an Irishman, was simply a difference of opinion. Casement's view was no more treasonable than his own.

But as Casement was not going to be tried before a jury of his countrymen, Shaw continued, he must adopt a slightly different stance. He should admit the facts which the Prosecution would bring up against him; it would be futile to try to deny them. His plea of Not Guilty, he should explain to the Court, was based on a denial that guilt should necessarily attach to the facts. He should tell the jury of his hope

> that in a very humble way he might do for his country what Garibaldi had been honoured in England for doing for his country. The court might smile at his vanity now that he had failed, but the Court knew that nations were not freed by personal modesty any more than by personal vanity, and a nation which could not produce a Garibaldi had to be content with Casements, and the Casements must do their best. ... He therefore very naturally and properly sought to obtain, and to a certain extent did obtain the assistance of the German Empire in his enterprise. He had no apology whatever to make for that; it was his plain duty to his country.

But Casement, Shaw went on, should make it clear that he no more wanted a German occupation of Ireland than the jury wanted a Russian occupation of England—however friendly an ally Russia might be. He had not asked for German soldiers—only for German arms and Irish soldiers. And to the accusation that he had taken England's pay while holding such views, he should reply that this did not commit him to continue to serve her, any more than the acceptance of briefs by the Attorney-General committed him to continue to serve men he had defended. In the long run, his loyalty could only be to his own country, Ireland.

By this time, Shaw had so thoroughly involved himself with Casement's defence that, writing it, he began to visualise himself in the dock, haranguing the court; and he slipped into the first person:

> I am neither an Englishman nor a traitor; I am an Irishman, captured in a fair attempt to achieve the independence of my country; and you can no more deprive me of the honours of that position, or destroy the effects of my effort, than the

abominable cruelties afflicted six hundred years ago on William Wallace, in this city, when he met a precisely similar
indictment with a precisely similar reply, have prevented
that brave and honourable Scot from becoming the national
hero of his country.

He should then, Shaw concluded, warn the jury that the Lord
Chief Justice would certainly tell them that they were to find a
verdict on the facts of the case—that they need not concern
themselves with the issue whether what had been done was
treasonable in law, which was for the Bench to decide. The jury
must not listen to this advice. They must ask themselves the
real question; was Casement, in the wider sense, a traitor to
his country? And if there was one member of the jury who
would answer, no, this would preclude the unanimity needed for
a verdict of Guilty.

In the meantime, Casement had been working out his own
defence. He, too, planned to make the most of the analogy with
other 'traitors' like Garibaldi, who had been helped—and indeed
revered—by the English in the past. He wanted, though, to
bring it up to date, by citing contemporary examples. He asked
Gavan Duffy to get either Alice Green or Robert Lynd—an
Irish friend, working as a journalist in London—to seek the
evidence he needed; 'try to find me in the English press any
references to the "Polish Legion", the "Czech Legion", the
"Alsatian Corps" or any other of the numerous bodies of
"traitors" and "renegades" being "seduced from their allegiance" on behalf of the immortal allies to fight against their
own sovereigns'. The case of the Czechs seemed to him particularly relevant; and it was actually even closer than he could
have known. They had achieved Home Rule before the war;
their leader in exile, Thomas Masaryk, had been a member of
the Czech legislature, and had pledged allegiance to the Emperor Franz Joseph. It had been the personal intervention of the
Emperor, too, which had secured him his university professor-
ship—because he had been regarded as a moderate. Yet when
war broke out, he had chosen to become a traitor to his country;
and in December 1915 he had obtained from Asquith a declaration similar in character to the one which Casement had obtained from the German Government, accepting Czechoslovak
aspirations. Masaryk, too, had refused allied money, but

accepted it from his compatriots in the United States. 'There are said to be twelve regiments in the Russian service now fighting "to free Bohemia" ' — Casement observed; 'and yet Bohemia *has* her parliament, and the Czech language is spoken in it. And Ireland? Ireland has got Mr. Redmond, and Sir E. Carson, and Galloper Smith prosecuting *me*, and Home Rule on the Statute Book, be Jabers.' It would be useful for his defence, he felt, to have a collection of English expressions of approbation of what the Czechs were doing, to set off against their disapprobation of an Irishman who had tried to do the same thing.

In an outline of his proposed defence, which he set out in a letter to Gavan Duffy, Casement said he had decided to admit full responsibility and accept all the consequences of what he had done in Germany, but—

> to show that the idea, the aim, the responsibility for the re-
> bellion arose with Irishmen, in Ireland, and was carried to an
> issue by 'themselves alone', that in very truth it was a *Sinn
> Fein* rebellion. My going to Germany was only to get guns and
> such help as was possible to allow of Irishmen at home fight-
> ing, instead of talking. We have to show that it was no
> 'German plot', that there was no 'German gold' in it, and
> that it sprang from the fixed resolution of the Irishmen them-
> selves. This I can do. For it *is* the truth, and in accepting, to
> the full, responsibility for my share in inspiring that action, I
> am only shouldering the burden that is mine.

When Shaw's proposed defence line was handed to him, a day or two later, Casement was naturally delighted to find how closely it accorded with his own. 'I shall be so grateful if you will convey to Bernard Shaw my warmest thanks,' he told Gavan Duffy; 'his view is mine, with this exception—that I should never suggest to an English court of jury that they should let me off as a prisoner of war, but tell them "You may hang me, and be damned to you".' He was certainly going to dispute their right to try an Irish rebel in an English court; but 'as they have my body, they may do with it what they please, while the rest of me will remain unconvicted still'.

Nevertheless Shaw's defence was not the kind of help Alice Green and Gertrude Bannister had been looking for. What he wanted to do, Beatrice Webb noted with some asperity, was 'produce' the defence, 'as a national dramatic event'. When

Alice Green and Gertrude Bannister told him that Casement's health was too precarious to stand the strain of defending himself, and that he would need to have Counsel, Shaw lost interest. It would be difficult, he said, to find any one who would agree to take the defence line which he had composed for Casement, and even if he did, he would be unlikely to undertake it 'with the necessary wholeheartedness'. In the circumstances, he declined to waste his or his wife's money by contributing to the defence costs.

Serjeant Sullivan

Shaw's instinct, as things turned out, was sound. The barrister whom Gavan Duffy had to fall back on would have nothing to do with the proposed line of defence.

Alexander Martin Sullivan was in his early forties, a 'Serjeant' (one of the species familiar in Dickens' day) at the Irish Bar. Although the son of an Irish Nationalist M.P. — the A. M. Sullivan whose account of the Manchester Martyrs had so moved Casement — he was on the council which had been set up in Ireland to encourage recruiting for the British forces, and he was a law officer of the Crown. This made him an unlikely choice to defend Casement. But he happened to be Gavan Duffy's brother-in-law; and little sympathy though the two men can have had for each other politically, Duffy happened to know that as a young man, he had been called to the English Bar. Although he had never practised there he was technically qualified to plead; and this gave him what Gavan Duffy felt would be a 'magnificent opportunity' to make his name.

Sullivan was doubtful. As a Crown law officer, he was not permitted to accept briefs against the State in Ireland, and he feared the ban might apply in England too. He was also worried about his standing in an English court, where he would be a junior counsel (his Irish seniority did not count). 'I would reluctantly go into the business,' he replied, 'provided I was handsomely paid.' Offered five hundred guineas — handsome indeed, by his standards — and reassured that his position in Ireland need not affect his appearing against the Crown in England, he decided to accept.

But when he came to Brixton gaol on June 22nd, Sullivan made it clear that Casement must adhere to a line of defence which he had decided on. His plea was to be that no treason had been committed within the meaning of the statute under which he was being prosecuted. This dated from the reign of Edward III who, in need of funds, had hit upon a simple way to obtain them; it was to be treason 'if a man be adherent to the King's enemies in his realm', and all the worldly goods of that man would be forfeit to the Crown. But Casement had not been adherent to the King's enemies *in his realm*.

The legal argument was in fact more insidiously complex; but the essential point, so far as Casement was concerned, was that Sullivan would not be arguing on the issue whether or not he had committed treason; only on whether or not he had committed treason within the meaning of the Act. The weakness of Sullivan's line was that the Courts ordinarily followed precedent; and the precedents were uniformly discouraging. In the most recent case one of the leaders of the Irish Brigade formed by the Boers, Colonel Arthur Lynch, had been found guilty and sentenced to death, though his misdeeds had been committed even further from the realm. There could be no doubt, then, that the defence would fail; certainly Sullivan was under no illusions that it had any prospects of success. But at the end of it all, Casement might hope to be reprieved—as Lynch had been.

Casement was unhappy with Sullivan's line. 'At the end of a defence of his making,' he complained to Gavan Duffy,

> I should find myself without a case, and debarred from the only defence possible, viz., my own plan and that of G.B.S. I owe it to Ireland, to the Irish in the U.S.A. who so loyally helped, and to Germany, and even to my own wretched self to adopt the only course and conduct the case myself. I should be in a far less false position, and could at least make my position clear, leave it on record, justify the cause of Ireland before the world and leave the British Government to do what it pleased.
>
> In any case, as G.B.S. says, I have nothing to lose—I've lost it already—and the only thing to fight for now is the cause of others, not my life, or fate at this trial. . . .

He had passed a wretched day and night, he went on, since Sullivan left; but he had come to the conclusion that 'today I see no right course but the one—to go my road alone.'

Alice Green and Gertrude Bannister united with Gavan Duffy to dissuade him. They were convinced he would be unable to stand up to the gruelling cross-examination which he would be given by Smith and the rest of the prosecuting team. If he followed the course Sullivan suggested, it was pointed out to him, he would not be cross-examined, because the argument would be on legal technicalities. Should Sullivan's defence succeed, he would then be free. If it failed—well, as he knew, there was always the condemned prisoner's speech from the dock, to justify the cause. He gave in, and agreed to let Sullivan prepare the defence his way.

There was, in fact, another reason for persuading him to accept a defence which would not require him to undergo cross-examination. He had left some of his possessions in his old Ebury Street lodgings; and among them were the diaries for 1903, 1910, and 1911, and the account book for 1911—which Basil Thomson described, after they had been brought to him at Scotland Yard, as containing material which could not be printed 'in any age, in any language'—though this had not prevented Hall from showing copies of parts of the diaries to English and American journalists.

When the decision was made to try Casement for treason, they had been handed over to the Prosecution; and Smith had decided to pass them to Artemus Jones, suggesting that the defence, to save Casement's life, might like to put in a plea of 'guilty but insane' by using passages pointing to mental instability. He was later to receive some credit for this gesture; but not, significantly, from those who admired his legal acumen. Whatever else the diaries might have done, they certainly would not have helped to secure a verdict of guilty but insane. Under the legal code prevailing at the time, insanity was defined in ways which, as Smith well knew, could not have applied to Casement.

Serjeant Sullivan, therefore, had good reason to reject Smith's offer. But he did not merely reject it; he refused even to look at the diaries. He was later to give varying explanations, but there is no reason to doubt the truth of the one he gave at the time. He already knew 'of their nature and contents, from many people who were strangers to the case'; and, as he had made up his mind on a different line of defence, there was no point in his looking at them.

It was a plausible enough excuse; but not wholly convincing. To defend Casement successfully, Sullivan ought to have known all the weapons the Prosecution possessed; and the very fact that the contents of the diaries were already known, even to people who were strangers to the case, should have prompted him to read them. Why did he not care to do so?

The most likely explanation is the one Gertrude Bannister put forward for the general course Sullivan took: that he was determined to do nothing which would spoil his main chance — entry into the English Bar. He was shrewd enough to see that his prospects in Ireland were uncertain. There would be little enthusiasm there for Crown lawyers. And although he disliked the English legal system, contrasted with the Irish, he loved the English Bar as an institution, with its traditions, its camaraderie, its port and its jests. Here was this opportunity to secure his ticket of entry, by making a good impression on the Court, and on the Bar. But he could not hope to do this on a plea of guilty but insane; because it would give him no chance to display his legal knowledge. He must plead, with all the skill at his command, the kind of case which would give the judges plenty to think about but nothing to fear.

Forty years later, Sullivan was to claim that Casement had admitted his homosexuality, and had wanted him to make a 'rhapsodical justification' of his homosexual practices, as 'inseparable from the true genius'. But this would have been wholly out of character. When Dick Morten visited him in Brixton, and asked 'what about the other thing, Roddie?' Professor Morgan, who was present, noticed that Casement was grieved that his oldest friend should have heard the rumours — 'Dick; you've upset me!' As none of his friends had suspected that he was a homosexual, he must have realised what a blow the revelation would be to them. Even more important to him, though, at that period of his life, was that he should get the chance to explain and justify the Irish cause. If the Prosecution could make use of the diaries, he would be discredited, and of what value to the Irish cause would his speech from the dock be then? But if he adopted the strategy which Sullivan proposed, the diaries could not be used by the Prosecution, because they could be challenged as irrelevant to the legal issue on which Sullivan was basing his defence.

This would have seemed all the more important to him because, though he was still certain he must be found guilty, he was coming to the conclusion that he would not be executed. As he wrote to Gavan Duffy on June 14th:

> The English mob and vast majority of the people would like to see me hanged and want it badly. The British Government *dare not* hang me (they don't want to either—as individuals I think). They simply dare not. They would willingly bring back to life poor Sean MacDermott, Connolly, Pearse, Colbert (and the other victims of their military autocrats of Easter Week) and they are assuredly not going to add to the roll of victims, me. They know quite well what the world would say of that, and what America would say of it.

At first, the American newspapers, the majority of which were pro-ally, had tended to regard the Easter Rising as treacherous, and Casement as a traitor. But after the executions, feeling had begun to turn against the British. Even the *New York Times*, which had been solidly on their side, described their attitude as neurasthenic. And it began to be accepted that Casement was not a traitor, but a man—as the *World* put it in an article on May 24th—with 'a screw loose'. Authority was lent to this view by his old friend Poultney Bigelow, in a letter on the same day in the *New York Times*. The correspondence he had had with Casement, Bigelow said, revealed him to be a paranoiac, who ought to be locked up. Enclosing Bigelow's comments in a despatch to Grey, the British Ambassador in Washington, Sir Cecil Spring-Rice, commented that the general impression in America was that Casement's mind had suffered owing to his experiences in the tropics. To execute him, therefore, even if that were justified, would be just what the pro-German agitators in America were hoping for—a view which he reiterated on May 30th, adding that it was shared by the White House. And on June 9th, he set out his views in detail. American opinion, he said, might have condoned the executions in Dublin, but not the way they had been carried out.

As to Casement; the Irish might regard his execution as a small matter in comparison with the others. But the great bulk of American public opinion, while it might excuse executions in hot blood, would very greatly regret an execution some time after the event. This is a view of important friends of ours here who have nothing to do with the Irish movement. It is far better to make Casement ridiculous than a martyr. The universal impression here seems to be that when here, he acted almost like a madman. There is no doubt whatever that Germans here look forward with great interest to his execution, of which they will take full advantage.

Casement could not have known of Spring-Rice's views; but he learned the state of American opinion from an American lawyer, Michael Francis Doyle, who was sent to London by Devoy to do what he could to help in the defence. Doyle sympathised with the Irish cause and admired Casement (by Doyle's account, he flatly denied having written a homosexual diary, and Doyle believed him). Assuming that Doyle's estimate of American opinion was correct, the British Government were unlikely to risk inflaming it, and thereby further jeopardising the prospects of American entry into the war on the side of the allies. The likelihood, then, was that Casement would be found guilty, but reprieved. And if he were reprieved, he could presumably get the diaries back, and if necessary destroy them. As he told Gavan Duffy, 'they had no right to retain any papers or documents of mine—diaries, books, or anything *not* used at the trial against me'; and anything of that kind not so used should legally be recoverable.

CHAPTER TWO

JUDGMENT

Old Bailey   *June 1916*

The fact that Casement was now in the hands of his lawyers at least took some of the pressure off him in the days immediately before the trial was due to open. He was even able to obtain some wry amusement, from a cable which reached him from South America. The news of his capture and impending trial had attracted some attention in the world's press, particularly in Peru, where the papers—Ernest Rennie, who had succeeded des Graz as Ambassador, complained—were full of it. Rennie's instructions had been to continue to press for action to bring the Putumayo criminals to trial, but nothing had been done; and on May 29th, 1915, nine of them awaiting trial had escaped. 'Some of the worst of the lot', Spicer had minuted; 'I suppose we must maintain a show of interest and urge the Peruvian Government to recapture them. They are probably over the border long ago.' They were: and in Lima there was a disposition, Rennie had remarked, 'to hope that in the present crisis of the world's history, the Putumayo affair may be overlooked'. Inevitably, Casement's arrest was seized upon by the Lima newspapers, to show that his Putumayo testimony could now be regarded as worthless; and this was the theme of the cable he received, addressed to him at the Tower of London:

> Am informed you will be tried for High Treason on 26 June—want of time unables me to write you being obliged to wire you asking you to be fully just confessing before the human tribunal your guilt only known by Divine Justice regarding your dealings in the Putumayo business. They were all suggested by *Truth* Anti-Slavery Society Colombian Government Agents ... inventing deeds and influencing Barbadians to confirm unanimously facts never happened invented by Saldana thief Hardenburg etc. etc. I hold some Barbadians declaration denying all you obliged them to declare pressing upon them

as English consul and frightening them in the King's name with prison if refusing to sign. . . .

You tried by all means to appear a humaniser in order to obtain titles, fortune, not caring for the consequences of your calumnies and defamation against Peru and myself doing me enormous damage. I pardon you but it is necessary that you should declare now fully and truly all the true facts that nobody knows better than yourself.

Julio Arana

Basil Thomson, who saw the cable, was impressed. Perhaps, he thought, Casement really had deceived them. The Foreign Office knew Arana too well; the fact that Casement had committed treason, Spicer pointed out, could not exonerate the Putumayo criminals. But he could only agree with Rennie that it would be unwise to continue to press for proceedings against them. Casement was entertained by the cable's sheer effrontery —'think of it!' he wrote to tell Dick Morten; 'from Para, asking me to confess my "crimes" against him!' But he was also saddened by the implication: ' the poor Indians . . .'.

Another ghost from his past attempted, at this time, to return to haunt him; Christensen wrote to the Foreign Office from the United States suggesting they might like to have his testimony against the traitor. According to Devoy, the *Clan* stopped him from leaving; and the Foreign Office were probably relieved that they did.

The trial opened at the Old Bailey on June 26th, before three judges. Sir Rufus Isaacs had managed to survive the Marconi Shares scandal in 1913. Had the case against him been better handled, Winston Churchill—one of his Cabinet colleagues—believed, his political career would have been ended; but a Committee of Inquiry came to the conclusion that though he and Lloyd George had been indiscreet, technically they had committed no offence. A few months later, Asquith had appointed Isaacs Lord Chief Justice—timing which provoked Kipling into one of the most savage of his diatribes:

> Well done, well done, Gehazi!
> Stretch forth thy ready hand
> Thou barely 'scaped from judgment
> Take oath to judge the land . . .

Isaac's smooth diplomacy had been too valuable to the Government, during the war, to be wasted on the Bench. While Casement was trying to collect his Irish Brigade to fight the English, Isaacs had been in the United States as president of an Anglo-French commission sent there to try to raise a war loan for the allies. In this he had succeeded beyond expectations; and for this service, just three weeks before he was due to try Casement, he had been raised to the peerage as Viscount Reading.

Of the other two judges. Mr. Justice Avory was already acquiring a reputation for ruthlessness. Even Patrick Hastings, who admired him, had to admit that he would not have cared to appear before Avory on any charge of which he knew he was guilty—as Casement knew he was. Mr. Justice Horridge had been an obscure Liberal politician who had used his services to his party as the traditional stepping-stone to the Bench; he was to be remembered mainly for his ferocious facial tic.

Appearing for the Crown, with Smith, were the Solicitor-General, Sir George Cave; Bodkin, Humphreys and another junior, G. A. H. Branson. The prisoner was allowed two counsel, both juniors—Sullivan and Artemus Jones; and Professor Morgan was permitted to help the Defence elucidate knotty legal issues; Michael Francis Doyle had no standing. He could assist Gavan Duffy informally, but the line of defence which Sullivan had chosen to take offered him little scope. When he offered to go to Germany to collect evidence for Casement, he was told that if he did, he would not be allowed back into Britain.

Smith's opening speech, on the pattern indicated at Bow Street, was brief. Casement, he claimed, had been a loyal subject of the Crown until 1911, when he had written what Smith described as his 'fulsome' letter of thanks for his knighthood to Grey; and he had also continued to draw his pension until October 1914—in other words, after war had broken out. But then, he had made his way to Germany, to try to seduce British prisoners of war from their allegiance. Those who refused had been punished, by being put on a lower ration scale. Finally, Casement had arrived from Germany off the Irish Coast—how, Smith was not prepared to state, but obviously it was in conjunction with the cargo of arms which was to have been landed from the *Aud*. The *Aud*, however, had been intercepted, and so had Casement. 'Such, gentlemen'—Smith concluded—

in general outline, is the case which the Crown undertakes to prove, and upon which the Crown relies. I have, I hope, outlined these facts without heat and without feeling. Neither, in my position, would be proper, and fortunately neither is required. Rhetoric would be misplaced, for the proved facts are more eloquent than words. The prisoner, blinded by a hatred to this country, as malignant in quality as it was sudden in origin, has played a desperate hazard. He has played it, and he has lost it. Today, the forfeit is claimed.

It was a travesty of Casement's actions and motives, but no worse than he could have expected; and in a memorandum to Robert Lynd and Alice Green, he was chiefly concerned about the unimportant, but to him wounding, accusation that his letter to Grey had been fulsome. On the contrary, he felt, it had been perfunctory. As a result, he failed to rebut the more serious insinuation that he had continued to draw his pension after war broke out. When the Crown began to produce its witnesses, an official in His Majesty's Paymaster's Office produced a receipt, purporting to be signed by Casement, dated October 7th, 1914 —when he was on his way to Norway. He had in fact made the standard application for his next quarter's pension at the beginning of September 1914, not because he had any intention of drawing it, but because his *Clan-na-Gael* friends had advised him to do nothing, at that stage, to excite Foreign Office suspicion. Sullivan noticed that the date on the receipt had been altered, but did not press the point. There might have been an innocent explanation; in an Irish court, though, Sullivan would certainly have pounced on the changed date, in the hope of embarrassing the Prosecution.

The witnesses from Limburg did much less harm to Casement's reputation than could have been expected. With one exception, they agreed that he had told them that they were not going to be asked to fight for Germany—only for Ireland; and the evidence of the exception, who claimed that he told them they might be asked to fight with the Turks against the Russians, was later withdrawn. From one of the Limburg men, too, Sullivan managed to extract the information that he had heard Casement speak at the Volunteer meeting in Cork in 1913, which at least pushed back the date of his change of heart to well before the war had begun.

The Banna Strand witnesses, who followed, were called simply to prove that Casement had landed there. Sullivan could expect to get nothing out of them except a little light relief, which he did, by asking what got them up so early on a Good Friday morning. From one of the members of the local constabulary, he secured further confirmation of Casement's version of what had happened before the war; recollections of the ferment in Ireland over the Home Rule bill, and the Volunteers. But there was little else he could do; and soon, the Prosecution were content to rest their case.

At this point, Sullivan was permitted to air his knowledge of the law of treason, on his motion to quash the indictment. The judges, Professor Morgan, and the Attorney-General discussed the points he brought up; and at the end of it all the Lord Chief Justice announced that 'notwithstanding the learned and able arguments that have been addressed to us,' the motion must be refused—as everybody in the Court must have known he would. His fellow judges concurred. As Sullivan had staked everything on the technicality, he could not now take up a different defence line, and call witnesses, before he delivered his address to the jury.

First, though, Casement was permitted to make a brief statement—unsworn, so that he could not be cross-examined. He wanted to say a few words, he explained, with reference to some of the points made by the prosecution. His pension he had earned by service, and it was assigned by law. His knighthood he had not been in a position to refuse (except by resigning from the Service, which, at that stage of the Putumayo inquiry, he had not wished to do). He had not asked Irishmen to fight for any country except their own; and 'the horrible insinuation that I got my own people's rations reduced to starvation point because they did not join the Irish Brigade was an abominable falsehood'—it was the allied blockade of Germany which had compelled a general reduction in rations for all prisoners of war. As for the imputation that he had taken German gold, 'those who know me, know the incredibility of this malicious suggestion'. The Easter Rising had been made in Ireland; not one penny of German gold went to finance it. 'I have touched on these personal matters alone,' he concluded, 'because intended as they were to reflect on my honour, they were calculated to tarnish the cause I hold dear. That is all, my Lords.'

Sullivan then made his address to the jury; and he began, quite skilfully, to shift his own defence towards the one which Casement and Shaw had suggested. The jury must apply themselves to the issue whether Casement had 'adhered to the King's enemies' in Germany. On the evidence of the Prosecution's witnesses, he suggested, he had not adhered to the King's enemies there; on the contrary, he had gone to great pains to insist that the Irish Brigade were to adhere only to Ireland, and not to the Germans. But why—he still had to explain—had Casement gone to Germany? He now revealed what had been in his mind during his cross-examination of the Irish witnesses, harking back to the state of Ireland before the war. 'What are you to do,' he asked the jury,

> when after years of labour, your representatives may have won something that you yearn for, for many a long day; won it under the Constitution, had it guaranteed by the King and the Commons, and you are informed that you should not possess it because those who disliked it were arming to resist the King and Commons, and to blow the Statute off the Book with powder? The civil police could not protect you, and the military force would perhaps prove inadequate for your support. You may lie down under it, but, if you are men, to arms! When all else fails, defend yourself.

On this point, Sullivan could feel more conviction than he had previously shown, because, as a constitutionalist, he regarded what had happened in Ulster with even greater distaste than Casement had. Carried away, he warmed to his theme:

> There were found men who, distrusting the truce proclaimed in Ireland, seeing that one man would observe his neighbour had not given up his rifle, another that another had got a new gun, he would arm himself; and one by one, in small quantities, you have the danger of the arms still coming in, and people fearing that the truce was not real, and that any moment there might break out. . . .

Here, Sullivan was interrupted by the Chief Justice, who asked him for his evidence. The Attorney-General remarked that he had been loath to intervene, but he had heard a great many uncorroborated statements. 'I think you are stating matter,' Reading told Sullivan, 'which is not in evidence.' Suddenly, Sullivan saw the chasm which had opened up in front of him. He could go on to argue that what had happened in Ulster was very relevant to the defence. The Ulster Protestant leaders had not merely admitted that what they were doing was treason; they had boasted about it—Carson, Smith. ... But here, in court, was Sir Frederick Smith, Attorney-General, a member of the Government. He would not be at all pleased to be reminded of what he had said, before the war. Nor would Lord Reading. He had been a supporter of Home Rule under the Liberal Government; but now, he was concerned with the war effort, and he would not welcome the dredging up of the embarrassing past. Up to this point, Sullivan had clearly relished pitting his forensic skill against the great ones of the English Bar. But he had let himself be carried away. He must apologise. And he did: abjectly. 'I am exceedingly sorry your Lordship did not intervene sooner. ... I am exceedingly sorry I have gone outside what I ought'; and again a little later, 'I am sorry if I transgressed, and regret that the rein was not applied.' The Chief Justice, mollified, intimated he would say no more. But Sullivan, unable to pursue the line he had taken, found that when he tried to cary on his address to the jury, he was lost. He groped around for a while, searching for a way out; came to a stop; and then said, 'I regret, my lord, to say that I have completely broken down.'

The Court adjourned; and the next day, Artemus Jones reported that on medical advice, Sullivan had decided he would not be able to continue. He had to try to carry on from where the Defence had broken off. He had been impressed by Casement; the qualities which most struck him, he was to recall, were his sincerity and his intellectual integrity. It was in Jones's own interest, too, to make an impression. But he had no sympathy with Irish nationalism; and in any case, the judges' intervention to check Sullivan had left him little room for manoeuvre. He mentioned a passage which had been quoted in the evidence from the *Irish Times* of July 14th, 1913: 'if the resolution of Ulster were put to the test, they would find those in England who had felt it their duty to encourage the men of Ulster in their attitude, and who would be prepared to prove by their deeds that when they said that Ulster was right they meant that Ulster was right, and who would be prepared to share the risk'; but he did not follow it up with examples of what the *Irish Times* was referring to—extracts, say, from the speeches of the Unionist leaders, in which they boasted they were committing treason. He was content to leave it to the imagination of the jury, who were not likely to remember just how far the men of Ulster, and their Unionist supporters, had gone, three years before.

Jones made no attempt to draw the parallel with the Czech brigades; and when he tried to return to a consideration of what the term 'aid and comfort' implied, he was interrupted by the Chief Justice, who claimed—as Shaw had warned he would do—that the words of the statute were to be interpreted according to law, 'and therefore they are not for the jury, but for us'. Although he did his best for Casement by reiterating the point that it was Ireland, not Germany, that he was serving, his peroration virtually handed the victory to the Prosecution: 'the history of Ireland contained many melancholy and sad chapters, and not the least sad is the chapter which tells and speaks of so many mistaken sons of that unfortunate country who have gone to the scaffold, as they think, for the sake of their native land'.

Smith had insisted on his right to address the jury after the Defence, as in a trial for treason he was entitled to do. But he hardly needed that advantage. 'I respectfully accept'—he unctuously explained—'as I should be bound to accept, the indication which my Lord, the Lord Chief Justice, gave to my learned friend as to the direction which he proposed to give you on the question of law, which is for my Lord.' But having said that, he went on subtly to paraphrase the Lord Chief Justice's direction in a way which made it sound as if, in law, Casement was unquestionably guilty:

My Lord said this, that he should direct you that anything was an aiding and comforting of the King's enemies which strengthened the enemy for the purpose of his struggle with this country, or which weakened this country for the purpose of its struggle with the enemy. ... Apply that test. Supposing that Germany did win a naval success, giving her temporary control of the seas, giving it her for long enough to land Irish and German soldiers in Ireland; supposing that had taken place, would that or would it not have strengthened the enemy Germany in her struggles with this country; I ask you, would it or would it not?

On the same test, a newspaper article criticising British strategy could equally have been regarded as treasonable.

In his summing-up, the Chief Justice was concerned only to make sure that no member of the jury might have missed the point. He repeated his direction, with more emphasis: 'it does not need a very vivid imagination to see that if Germany could introduce arms and ammunition into Ireland for the purpose of helping to create a rebellion there, or strife of a serious character, so as to occupy the attention of the British Executive, and also to necessitate the maintaining of a considerable number of His Majesty's soldiers in Ireland, that that would be assisting Germany'. And when the jury retired, it took them less than an hour to reach their verdict: Guilty.

In such trials, the convicted prisoner was entitled to his speech from the dock, to give his reasons why the Court should not pass sentence and judgment upon him according to law. Casement's was designed simply as an explanation of the reasons why he, and the executed leaders of the Dublin rising, had taken the course they did. He read it; nervously at first, *The Times* reporter observed, with trembling hands, but growing more confident as he proceeded.

There was nothing to be gained, Casement knew, from trying to impress his hearers: his argument was addressed 'not to this Court, but to my own countrymen'. He owed no loyalty to England: loyalty, he claimed, 'is a sentiment, not a law. It rests on love, not restraint.' As the Government of Ireland by England rested on restraint, and not on love, it could evoke no loyalty. In any case, the ancient statute under which he had been tried was an absurd anachronism. He therefore did not feel called upon to reply to the Lord Chief Justice's question, why sentence should not be passed upon him.

I hope I shall be acquitted of presumption if I say that the Court I see before me now is not this High Court of Justice of England, but a far greater, a far higher, a far older assemblage of justices — that of the people of Ireland. Since in the acts which have led to this trial it was the people of Ireland I sought to serve, and them alone, I leave my judgment and my sentence in their hands.

He went on to describe and justify his aims, and his actions, from the time of the founding of the Volunteers. It was not the Volunteers who had broken the law, he recalled; it was a British political party, the party 'of law and order'—denounced by the then Lord Chancellor as grossly illegal. But 'since lawlessness sat in high places in England, and laughed at the law as at the custodians of the law, what wonder was it that Irishmen refused to accept the verbal protestations of an English Lord Chancellor as a sufficient safeguard for their lives and their liberties?' For himself, Casement had decided to go to America, to seek help there. 'If, as the Right Honourable Gentleman, the present Attorney-General asserted in a speech at Manchester, nationalists would neither fight for Home Rule nor pay for it, it was our duty to show him we knew how to do both.' Then, the war had intervened. After what had happened in the Curragh, where the English army of occupation had refused to obey their orders, he could not see why Irishmen should listen to the plea that it should be their first duty to enter that army, 'in return for a promissory note, payable after death'—a scrap of paper that might or might not be redeemed. The Unionists had already proclaimed their doctrine of loyalty: 'Mausers and Kaisers and any king you like'. Why should he not follow their example?

The difference between us was that the Unionist champions chose a path they felt would lead to the Woolsack; while I went a road which I knew must lead to the dock. And the event proves we were both right. The difference between us proves that my 'treason' was based on a ruthless sincerity that forced me to attempt in time and season to carry out in action what I said in word—whereas their treason lay in verbal incitements that they knew need never be made good in their bodies. And so I am prouder to stand here today in the traitor's dock to answer this impeachment than to fill the place of my right honourable accusers.

The Irish had been held out the hope that after the war they would be given self-government. But self-government was theirs by right, 'a thing no more to be doled out to us or withheld from us by another people than the right to life itself'. If it were treason to fight for it, Casement claimed, he was proud to be a rebel; 'it is a braver, a saner and a truer thing, to be a rebel in such circumstances as these than tamely to accept it as the natural lot of men'. And with that, he concluded—though he went on briefly to beg the jury not to take what he had said about preferring to be tried by his own people as any reflection on their integrity; how would they feel, if they heard an Englishman had been carried off to Ireland, there to be tried by a jury 'in a land inflamed against him, and believing him to be a criminal, when his only crime was that he had cared for England more than Ireland?'

The flavour of the speech does not come out in any summary —or, indeed, even when it is read in full;* it is best listened to, read or spoken. Naturally the opinion of those who heard it delivered in the Old Bailey tended to be coloured by their preconceptions; 'very silly and fatuous' was one reporter's comment. To Gertrude Bannister, it was 'beautifully worded and perfectly delivered; his voice was calm, and his manner, simple and direct'; and Artemus Jones was to recall that in spite of the fact that the Old Bailey was stifling, on that hot June day, it held the attention of the entire court from first to last; 'the great speech of Sir Roger Casement before sentence', he thought, would 'be read by his fellow-Irishmen generations after his judges, his prosecutors, his lawyers and his calumniators have been forgotten'. Reading it, Wilfred Blunt—a connoisseur in such matters—thought it 'the finest document in patriotic history, finer than anything in Plutarch or elsewhere in Pagan literature'; and it moved him to 'anger and delight that anything so perfect should have come from the mouth of a man of our time condemned to death'. Years later, Pandit Nehru was to describe the profound impression the 'extraordinarily moving and eloquent' statement had made on him: 'it seemed to point out exactly how a subject nation should feel'.

Court officials had been waiting behind the judges while Casement spoke, holding the black caps which, tradition demanded, should be worn when sentence of death was being pronounced. They were tired; and the caps were set askew on the heads of the judges, whose appearance was made even more macabre by

* See Appendix I.

Horridge's facial tic; it made him look as if he were reacting to the ancient and repulsive formula—'that you be taken hence to a lawful prison, and thence to a place of execution, and that you be there hanged by the neck until you are dead'—with a fit of uncontrollable satanic laughter. And with Mr. Justice Avory's 'Amen!' the case concluded.

The appeal   July 1916

The 'lawful prison' to which Casement was consigned was to be Pentonville. As he had been convicted, he now had to wear convict's dress—which mortified his cousin, when she came to see him, but only reminded Casement that 'a felon's cap's the brightest crown an Irish head can wear'. Nor was he likely to be disturbed by the news, published the day after his trial ended, that he had been formally degraded from knighthood—the first case of its kind for nearly three centuries.

His trial, though, was not yet over: an appeal had been lodged by the Defence. He had no illusions about its prospect of success but, as he told Alice Green, 'I am advised I *should* go', and it would mean 'I shall see you and the others, I hope, again —and I shall be a spectator this time—sitting in a reserved box and looking on at the actors with a quite detached and even cynical smile—especially the wigs'.

The advice to appeal came from Serjeant Sullivan, who had made a rapid recovery, and was anxious to take the opportunity to remove any unfortunate impressions that might have been left by his lapse into temerity during his speech in Casement's defence. On July 17th, before the Appeal Court, he went over the same legal points he had made in his motion to quash the indictment, though in greater detail, and quoting some fresh authorities. The judges rejected his plea without even bothering to call on the Attorney-General to reply.

It only remained for Sullivan to appeal to the House of Lords, on the ground that the legal issue was of exceptional public importance. But to do this it was necessary to obtain leave from, of all people, the Attorney-General; and Smith refused it. Smith's explanation was that though it would have been easy to give his consent, he felt that as Sullivan's case had been rejected by two sets of judges, it would have been a negation of his duty to inflict it on a third set—a view with which his juniors, whom he consulted, agreed. And unquestionably, it would have been effort wasted, so far as the Defence were concerned. But the fact that Smith had been one of the leaders of the treasonable campaign in Ulster was, as H. G. Wells described it in his *Outline of History*, 'a shocking conjunction'; for justice to be seen to be done, he ought to have let the appeal go forward, especially as Professor Morgan had indeed raised points of law which deserved further consideration. Gavan Duffy took up the charge in a letter to *The Times*:

If the determination of what is high treason is not of 'exceptional public importance', the statute being worded as it is, what can be? And is it not in the public interest of this country that the point should be dealt with and settled by the Highest Court in the land, and that no man, and particularly at this period of Irish history, no Irishman, should have the power to say that the determination of such a matter —one on which the life of an Irishman depends—was withheld? Yet Sir F. E. Smith (from whom there is no appeal), whose antecedents in Ulster are well remembered, has refused the certificate.

Casement was not worried; he felt sure an appeal would have been a futile exercise—as conducted by Sullivan. If it could have been taken to the Lords by Morgan and Jones, that would have been different; 'I wish I had stuck to my two Welshmen', he wrote in his farewell letter to Dick Morten, 'and not brought the other in at all.' He now realised that 'the other' had deceived him. He had begged Sullivan not to concentrate exclusively, in the appeal, on the issue of the legal interpretation of the statute; but to bring up the wider issues. Sullivan had promised he would, but in the event, he had confined himself to the interpretation of the statute, to the arguments of the Cokes and the Blackstones—'God deliver me, I say, from such antiquaries as these, to hang a man's life upon a comma, and throttle him with a semi-colon'. His Counsel, he complained, had 'played me a sad trick in dropping so important a part of my appeal without a word of notice'. And that Sullivan knew what he was doing is clear from a letter he wrote to Smith after he returned to Dublin. The trial, he told Smith, was one of which you and your countrymen may well be proud. It was a splendid demonstration of the manner in which justice should be administered. The calm and noble dignity of the tribunal and the high plane of thought on which you placed all controversy from the start were both eclipsed by the profound manifestation of the desire to be chivalrous and generous to the weaker side.

Then, he proceeded to the main chance:

I greatly dreaded that in that last dreadful hour, when my brain refused to answer the helm, I had failed to maintain the tone and temper deserving of the occasion. If so, I am deeply grieved and repentant.

He was to have his reward a few years later, when Smith, by then Lord Chancellor, called him to the Inner Bar, along with thirty-eight other barristers. They were described, Sullivan recalled in his memoirs, as the Thirty-Nine Articles — Smith having thoughtfully struck one man off the list, in case they should become known as the Forty Thieves.

Casement had known all along that there could only be one verdict, 'Judge, jury, prosecution, all are one'; it was like 'referring the keeping of Lent to a jury of butchers'. Yet in the annals of the English Bar, the trial was regarded then, and has continued to be since, as a monument to the magnificent impartiality of English law. Even Artemus Jones thought that 'in its fairness, in its strict impartiality, Casement's trial was beyond criticism'; and according to Lord Reading's biographer, Derek Walker Smith, 'History can show no finer example of the rule of law in this country, and can adduce no greater testimony to the unswerving fairness of our courts.' Such is the capacity of the legal mind to assume that justice is done provided all the outward observances are adhered to, that Lord Reading himself would probably have agreed. Yet he himself at the trial was guilty of one of the most striking examples of Pecksniffery in the history of the Bench. 'It is the proud privilege of the Bar of England,' he told the jury, 'that it is ready to come into court and to defend a person accused, however grave the charge may be.' He must have known that Gavan Duffy had been unable to persuade any practising member of the Bar of England to justify his boast; that was why the defence had had to import Serjeant Sullivan.

The trial was in reality an elaborate show trial, giving out the impression that justice was being done, while taking care that the predetermined conclusion—sentence of death—was reached. As Alfred Noyes was to point out, the Chief Justice and Attorney-General—who were old legal colleagues, as Smith had appeared for Reading in a libel action in connection with the Marconi shares scandal—were even prepared to indulge in one of those collusive by-plays which so delight connoisseurs of court procedure. Smith had referred to the 'diary' which had been found on Casement at the time of his arrest—the one containing such entries as 'left Wicklow on Willie's yacht'. By this time, it was widely known that diaries had been found revealing his homosexual activities; and, presumably because he felt that the brief entries in the diary found in Casement's pocket would be an anti-climax, Smith decided to exploit it in court simply by referring to it, and then telling the jury—having whetted their interest—that he would not waste their time further with it. Reading saw his opportunity. 'Mr. Attorney,' he interrupted,

You mentioned a passage in the diary. Is there any evidence whose diary it is?

The Attorney-General. It was a diary. I will give your Lordship the evidence of it. It was a diary found.

The Chief Justice. I know, but so far as my recollection goes there was no further evidence given beyond the fact that it was found. Whose writing it is, or whose diary it is, there is no evidence.

The Attorney-General. My Lord, I did not say it was a diary of any particular person. I said 'the diary'. By 'the diary' I mean the diary which was found, and is in evidence as having been found.

The Chief Justice. I thought it right to indicate that, because it might have been conveyed to the jury that it was Casement's diary. There is no evidence of it.

The Attorney-General. You have heard, gentlemen, what my lord has said. If there was any misunderstanding I am glad it should be removed. It was a diary found with three men as to whom I make the suggestion that they all come from

Germany. There is no evidence before you as to which of the three the diary belonged. . . .

'There is no evidence *before you*' Smith told the jury. But Smith must have known it was Casement's, as he had made no secret of it, during his interrogation. 'The misunderstanding was deliberately contrived,' Noyes believed, 'with a most cunning and elaborate misuse of associated ideas, for the benefit of the jury and of the public who had already heard rumours of the "*diary found*".'

Smith's attitude to the trial can also be gauged from the memoirs of one of his junior Counsel, Travers Humphreys. The night before the trial opened, he showed his juniors the speech which he proposed to make for the Prosecution the following day. When Humphreys suggested some alterations, he replied, 'It's too late to alter it; the whole speech has been cabled to America, where it will be published tomorrow morning.' His excuse was that the speech would not be read at New York breakfast tables until after he had delivered it. Nevertheless it was a clear breach of legal convention, because it meant that New York editors and compositors knew what Smith was going to say before the Court did.

From the start, in short, the trial was a staged drama. Sullivan's line of defence simply made it easier for the court to reach the preordained decision without seeming to have ordained it. 'Of course,' Shaw commented,

it was knocked to pieces with contemptuous ease by Counsel for the Crown; and when the Lord Chief Justice had solemnly complimented Casement's counsel on having done everything for his client that human forensic skill could achieve, the verdict of Guilty was duly delivered. Then, if you please, the virtually dead man got up and made his speech. A couple of members of the jury were, I am told, good enough to say that if they had heard it before the verdict they would have dissented. But that possibility, on which I had banked, had been averted by the best possible legal advice.

Casement agreed. He was not responsible, he insisted, for Sullivan's defence. 'It was his line—he took it and kept me silent —and I am very sorry I did not act on my earliest judgment and have no counsel at all.'

CHAPTER THREE

EXECUTION

The reprieve campaign

The date fixed for Casement's execution was August 3rd—giving his friends just over a fortnight in which to persuade the Government to grant a reprieve. Some of them had already begun to bring pressure to bear; Alice Green had been so certain of the verdict that even before his trial she had written to the South African leader, General Botha, whom she had once met, to tell him that his name and his example had been constantly invoked since the Dublin rising, because the South African Government had treated their rebel element earlier in the war with clemency. No voice, she felt, would be so powerful in turning the British public to a more charitable mood.

In Ireland, most of Casement's associates from his Volunteers days were in prison but there were some who—though they had been horrified by his decision to go to Germany—felt that, as Armour of Ballymoney put it, 'his services to the Empire and humanity were very real, as he had an inborn hatred of tyranny and cruelty, and few deserved better of his country than Sir Roger'. Colonel Maurice Moore had sided with Redmond in the Volunteers split after war broke out; but he and Agnes O'Farrelly—a professor at the National University—formed a reprieve committee consisting of, among others, Monsignor Ryan, Douglas Hyde, and Lorcan Sherlock, a former Lord Mayor of Dublin. A petition was drawn up, and circulated to likely signatories. On balance the replies were charitable—though one citizen, whose name was later erased from his letter of reply, said 'I would as soon ask for clemency for Judas Iscariot'. Even Cardinal Logue, the Catholic Primate, regarded by the republicans as their most implacable opponent, agreed to sign, 'from motives of mercy and charity'. W. B. Yeats wrote personally to Asquith, from Calvados, claiming that though he had never approached a minister of the Crown before, he must express his opinion that the execution of Casement would be evil. And one of the Irish Party leaders, T. P. O'Connor—who in 1913 had called Casement 'one of the finest figures in our imperial history'—intervened on his behalf, writing to Asquith to remind him of the Battisi case. Battisi was an Italian living in Austrian-occupied territory, who had been a member of the Austrian parliament. When war broke out, he had fought for what he regarded as his country—Italy; and, captured by the Austrians, he had been executed as a traitor. 'Legally, of course, his execution was justified; politically it was a profound mistake, and our own papers and all reasonable people in the world united in condemning the execution.'

In London, Conan Doyle organised a petition which was signed by a notable collection of distinguished authors—including Arnold Bennett, G. K. Chesterton, Sir James Frazer, John Galsworthy, Jerome K. Jerome—and editors—G. P. Gooch, of the *Contemporary Review*, A. G. Gardiner of the *Daily News*, H. W. Massingham of the *Nation*, C. P. Scott of the *Manchester Guardian* and Clement Shorter of the *Sphere*; along with the president of the Royal College of Physicians, the president of the National Free Church Council, and the president of the Baptist Union. Of those who refused to sign, only one name brought Casement sorrow; Herbert Ward, who could not bring himself to forgive him for going over to the enemy. Morel also chose to dissociate himself from the campaign, but in his case there was a reasonable excuse. His fellow council-members of the Union for Democratic Control, who had been arguing that the war was as much the fault of the Foreign Office as of the Kaiser, warned him that they were suspect enough without it being said that one of them was identified with a traitor. Alice Green reassured him. Casement, she wrote, believed he was quite right to accept his colleagues' request.

The Archbishop of Canterbury felt it would be wrong for a man in his position to try to bring pressure publicly to bear on the Cabinet on what was really a political issue; but he saw the Lord Chancellor and the Home Secretary privately to express to them his support for a reprieve. He had been in contact with Casement at the time of the Congo and Putumayo investigations, he told Herbert Samuel, and was 'always impressed by his capacity, his enthusiasm, and his apparent straightforwardness'. Bernard Shaw also declined to sign Conan Doyle's petition, but only on the ground that it might deter other people from putting their names to it if they saw his. Instead, he wrote one of his own, and sent it to Asquith, repeating the arguments he had used against the execution of the leaders of the rising. Up to the time of his trial, Shaw contended, Casement had no serious hold on the Irish people; and presumably Asquith had no desire to make him into a national hero.

There is, however, one infallible way in which that can be done; and that way is to hang him. His trial and sentence have already raised his status in nationalist Ireland; but it lacks the final consecration of death. We urge you very strongly not to effect that consecration.

In a letter * in the *Manchester Guardian* (*The Times* refused it) on July 22nd, Shaw expanded on this argument, recalling that although Casement had had a fair trial, the Defence had failed to raise certain important issues — the treason of the Unionist leaders over Ulster, for one: what about those unconvicted 'and indeed unprosecuted traitors, whose action, helped very powerfully to convince Germany that she might attack France without incurring our active hostility?' The jury, too, ought to have been shown that Ireland's being a part of the United Kingdom no more prohibited Casement from doing what he had done, than five centuries of Turkish rule in the Balkans had abrogated the right of a Serbian to fight for his country's independence. And it ought to have been emphasised to them that the fact Casement had been in the pay of the British Government did not make him a traitor to Britain, any more than Shaw's acceptance of thousands of pounds in royalties from Germany (far more, he remarked, than he had received from British sources) made him a traitor to Germany. But his essential point was that Casement would be regarded in Ireland as a national hero, if he was executed —

and quite possibly as a spy, if he is not. For that reason, it may very well be that he would object very strongly to my attempt to prevent his canonisation. But Ireland has enough heroes and martyrs already, and if England has not by this time had enough of manufacturing them in fits of temper, experience is thrown away on her.

* See Appendix II.

Before he received Shaw's letter for the *Manchester Guardian*, C. P. Scott had himself written an editorial along much the same lines, and had also written privately to Lloyd George:

Is it politically possible to save Casement's life? I think it would be in the highest degree politically expedient. His health was quite broken by what he went through in that dreadful Putumayo business, and I think he is at least as much off his head as the religious fanatic who murdered Sheehy-Skeffington and two other men and who — rightly, I think — is not going to be hung.

I write to you because you have a freer mind than anybody else and because you have been chosen by the Cabinet as a pacifier of Ireland and ought to be listened to on such a matter.

If the execution had threatened to come between Lloyd George and the attempted pacification to which Scott was referring, in all probability there would have been a reprieve. Shaken by the rising and by the reaction to the execution of its leaders, Asquith had been forced to the conclusion that now, if ever, was the time for the Government to offer concessions which would reassure the moderates in Ireland that Home Rule was not in jeopardy. The Irish Party, he calculated, would be the beneficiaries; popular support would once again swing in behind Redmond; recruiting would revive; and American opinion would be mollified. After visiting Dublin, to express his desire for a settlement based on goodwill, he had appointed Lloyd George to try to find one which would be acceptable to both the Irish Party and the Unionists. Lloyd George's method was simple. He told the Irish Party they could have Home Rule if they agreed to the temporary exclusion of Ulster, or part of Ulster; but he told Carson and Craig that if they agreed to Home Rule for the rest of Ireland, that exclusion would be permanent. Redmond, Carson and Craig were reluctantly prepared to accept; so were Bonar Law and Smith, in office, as no more political capital could be made out of Unionism. Lansdowne and other diehard Unionists, however, could not be persuaded to accept Lloyd George's plan. It had to be abandoned; and when on July 22nd his duplicity over Ulster was revealed to Redmond, the Government irrevocably lost the confidence of the Irish Party.

It was to take time for realisation how the Home Rule movement had been undermined to penetrate through to the Irish electorate; but even before the end of July, the Inspector-General of the Royal Irish Constabulary concluded his report on the state of the country with the admission that the only beneficiaries had been *Sinn Fein*; it had 'thrown into their ranks many who had previously shown no sympathy for them'.

Asquith, therefore, had no political advantage to gain from attempting to conciliate Irish opinion. And he knew that there would be unwelcome political repercussions in England, if Casement were reprieved. How deep the bitterness was against him as a traitor to his country, and his class, was made clear to Alice Green when she sent Gertrude Bannister's petition to about twenty influential people. All of them—though it was to be sent to Asquith privately—refused to sign. 'The upper classes are intensely hostile', she wrote to tell Cadbury, with the clergy outdoing the laity in their imperialism; 'the war has formed all minds into a single groove'. The course the war was taking further increased hostility to Casement. In the Middle East there had been 'the humiliation of the surrender at Kut, and the growing Turkish threat to the Suez canal. In France, the Germans were still battering at Verdun. Although the North Sea battle of Jutland, early in June, was claimed as a victory, the losses had been disturbing. Zeppelin raids on London had begun. And— for the prospects of a reprieve, most serious of all—in the weeks after the rising hardly a day passed without some report in the press of the gallantry of the Irish regiments, from both North and South, on the western front; and of their heavy losses. Were those loyal men to die, and Casement to live?

Woodrow Wilson

There was only one source from which pressure could have been successfully exerted to secure a reprieve: the United States. From the time he heard Casement had been captured, Spring-Rice had continued to argue that it would be politically unwise to execute him, with the Presidential and Congressional elections coming up that winter. It was not so much the Irish vote he was worried about. Whether or not Casement was executed was unlikely to make any difference to that. Spring-Rice's fear was that influential pro-allied citizens in America, who had been annoyed by the Easter Rising but shocked by the executions, would react still more unfavourably if he were hanged.

During July, letters and petitions began to find their way to the British embassy in Washington suggesting that his fears were justified. Individuals and societies who had nothing to do with Ireland were expressing concern; and some Congressmen took up the cause. On July 22nd, one of the Senators for New Jersey moved:

Whereas the Senate of the United States have heard with deep regret that the sentence of death has been pronounced upon Sir Roger Casement after a hasty (so-called) trial; there-fore, let it be resolved, that the President of the United States be, and is hereby, requested to ask a stay in the execution of said sentence in order that new facts may be introduced.

Motions in the Senate, though, were unlikely to have any impact in London unless they were transmitted with some in-timation of Presidential backing—or at least, with a Presidential warning that they ought to be taken seriously. As soon as Case-ment's sister Nina had heard he had been captured, she had written to Wilson asking him to intervene on the ground of her brother's service to humanity. Wilson refused. 'We have no choice in a matter of this sort,' he told his Secretary, Joseph Tumulty, on May 2nd. 'It is absolutely necessary to say that I could take no action of any kind regarding it.' His excuse was that he would have a right to intervene only if Casement were an American citizen. This was in fact incorrect—as petitioners on Casement's behalf soon pointed out; past Presidents had on several occasions pleaded for clemency for men who were not American; and Doyle told Tumulty that both Redmond and Lord Northcliffe had assured him that a word from the President would be enough to save Casement. But Wilson remained ada-mant, even after the appeal had been rejected. 'It would be in-excusable to touch this,' he told Tumulty on July 20th. 'It would involve serious international embarrassment.'

The reason Wilson was so positive that he could do nothing, when historical precedent indicated that he could, was to be hinted at by Spring-Rice, a few months later: 'the President is by descent an Orangeman and by education a Presbyterian'. Wilson's sympathies were with the allies, and with Ulster. If the execution of Casement posed a serious threat to his re-election, he might have acted differently; knowing—as presumably he did, if Spring-Rice knew—that Devoy was not going to bring the Irish voters out against him simply for the sake of Casement's memory, he felt no compulsion to intervene.

The Black Diaries

The decisive reason, though, for the failure of the campaign for a reprieve was that Casement's diaries had been found in his Ebury Street lodgings. They were effectively used to head off influential citizens who might otherwise have supported it. Copies were made which—according to Alfred Noyes, who was shown them at the time—'were circulated behind the scenes of the trial, through London clubs, among Members of Parliament and others who might be thought to influence public opinion'. They were shown, for example, to King George V—and by him to Bishop Hensley Henson, who of all the eminent Churchmen of the time was the one most likely to campaign on Casement's behalf. The Archbishop of Canterbury was invited to examine them, but on reflection decided to ask John Harris of the Anti-Slavery Society to undertake the inspection for him; and Harris, who had known and admired Casement since they had met in the Congo, was so shattered by what he found that he almost fainted. According to Stephen Gwynn, it was the diaries which decided John Redmond to have nothing to do with the reprieve campaign. Particular care was taken that influential Americans in Britain should see extracts. Captain Hall showed them to Associated Press representative in London, Ben Allen; and they were shown to Walter Page, the Anglophile American Ambassador—who, even before he had seen them, had written to say he had been privately informed that much information about Casement 'of an unspeakable filthy character' was available, but had been withheld at his trial; 'if all the facts about Casement ever become public, it will be well that our Government had nothing to do with him or his case, even indirectly!' And they were shown to crusading journalists in Britain who could be expected to take up the reprieve cause, notably H. W. Massingham, editor of the Nation, who went to the authorities and demanded to be told the truth about the diaries. When he came afterwards to see the Shaws his report on them, according to Charlotte, was 'a crushing blow. We were (or rather our little committee was) rather knocked to pieces . . . the thing entirely killed any English sympathy there might have been for Casement.'

According to Casement's biographer Denis Gwynn, one of the principal officers at the Ministry of Information, G. H. Mair, used to boast that he had had the responsibility for getting the diaries copied. What has remained obscure is who actually gave the authorisation to show the copies around. Inevitably, suspicion fell on F. E. Smith. He showed them to friends; Sir James O'Connor, the Irish Attorney-General, told Bulmer Hobson how shocked and disgusted he had been 'at the impropriety of the Attorney-General of England peddling dirty stories in this way about a man he was prosecuting on a charge of treason'. But Smith's interest, apparently, was only scatological; when he heard that the Foreign Office was proposing to photograph portions of the diary, with a view to influencing opinion, he told Grey he thought it was 'rather a ghoulish proposal'. Grey agreed: it would not be proceeded with, unless the Cabinet gave its authority.

But the Cabinet did not use its authority to prevent the circulation of copies of the diaries; and even before the appeal had been heard, newspapers were referring to them. On July 16th Northcliffe's *Weekly Dispatch* inquired whether Clement Shorter and Sir Arthur Conan Doyle, who were working for a reprieve, knew their contents; and the *News of the World* claimed that nobody who saw them 'would ever mention Casement's name again without loathing and contempt'.

There can be now little doubt who had the chief responsibility: the legal adviser to the Home Office, Ernley Blackwell. Blackwell had what can only be described as a malignant hatred of Casement. 'A pale, narrow-faced, thin-lipped man', Gertrude Bannister found him, when she went to try to get permission to send in food for her cousin during the trial, 'with the sort of expression I knew by much bitter experience meant. "Get through with what you have to say quickly—I will consent to nothing you want".' He tried to pretend to her it was not within his legal power to grant her request, though she had found out for herself beforehand that it was. And when the Cabinet papers from the period were released for inspection, they showed how Blackwell had set himself to prevent ministers from weakening in their resolve that there should not be a reprieve.

On July 15th—before the hearing of the appeal—Blackwell and a colleague, Sir Edward Troup, prepared a memorandum for the Cabinet on Casement, which might have been written by one of the Counsel for the Prosecution. 'It is difficult,' they wrote,

> to imagine a worse case of High Treason than Casement's. It is aggravated rather than mitigated by his previous career in the public service, and his private character—although it really has no relation to the actual offence with which he is charged—certainly cannot be pleaded in his favour.
>
> If the decision is to be taken in accordance with the rules which ordinarily govern Home Office practice, there are no possible grounds for interference with the sentence.

In a separate memorandum, Blackwell went into the issue of the diaries. Some members of the Government, Blackwell knew, including Grey and Lansdowne, were of the opinion that Casement should be confined in a criminal lunatic asylum; because, they argued, if he were executed 'without any smirch on his character' he would be canonised as a martyr, in America as well as in Ireland. The decision was therefore taken to submit the diaries to psychiatrists. Their verdict, predictably, was that though Casement was abnormal, he was not as the law stood certifiably insane. Blackwell added his own commentary:

> Of later years he seems to have completed the full cycle of sexual degeneracy and from a pervert has become an invert—a woman, or pathic, who derives his satisfaction from attracting men and inducing them to use him. The point is worth noting, for the Attorney-General had given Sir E. Grey the impression that Casement's own account of the frequency of his performances was incredible and of itself suggested he was labouring under hallucination in this respect. I think the idea may be dismissed. I believe the diaries are a faithful and accurate record of his acts, thoughts and feelings just as they occurred and presented themselves to him. No one ... could doubt for a moment that Casement, intellectually at any rate, is very far removed from anything that could properly be described as insanity. His excesses may have warped his judgment and in themselves they are of course evidence of dis-

ordered sexual instincts, but they have not in my opinion any relevance in consideration of his crime.

In any case, Blackwell argued, there was no need for members of the Government to worry that if Casement were hanged, his reputation would remain unsullied: 'I see not the slightest objection to hanging Casement and *afterwards* giving as much publicity to the contents of his diary as decency permits.'

When Casement's appeal was rejected on July 18th Blackwell presented the memorandum he had prepared jointly with Troup to the Cabinet. It had the desired effect; ministers agreed unanimously that Casement must hang. But Blackwell apparently kept his second memorandum in reserve, in case they should be tempted to change their minds for reasons of political expediency. It proved a sensible precaution. When the news came on July 24th of the American Senate resolution, Blackwell had his reply ready; Casement could be hanged *and* smirched.

Blackwell did not need authorisation to show the diaries around. All that he required was the Cabinet's tacit consent. And this would have suited the Cabinet, for formal authorisation would have meant putting the responsibility on some individual minister, who would leave himself personally open to the kind of general denunciation Nevinson made in the *Manchester Guardian* on July 25th, about the peddlers of rumours of Casement's immorality: 'anyone who may have attempted by such means to blacken the character of, and prejudice our feelings towards, a man who stands in acute danger of a degrading and hideous death, is, in my opinion, guilty of a far meaner and more loathsome crime than the worst that could possibly be unearthed in the career of the criminal himself'. As Home Secretary, Herbert Samuel was technically responsible. 'Something of a kindred spirit', Casement had called him, in 1905; but he appears from his correspondence to have found the subject so distasteful that he preferred not to think about it. Even so, it seems inconceivable that he did not know—and still more inconceivable that Smith, who as Attorney-General also held some responsibility, did not know. Yet when Jones and Morgan went to see him on July 29th, to try to get him to reconsider his refusal to grant leave to appeal to the Lords, and mentioned the campaign to discredit Casement, Smith claimed there was 'not a word of truth' in it.

The Foreign Office was also involved—Alfred Noyes was shown extracts there. This would have helped to make it more difficult to pin down the source. 'If I could only ascertain which Government Department is responsible for the propagation of the story,' Gavan Duffy wrote to Colonel Moore a few days before the date set for the execution, 'I could take effective measures; but so far it has not been possible to get the necessary evidence.' But the operation must have been conducted from the Home Office; and the likelihood is that Blackwell was the chief organiser—as Noyes later asserted.

Energetically though the diaries were used, however, the reprieve campaign continued to build up, causing ministers concern. John Dillon appealed to Asquith on Casement's behalf; and in Ireland, Colonel Moore's petition was signed by eighteen Archbishops and Bishops, and over two hundred and fifty members of university staffs and learned societies. Although Redmond to the last refused to intercede—when Nevinson went to the Commons to make a final appeal to him, he turned away at the mention of Casement's name, saying, 'Please don't!'—a deputation from the Irish Party to Asquith on July 26th brought a petition signed by thirty-nine of its members. And in the United States, William Randolph Hearst threw his newspapers behind the cause. According to his wife, even after he had to undergo surgery he was composing an editorial on the subject within an hour of leaving the operating table. If Casement were guilty, Hearst's theme was, so were John Adams and the other signatories of the Declaration of Independence; all should have been hanged.

On July 29th a resolution was introduced by Senator Pittman of Nevada 'that the Senate expresses the hope that the British Government may exercise clemency in the treatment of Irish political prisoners, and that the President be requested to transmit this resolution to that Government'. The fact that Casement was not named made it easier for Senators to accept; the earlier motion was dropped, and the new resolution passed by forty-six votes to nineteen. And although a series of well-timed delays spared the British Government from having to give formal consideration to this plea—owing to an intervening week-end, the copy of the resolution did not reach the White House until the morning of July 31st; and then its transmission to London was not sanctioned until August 2nd, just too late for it to reach

London in time to be handed to Asquith that day—Cabinet ministers, when they met that morning, had been told it was on its way. They devoted part of the meeting to a final discussion of the case, in the light of 'some further material', as Asquith described it, 'and the urgent appeals for mercy from authoritative and friendly quarters in the United States'.

'Some further material' was an understatement. The Cabinet that morning were confronted by a formidable quantity of evidence requiring their consideration, all of it pointing towards the desirability of a reprieve.

Although little use had been made of the Czech parallel at the trial, friends of Casement had been drawing attention to it; and in a letter to the *Guardian* on July 27th, Alice Green had been able to show that at a State Banquet in Paris, given by the French President, four 'traitors' had been honoured for their services to the allies: 'all four men had left their native land, and were occupied in raising troops of their fellow countrymen, whether prisoners of war or émigrés, to fight against the Austrian and German Empire'. On the same day, too, it had been reported that the captain of a British merchant ship had been executed by the Germans for attempting to ram a German U-boat. There was a wave of anger, in the United States as well as in Britain; and in a letter to the *Daily News*, published on August 2nd, Bernard Shaw drew attention to the implications. 'The extraordinary luck which never seems to desert England,' he wrote, 'has ordained that the Lusitanicide Germans should again select just the wrong moment (for themselves) to produce a new revulsion in our favour by shooting, on technical grounds, a man whom all the rest of the world regards as a prisoner of war.' The anger it had aroused across the Atlantic had revived hopes of the Americans coming in with the allies; was this hope to be extinguished again, Shaw asked, by the execution of Casement?

The Cabinet were unlikely, at this stage, to pay much attention to Shaw; but it happened that they had just received a plea for mercy, based on the same argument, from a man who they had good reason to attend to—the influential American Senator, Cabot Lodge. Lodge, Spring-Rice had cabled, 'thinks contrast between last German atrocity and British clemency would be a striking object-lesson to the general public'. It was not the Irish Americans who were the worry, Spring-Rice reiterated—they actually wanted Casement's execution for its propaganda value.

It was the general public. And what the general public felt was reflected in another petition transmitted from New York on July 28th, with twenty-four signatures, including that of John Quinn:

> The undersigned American citizens, all of whom have been and are pro-ally in their sympathies, respectfully appeal in the interests of humanity for clemency in the case of Roger Casement, and are profoundly convinced that the clemency would be wise policy on the part of the British Government at this juncture and in this great crisis in the history of our race.

The fact that the signatories were not politicians, angling for the Irish vote, gave their plea added weight—as Grey recognised, when he directed that it should be brought to the Cabinet's attention. Presumably, too, ministers were told that Bryce had addressed a last-minute appeal to them, through Lloyd George.

> I earnestly hope that Casement will not be executed. To me it seems a matter of policy and nothing else. It would be in the highest degree impolitic to hang him, and give the Irish, and still more the Americans, another martyr. His brain is, I believe, disordered.

Bryce mentioned he had heard that the coloured people were getting up a petition for a reprieve; and the Cabinet had one before them that morning, forwarded by Spring-Rice:

> The Negro Fellowship League, an organisation composed of members of the coloured race and of which I have the honour to be President, unanimously voted last Sunday, July 9th, to address this communication to you and the British Government asking clemency for Roger Casement. We feel so deeply grateful to this man for the revelations he made while British Consul in Africa, touching the treatment of natives in the Congo. But for him, the world might not know of the barbarous cruelties practised upon the helpless natives. Because of this great service to humanity, as well as to the Congo natives, we feel impelled to beg for mercy on his behalf.

There are so few heroic souls in the world who dare to lift their voices in defence of the oppressed who are born with black skins, that the entire Negro race would be guilty of the blackest ingratitude did we not raise our voices on behalf of the unfortunate man who permitted himself in an evil hour to raise his hands against his own Government. . . .

The Cabinet also had before them an appeal from South America. Earlier, Mitchell Innes had cabled from Montevideo, where he had been appointed minister, saying that articles were appearing in the press in South America stressing Casement's services to humanity; and though they were in general friendly to Britain, it was evident that the exercise of mercy would be received with rejoicing—especially (he added with a touch of malice) in the more advanced countries, where the death sentence had either been abolished or was practically obsolete. And on August 1st, the Colombian minister in London handed in a plea from the President of Colombia, transmitting Resolutions passed in the Senate and the Chamber of Deputies there recalling Casement's 'humanitarian efforts to save so many lives in the Amazon region, for which the Colombian people are sincerely grateful', and asking that they should be taken into account. If, as Wyndham Childs believed, Casement's trial had been laid on to impress neutrals, it now began to look as if it was going to have the opposite effect.

But the most important, and for ministers potentially the most disconcerting, piece of 'further material' confronting them that morning was a document transmitted from the Vatican. It confirmed that Casement had not gone to Ireland to lead the rising, but to try to prevent it.

Just before the appeal was heard, Gavan Duffy had received a letter from Father Ryan of Tralee, who had visited Casement when he was under arrest there, testifying that Casement had told him his real reason for coming to Ireland; and Eva Gore-Booth, who had not known Casement before, but had attended his trial and had been much moved by his demeanour, wrote to C. P. Scott and to members of the Cabinet to draw their attention to Ryan's testimony. When it was brought up at a Cabinet meeting on July 21st, however, Blackwell ridiculed it; 'the idea of saying that he had come with the intention and for the purpose of stopping the rising appears to have occurred to Casement only after his capture. It is at any rate entirely inconsistent with the known facts'. Ministers had allowed themselves to be convinced. But on July 27th, the Cardinal Secretary of State at the Vatican asked the British minister there to bring to his Government's notice some information received in a letter from Dr. Charles Curry, of Munich, and it reached the Foreign Office on August 1st. By quoting Casement's letters to him, Curry was able to confirm that his object had indeed been to prevent the rising; a decision taken, Curry felt — like his earlier efforts in the Congo and the Putumayo — on humanitarian principles, to avoid the useless shedding of blood. And in his covering letter, the Cardinal Secretary of State added that in view of this evidence, there was reason to believe that Casement's execution would have an unfortunate effect in Ireland and in America. It would be politically wise, he suggested, to commute the sentence.

Seldom can such a weight of testimony have been advanced at the last moment in favour of a reprieve. It was wasted. Secure in the knowledge that Casement's reputation could later be destroyed, Asquith was unconcerned. On the night before the Cabinet meeting at which Casement's fate would finally be decided, he told the American Ambassador, who was his guest for dinner, that the Cabinet had practically determined not to intervene. He asked Page if he had heard about the diary; Page replied that he had already seen it, and had been given photographed copies of some of it. 'Excellent,' Asquith remarked, 'and you need not be particular about keeping it to yourself.'

So although the Cabinet devoted an hour and a half to a discussion on the case, when they met on August 2nd, there was never any real prospect of ministers changing their minds. 'Much pressure has been brought to bear,' Herbert Samuel wrote to his wife, after the Cabinet meeting,

from many quarters — here, in Ireland, and in America — in favour of a reprieve. There has been much doubting in the Cabinet — among a few. The question has been discussed there three times, this morning for an hour and a half. I have had no doubt all through that, as the man is certainly not insane, there is no ground on which he could be reprieved. Although his execution will create a (somewhat artificial) row in America, and give rise to a certain amount of passion in Ireland, and although the *Manchester Guardian* and the *Nation* will denounce us, his reprieve would let loose a tornado of condemnation, would be bitterly resented by the great mass of the people in Great Britain and by the whole of the army, and would profoundly and permanently shake public confidence in the sincerity and courage of the Government. In the end the Cabinet unanimously came to this conclusion. But there are moments when a Home Secretaryship is a post far from agreeable. Had Casement not been a man of atrocious moral character, the situation would have been even more difficult.

The Archbishop of Canterbury, who had continued his private efforts to obtain a reprieve, heard the same explanation from the Lord Chancellor. The decisive fact, he was told, had been the fate of 'certain Irish prisoners in Germany, some of whom had been returned to England invalided, their illness being due to German ill-treatment consequent on their refusal to listen to Casement's treasonable blandishments'. Casement had passionately denied this, and there was no truth in it; but for the Government's purpose, it was desirable that it should continue to be believed. It was also desirable to maintain the fiction that he had come to Ireland to lead the rising. The Cabinet had already asked the Foreign Office and the Home Office to draw up a statement, which could be used to justify the decision not to grant a reprieve. The Foreign Secretary, who on July 27th became Viscount Grey of Falloden, was responsible for the final draft. 'There is the clearest evidence,' he instructed Spring-Rice to tell Senator Lodge,

that his object was absolutely hostile to this country and the *ex post facto* statement that he tried to stop the rising was not raised at the trial and is demonstrably untrue. His whole action in the matter was more particularly hostile and malevolent than that of any of the leaders, extreme though some of these were in Ireland. Irish soldiers, prisoners of war in Germany, who resisted Casement's exhortations to disloyalty, were subjected to rigorous treatment by the Germans; some of them have since been exchanged as invalids and have died in this country regarding Casement as their murderer.

To the scaffold

Although even before the appeal was heard, Casement had realised his earlier assumption that he would not be hanged was unfounded, the growing certainty that he must die only served to calm him. Visiting him in Pentonville would have been a desolation—Alice Green told Morel—but for 'his gentle dignity, his serenity, his confidence in his friends and absence of mistrust'; and, writing to her the following day, Casement confirmed her opinion: 'I have a happier mind than I had for a long time.' The only reason he had allowed his lawyers to appeal was that it would give him a chance to see her and other friends again; 'again goodbye, my true-hearted, ever-faithful friend'.

When the appeal was dismissed, Casement had made up his mind that he wanted to be received into the Catholic Church. It was not a sudden decision. As long before as 1912, he had declined to subscribe to a Protestant charity on the ground, among others, that he was not a Protestant; and although the Catholic Church's apathy about, and sometimes hostility to, the Irish language and Irish nationalism had kept him at a distance until 1914, he had never abandoned the search for a faith which had taken him to the Mission Station in his Congo days. In the new year of 1914 he revealed his feelings in a sonnet, which the *Irish Review* printed in March:

> Weep not that you no longer feel the tide
> High-breasting sun and storm that bore along
> Your youth on currents of perpetual song;
> For in these mid-sea waters, still and wide,
> A sleepless purpose the great Deep doth hide.
> Here spring the mighty fountains, pure and strong
> That bear sweet change of breath to city throng
> Who, had the sea no breeze, would soon have died
> So, though the sun shines not in such a blue
> Nor have the stars the meaning youth devised
> The heavens are nigher, and a light shines through
> The brightness that nor Sun nor Stars sufficed
> And on this lonely waste we find it true
> Lost youth and love, not lost, are hid with Christ.

By the time Monteith met him in Germany he already had

decided leanings to the Catholic Church; he always carried a prayer book with him, Monteith recalled, or some manual of instruction, his favourite being the *Imitation of Christ*. According to Father Crotty, he actually contemplated becoming a Catholic while he was at Limburg.

Finding Casement well-versed in Catholic teaching, Father Carey, the prison chaplain at Pentonville, made the standard application to the Archbishop, Cardinal Bourne, for authorisation to receive him into the Church. Bourne, however, stipulated that he must first express sorrow 'for any scandal he might have caused by his acts, public or private'. Casement rebelled; it might be used to imply that he was apologising for the part he had played in Germany. 'They are trying,' he told his cousin, 'to make me betray my soul.'

In the course of their discussions, however, Carey found that Casement's mother had had him baptised as a Catholic, along with his brothers and sister, when he was a small child. It was enough; if he were already a Catholic, Carey was no longer confronted simply with the absorbing spiritual exercise of conversion. It became a positive obligation on him to reconcile Casement, *in articulo mortis*, to the Church.

Even then, difficulties remained. According to Blackwell, who had appointed himself censor of the condemned man's correspondence, he regarded his past 'excesses' as no more than 'follies'. This outraged Blackwell; but it was characteristic of Casement, who was less concerned with what he had done than its effect, asking for prayers 'that any evil that may have come from his folly and imprudence may not live long'. Though he and Carey had some protracted arguments on doctrinal issues, they were of a kind which he could enjoy; they soothed, rather than provoked him. Fenner Brockway—in Pentonville for his socialist and pacifist convictions—saw him from his cell window; his face 'wonderfully calm . . . he seemed already to be living in another world; there was not a trace of anxiety or fear in his features' (by a coincidence, another inmate of Pentonville, transferred there just before Casement was due to be hanged, was Captain White of the Citizen Army, arrested for trying to organise protests against the execution of James Connolly; 'it was not the Government's intention, but Casement and I were reconciled, even united, at last').

Casement read avidly, in those final days; although the prison governor shared the prevailing detestation of him as a traitor, he was allowed what books he wanted, even Wolfe Tone's diaries. He also found, and was delighted by, poems of Francis Ledwidge, a young Irishman who, like Will Redmond—John's brother—had joined the British army; both 'soon to be killed on the Western Front. And he wrote farewell letters to those he had worked with, and been helped by, during his career; among them Cadbury and his wife, who had been 'like a brother and sister . . . farewell, dear gentle hearts'. Blackwell censored most of the letter, on the ground that it contravened Defence Regulations.

On July 27th, Casement was allowed a last visit from Gertrude Bannister. He was unhappy, because the Governor had just reviled him for the course he had chosen to take, and because a final attempt at a reconciliation with Herbert Ward had failed. It worried him, too, that he was to be buried in Pentonville. 'Don't let me lie here in this dreadful place,' he begged her, 'take my body back with you and let it lie in the old churchyard in Murlough Bay.' They wept together—the only time she had ever been in tears when she was with him—until they told her she must leave:

> I wanted to shriek and beat on the gate with my hands. My lips kept saying 'let him out. Let him out!' I staggered down the road crying out loud, and people gazed at me. I got home somehow. Now, writing it down, I cry and cry and want to scream out, but what's the good. . . . He was there waiting for death, such a death. I was outside, and I wanted to die.

Two days later, the governors of Queen Anne's School, Caversham, who had earlier intimated their disapproval of her efforts on her cousin's behalf, sent her a cheque for £40, in lieu of notice.

After the Cabinet meeting on August 2nd, Asquith at least had the courtesy to write personally to Gertrude Bannister to tell her of the final decision. Casement, too, was told. 'Tomorrow, St Stephen's Day,' he wrote to her, 'I die the death I sought, and may God forgive the mistakes and receive the intent.' A message which arrived from his sister Nina—'keep up heart, my dearest brother. Am doing everything possible' was not delivered, on the charitable ground that it would be an act of refined cruelty to give him a message which might raise hopes for which there was no foundation. He made his confession, and was reconciled with the Church. He also wrote a last apologia, which Blackwell suppressed; but one of the priests who were with him managed to make some rough notes of its contents. He was chiefly concerned to show why he had done what he did—'my dominating thought was to keep Ireland out of the war'—and to explain his decision to die a Catholic. The Church had at last given him what he had looked for. 'In Protestant coldness I could not find it, but I saw it in the faces of the Irish. Now I know what it was I loved in them. The chivalry of Christ speaking through human eyes.'

Although Casement had still not entirely put out of his mind the possibility that there might be a last-minute reprieve, he no longer desired it—'It is better that I die thus on the scaffold ... it is a glorious death, for Ireland's sake.' But he must die bravely. 'If it be said I shed tears, remember they came not from cowardice but from sorrow ... I hope I shall not weep, but if I do it shall be nature's tribute wrung from me—one who has never hurt a human being—and whose heart was always compassionate and pitiful for the grief of others.' When the time came, he did not weep. He had taken his first Communion, and spent an hour at prayer with Father Carey. 'He feared not death,' Carey wrote, describing the last moments; 'he marched to the scaffold with the dignity of a prince.' To Ellis, the hangman, he appeared to be 'the bravest man it fell to my unhappy lot to execute'.

As the prison bell announcing his execution began to toll, a small crowd which had gathered in the street outside raised a derisory cheer. It would have grieved Casement that ordinary men and women—most of them workers in a nearby munitions factory—should have felt that way. 'It is a cruel thing to die,' he had written in his last letter to his sister Nina, 'with all men misunderstanding.' But now, it no longer mattered. He had followed Swift, where cruel rage could tear the heart no more.

PART SEVEN

THE GHOST OF ROGER CASEMENT

CHAPTER ONE

THE FORGERY CONTROVERSY

'Inspired innuendoes'

On the day after Casement's execution the Cabinet took the unusual step of issuing a statement, justifying their refusal to grant a reprieve:

> All the circumstances in the case of Roger Casement were carefully and repeatedly considered by the Government before the decision was reached not to interfere with the sentence of the Law. He was convicted and punished for treachery of the worst kind to the Empire he had served, and as a willing agent of Germany.
>
> The Irish rebellion resulted in much loss of life, both among soldiers and civilians. Casement invoked and organised German assistance to the insurrection. In addition, though himself for many years a British official, he undertook the task of trying to induce soldiers of the British army, prisoners in the hands of Germany, to forswear their oath of allegiance and join their country's enemies. Conclusive evidence has come into the hands of the Government since the trial that he entered into an agreement with the German Government which explicitly provided that the Brigade which he was trying to raise among the Irish soldier prisoners might be employed in Egypt against the British Crown. Those among the Irish soldier prisoners in Germany were subjected to treatment of exceptional severity by the Germans; some of them have since been exchanged, and have died in this country, regarding Casement as their murderer.

Up to this point, the Government statement kept reasonably within the bounds of justified comment. Admittedly Casement had not been responsible for the German treatment of Irish prisoners of war. But they could not have known this. Fearing, though, that the statement was not yet convincing enough, the Government had authorised a further assertion:

> The suggestion that Casement left Germany for the purpose of trying to stop the Irish rising was not raised at the trial, and is conclusively disproved not only by the facts there disclosed but by further evidence which has since become available.

For obvious reasons, Casement had not claimed in his speech from the dock that he had come to Ireland to try to stop the rising: to have done so would have left himself open to the charge that he was whining for mercy. If the British Government had made the point that he was concerned to stop the rising only because he feared it would be a failure, that would have been reasonable. But to deny that he had come to Ireland for that purpose, and to pretend that fresh evidence had come in to disprove it, was a deliberate falsehood. The evidence which had become available—in particular, Curry's letter—made it very clear why Casement had left Germany.

But this raises the question: had the Cabinet seen the letter? As soon as Blackwell heard of it, he had asked the Foreign Office for a copy. It would have been his function to lay it before the Cabinet, at their final meeting on August 2nd. But did he do so? If he did not, he could easily have deceived them into accepting the statement, which bears all the signs of being composed by Blackwell himself: It concluded:

> Another suggestion, that Casement was out of his mind, is equally without foundation. Materials bearing on his mental condition were placed at the disposal of his Counsel, who did not raise the plea of insanity. Casement's demeanour since his arrest, and throughout and since the trial, gave no ground for any such defence, and indeed were sufficient to disprove it.

Although the statement gave no clue to the nature of the 'materials bearing on Casement's mental condition', the reference was obviously to his diaries; and in an editorial commenting on points made in it, *The Times* belatedly criticised the Government for its use of them:

We cannot help protesting against certain other attempts which have been made to use the press for the purpose of raising issues which are utterly damaging to Casement's character but which have no connection whatever with the charges on which he was tried. These should either have been raised in a public or straightforward manner, or they should have been left severely alone ... if there was ever any virtue in the pomp and circumstance of a great State Trial, it can only be weakened by inspired innuendoes which, whatever their substance, are now irrelevant, improper, and un-English.

Improper and un-English they might be, but so far as the Foreign Office were concerned, they were still far from irrelevant. Blackwell's suggestion that they should be used to silence criticism of the Government after Casement's execution was carried out. 'The English have been circulating reports on Casement's degeneracy', John Quinn wrote from New York to tell Gavan Duffy a month later; 'They came to me from all quarters.' Disgusted, Quinn had written to Spring-Rice to say that if the showing around of the photographed copies of the diaries continued, he would recall how the Pigott forgeries were used to try to discredit Parnell. The hint, he thought, had worked. Grey had given instructions that the circulation of the copies must stop.

By that time, though, they had fulfilled their purpose. There had consequently been far less of a reaction to the news of Casement's execution than Spring-Rice had feared. If the story in some American papers on August 2nd—that the President had sent a plea for mercy—had been true, he pointed out two days later, it would have been serious; fortunately, he found, it had been a rumour. Apart from the fact that some of the Hearst newspapers had gone into 'mourning', there had been no immediate repercussions. A few days later, expressing his relief that the press had not gone overboard about Casement, he attributed their caution to the 'timely warnings' he had given; he had personally warned the Apostolic delegate about the risk to the Catholic Church of trying to make Casement into a martyr. In other countries, where the ambassadorial briefing had been less intensive, there were some manifestations of anger: Hardinge reported from San Sebastian that the Spanish Liberal newspapers in Spain had denounced the execution as cruel and impolitic, and the Catholic newspapers, as a martyr-dom. But Spanish opinion was not, at that time, of great concern to the British Government.

'They touch the lowest depths ...'
So Blackwell's prescription had worked, at least where it mattered. But it worked, as things turned out, only in the short term. Among the ballads which came on the Dublin streets soon afterwards, there was one which was to prove prophetic:

> O lordly Roger Casement,
>   you gave all a man could give
> That justice be not mocked at
>   and that liberty might live.
> But you hurt the high and mighty ones
>   in pocket and in pride
> And that is why they hated you,
>   and that is why you died.
>
> Aye, they stripped you of your honours
>   and they hounded you to death
> And their blood lust was not sated
>   as you gasped your dying breath
> They tried to foul your memory
>   as they burned your corpse with lime
> But God is not an Englishman
>   and truth will tell in time.

That Casement was buried in Pentonville, and that such ugly aspersions had been cast on his private character, were to be the subject of sporadic and often bitter controversy for the next fifty years.

The first intimation of trouble in store came to the poet Alfred Noyes, when he was about to give a lecture in the winter of 1916 in Philadelphia. Noyes was a professor of English Literature at Princeton, and in this capacity was employed by the British Government as a propagandist, a job which ordinarily he did with finesse, emphasising the essentially civilised nature of the allies, as compared to the Germans. But after he had seen the diaries—and, he was later careful to stress, after Casement's execution—he had included a paragraph about them in one of his articles. Denouncing the Irish rebels—who, 'beyond the shadow of doubt, did murder, ruthlessly, deliberately and indiscriminately, men, women and children'—Noyes went on to write:

And the chief leader of these rebels—I cannot print his own written confessions about himself, for they are filthy beyond all description. But I have seen and read them and they touch the lowest depths that human degradation has ever touched. Page after page of his diary would be an insult to a pig's trough to let the foul record touch it. The Irish will canonise these things at their own peril.

The article was published in a Philadelphia newspaper; and when Noyes was about to give his lecture there, a lady in the audience rose and denounced him, identifying herself as Casement's sister, Nina. Distraught as she was, Noyes was to recall, 'there was a strange irrational nobility shining through all her wild charges'. Nina's assumption, from her knowledge of her brother, was that the diaries must have been forged; and this became the commonly accepted view among the Irish-Americans, and in Ireland. For a variety of reasons, the theory seemed plausible; chief among them the fact that there had never been the least suspicion that Casement was a homosexual. As his cousin Gertrude Bannister—she had become Mrs. Sidney Parry —put it, Casement had many friends, 'both men and women, and *not one* of these friends ever had the smallest reason to doubt Roger's moral integrity'. Still more surprising, not one of his enemies—and he had had powerful ones—had cast doubt on his morals (the Foreign Office were in a position to offer some confirmation of the charge; but as, to do so, they would have had to recall the Christensen affair, they understandably kept silent).

Nor was it possible to protest that no British Government would have stooped to so vile a deception. If, as Austen Chamberlain admitted, they had published forged documents suggesting that the Germans were melting down the corpses of soldiers killed at the front to provide additional fat, they were unlikely to worry about forging a diary; and every Irishman knew how an earlier British Government had tried to exploit Pigott's forged letters to destroy Parnell. And—very damning it seemed, at the time—the man who had claimed to have discovered the diaries, Sir Basil Thomson,* himself fell under a cloud. Not merely did he give suspiciously different accounts of how they had been found; in 1925 he was arrested in Hyde Park for indecent behaviour with a woman whose profession was adequately indicated by her name on the charge sheet: Thelma de Lava. In spite of some influential witnesses to his character, he was convicted, and fined £5, a verdict upheld on appeal.

If the Irish Government had taken up the cause, the British Government might have felt it wise to allow the diaries to be inspected; but at the time of the negotiations which led up to the Treaty of 1921, they had been shown to Michael Collins by the Lord Chancellor, Birkenhead—as Sir Frederick Smith had become, fulfilling Casement's prophecy about the Unionist path leading to the Woolsack. Collins, who claimed to know Casement's handwriting, had been convinced they were genuine—a verdict which discouraged the first Free State Government, and its successors, from making formal representations. And to individual inquirers, the Home Office simply denied knowledge of the diaries' existence. In the late 1920s T. E. Lawrence contemplated writing a life of Casement—a project which won the Shaws' approval. 'As you say, he understood,' Shaw wrote to Gertrude Parry after Lawrence's death. 'I remember what a bound my heart gave when he said he would like to write about Roger. Perhaps he would have—who knows! But I think it was just a passing inspiration.' Perhaps it was; but the reason Lawrence gave to John Buchan for not going ahead with the idea was that he had been refused access to the diaries; and without them, he felt, a life of Casement could not be written.

The thesis that they had been faked was eventually documented by an Irish-American, William J. Maloney, in *The Forged Casement Diaries*, published in 1936. Although Maloney was too much in the grip of his own thesis to produce a balanced onslaught, his evidence looked damning; and he also had what appeared a reasonable hypothesis of how the forgery had been accomplished. Casement had told friends he had brought back a diary of Armando Normand's from the Putumayo, recording unnatural crimes. All that the forger would have had to do, therefore, was fuse them into Casement's own Putumayo

* He was knighted in 1919.

diary—either directly, or by manufacturing a new diary, forged in its entirety.

Maloney's thesis deeply moved Yeats. He wrote two poems on the theme, and read them to Joseph Hone, who was astonished at the ferocity of his feelings—so worked up did Yeats get that he had to have a glass of port to calm himself. One of these included the verse:

> Come, Alfred Noyes, come all the troop *
> That cried it far and wide
> Come from the forger and his desk
> Desert the perjurer's side

Noyes was provoked into writing a letter to the *Irish Press* (which had published the poems) explaining how he had come to be involved, admitting that he might have been deliberately misled in 1916, and suggesting that the only way to settle the issue would be to have the diaries examined by experts. But the Irish Government declined to intervene; and some sympathisers with Casement remained unconvinced by Maloney's theory—Bernard Shaw, for one, who could not believe that the people supposed to have been involved would have authorised such a deed. He had known F. E. Smith as 'the boldest and most unscrupulous political reactionary of his day', who had

notoriously committed the very offence with which Casement was charged, that of levying arms against the Crown. And he was not in the least put out by it. Later, he stepped brazenly and cynically down from the Woolsack into the City. He drank shamelessly. Yet he was an irresistibly likeable man. I never met anyone who knew him personally who disliked him; and I found it impossible to dislike him myself. As to Admiral Hall, there is no evidence in his record and no suggestion in his personality that he is a melodramatic villain. That these two men were capable of committing a diabolical fraud on public opinion to secure the conviction of a distinguished public servant of their own class, whose pardon would not have done them the slightest harm, is too improbable to be believed without overwhelming proof.

For a while, the forgery agitation died away; but it revived

* Later amended to: 'Come Tom and Dick, come all the troop'.

twenty years later following a book on Casement by H. O. Mackey, an Irish doctor, and an article in the *Spectator* by Sir William James, the biographer of Admiral Hall. The use to which Hall had put Casement's diaries, James argued, could be faulted; but surely there could no longer be serious doubt about their authenticity? A number of correspondents wrote to point out that they *did* doubt their authenticity and would continue to do so until the diaries were made available for inspection. In the House of Commons, Montgomery Hyde, Emrys Hughes and Hugh Delargy began to press the Government for information, and in May 1956 they secured an Adjournment Debate on the subject which, if it did nothing else, revealed how flimsy the Government's case was for continued concealment. The debate also roused Alfred Noyes, whose name had been dragged into it, to announce in a letter to *The Times* that he had been forced to the conclusion that the diaries were spurious (he was to document the reasons for his conversion in *The Accusing Ghost*). In 1956, too, René MacColl's biography of Casement was published; and the author's assumption—though he did not provide evidence to support it—that the diaries were genuine, kept the controversy alive.

MacColl, in fact—as he was eventually able to show—had been in possession of the required evidence; but he had not been permitted to disclose it. He had been shown typed copies of the 1903 and 1910 diaries, and the 1911 cash register, which had come into the possession of Peter Singleton-Gates in the early 1920s. Singleton-Gates had also seen the originals; and if, as he claimed, the transcripts were an accurate copy, that damaged the Normand theory, because in 1903 Casement had been in the Congo. In any case, he described homosexual episodes in London and Belfast; and Singleton-Gates was certain that they could not have been added later, as they were interspersed through the diary entries.

Still it seemed sensible to suspend final judgment until the diaries themselves were opened for inspection, and after the publication of *The Black Diaries*, by Singleton-Gates and Maurice Girodias, in 1959—based on the typed transcripts—the Home Secretary, R. A. Butler, announced that he would grant facilities for historians and other responsible persons to see the originals at the Public Record Office. Inspection confirmed that Singleton-Gate's recollection had been correct. Interpolation of homosexual material would not have been possible. There were plenty of comments added later; but these only pointed to the reason why Casement kept the diaries; as a reminder of times past. He liked to note pleasant recollections much as some readers like to make marginal comments in a library book. But much of the homosexual material was embodied in his day-by-day commentary. If the diaries had been forged, therefore, they must have been forged in their entirety; and that would have taken even the most accomplished forger years to complete.

Allowing the diaries to be inspected did not end the controversy. After seeing them Professor Roger MacHugh, of the National University of Ireland, wrote an article for the magazine *Threshold* restating the case that they had been forged. And that case, as presented, still looks very strong. How could Casement have lived his double life in the Putumayo, particularly on that second visit, without its being noticed by friends — such as Dr. H. S. Dickey, who accompanied him on the river steamer, and was with him in Iquitos? Still more baffling, why was he not trapped by Arana's men? * And the whole story of the finding of the diaries, their use by the Home Office, and their subsequent suppression, reeked of foul play on the part of the authorities. Nevertheless, the case against the forgery theory remains unshaken. No person or persons, in their right mind, would have gone to so much trouble and expense to damn a traitor, when a single diary would have sufficed. To ask the forger to fake the other two diaries and the cash register (and if one was forged, all of them were) would have been simply to ask for detection, because a single mistake in any of them would have destroyed the whole ugly enterprise. Besides, where could the money have been found? Government servants may sometimes be unscrupulous, but they are always tight-fisted. Why should they pay a forger to do more than was strictly necessary for the immediate requirements?

---

* Richard West, in his biography of Brazza, notes a curious parallel between Casement and André Gide (he was also to publish a disturbing indictment of what was happening in the Congo on the French side of the border): 'Both men were practising, even rapacious homosexuals. Both men were conducting investigations that would embarrass, to say the least, certain important commercial interests which laid them open to disgrace or to being blackmailed into silence.' West could only hazard the guess that Gide's servants liked him, and therefore kept his secret.

'The love God made ...'

Even allowing for an element of fantasy, then—and there are many indications of that—Casement was a practising homosexual. Did it affect his career?

There is a passage in Proust's *Remembrance of Things Past*, on the subject of the Baron de Charlus, which is relevant—in spite of the two men's dissimilarity:

> He belonged to that race of beings, less paradoxical than they appear, whose ideal is manly simply because their temperament is feminine, and who in their life resemble in appearance only the rest of men; there where each of us carries, inscribed in those eyes through which he beholds everything in the universe, a human outline engraved on the surface of the pupil, for them it is that not of a nymph but of a youth. Race upon which a curse weighs, and which must live amid falsehood and perjury, because it knows the world to regard as a punishable and a scandalous, as an inadmissible thing, its desire, that which constitutes for every human creature the greatest happiness in life; which must deny its God, since even Christians, when at the bar of justice they appear and are arraigned, must before Christ and in His Name defend themselves, as from a calumny, from a charge of what to them is life itself ... lovers from whom is always precluded the possibility of that love the hope of which gives them the strength to endure so many risks and so much loneliness, since they fall in love with precisely that type of man who has nothing feminine about him, who is not an invert and consequently cannot love them in return; with the result that their desire would be forever insatiable did not their money procure for them real men, and their imagination ends by making them take for real men the inverts to whom they had prostituted themselves.

Casement could have subscribed to that commentary—except, perhaps, to the suggestion that he would have to deny his God. He expressed his view about that in a poem:

> No human hand to steal to mine
> No loving eye to answering shine,

Earth's cruel heart of dust alone
To give me breath and strength to groan.

I look beyond the stricken sky
Where sunset paints its hopeless lie
That way the flaming angel went
That sought by pride love's battlement.

I sought by love alone to go
Where God had writ an awful no
Pride gave a guilty God to hell
I have no pride—by love I fell.

Love took me by the heart at birth
And wrought out from its common earth—
With soul at his own skill aghast—
A furnace my own breath should blast.

Why this was done I cannot tell
The mystery is inscrutable
I only know I pay the cost
With heart and soul and honour lost.

I only know tis death to give
My love; yet loveless can I live?
I only know I cannot die
And leave this love God made, not I.

God made this love; there let it rest
Perchance it needs a riven breast
To heavenly eyes the scheme to show
My broken heart must never know.

When he met his Creator, clearly, Casement did not propose
to accept that the fault lay all on one side.

In one respect, Casement was luckier than Charlus—or Oscar
Wilde. He had the opportunity to meet Indian youths whom he
could love in a way that was difficult to do in Europe. A passage
in a recent work of fiction comes close to expressing what he
felt: a description by James Steede, the central figure in Robin
Maugham's novel *The Link*:

I think I was more attracted to the Indians than to any other people I met during these days. I was astonished by their beauty, I marvelled at their smooth skins gleaming like polished mahogany, and their graceful slender limbs which concealed an immense strength, and their strange mixture of gentleness and virility. Their desire, I found with some of them, was as unimpeded by shame as was my own, and when I found one who seemed fond of me, I only wished we could converse in words as fluently as we made love, so I could form a permanent friendship with him. But when the session came to an end we would smile, rather helplessly, sadly even, and then we would part.

Casement, too, craved to love, and to be loved. And if he could have come to terms with his homosexuality, his development might have been very different. But he could not do so. Perhaps his feelings were ambivalent. According to Gertrude Bannister, as a youth he had fallen in love with another cousin of his, Eva Lampier; and later, he had expressed a desire for marriage, but said that he felt he could not condemn any woman to the life his Bannister aunt had had to live, with her husband away in West Africa for three or four years at a time. Whatever the reasons, he regarded homosexuality as an affliction; for the individual, unfortunate, and for the community, unhealthy (a term he actually used, criticising the proposal to bring Chinese labour to South Africa on the ground that Chinamen were known to have views on sex 'not in favour in Europe since the days of Greece and Rome').

It must have been continually galling for a man of his passionate nature to be unable to disclose his feelings to his closest friends. To make it all the more difficult, the devotion he inspired in them was inextricably linked, in their minds, with the assumption of his utter integrity. While he was in prison, a letter reached him from a woman he had known as a girl, thirty years earlier, addressed to 'my dearly loved friend of long ago', saying she knew that 'that dear great generous heart of yours would prompt you only to deeds of good intent'. Over and over again such tributes recur. 'I am quite sure,' Lady ffrench wrote of him, 'that even in his most condemned actions, he had the highest motives for what he did. He saw things like that, and he could not see them otherwise. Moreover, unlike most idealists he was prepared to sacrifice himself.' To Nevinson, he was 'one of the most courteous, generous and fine-spirited men I have known ... a man of sensitive imagination and conspicuous courage, utterly regardless of self-interest'. In his dedication to *Casement's Last Adventure*, Monteith described him as 'the man who eliminated self'. Nobody who ever met him, his biographer Dennis Gwynn wrote, could 'fail to be impressed by his transcendent sincerity and idealism'; and he quoted one of Casement's Congo colleagues as having called him a man who 'always represented what is meant by the words honour and courage'. 'I have known no one who was more single-minded, more unselfishly devoted to the causes he believed in.' Bulmer Hobson wrote:

> I have known no one who was so stirred at the thought of injustice and wrong, whether it was in Africa, America or Ireland. I have not met his equal for courtesy or kindliness or generosity ... I do not expect to meet his like again.

All those who knew Roger Casement, Stephen Gwynn claimed in the entry he wrote on him for the *Dictionary of National Biography*, 'knew him to be honourable and chivalrous'. Writing in the *Nation* after Casement had been sentenced to death, Robert Lynd described him as 'one of the least self-seeking and most open-handed of men—a man who has lived not for his career, but for the liberation of those who are oppressed and poor and enslaved ... Even those who, like myself, have been diametrically opposed to his recent policy, can never lose our admiration and affection for everything in him that was noble and compassionate.'

All these men and women—and others who had known him even better; Edmund Morel, Alice Green, Gertrude Bannister—were unaware that Casement was homosexual. Many of them remained convinced to the end of their lives that it was inconceivable. And as Proust observed, in the passage on Charlus, such men must in fact be

> friends without friendships, despite all those which their charm, frequently recognised, inspires and their hearts, often generous, would gladly feel; for can we describe as friendships those relations which flourish only by virtue of a lie, and

from which the first outburst of confidence and sincerity in which they might be tempted to indulge would make them be expelled with disgust?

The Foreign Office

Nor was it simply the need to conceal his homosexuality that fragmented Casement's personality. Outside forces were also at work on him, chief among them his need, if he was to do what he wanted to do, to remain a member of the Consular Service and, as such, an appendage of the Foreign Office.

He had two reasons for hating the Foreign Office; one being its almost paranoid anti-German attitude. In *Diplomacy Old and New* George Young—who was in the Washington embassy when Casement came through in 1912, but who resigned from the Foreign Service during the war—was to describe how it had functioned as a self-perpetuating oligarchy, resistant to democratic ideas, and dictating to the Government (rather than vice-versa), the policy of encirclement of Germany, through the alliances with France and Tsarist Russia. Casement, like Morel, believed this policy could only precipitate the conflict which it was designed to avoid; and, years later, Lord Grey was to admit that it had. 'The lesson of history,' he conceded in his retirement, 'is plain. It is that no enduring security can be found in competing armaments and in separate alliances; there is no security for any Power unless it be security in which its neighbours have an equal share.' This was precisely what Casement had pleaded for, in his articles and letters on the international situation in the years immediately before the war.

But even more destructive of Casement's confidence in his employers was that their concern was always with government, rather than with people. Casement could not be a good civil servant because, as Morel put it, 'the official was sunk in the man. The man was ablaze with passionate pity for the helpless.' Bulmer Hobson agreed; Casement, he recalled, 'felt the tortures and the wrongs inflicted on a primitive and distant people as keenly as if they had been inflicted on his own'. Yet only by working for the Foreign Office could he hope to do anything for the natives who were being tortured and wronged. It was consequently agonising, feeling as he did, to have to work for Lansdowne, or Grey. How little Grey cared about the Congo or the Putumayo can be gauged from his autobiography. He mentioned them only in passing, whereas the trivial but tortuous diplomatic manoeuvres which so absorbed him were chronicled in loving detail.

Working for the Foreign Office also helped indirectly to preserve a side of Casement's character which it would have been healthier for him to reject—or at least to reassess. He had been brought up to believe that he was a gentleman, and that the standards which gentlemen of his class accepted ought to regulate his behaviour; and in this belief he never wavered. 'The Irishman,' he once wrote, with evident pride, 'whether he be a peasant, a farm labourer, however low in the process of Anglicisation he has sunk, is still in imagination, if not always in manner, a gentleman. The Englishman is a gentleman by chance, by force of circumstances, by luck of birth, or some rare opportunity of early fellowship. The Irishman is a gentleman by instinct.' Bernard Shaw agreed: an Irishman, he remarked, could be a gentleman, 'a species now extinct in England'. But he added, 'and nobody a penny the worse'; and he was not just being facetious. The 'quality', as they liked to be called, had many endearing traits, exemplified in Major Sinclair Yeats, the Irish R.M.; but their morality had its eccentric side. Their seven deadly sins—H. M. Pim observed in 1915—were 'bad form, poverty, patriotism, activity, nationality, curiosity and Popery' (the objections to patriotism and nationality being to the Irish versions). Casement rejected all these except one; 'bad form', for him, remained a deadly sin. He continued to believe there were gentlemen, and there were others—who, like Gielgud, must be snubbed if they tried to behave as his equal. One of his poems, revealingly entitled 'To one who loved beneath him', began

> Come up beside me, then, and be as one
> Who hath a right to lean upon my heart

It was fantasy; none but a gentleman could have had that right. But circumstances precluded gentlemen from being allowed to stake a claim: the nearest Casement came to a Lord Alfred Douglas was the wretched Adler Christensen.

To maintain his sanity, Casement had two resources, when his work did not absorb him. One was his poetry. In it he was able, up to a point, to release his feelings; as in his 'Quo Vadis'?

> Is it never to cease, the anguish? Is it never to end, the toil
> Of a heart that is filled with longing and maketh the soul its
>   spoil?
> Of a hunger for things unholy, we loathe while we still prefer?
> For the Gods of good die slowly, and dying, they still demur.

The construction might be tortuous, and the language archaic, but the feeling often burst through; and the love:

> O, what cares love for a wounded breast?
> Love shows his own, with a broader scar
> 'Tis only those who have loved the best
> Can say where the wounds of loving are.

'If poetry comes out of intensity of vision,' Padraic Colum felt, 'Roger Casement was potentially a great poet'.

His other resource was religion; but here he was blocked, until the very end of his life. Tha Protestantism of his childhood was no good to him; as he recalled in Pentonville, it was too cold. And the simplicity of the missionaries' faith, though it attracted him in the Congo, lost its hold on him after he left. Then, in Ireland, he was repelled by the prevailing political attitude in the Catholic Church, and by the tameness with which it was accepted. 'The Irish Catholic, man for man,' he wrote to Bulmer Hobson in 1909, 'is a poor crawling coward as a rule. Afraid of his miserable soul and fearing the Priest like the Devil. . . .' Freedom could come to Ireland, he thought, 'only through Irish Protestants, because they are not afraid of any Bogey'; a view he was often to reiterate in 1914. It was not until he reached Germany that he could begin to strip Catholicism of its unwelcome political and social accretions; and by then, it was too late to save him from black despair. Only in his last days did it provide him with serenity.

Disintegration

In his article on the forgery issue, Professor MacHugh observed that the impression 'of a deranged man in a psychopathic state' given by the later diaries is inconsistent with the contemporary record of Casement's character. But in fact, the diaries help to explain why Casement was so continually afflicted by illness, mental and physical.

Homosexuals, Richard Krafft-Ebing claimed in his *Psycho-pathia Sexualis*, published in 1886, were in his experience almost always neuropathic, torn as they were between the impulse they felt towards persons of their own sex which was frequently abnormally intense, and their fear of public opinion and the law.

> Before them lies mental despair—even insanity and suicide— at the very least, nervous disease; behind them shame, loss of position, etc. It cannot be doubted that under these cir- cumstances, states of stress and compulsion may be created by an unfortunate natural disposition and constitution. Society and the law should understand and appreciate these facts. The former should pity, and not despise, these unfor- tunates; the latter must cease to punish them.

In Casement's time there was still no sign of understanding; and this helps to account for the gradual disintegration of his personality. In his thirties, he was already being diagnosed as what in those days was termed as a neurasthenic; and by the time he was in his forties, the evidence suggests that he was what would now be called a manic depressive. At times, he was literally cracked.

CHAPTER TWO

ACHIEVEMENT

The fact that Casement was so fragmented a character, though, only makes his achievement more remarkable. It is not given to many men, outside the ranks of statesmen, to become internationally celebrated on three separate occasions during their lives, as he did; and his campaigns on behalf of the natives in the Congo and the Putumayo moved public opinion to the point when Governments actually had to treat it with respect. He 'inoculated the diplomacy of this country with a moral toxin', Morel felt; 'Historians will cherish these occasions as the only two in which British diplomacy rose above the commonplace'.

The Congo

Casement himself was more cautious about his own achievement. 'I made awful mistakes'—he wrote in his last letter to Dick Morten—

> and did heaps of things wrong, confused much, and failed at much—but I very near came to doing some big things ... on the Congo and elsewhere. It was only a shadow they tried on June 26; the real man was gone. The best thing was the Congo, because there was more against me there and far cleverer rascals than the Putumayo ruffians.

Considering that Casement's report on the Congo was accepted by Leopold's own Commission, and began the process by which Leopold was eventually forced to give up his Empire, it might be thought that Casement was being unnecessarily modest. But as René MacColl was interested to find, working on his biography forty years after his death, there were apparently knowledgeable people who denied Casement even that limited amount of credit; and to this day, doubt is sometimes cast on the reliability of his Congo testimony.

It can be traced back to the dispute between the Belgian and

British Governments over the annexation of the Congo. The Belgians, anxious to have freedom of action there, wanted to minimise the evils of the system, and therefore tended to argue, and eventually to believe, that British criticism had been prejudiced. Naturally Casement's trial and execution was welcomed by Leopold's apologists; as was the news, a few months later, that Morel had been given a prison sentence (he had sent copies of a pamphlet criticising the Tzarist regime to Romain Rolland in Switzerland, thereby breaking a wartime regulation; anybody else could have been expected to get off with a caution, or at worst a fine, but Morel, known as a critic of the Government for the policies which had led to war with Germany, was given six months). 'We have learned the worth of the two instigators of this movement,' an apologist for Leopold, O. Louwers, claimed; 'the first, Casement, has been hanged well and high for treason in the service of Germany. The second, Morel, cast into prison whither he was brought by his defeatism, his over-enthusiasm for Germany. These men were undoubtedly the devoted servants of the German cause. Under cover of a civilising campaign they were working in her interests.' In the memorandum which was drawn up for the guidance of the Belgian delegates to the Versailles Peace Conference, they were told that the line they should take was that although the Congo regime had been 'not perhaps perfect', it had much to its credit; and as the Germanophilia of Casement and Morel had since come to light, they need not be taken seriously.

After the war, Morel courageously fought his way back into public life. He defeated Churchill in a by-election in 1922; and the following year, in A. J. P. Taylor's estimation, would have become Foreign Secretary in the first Labour Government, if Ramsay MacDonald had not been so interested in foreign affairs himself; his was 'the only name big enough to keep out E. D. Morel'. But Morel had been so horrified at the disclosures of Casement's homosexuality that he could not bring himself to finish the *History of the Congo Reform Association*, with its vindication of Casement's work; and Morel's biographer, Cocks, in his anxiety not to allow Morel to be defiled, almost achieved the remarkable feat of avoiding all reference to Casement; he mentioned the Congo Report, but not the two men's friendship. The belief lingered that Morel and Casement had been acting for Germany: Tim Healy still accepted it in 1928; and Pierre Daye, in a biography of Leopold published in Paris in 1934, claimed that the fact that Casement had been hanged, and Morel gaoled, was enough 'to show the moral worth of the two principal architects of the anti-Congo campaign'. (By the same token, Pierre Daye's moral worth might be assessed from the fact he was sentenced to death *in absentia* for collaboration with the Germans during the Second World War.)

More serious historians have rejected this interpretation—from the anthropologist Sir Arthur Berriedale Keith, shortly after the end of the First World War, to Robert Cornevin, in his history of the Congo published in Paris in 1963. But for those who disapprove of Casement on political or moral grounds, the temptation has inevitably been to believe the worst of him. His investigation of the Congo was 'far too brief and cursory for so important a matter', René MacColl was told; 'the whole tone and tenor of his subsequent report was wildly exaggerated and based on highly debatable evidence'—criticisms which, MacColl emphasised, were made to him not by Belgians, but by 'reputable British officials'. And in 1962 they were echoed in George Martelli's *Leopold to Lumumba*, which spoke of 'the patent bias of much of the Report' and 'the holes which were afterwards picked in it'. Martelli actually claimed that Leopold had been wronged; 'his intentions, even when misguided, were always public-spirited'.

What Leopold's intentions really were has remained a fruitful source of speculation. The interpretations range from Cecil Rhodes's awed comment, after he met Leopold, 'Satan! I tell you that man is Satan!' to Professor Jean Stenger's suggestion that although Leopold was obsessed with money, it was 'not with his own fortune, but with the embellishment of his country'. Whatever Leopold's motives, though, it is clear from Stengers's patient unravelling of his serpentine financial dealings, and from Neal Ascherson's biography, that he was one of the most skilful embezzlers in history; that he systematically swindled his own countrymen, to obtain the funds with which he could pursue his dream of a great Central African Empire, controlling the Upper Nile as well as the Congo; and that he cold-bloodedly sacrificed the Congo natives for that purpose. It was Casement who brought the cruelty involved in making this human sacrifice to the world's attention; and it was Casement who inspired Morel to set up the organisation which even-

ually prised the Congo from Leopold's grasp. It took time; even
after annexation, the system remained, though in a modified
form. The Congo was never to come near to matching the
original Berlin specifications. But this was not Casement's fault.
He had warned what was likely to happen, if the system was not
changed. And half a century later, the Belgians were to suffer the
fate he had predicted.*

In one respect, though, it seems probable that Casement did
more for the African natives than anybody, including himself,
realised. In 1907 the British colonial administrations in West
Africa refused to allow Lever Brothers to set up a plantation
system to produce palm oil; and again, in 1920. As the Governor
of Nigeria put it in 1926, British colonial policy was not to
develop the land for the benefit of Britain, but to aim primarily
'at the development of the agricultural resources of these countries through the agency of their indigenous populations'. The
economic development as a consequence was slower, in British
colonies; but the natives suffered far less from exploitation. And
for this, the shock administered by Casement's Report on the
Congo must have had some responsibility.

Putumayo

The results of Casement's Putumayo campaign, were less striking. They were also to be more ephemeral. Tizon left the Putumayo in 1913, and three years later—a few days after
Casement's execution—the Indians in the Athens section of the
Putumayo rebelled, killing thirteen of the company's white employees. According to the missionary Father Sanbrook, they
had been goaded to desperation by ill-treatment,

> though the wholesale crimes of former times have disappeared
> —the shootings, tortures and all the villainy Casement ex-
> posed—still the Indian has been constantly punished with
> whips, chains, kicks and stocks for shortage of rubber. Occa-
> sional cases of death have also taken place, both on the part
> of certain whites, but chiefly through the native 'muchachos'.

* And, as Richard West has put it, 'The present rulers of Africa are
the heirs not of Brazza but of Leopold. They will not easily be removed
because they command wealth greater than Leopold's and an even more
servile pack of journalists and race relations men.'

And Whites also have simply played havoc with the nativ
women.

There could be no real change so long as Arana and Zumaeta
remained in charge—and the fact that Zumaeta was elected
Mayor of Iquitos in 1914 showed how effectively in charge they
remained. In 1923, when a survey of the Upper Amazon was
carried out by a United States Government-sponsored commission, its members reported that they had not found it necessary
to visit the Putumayo because 'stories of former "atrocities"
are now greatly discounted by the calmer and more unprejudiced judgment of those who were actually familiar with the
conditions'. The source of the 'calmer and more unprejudiced
judgment' was revealed in the commission's expression of their
gratitude to an Iquitos citizen 'whose kindness they took pleasure in acknowledging'—Julio César Arana, by that time Senator
for the Loreto Province.*

Although the use of plantations began to make it less profitable to collect wild rubber, the Amazon natives continued to be
exploited by forced labour—slavery in all but name, because the
alternative, wherever a white individual or company controlled
the region, was starvation. Leonard Clark, an American who
explored the region in the late 1940s, arrived there assuming
that as the companies must have reformed, conditions would
have changed since Casement's time: 'they did not reform', he
found; 'the slave conditions have not changed'. Even the missionaries had been sucked into the slave trade. And a report to
the World Council of Churches in 1970 revealed that the arrival
of settlers from Colombia, staking out extensive claims to what
had been tribal Amazon territory, employing forced labour to
clear the land and using army units to enforce 'discipline', had
led many natives to try to escape by going deeper into the
jungle, where they were dying from malnutrition and disease.

At most, then, Casement's visit to the Putumayo secured
only some temporary relief for the natives there. Following the
report of Roberts's Select Committee, its recommendations
were embodied in a circular sent to British Consuls in all countries where there was any possibility of British firms following
the same course as the Peruvian Amazon Company; but this was
more for the protection of the Foreign Office than of the natives.

* He lived on in Lima until 1952, dying at the age of eighty-eight.

And although, again, Casement could hardly be blamed for having failed to rouse Grey to more effective action, his handling of the Putumayo campaign was less skilful than his Congo effort. Partly this was because he had no Morel to take up the cause. But it was also because he had tended to forget the importance of the lesson he had endlessly taught: that what mattered was not the individuals who were responsible for the treatment of the natives, but the system which they operated —or which operated them.

For years past, Socialist writers had condemned colonialism for its pretence that it was bringing civilisation to primitive peoples, when in fact it was exploiting them for profit. But Casement was the first Foreign Service official to document at first hand the way in which slavery could be reintroduced under the guise of *laissez faire* capitalism, wherever the capitalists were able to secure a monopoly of the land. If he had gone ahead with the project he outlined in 1913, the 'movement of human liberation'—or, better still, if he had persuaded Morel to take it up—he might have shown just how destructive the combination of land monopoly and economic control could be. But he had not read the signs so clearly, in the Putumayo; and then Ireland distracted him.

Ireland

There remains the question what Casement did for his country; an achievement which has only recently come to be better appreciated.

For a time, his reputation suffered because his part in 1916 was misunderstood not only by the British, who continued to regard him as a traitor seduced by German gold, but also by the Irish. In a letter to Laurence de Lacy, written shortly before the date set for execution, John Devoy explained how the rising had suffered from the discovery, by United States Intelligence, following a raid on the German embassy, of the plans for the arms ship:

> Casement did the rest. He landed on Friday and sent a message to MacNeill to stop it; that it was hopeless etc. MacNeill got it on Saturday and issued his countermand.

Devoy went on to denounce Casement for his 'utter impractica-
bility ... we knew he would meddle in his honest but visionary
way to such an extent as to spoil things, but we did not dream
that he would ruin everything as he has done'. And although in
his memoirs he was to relent sufficiently to call Casement 'one
of the most single-minded of Ireland's patriot heroes', he continued
to believe that his intervention had spoiled the chances
of the rising's military success.

Devoy was mistaken; Casement's message did not in fact
reach MacNeill, and he was not responsible for the counter-
mand order, except in so far as MacNeill was influenced to make
it by the news that he had been captured. But the fact that the
rising went ahead without German assistance inevitably meant
that the men who were executed for their part in it became the
martyrs; although being hanged for treason gave him a place
in the Pantheon, it was not with the others. There was even
some disposition to dismiss his work in Germany—because of
the failure of the Irish Brigade. Almost the entire Brigade,
according to Sir Wyndham Childs, claimed to have joined it
only in the hope of securing better treatment—and he felt they
were telling the truth; only one of them, apparently, linked up
with *Sinn Fein* later—Timothy Quinlisk, whom Casement had
mistrusted, and who turned out to be working for the British
authorities (he was executed, on the orders of Michael Collins).
Might it not be—Richard Dawson suggested in his *Red Terror
and Green*—that Casement really was a German agent; that he
had been sent to organise the Volunteers in the hope they would
pin British troops down in Ireland? What with the possibility,
too, that the black diaries were his, he was understandably set
apart; admired for his life's work, more than for what he had
done for Ireland. Such was the Casement of Eimar O'Duffy's
historical novel *The Wasted Island*, his eyes 'sad with memories
of unforgettable horrors witnessed in the forests of the Congo
and Putumayo'.

But there were always Irish writers who perceived that Casement was not an isolated, eccentric figure on the fringes of the
national movement. 'There now steps upon our stage a man who
is, perhaps, its most tragic figure,' Shaw Desmond wrote in his
study of *Sinn Fein* in 1923. 'Look well on this man, because he
carries in himself the whole story of Ireland. Learn the secret of
this man, and you have learnt the secret of Ireland.' Later Des-

mond Ryan was to put Casement's work in a clearer perspective.
What has still not had full recognition, though, is the influence
which Casement exerted on the national movement from the
time he returned from the Congo, in 1904. He provided funds,
sympathy, enthusiasm, at a time when the men and women
working in the national movement were much in need of them;
and from genuine love, not from a superfluity of wealth seeking
an easy outlet. In return, he inspired love. Only rarely was there
a querulous reaction—such as A.E.'s remark that he was 'dubious about the nationality of men who cannot live in Ireland,
but must always be inventing grandiose schemes for us at the
other end of the earth'. In general he won remarkable devotion.
He was an enthusiast, but fired by his determination to learn,
rather than to dominate. And he was not, as such tyros can be,
embarrassingly naive. On the contrary, his assessments of the
Gaelic League and *Sinn Fein* were perceptive. He was the first,
too, to appreciate the real significance of the Ulster Volunteers,
and insist they should be regarded as a model, not as a threat.
More than any other man, he was responsible for the rapid
recruitment of the Irish Volunteers in the early months of 1914.
And it was he who laid the plans, and secured the funds, for
the arms landed in 1914, without which the Easter Rising could
hardly have taken place.

As things turned out, it was a mistake for Casement to go to
Germany, after the outbreak of war—if for no other reason
than that Germany was not going to win it. And he made further
mistakes while he was there. Nevertheless, what he did was not
treasonable, except in the sense that what William Wallace—
and the American revolutionaries—did was treasonable. The
closest parallel is with Thomas Masaryk, who was being lionised
by the allies at the same time that 'the pitiable Casement', as
he referred to him, was awaiting death. How close it is can be
judged from a passage in Wickham Steed's introduction to
Masaryk's memoirs, which Maloney used to introduce his own
book on the diaries.

To Masaryk and to the Czechs, the name 'Austria' meant
every device that could kill the soul of a people, corrupt it
with a modicum of well-being, deprive it of freedom of conscience and thought, undermine its sturdiness, sap its stead-
fastness, and turn it from the pursuit of its ideal. Since the

Hapsburgs with their army, their Church, their police and their bureaucracy were the living embodiment of this system, Masaryk after long hesitation turned against them and opposed them in the name of every tradition, conviction and principle he held dear. He knew the dimensions of the venture ... it would mean a choice between a Hapsburg gallows and lifelong exile.

Like Masaryk, Casement turned against the country to which he had given his allegiance because he felt that his own people were being stifled, body and soul; a process which he likened to the way in which the *Sipo Matador*, an Amazon fig vine, destroyed the tree to which it attached itself. According to the naturalist H. W. Bates, the vine first spread its mould over one side of the tree ('the Pale!', Casement commented) until the flow of sap ceased; 'the strange spectacle then remains of the selfish parasite clasping in its arms the lifeless and decaying body of its victim, which had been a help to its own growth.' It had been the gradual realisation that the English, sincerely believing that they were sustaining poor Ireland, were incapable of admitting to themselves that they were arresting her development, which compelled him first to become a separatist, and then to seek Germany's help to secure that separation.

In this, as Shaw insisted, Casement was being logical. But it left the impression that he was being treacherous—as a convert usually does, in the period when his loyalties are divided; and the violence with which he expressed his anti-English feelings has continued to lend colour to the allegation that his Irish nationalism developed out of pique at his treatment by the Foreign Office. 'I do not believe that patriotism was his primary motive in joining the nationalist movement,' MacColl asserted. 'I consider it was due to wounded vanity.' But MacColl, who as he admitted knew little about the Irish background, was under the mistaken impression that his vanity was wounded at being snubbed by 'the elegant professionals of the Foreign Office' because he was 'only a poor boy from Antrim, who had gone to the wrong sort of schools'. Boys of Casement's background from Antrim were not, and are not, impressed by Englishmen who had been to the right sort of school; from the moment he joined the Foreign Service he regarded them with contempt. Inevitably his growing nationalism was fanned by his irritation with them;

but it was always there—in his childhood, as his Bannister cousins recalled; in his early verses; in his Congo days, as Puleston testified—the 'fatal disease', Birrell described it, 'deep buried in certain Irish men and women—Casements, Greens, Devoys, Wolfe Tones'. And by the time he went to South America, it was indeed a disease; an obsession, disturbing even those who most admired him, like H. L. Mason, who worked with him, and thought he had 'only one serious fault . . . a fanatical view of the Irish situation amounting to mania, so that his friends most carefully avoided ever mentioning the subject'.

Musing over the leaders of 1916, Yeats asked,

> And what if excess of love
> Bewildered them till they died?

—a painfully apt diagnosis of Casement. But at least he had the consolation, denied to the others, of living long enough to know that they had achieved what they had set out to do. 'Irishmen!', he wrote in his last message, the day before he was hanged,

> live unselfishly and die bravely for Ireland, as the men of 1916 have done, and no power of man nor Empire of Gold can withhold freedom. Ireland alone went forth to assail evil, as David, Goliath; unarmed, save with a pebble; and she has slain, I pray to God, the power and boast and pride of Empire. That is the achievement of the boys of 1916, and on it the living shall build with a sterner purpose and bring it to a greater end.

What the living eventually built owes something to Casement's example, and something to his ideas. After his death, his influence lived on in the hearts of those whom he had impressed (de Valera named a son, born a few months later, after him: Griffith kept his photograph, which British troops who came to arrest him in 1920 seized as evidence against him), and their policies. Almost by accident, *Sinn Fein* found itself the beneficiary of the Easter Rising (or the authorities' mishandling of the situation); militant nationalism united under the *Sinn Fein* banner, and in 1918 swept the old constitutional Irish Party aside. And *Sinn Fein* did not live on in name alone. The policies which Griffith had formulated (though he had hoped to avoid force in introducing them), and which Casement had helped to popularise, were accepted. Westminster was boycotted; the elected *Sinn Fein* M.P.s set up an assembly of their own in Ireland; a *Sinn Fein* administration and judiciary were established; and by 1920 they were effectively in control of many areas. '*Sinn Fein* rules the County'; a friend of Walter Long's wrote to tell him from Limerick, 'and rules it admirably.' By the following year, Tim Healy was conceding that 'the main fact strikes you in the face; that the *Sinn Feiners* won in three years what we did not win in forty'.

Unlike many of the men in 1916, Casement had never wavered in his belief in *Sinn Fein*; and he himself provided some of the policies which it was to adopt. According to Padraic Colum in his biography of Griffith, the decision to approach the Versailles Conference for recognition stemmed from Casement's proposals for an independent neutral Ireland; and they were brought up again by Griffith in the negotiations leading up to the treaty of 1921—only to be rejected by Lloyd George, on the ground that 'neutrality repudiates association'. De Valera, too, took up an idea of Casement's, that Britain should apply a kind of Monroe Doctrine to Ireland, allowing Ireland to be categorised as a neutral country, as Cuba was. In 1939 he felt confident enough to take the risk of declaring Ireland neutral, even without such a guarantee; and in 1948 Bernard Shaw, in the last pronouncement he made on the Irish question, recalled that 'such independence was Casement's aim'. Shaw feared that Ireland's neutrality would not be respected; but as the threat of a third world war receded, her freedom from military alliances actually enabled her to enjoy a new role as a bridge between the western powers and the colonies, acquiring nationhood, at the United Nations and elsewhere—a development which would have given Casement much satisfaction.

Glasnevin   *1914*

Casement could hardly have predicted what was eventually going to happen in his loved Ulster. But he came nearer to grasping the essential point, sadly missed by the leaders of the new Ireland after 1921, that if Ireland was ever to be united, it could only be by winning the trust of the Ulster Protestants. Eventu-

ally de Valera, whose own attitude to the North had been equivocal—he thought force would be morally justified, to restore
unity, though he admitted that it was impracticable to apply it
—recognised this contribution, when Casement's remains were
at last returned to Ireland.

After his execution, Professor Morgan had made formal application to the Home Secretary on Gertrude Bannister's behalf
that the body should be handed over for private burial. The
Home Office refused—which prompted Eva Gore-Booth to
write:

> No cairn-shaped mound on a high windy hill
> With Irish earth the hero's heart enfolds
> But a burning grave at Pentonville
> The broken heart of Ireland holds.

For the next half century, alongside the campaign to get at the
truth about the diaries, sporadic efforts were made to secure
the release of the remains—by individuals like Nevinson; by
groups like the Roger Casement Committee, which functioned
for a time in the mid-1930s; and by the Irish Government,
which on this issue had no inhibitions. When Churchill explained
to de Valera in 1953 that the law on the subject was 'specific
and binding', and that in any case 'we should avoid the risk of
reviving old controversies and reawakening the bitter memories
of old differences', de Valera replied that those bitter memories
would continue to be revived so long as Casement's body lay
within prison walls. They often were, until Harold Wilson decided in 1964—Casement's centenary year—that though the
law might be specific, it need not be binding. On February 23rd,
1965, the remains were returned to Ireland.

By that time, the mystique of 1916 was beginning to fade;
and although the press made the most of the occasion—'not
since the return of the remains of O'Donovan Rossa', the *Cork
Examiner* claimed, 'have there been such stirrings of melancholy pride'—there was some doubt what the public reaction
would be, and some flippancy: a popular rumour was that the
remains were not Casement's, but Crippen's. In the event the
cynics were confounded. Thousands of men and women filed past
the coffin as it lay in state at Arbour Hill; and crowds lined the
streets when it was borne to the Pro-Cathedral. That, ad-

mittedly, was on a sunny Sunday afternoon. The next day, when it was brought to Glasnevin cemetery, it was bitterly cold, with showers of sleet and snow. But still the silent crowds turned out, along the route.   •

De Valera, by this time President of the Republic of Ireland, was eighty-two years old, and he had been unwell. On the morning of the funeral, he was told that as he had been diagnosed as suffering from jaundice, he should not attend it. He insisted that he must. In that case, he was told, at least he should keep his head covered. 'Casement,' he replied, 'deserves better than that.' At the graveside, he delivered the funeral oration. When the Irish Volunteers were about to be released in 1917, he recalled, they had been sent for a day or two to Pentonville; he and MacNeill and a few others had sought out Casement's grave there, to pray beside it. He went on to praise Casement's services to the national movement, and to the Irish language; and then reminded his listeners of his background:

> Casement was of Ulster stock and he loved the Province of Ulster particularly, although he loved every inch of this country. He loved the Province of Ulster because of the part the people of Ulster had played throughout Ireland's history; and he loved it, also, because he knew that each one of us, next to our own native province, loves that province best.
>
> And as we stand here, each one of us will resolve that we shall do everything to work so that the people of that province and ourselves may be united in co-operation, that we will all be vying with each other in loving this land for which so many sacrifices have been made throughout the centuries.

Casement had made much the same point in his speech from the dock.

> We aimed at winning the Ulster Volunteers to the cause of a United Ireland. We aimed at uniting all Irishmen in a natural and national bond of cohesion based on mutual self-respect. Our hope was a natural one, and if left to ourselves, not hard to accomplish. If external forces of disintegration would but leave us alone, we were sure that Nature itself must bring us together.

Nature was given no chance: and it has been the final irony of Casement's career that he, of all Irish nationalists, the one whose memory is held in most execration in Protestant Ulster, should have been the one who tried hardest to prevent those external forces from fulfilling their destructive destiny.

CASEMENT'S SPEECH
FROM THE DOCK, 1916

My Lord Chief Justice, as I wish to reach a much wider audience than I see before me here, I intend to read all that I propose to say. What I read now is something I wrote more than twenty days ago. I may say, my Lord, at once, that I protest against the jurisdiction of this Court in my case on this charge, and the argument that I am now going to read is addressed not to this Court, but to my own countrymen.

There is an objection, possibly not good in law, but surely good on moral grounds, against the application to me here of this old English statute, 565 years old, that seeks to deprive an Irishman today of life and honour, not for 'adhering to the King's enemies', but for adhering to his own people.

When this statute was passed, in 1351, what was the state of men's minds on the question of a far higher allegiance—that of a man to God and His Kingdom? The law of that day did not permit a man to forsake his church or deny his God save with his life. The 'heretic' then had the same doom as the 'traitor'.

Today a man may forswear God and His heavenly kingdom without fear or penalty, all earlier statutes having gone the way of Nero's edicts against the Christians; but that Constitutional phantom, 'The King', can still dig up from the dungeons and torture chambers of the Dark Ages a law that takes a man's life and limb for an exercise of conscience.

If true religion rests on love, it is equally true that loyalty rests on love. The law I am charged under has no parentage in love and claims the allegiance of today on the ignorance and blindness of the past.

I am being tried, in truth, not by my peers of the live present, but by the peers of the dead past; not by the civilisation of the twentieth century, but by the brutality of the fourteenth; not even by a statute framed in the language of an enemy land—so antiquated is the law that must be sought today to slay an Irish-man, whose offence is that he puts Ireland first.

Loyalty is a sentiment, not a law. It rests on love, not on restraint. The Government of Ireland by England rests on re-straint and not on law; and since it demands no love it can evoke no loyalty.

But this statute is more absurd even than it is antiquated, and if it is potent to hang one Irishman, it is still more potent to gibbet all Englishmen.

Edward III was King not only of the realm of England, but also of the realm of France, and he was not King of Ireland. Yet his dead hand today may pull the noose around the Irishman's neck whose Sovereign he was not, but it can strain no strand around the Frenchman's throat whose Sovereign he was. For centuries the successors of Edward III claimed to be Kings of France, and quartered the arms of France on their royal shield down to the Union with Ireland on 1st January, 1801. Throughout these hun-dreds of years these 'Kings of France' were constantly at war with their realm of France and their French subjects, who should have gone from birth to death with an obvious fear of treason before their eyes. But did they? Did the 'Kings of France' resi-dent here at Windsor or in the Tower of London, hang, draw, and quarter as a traitor every Frenchman for 400 years who fell into their hands with arms in his hand? On the contrary, they received embassies of these traitors, presents from these traitors, even knighthood itself at the hands of these traitors, feasted with them, tilted with them, fought with them—but did not assassinate them by law. Judicial assassination today is re-served only for one race of the King's subjects, for Irishmen; for those who cannot forget their allegiance to the realm of Ireland.

The Kings of England as such had no rights in Ireland up to the time of Henry VIII, save such as rested on compact and mutual obligation entered between them and certain princes, chiefs, and lords of Ireland. This form of legal right, such as it was, gave no King of England lawful power to impeach an Irish-man for high treason under this statute of King Edward III of England until an Irish Act, known as Poyning's Law, the 10th of Henry VII, was passed in 1494 at Drogheda, by the Parliament of the Pale in Ireland, and enacted as law in that part of Ireland. But if by Poyning's Law an Irishman of the Pale could be indicted for high treason under this Act, he could be indicted only in one way and before one tribunal—by the laws of the realm of Ireland and in Ireland. The very law of Poyning's, which, I believe, applies this statute of Edward III to Ireland, enacted also for the Irishman's defence, 'All those laws by which England claims her liberty'. And what is the fundamental charter of an Englishman's liberty? That he shall be tried by his peers. With all respect I assert this Court is to me, an Irishman, not a jury of my peers to try me in this vital issue for it is patent to every man of conscience that I have a right, an indefeasible right, if tried at all, under this statute of high treason, to be tried in Ireland, before an Irish Court and by an Irish jury. This Court, this jury, the public opinion of this country, England, cannot but be prejudiced in varying degree against me, most of all in time of war. I did not land in England; I landed in Ireland. It was to Ireland I came; to Ireland I wanted to come; and the last place I desired to land in was England. But for the Attorney-General of England there is only 'England'—there is no Ireland, there is only the law of England—no right of Ireland; the liberty of Ireland and Irishmen is to be judged by the power of England. Yet for me, the Irish outlaw, there is a land of Ireland, a right of Ireland, and a charter for all Irishmen to appeal to, in the last resort, a charter that even the very statutes of England itself cannot deprive us of—nay, more, a charter that Englishmen themselves assert as the fundamental bond of law that connects the two kingdoms. This charge of high treason involves a moral responsibility as the very terms of the indictment against myself recite, inasmuch as I committed the acts I am charged with to the 'evil example of others in the like case'. What was this 'evil example' I set to others in the 'like case,' and who were these others? The 'evil example' charged is that I asserted the rights of my own country, and the 'others' I appealed to to aid my endeavour were my own countrymen. The example was given not to Englishmen, but to Irishmen, and the 'like case' can never arise in England, but only in Ireland. To Englishmen I set no evil example, for I made no appeal to them. I asked no Englishman to help me. I asked Irishmen to fight for their rights. The 'evil example' was only to other Irishmen who might come after me, and in 'like case' seek to do as I did. How, then, since neither my example nor my appeal was addressed to Englishmen, can I be rightfully tried by them?

If I did wrong in making that appeal to Irishmen to join with me in an effort to fight for Ireland, it is by Irishmen, and by them alone, I can be rightfully judged. From the Court and its jurisdiction I appeal to those I am alleged to have wronged, and to those I am alleged to have injured by my 'evil example,' and claim that they alone are competent to decide my guilt or my innocence. If they find me guilty, the statute may affix the penalty, but the statute does not override or annul my right to seek judgment at their hands.

This is so fundamental a right, so natural a right, so obvious a right, that it is clear the Crown were aware of it when they brought me by force and by stealth from Ireland to this country. It was not I who landed in England, but the Crown who dragged me here, away from my own country to which I had turned with a price upon my head, away from my own countrymen whose loyalty is not in doubt, and safe from the judgment of my peers whose judgment I do not shrink from. I admit no other judgment but theirs. I accept no verdict save at their hands. I assert from this dock that I am being tried here, not because it is just, but because it is unjust. Place me before a jury of my own countrymen, be it Protestant or Catholic, Unionist or Nationalist, *Sinn Feineach* or Orangemen, and I shall accept the verdict and bow to the statute and all its penalties. But I shall accept no meaner finding against me than that of those whose loyalty I endanger by my example and to whom alone I made appeal. If they adjudge me guilty, then guilty I am. It is not I who am afraid of their verdict; it is the Crown. If this be not so, why fear the test? I fear it not. I demand it as my right.

That, my lord, is the condemnation of English rule, of English-made law, of English Government in Ireland, that it dare not rest on the will of the Irish people, but it exists in defiance of their will—that it is a rule derived not from right, but from conquest. Conquest, my lord, gives no title, and if it exists over the body, it fails over the mind. It can exert no empire over men's reason and judgment and affections; and it is from this law of conquest without title to the reason, judgment, and affection of my own countrymen that I appeal.

My lord, I beg to say a few more words. As I say, that was my opinion arrived at many days ago while I was a prisoner. I have no hesitation in re-affirming it here, and I hope that the gentlemen of the press who did not hear me yesterday may have heard me distinctly today. I wish my words to go much beyond this Court.

I would add that the generous expressions of sympathy extended me from many quarters, particularly from America, have touched me very much. In that country, as in my own, I am sure my motives are understood and not misjudged—for the achievement of their liberties has been an abiding inspiration to Irishmen and to all men elsewhere rightly struggling to be free in like cause.

My Lord Chief Justice, if I may continue, I am not called upon, I conceive, to say anything in answer to the inquiry your lordship has addressed to me why sentence should not be passed upon me. Since I do not admit any verdict in this Court, I cannot, my lord, admit the fitness of the sentence that of necessity must follow it from this Court. I hope I shall be acquitted of presumption if I say that the Court I see before me now is not this High Court of Justice of England, but a far greater, a far higher, a far older assemblage of justices—that of the people of Ireland. Since in the acts which have led to this trial it was the people of Ireland I sought to serve—and them alone—I leave my judgment and my sentence in their hands.

Let me pass from myself and my own fate to a far more pressing, as it is a far more urgent theme—not the fate of the individual Irishman who may have tried and failed, but the claims and the fate of the country that has not failed. Ireland has outlived the failure of all her hopes—and yet she still hopes. Ireland has seen her sons—aye, and her daughters too—suffer from generation to generation always for the same cause, meeting always the same fate, and always at the hands of the same power; and always a fresh generation has passed on to withstand the same oppression. For if English authority be omnipotent—a power, as Mr. Gladstone phrased it, that reached to the very ends of the earth—Irish hope exceeds the dimensions of that power, excels its authority, and renews with each generation the claims of the last. The cause that begets this indomitable persistency, the faculty of preserving through centuries of misery the remembrance of lost liberty, this surely is the noblest cause men ever strove for, ever lived for, ever died for. If this be the case I stand here today indicted for, and convicted of sustaining, then I stand in a goodly company and a right noble succession.

My counsel has referred to the Ulster Volunteer movement, and I will not touch at length upon that ground save only to say this, that neither I nor any of the leaders of the Irish Volunteers who were founded in Dublin in November, 1913, had quarrel with the Ulster Volunteers, as such, who were born a year earlier. Our movement was not directed against them, but against the men who misused and misdirected the courage, the sincerity, and the local patriotism of the men of the North of Ireland. On the contrary, we welcomed the coming of the Ulster Volunteers, even while we deprecated the aims and intentions of those Englishmen who sought to pervert to an English party use —to the mean purposes of their own bid for place and power in England—the armed activities of simple Irishmen. We aimed at winning the Ulster Volunteers to the cause of a united Ireland. We aimed at uniting all Irishmen in a natural and national bond of cohesion based on mutual self-respect. Our hope was a natural one, and if left to ourselves, not hard to accomplish. If external influences of disintegration would but leave us alone, we were sure that Nature itself must bring us together. It was not we, the Irish Volunteers, who broke the law, but a British party. The Government had permitted the Ulster Volunteers to be armed by Englishmen, to threaten not merely an English party in its hold on office, but to threaten that party through the lives and blood of Irishmen. The battle was to be fought in Ireland in order that the political 'outs' of today should be the 'ins' of tomorrow in Great Britain. A law designed for the benefit of Ireland was to be met, not on the floor of Parliament, where the fight had indeed been won, but on the field of battle much nearer home, where the armies would be composed of Irishmen slaying each other for some English party gain; and the British navy would be the chartered 'transports' that were to bring to our shores a numerous assemblage of military and ex-military experts in the congenial and profitable business of holding down subject populations abroad. Our choice lay in submitting to foreign lawlessness or resisting it, and we did not hesitate to choose. But while the law breakers had armed their would-be agents openly, and had been permitted to arm them openly, we were met within a few days of the founding of our movement, that aimed at uniting Ireland from within, by Government action from without, directed against our obtaining any arms at all. The manifesto of the Irish Volunteers, promulgated at a

public meeting in Dublin on 25th November, 1913, stated with
sincerity the aims of the organisation as I have outlined them.
If the aims contained in that manifesto were a threat to the
unity of the British Empire, then so much the worse for the
Empire. An Empire that can only be held together by one section
of its governing population perpetually holding down and sow-
ing dissension among a smaller but none the less governing
section, must have some canker at its heart, some ruin at its
root. The Government that permitted the arming of those
whose leaders declared·that Irish national unity was a thing that
should be opposed by force of arms, within nine days of the
issue of our manifesto of goodwill to Irishmen of every creed and
class, took steps to nullify our effort by prohibiting the import
of all arms into Ireland as if it had been a hostile and blockaded
coast. And this proclamation of the 4th December, 1913, known
as the Arms Proclamation, was itself based on an illegal interpretation of the law, as the Chief Secretary has now publicly
confessed. The proclamation was met by the loyalists of Great
Britain with an act of still more lawless defiance—an act of
widespread gun-running into Ulster that was denounced by the
Lord Chancellor of England as 'grossly illegal and utterly unconstitutional'. How did the Irish Volunteers meet the incitements of civil war that were uttered by the party of law and
order in England when they saw the prospect of deriving political profit to themselves from bloodshed among Irishmen?

I can answer for my own acts and speeches. While one English
party was responsible for preaching a doctrine of hatred designed to bring about civil war in Ireland, the other, and that
the party in power, took no active steps to restrain a propaganda that found its advocates in the army, navy, and Privy
Council—in the Houses of Parliament and in the State Church
—a propaganda the methods of whose expression were so
'grossly illegal and utterly unconstitutional' that even the Lord
Chancellor of England could find only words and no repressive
action to apply to them. Since lawlessness sat in high places in
England and laughed at the law as at the custodians of the law,
what wonder was it that Irishmen should refuse to accept the
verbal protestations of an English Lord Chancellor as a sufficient
safeguard for their lives and their liberties? I know not how all
my colleagues on the Volunteer Committee in Dublin reviewed
the growing menace, but those with whom I was in closest co-

operation redoubled, in face of these threats from without, our efforts to unite all Irishmen from within. Our appeals were made to Protestant and Unionist as much almost as to Catholic and Nationalist Irishmen. We hoped that by the exhibition of affection and goodwill on our part towards our political opponents in Ireland we should yet succeed in winning them from the side of an English party whose sole interest in our country lay in its oppression in the past, and in the present in its degradation to the mean and narrow needs of their political animosities. It is true that they based their actions, so they averred, on 'fears for the Empire', and on a very diffuse loyalty that took in all the peoples of the Empire, save only the Irish. That blessed word 'Empire' that bears so paradoxical a resemblance to charity! For if charity begins at home, 'Empire' begins in other men's homes, and both may cover a multitude of sins. I for one was determined that Ireland was much more to me than 'Empire', and that if charity begins at home so must loyalty. Since arms were so necessary to make our organisation a reality, and to give to the minds of Irishmen menaced with the most outrageous threats a sense of security, it was our bounden duty to get arms before all else. I decided with this end in view to go to America, with surely a better right to appeal to Irishmen there for help in an hour of great national trial than those envoys of 'Empire' could assert for their weekend descents upon Ireland, on their appeals to Germany. If, as the right honourable gentleman, the present Attorney-General, asserted in a speech at Manchester, Nationalists would neither fight for Home Rule nor pay for it, it was our duty to show him that we knew how to do both. Within a few weeks of my arrival in the States the fund that had been opened to secure arms for the Volunteers of Ireland amounted to many thousands of pounds. In every case the money subscribed, whether it came from the purse of the wealthy man or the still readier pocket of the poor man, was Irish gold.

Then came the war. As Mr. Birrell said in his evidence recently laid before the commission of inquiry into the causes of the late rebellion in Ireland, 'the war upset all our calculations'. It upset mine no less than Mr. Birrell's, and put an end to my mission of peaceful effort in America. War between Great Britain and Germany meant, as I believed, ruin for all the hopes we had founded on the enrolment of the Irish Volunteers. A constitutional movement in Ireland is never very far from a breach of the constitution, as the Loyalists of Ulster had been so eager to show us. The cause is not far to seek. A constitution to be maintained intact must be the achievement and the pride of the people themselves; must rest on their own free will and on their own determination to sustain it, instead of being something resident in another land whose chief representative is an armed force—armed not to protect the population, but to hold it down. We had seen the working of the Irish constitution in the refusal of the army of occupation at the Curragh to obey the orders of the Crown. And now that we were told the first duty of an Irishman was to enter that army, in return for a promissory note, payable after death—a scrap of paper that might or might not be redeemed, I felt over there in America that my first duty was to keep Irishmen at home in the only army that could safe-guard our national existence. If small nationalities were to be the pawns in this game of embattled giants, I saw no reason why Ireland should shed her blood in any cause but her own, and if that be treason beyond the seas I am not ashamed to avow it or to answer for it here with my life. And when we had the doctrine of Unionist loyalty at last—'Mausers and Kaisers and any King you like', and I have heard that at Hamburg, not far from Limburg on the Lahn—I felt I needed no other warrant than that these words conveyed—to go forth and do likewise. The difference between us was that the Unionist champions chose a path they felt would lead to the Woolsack; while I went a road I knew must lead to the dock. And the event proves we were both right. The difference between us was that my 'treason' was based on a ruthless sincerity that forced me to attempt in time and season to carry out in action what I said in word—whereas their treason lay in verbal incitements that they knew need never be made good in their bodies. And so, I am prouder to stand here today in the traitor's dock to answer this impeach-ment than to fill the place of my right honourable accusers.

We have been told, we have been asked to hope, that after this war Ireland will get Home Rule, as a reward for the life-blood shed in a cause which whoever else its success may benefit can surely not benefit Ireland. And what will Home Rule be in return for what its vague promise has taken and still hopes to take away from Ireland? It is not necessary to climb the painful stairs of Irish history—that treadmill of a nation whose labours are as vain for her own uplifting as the convict's exertions are for his redemption—to review the long list of British promises made only to be broken—of Irish hopes raised only to be dashed to the ground. Home Rule when it comes, if come it does, will find an Ireland drained of all that is vital to its very existence—unless it be that unquenchable hope we build on the graves of the dead. We are told that if Irishmen go by the thousand to die, not for Ireland, but for Flanders, for Belgium, for a patch of sand on the deserts of Mesopotamia, or a rocky trench on the heights of Gallipoli, they are winning self-government for Ireland. But if they dare to lay down their lives on their native soil, if they dare to dream even that freedom can be won only at home by men resolved to fight for it there, then they are traitors to their country, and their dream and their deaths alike are phases of a dishonourable phantasy. But history is not so recorded in other lands. In Ireland alone in this twentieth century is loyalty held to be a crime. If loyalty be something less than love and more than law, then we have had enough of such loyalty for Ireland or Irishmen. If we are to be indicted as criminals, to be shot as murderers, to be imprisoned as convicts because our offence is that we love Ireland more than we value our lives, then I know not what virtue resides in any offer of self-government held out to brave men on such terms. Self-government is our right, a thing born in us at birth; a thing no more to be doled out to us or withheld from us by another people than the right to life itself—than the right to feel the sun or smell the flowers, or to love our kind. It is only from the convict these things are withheld for crimes committed and proven—and, Ireland, that has wronged no man, that has injured no land, that has sought no dominion over others—Ireland is treated today among the nations of the world as if she was a convicted criminal. If it be treason to fight against such an unnatural fate as this, then I am proud to be a rebel, and shall cling to my 'rebellion' with the last drop of my blood. If there be no right of rebellion against a state of things that no savage tribe would endure without resistance, then I am sure that it is better for men to fight and die without right than to live in such a state of right as this. Where all your rights become only an accumulated wrong; where men must beg with bated breath for leave to subsist in their own land, to think their own thoughts, to sing their own songs, to garner the fruits of their own labours

—and even while they beg, to see things inexorably withdrawn from them—then surely it is braver, a saner and a truer thing, to be a rebel in act and deed against such circumstances as these than tamely to accept it as the natural lot of men.

My Lord, I have done. Gentleman of the jury, I wish to thank you for your verdict. I hope you will not take amiss what I said, or think that I made any imputation upon your truthfulness or your integrity when I spoke and said that this was not a trial by my peers. I maintain that I have a natural right to be tried in that natural jurisdiction, Ireland, my own country, and I would put it to you, how would you feel in the converse case, or rather how would all men here feel in the converse case, if an Englishman had landed here in England and the Crown or the Government, for its own purposes, had conveyed him secretly from England to Ireland under a false name, committed him to prison under a false name, and brought him before a tribunal in Ireland under a statute which they knew involved a trial before an Irish jury? How would you feel yourselves as Englishmen if that man was to be submitted to trial by jury in a land inflamed against him and believing him to be a criminal, when his only crime was that he had cared for England more than for Ireland?

'SHALL ROGER CASEMENT HANG?'

BY G. B. SHAW

(Shaw's letter 'Shall Roger Casement Hang?'—rejected by *The Times*, London—was published in the *Manchester Guardian*, 22 July 1916, and reprinted in the *New York American*, 13 August 1916)

Sir,—As several English newspapers have answered the above question vehemently in the affirmative, may I, as an Irishman, be allowed to balance their judgment by a reminder of certain considerations, easily overlooked in England, which seem glaringly obvious in Ireland.

First let me say that I have no sentimental appeal to make. Casement (he is no longer technically Sir Roger: but I really cannot bring myself to throw Mister in his teeth at such a moment) has lived his life not without distinction. His estimate of the relative values of the political rights of his country as he conceives them and of the integrity of his neck may be more Irish than English (though I hope I have no right to say so); but at any rate he has staked his life and lost, and cannot with any sort of dignity ask, or allow anyone else to ask on his behalf, for sentimental privilege. There need be no hesitation to carry out the sentence if it should appear, on reflection, a sensible one. Indeed, with a view to extricating the discussion completely from the sentimental vein, I will go so far as to confess that there is a great deal to be said for hanging all public men at the age of fifty-two, though under such a regulation I should myself have perished eight years ago. Were it in force throughout Europe, the condition of the world at present would be much more prosperous.

I presume I may count on a general agreement that Casement's treatment should not be exceptional. This is important, because it happens that his case is not an isolated one just now. There are several traitors in the public eye at present. At the head of them stands Christian De Wet. If De Wet is spared and Casement hanged, the unavoidable conclusion will be that Casement will be hanged, not because he is a traitor, but because he is an Irishman. We have also a group of unconvicted, and indeed unprosecuted, traitors whose action helped very powerfully to convince Germany that she might attack France without incurring our active hostility. As all these gentlemen belong to the same political party, their impunity, if Casement be executed, will lead to the still closer conclusion that his real offence is not merely that of being on Irishman but of being a nationalist Irishman. I see no way of getting round this. If it was proper to reprieve De Wet, whose case was a very flagrant one, Casement cannot be executed except on the assumption that Casement is a more hateful person than De Wet; and there is no other apparent ground for this discrimination than the fact that Casement is an Irishman and De Wet a Boer. Now this is clearly a consideration that should not weight the scales of justice. It may represent a fierce feeling which, though neither general nor civilised, is real and natural; but its gratification in the exercise of the Royal prerogative would make all the difference between an execution and a political assassination.

Sir Harry Poland and Sir Homewood Crawford are obviously right in claiming that Casement's trial was conducted in a manner which was, if anything, unduly indulgent to the accused, though Sir Homewood might perhaps have found a more tactful precedent than the case of Wainewright the murderer. Nevertheless, the real case was not put before the Court at all. The Crown, sure of its verdict, contented itself with a perfunctory police-court charge. The defence, after manufacturing a legal point to provide technical ground for an appeal, put up the sort of excuse usual in criminal cases: that is, the excuse of a pickpocket. Accused, having—very unwisely in my opinion—allowed his case to be pleaded for him instead of pleading it himself, could not very well repudiate the defence he had thus brought on himself: he could only ignore it. It was then too late. But there is no reason why the real case should not be stated now. It is fully set forth in Casement's recent writings published in America. No one dares publish them here, apparently, though the works of Treitschke and Mr. Houston Chamberlain, under cover of derisory titles and prefaces that deceive no sensible reader, circulate freely.

Casement's contention is simple enough. He does not pretend that Ireland can be a Power. But Belgium is not a Power. Greece is not a Power. They exist politically because it suits the Powers to maintain them as 'buffer States' or 'open doors'. Casement, like Sir Edward Grey and all the professional diplomatists, knows that the sore point in the British position for the rest of the world is our command of the sea. He argued that, if Britain is ever defeated, the victor's first care will be to abolish our power of blockade, and he suggested that the most obvious and effectual means of doing this would be to establish an independent kingdom of Ireland, guaranteed as an open door by the non-British Powers. So far, his views are on record. I infer that he regarded a victory by the Central Empires in the present war as probable enough to justify him in opening negotiations with the German Government with a view to the eventuality he had forecast.

Now this was a perfectly legitimate political speculation. An Irishman cannot reasonably be deterred from entertaining it, and even acting on it, by any loyalty which he yet owes to the British Empire. My own objection to it, for instance, is expressed by pointing to the predicament of Belgium and Greece, and asking whether that sort of independence is really preferable to the integration of Austria or Bavaria, with adequate modern units of defensive force. It seems to me an obsolete speculation, but it implies no moral delinquency.

On the question of allegiance, Casement was equally explicit. He pointed out that five centuries of Turkish rule in the Balkans had not, in the opinion of the British nation, abrogated the right of every Serbian to strike for independence, and he concluded quite logically that the same period of British rule could not abrogate the right of every Irishman to do the same. In England we are still so strongly of that opinion so far as Serbia is concerned that we have not allowed an event which could be paralleled in these islands only by the assassination of the Prince of Wales in the streets of Dublin to shake our adherence to, and our support by armed force of, this principle of nationality. It seems to me that Casement is here quite unanswerable. In any case, the word traitor as applied to a rebel has always been a mere vituperation from the days of Wallace to those of Sir Edward Carson and Sir Frederick Smith, and in my opinion it should be disused in this sense by intelligent men. Certainly, no one outside Great Britain will have any desire to apply it, even for vituperative purposes, to Casement.

Public opinion seems to be influenced to some extent by the notion that because Casement received money for his work from the British Empire, and earned it with such distinction that he became personally famous and was knighted for it, and expressed himself as gentlemen do on such occasions, he is in the odious position of having bitten the hand that fed him. To the people who take this view I put my own case. I have been employed by Germany as a playwright for many years, and by the Austrian Emperor in the great theatre in Vienna which is part of his household. I have received thousands of pounds for my services. I was recognised in this way when the English theatres were contemptuously closed to me. I was compelled to produce my last important play [Pygmalion] in Berlin in order that it might not be prejudiced by the carefully telegraphed abuse of the English press. Am I to understand that it is therefore my duty to fight for Germany and Austria, and that, in taking advantage of the international reputation which I unquestionably owe to Germany more than to any other country to make the first statement of the case against her which could have convinced anybody outside England, I was biting the hand of the venerable Franz Josef, whose bread I had eaten? I cannot admit it for a moment. I hope I have not been ungrateful. I have refused to join in the popular game of throwing mud at the Germans, and I have said nothing against them that I did not say when many of our most ardent patriots were lighting illuminations and raising triumphal arches to welcome the Kaiser in London. But to Germany's attack on France I remain a conscientious objector, and I must take my side accordingly. Clearly, Casement may claim precisely the same right to take his side according to his convictions, all the more because his former services prove that he does so without malice.

The reasonable conclusion is that Casement should be treated as a prisoner of war. I believe this is the view that will be taken in the neutral countries, whose good opinion is much more important to us than the satisfaction of our resentment. In Ireland he will be regarded as a national hero if he is executed, and quite possibly a spy if he is not. For that reason it may well be that he would object very strongly to my attempt to prevent his canonisation. But Ireland has enough heroes and martyrs already, and if England has not by this time had enough of manufacturing them in fits of temper experience is thrown away on her, and she will continue to be governed, as she is at present to so great an extent unconsciously, by Casement's countrymen.

Yours, &c.,

G. Bernard Shaw.

THE CASEMENT DIARIES

Letter from the author to the 'Cork Examiner', 25 June 1973

Sir,—May I reply to points which Padraig O Maidin has brought up in the course of what (considering how far his views are removed from mine) was a very fair and sympathetic review of my biography of Roger Casement? O Maidin clearly believes that I failed to produce sufficient evidence to disprove the theory that the diaries now in the Public Record Office in London are forgeries. I think he is right; had I realised that so many people in Ireland continue to believe in the forgery theory, I would have devoted more space to it.

Referring to the homosexual episodes in the diaries in the P.R.O., O Maidin asks 'How is it that only the diaries that were in the possession of the British authorities contain such matter?'

Of the two other surviving diaries, one was written while he was in Germany, under constant police surveillance he would have been unwise to include any compromising material. The other was a copy of his Putumayo diary, which he made for the use of the Select Committee investigating the affair. As he told the Chairman, he was sending the copy because 'naturally there is in it (the original diary) something I should not wish anyone else to see.' Other diaries and letters were left with Casement's friend, F. J. Bigger in Belfast. Bigger's son, Professor of Pathology in T.C.D., told J. J. Horgan that when his father opened the trunk containing them, after Casement's death, he was so horrified at the relevations they contained of Casement's homosexual relationships that he burned them. Rene MacColl reported this in his biography, though as Horgan did not wish his identity to be disclosed in his lifetime, the story was attributed to 'a well-known resident of Cork.'

'It can be accepted,' O Maidin continued, 'that the trunk (containing the diaries now in the Public Record Office) was removed from Casement's lodgings as soon as Hall and Thomson became aware that Casement was on his way to Germany in October

1914.' It can be accepted, but it should not be, as all the evidence is that the diaries were found after Casement's arrest in 1916.

The only 'evidence' that I am aware of for the hypothesis that the diaries were found in 1914 rests on the acknowledgment that it would have been difficult to forge them in the brief period between his arrest and the time before his trial, when they were first shown around.

'A single forged diary would have exposed the plot,' O Maidin argues; 'Casement was never shown the diaries.' True; but what O Maidin forgets is that the diaries were shown by Sir Frederick Smith to Casement's lawyers. Artemus Jones, Serjeant Sullivan's Junior Counsel, saw them; and passed them to Sullivan. It happened that Sullivan refused to look at them—believing, as he did, that they were genuine, and not wanting to have to change his defence line to accommodate that unwelcome fact. But Smith could not have known that Sullivan would refuse to look at them. His hope was that the defence would be compelled to plead insanity—which would not have saved Casement; he would have been hanged and discredited. Smith, in other words, believed that the diaries were genuine—or why would he have risked obloquy by letting Casement see them, and prove they had been forged?

Brian Inglis.

ACKNOWLEDGMENTS

I am very grateful to Dr. Patrick Henchy and the staff of the National Library of Ireland—in particular the MSS. section; to John Walford of the Public Record Office, who went to a great deal of trouble to help track down material even when, for one reason or another, it was not in the files there—and the P.R.O. staff, in Fetter Lane and in Portugal Street; my thanks, too, to the staff of the Rhodes House Library; the London School of Economics Library; the Beaverbrook Library; the Baptist Missionary Society; and the House of Lords Record Office; the Trinity College, Dublin Library; and, as always, the London Library.

I am grateful, too, to those who read and commented on segments of the book while it was in typescript—Bill Grundy actually read the lot, and very useful some of his trenchantly expressed criticisms were.

So were Bernard Levin's, of the proofs. Robert Kee also read them, and made some valuable suggestions, which I have incorporated—as did Geoffrey Parminter, whose biography of Casement appeared in 1936. And for help of various kinds, my thanks to David Ayerst, Robert Barton, Ernest Blythe, Erskine Childers, Sylvanus Cookey, Dr. Ruadhri de Valera, Maurice Girodias, Colin Harding, Alexander Irvine, Seamus Kelly, Mrs. Ted R. Kunstling, Dr. Sheila Marks, Mrs. Hermione MacColl, Professor R. B. McDowell, Professor Roger McHugh, Bryan Moser, Mrs. Freda Obregon, Conor Cruise O'Brien, Leon O Broin, Ulick O'Connor, Michelle Proud, Robert J. Stopford, Professor Michael Tierney and Richard West.

But my chief debt is to Ann Froshaug. Ann acted as pathfinder—pursuing the sources to their files, elucidating the complexities of the Public Record Office's filing system—and guide. Fortunately for me, too, she was able to provide a commentary on the draft typescript, before departing to resume her academic career.

At any time, the prospect of another book on Roger Casement

would have been viewed with misgiving by members of his family. They could be forgiven for declining to co-operate; indeed, I was reluctant even to approach them. However, I wrote to the late Mrs. Mabel Casement and—mainly, I am sure, out of longstanding friendship with my mother—she wrote to explain the family's attitude to Roger, and their reasons for their unwillingness to make available such letters of his as they possess —which are apparently few.

INDEX

JENNIFER JOHNSTON

THE CAPTAINS AND THE KINGS

'Elegantly written, with a depth of understanding of old age which is remarkable. The book is truth itself . . . Miss Johnston knows her Ireland as well as she knows human nature . . . This is her first novel: I hope it will the first of many'
Irish Times

'Cumulative power . . . The author portrays, without over-emphasis, the specific and inescapable pain of old age'
Times Literary Supplement

'*The Captains and the Kings*, a perceptive and beautifully balanced book, has not a wrong note in it . . . Diarmid and Prendergast are as real as growing pains and arthritis'
Yorkshire Post

'A piece of writing I shall long remember — sensitive, under-played and with deep meaning . . . Altogether an enjoyable book that should make many a reader eager for her next novel'
Cork Examiner

'This is a first novel of distinction, written with that loving care for words that is becoming increasingly rare today'
Irish Independent

'The two central figures are finely vivid . . . A most assured and skilful first novel'
Sunday Times

THE GATES

'It was predicted that if her second novel turned out as good, that she would take her place in the front rank of Irish writers. With *The Gates* she has succeeded in doing just that. It is a marvellous novel, absorbing in its brooding tension'
PATRICK BOYLE (*Irish Independent*)

'Assured, skilful, delicately comic and mutedly sad . . . Miss Johnston is a very good writer'
JULIAN SYMONS (*Sunday Times*)

ALSO IN CORONET

All these books are available at your bookshop or newsagent, or can be ordered direct from the publisher. Just tick the titles you want and fill in the form below

....

CORONET BOOKS, P.O. Box 11, Falmouth, Cornwall.

Please send cheque or postal order. No currency, and allow the following for postage and packing:

1 book—10p, 2 books—15p, 3 books—20p, 4-5 books—25p, 6-9 books—4p per copy, 10-15 books—2½p per copy, over 30 books free within the U.K.

Overseas—please allow 10p for the first book and 5p per copy for each additional book.

Name...

Address..

....